CW01425861

Makers of Nuclear Strategy

Makers of
Nuclear Strategy

Edited by

John Baylis and John Garnett

Pinter Publishers
London

© John Baylis and John Garnett, 1991

First published in Great Britain in 1991 by
Pinter Publishers Limited
25 Floral Street, London WC2E 9DS

British Library Cataloguing in Publication Data

A CIP catalogue record for this book is available from the
British Library
ISBN 1 85567 025 9

Typeset by Witwell Ltd, Southport
Printed and bound in Great Britain by Biddles Ltd., Guildford and King's Lynn

Contents

Notes on the contributors

John Baylis is a Reader in the International Politics Department at the University of Wales, Aberystwyth.

Ken Booth is a Professor in the International Politics Department at the University of Wales, Aberystwyth.

Lawrence Freedman is Professor of War Studies at King's College, University of London.

John Garnett is Woodrow Wilson Professor of International Politics at the University of Wales, Aberystwyth.

Sir Michael Howard is Robert A. Lovett Professor of Military and Naval History at Yale University.

Neil MacFarlane is a Professor of Political Studies at Queen's University, Kingston, Ontario, Canada.

François de Rose was a member of the ruling body of the French Commissariat à l'Energie Atomique, Deputy Chief of Staff of National Defense and Ambassador to the North Atlantic Council. He is now retired.

Richard Rosecrance is the Walter S. Carpenter Jr. Professor of International and Comparative Politics at Cornell University.

Phil Williams is a Professor in the Graduate School of Public and International Affairs at the University of Pittsburgh.

INTRODUCTION

John Baylis and John Garnett

Many of the weapons developed during the twentieth century have been frightful. Chemical and biological weapons, in particular, have caused widespread revulsion among civilized peoples, but it is probably true that no weapon has provoked more fear and horror than the atomic bomb. The lasting images of Hiroshima and Nagasaki have seen to that. Bernard Brodie, as impressed as anyone by the awesome power of the fission bomb, described it as 'the absolute weapon'. He was, of course, wrong for two reasons: although in 1945 it epitomized the ultimate in human destructiveness, it paled into insignificance when compared with the fusion weapons which came along shortly afterwards; second, since there are no technological plateaux in the endless process of weapon innovation, there can be no 'absolute weapons'.

Nevertheless, Brodie's phrase perfectly captured the popular consensus that the world was entering a new, ominous and qualitatively different period of history. For the first time human beings had acquired the capacity to destroy both themselves and the planet on which they lived. This was a sobering prospect, and, as the post war years unfolded, the problem of managing the peace was further exacerbated by the superpower arms race which had so quickly dashed hopes of the victorious allies' continuing collaboration. By the late 1950s the stockpile of nuclear and thermonuclear weapons in the arsenals of the superpowers could be numbered in hundreds; by the 1960s, thousands of these weapons existed; by the 1980s the Americans and Soviets controlled tens of thousands of nuclear and thermonuclear weapons with delivery systems capable of dropping them with a very high degree of accuracy anywhere in the world.

Inevitably, the nuclear revolution spurred new thinking about military power. Strategists struggled to make sense of new weapons which seemed to turn conventional military wisdom upside down. When nuclear war threatened to destroy both vanquished and victor alike, the widely accepted Clausewitzian idea of war as an instrument of policy began to look decidedly odd. Similarly, traditional strategic concerns with winning wars now had a very anachronistic flavour. As Liddell Hart put it: 'old concepts and old definitions of strategy have become not only obsolete but nonsensical with the development of nuclear weapons. To aim at winning a war, to take victory as your object, is no more than a state of lunacy.'[1]

The strategic thinkers considered in this book were among the first to grapple with the new intellectual and military problems of the nuclear age. Of course they were not the only ones trying to think constructively about the momentous issues thrown up by a new technology of unprecedented destructiveness. Around them — at least around the Americans — there developed an enormous industry of specialists dealing with nuclear strategy. This intellectual community has been described as 'the War-Peace Establishment'. It was not an establishment in the usual sense of being an institution, but 'one of ideas and theory' which wielded enormous influence, not only over the way an entire generation's thoughts about military issues were shaped but also over the formulation of defence policy in the nuclear-weapon states.

Choosing 'the makers of nuclear strategy' from the hundreds of defence analysts who contributed to the intellectual milieu which mushroomed in the post-war years has not been easy. Indeed, the editors remain conscious of an element of arbitrariness in the selection. If Sir Anthony Buzzard is included, why not Sir John Slessor? If General Beaufré makes the grade, why not General Gallois? If Henry Kissinger is included, why not William Kaufmann, Klaus Knorr, Hedley Bull and all the others whose names dominated the strategic journals of the 1950s and 1960s? In a book of limited size some hard choices had to be made, and we are not at all sure that we got our selectivity exercise right. Nevertheless we do believe that the thinkers we have chosen are both creative and influential. Serious students of nuclear thinking may need to cast their net wider than these strategists, but they will certainly not be able to ignore our choices.

We were particularly conscious of the problem of attributing ideas to particular individuals who in reality may have merely publicized them or unconsciously absorbed them from the strategic milieu in which they lived. Once articulated, however informally, ideas have a life of their own. They are so frequently contested, amended, forgotten, revived, embellished and developed by analysts who play with them that it is often impossible either to trace their origins or allocate responsibility for them. Even the most original thinker is sometimes saddened to learn either that his best ideas have been thought of before or that they had their origins in the half-recollected thoughts of others.

The problem arises in an acute form with Herman Kahn, whose reputation rested partly on the publication of ideas which were not his and which had hitherto circulated only in a very restricted RAND environment. But many of the writers considered in this volume fed upon each other's ideas and owed a considerable debt to the intellectual ferment which characterised the strategic debates of the late 1950s and 1960s. Henry Kissinger, for example, relied heavily on ideas currently fashionable among the strategic community. He wrote clearly and he contributed substantially to the policy debates about American nuclear policy; but the raw material with which he worked was almost entirely devised by others. In a sense he was an *applied* strategist rather than a maker of modern strategy.

The strategists in this book were among the first to consider the implications of the nuclear age, but in trying to make sense of a technological environment which totally transformed the military scene, they also had to grapple with a political environment which was equally revolutionary — a world dominated by two superpowers locked in a Cold War relationship. All of the makers of nuclear strategy were reared in the politics of the Cold War, and it was this context which provided the political backdrop for their strategic speculation.

Looking back on it, with the benefit of hindsight, the historian may see the Cold War and the division of Europe as a rather peculiar aberration which temporarily interrupted a much more fluid system of balance-of-power politics. But at the time it seemed a permanent feature of international life which the strategists took for granted. The notion that in the late 1980s and early 1990s it would simply fade away would have seemed preposterous to all of them. Almost every bit of their analysis was predicated on the international conditions caused by superpower rivalry and a divided world.

The United States recognized only one enemy, the Soviet Union, and strategic thought was obsessed with the Soviet threat. Deterrence theory concentrated on the strategic balance between the United States and the Soviet Union. The central questions of the day related to the problem of acquiring and maintaining effective retaliatory capability, and of perpetuating a stable balance in the face of dramatic innovations in weapon technology. Arms Control negotiations were mainly American–Soviet discussions designed to limit the arms race without destabilizing deterrence. Whatever successes were recorded happened largely because decision-makers in Washington and Moscow were able to agree. Whatever failures occurred happened because the superpowers failed to agree. The doctrine of limited war wrestled with problems of reconciling the possibility of American–Soviet conflict, with the near certainty of nuclear oblivion if neither side practised restraint. Techniques of crisis management were largely developed to deal with an American–Soviet confrontation on the model of the Cuban missile crisis. Strategies of 'massive retaliation', 'pause', 'trip wire' and 'flexible response' were similarly designed to meet the requirements of East–West confrontation. Thus, behind almost every aspect of military thought and giving point to it, lay the assumptions of the 'Cold War' — a bipolar world permanently divided into two armed camps led by two superpowers whose leaders were the only significant decisionmakers.

Now that the Cold War is over and the influence of the superpowers is in decline, many of the ideas elaborated by the nuclear strategists have a rather dated, even parochial, flavour about them. Future generations of students may find it very difficult to understand the obsession with nuclear war and East–West relations which affected all the nuclear strategists. Even horizontal nuclear proliferation was regarded as a 'problem' largely from the perspective of existing nuclear states who did not want the nuclear club to become less exclusive. The problems of the Third World and 'North–South' issues hardly figured at all in the speculation of these thinkers whose theories were geared almost exclusively to a unique and, as it has turned out, transitory political situation. It remains to be seen how well their thoughts will translate into the more fluid, multi-polar world of the 1990s and beyond. Our guess is that though the basic philosophical reflections and theoretical work will live on to illuminate future strategic issues, much of the detailed analysis of defence policies will be of interest only to historians.

The other aspect of nuclear thought which may strike future students as slightly odd is the particular set of assumptions which the nuclear thinkers shared and which underpinned much of their speculation. Though they differed in all sorts of ways and frequently disagreed with each other, they were, in an important sense, all tuned to the same intellectual wavelength. To a large extent — and with the possible exception of Sokolovskii and his collaborators — the makers of nuclear strategy shared a common set of assumptions about the nature of international politics and the kind of reasoning which is appropriate for handling political/strategic problems.

In particular, either consciously or unconsciously, they had all absorbed the 'Realist' approach to international politics which dominated thinking about the subject in the post-war years. 'Realism' provided a sophisticated intellectual perspective on the world — more sophisticated than some of its critics have realized — and one which was particularly suited to the harsh mood and temper of the Cold War years. It is impossible to summarize a profound body of thought in a few sentences. Suffice it to say that Realists tended to be conservative in their views and pessimistic about what could be done to ameliorate the human condition. They tended to accept a world divided into independent sovereign states as being the normal, if not the permanent, condition of international society, and they regarded 'power politics' as the driving force in state behaviour.

Realists were sceptical about the restraining influence of international law and the possibility of permanent peace and scornful of ideas of general and comprehensive disarmament, world government and collective security. They had little faith in the powers of human reason and not much confidence in the power of morality to constrain state behaviour. At the heart of their philosophy was first, a rather jaundiced view of human nature which emphasized man's egotism, selfishness and his aggressive impulses and second, an interpretation of politics which allocated a central role to the pursuit of power and the promotion of the national interest. The Realist tradition may have fitted the grim mood of the Cold War years, but in the softer climate of superpower *rapprochement*, disintegrating alliances, *glasnost*, arms control and disarmament, it seems excessively tough minded — even cynical.

More seriously, it no longer mirrors political reality. In the 1990s nuclear war has virtually slipped off the agenda. It remains a possibility, but virtually nobody now believes that the 'doomsday clock' is set at five minutes to midnight. Fears of nuclear Armaggedon have been replaced by new obsessions. Environmental issues connected with population control and global warming are now centre stage. Ecological disaster now seems a more likely threat to the planet than a nuclear winter.

In a sense, therefore, the nuclear age may be over. Not, of course, in the sense that nuclear weapons are likely to disappear or that nuclear war is becoming impossible (indeed, if horizontal proliferation continues it may actually become more likely); but in two other senses: first, in that other issues are now capturing the public imagination and attracting the attention of students of international relations; second, in that the nuclear thinkers did their job almost too well. They provided an intellectual apparatus that has stood the test of time very well.

Many of the theoretical insights and political judgements about deterrence, arms control, crisis management and limited war are as relevant today as they ever were. But most of them were well articulated before the mid-1960s. After this date, original and striking contributions to the basic literature of strategy virtually ceased. The hard truth is that today there is not much more of a fundamental nature to say about nuclear strategy. Of course, the output of strategic writing is as voluminous as ever but much of it is highly specialized writing dealing with the minutiae of the subject rather than conceptual and original thinking. The 'golden age' of nuclear strategy — to which all the writers examined in this book contributed — has now been over for twenty years. In a sense the demise of the Cold War and the new, more relaxed, climate of international relations has simply confirmed a process of decline which has been evident for many years.

Arguably, we are still too close to the nuclear age to reflect objectively on its thinkers, but it did seem appropriate to make a tentative assessment and to gather their thoughts in a single book. Edward Meade Earle's classic *Makers of Modern Strategy* provided us with a model, and if we are half as successful in describing some of the makers of nuclear strategy as he was in explaining the thoughts of earlier generations of military thinkers, we shall be content.

It is fitting that the first chapter should focus on the work of Bernard Brodie, whom Ken Booth describes as 'the quintessential strategist of the first generation of the nuclear age'. *The Absolute Weapon: Atomic Power and World Order*, edited by Brodie in 1946, was a major landmark in the story of thinking about nuclear weapons. It was the first book on deterrence in the atomic age and the first comprehensive exposition of American strategy in that age. In his contribution to the book Brodie emphasized that the unique destructiveness of the new weapons meant that the avoidance of war was now all-important. Nuclear weapons, he argued, could have almost no other purpose than averting war. With this argument Brodie opened the debate and set down an agenda for deterrence which became the main preoccupation for nuclear strategists for decades ahead.

Ken Booth agrees with Thomas Schelling's generous assessment of Brodie as the first of the nuclear strategists 'both in time and in distinction'. Brodie's work was outstanding in the way it explained the new and frequently ambiguous interrelationship between war, politics and strategy. Future generations are likely to acclaim Brodie as 'the Clausewitz of the age of nuclear deterrence'. He was a 'strategist's strategist' whose importance, Ken Booth argues, lies not so much in his direct influence of policy (indeed he was 'marginalized' in the 1960s when many of his contemporaries were offered jobs in the Kennedy administration), but in the general and indirect influence he had in shaping the sensibilities of numerous individual strategists. For thirty years or more he was 'on the sidelines, helping to set the agenda, writing the literature and stimulating thinking of the new strategy'.

Ken Booth traces the evolution of Brodie's thinking about nuclear strategy from *The Absolute Weapon* in 1946 to his last article on 'The Development of Nuclear Strategy' written in 1978. He shows how Brodie wrestled continuously and open-mindedly with one of the central paradoxes of nuclear deterrence: how to create a strategy which would deter — through the possibility of losing all control — while at the same time maintaining as much control as possible. In an attempt to resolve this paradox Brodie was one of the first to advocate limitations and restraints in atomic war through discriminate target selection. He argued forcefully that limited war was preferable to all-out war, and he helped to provide a major critique of the doctrine of 'massive retaliation'. Like the other nuclear strategists of his day he focused on the search for a wider range of strategic options than the prevailing strategy allowed.

Despite this interest in limited war Brodie became increasingly concerned that the development of thermonuclear weapons would undermine the prospects for restraint. Ken Booth argues that the H-Bomb negated the political philosophy of war which Brodie inherited from Clausewitz. As a result he found it increasingly difficult to fit the new weapons into the traditional framework of thinking about war and politics.

Brodie's *Strategy in the Missile Age*, written in 1959, reflected the author's inner turmoil and exposed 'the human dimensions of a humane and imaginative strategist'. Although the book represented one of his key statements on limited war, it also reflected his unease over the effect thermonuclear weapons would have on the prospects of keeping wars limited. Nevertheless, he was still not prepared to oppose such weapons. Ken Booth argues that although Brodie had reservations about the controllability of limited nuclear war, the dissonance in his mind was itself controlled by his growing conviction that the probability of an American–Soviet war was very low.

Brodie's unease brought him into conflict with colleagues at the RAND Corporation. Differences emerged in two important areas. First, he was more sensitive to moral issues than most of the other nuclear strategists. He believed that moral values had an important role to play in the formulation of American strategic policy. And second, he favoured traditional approaches to the subject rather than the fashionable systems-analysis approach promoted by strategists like Albert Wohlstetter. Despite the importance and influence of Wohlstetter, Booth's judgement is that 'in the history of strategic thought Brodie will stand ahead of Wohlstetter just as Clausewitz now stands clearly ahead of Jomini'. Systems analysis was influential, particularly during the McNamara era, but ultimately it proved to be a transitory fashion. Brodie's thought, on the other hand, with its emphasis on history, politics and philosophy, enjoys a 'secure reputation'.

Even so, Ken Booth is not uncritical of Brodie. He points out that there were omissions, mistakes and inconsistencies in his writing. In particular Booth is critical of Brodie's short-sightedness in the late 1950s in believing that NATO would retain its superiority over the Soviet Union and that escalation to the nuclear level might be a useful tactic.

These minor weaknesses, however, have to be set against Brodie's open-mindedness and his willingness to consider new ideas. Throughout his career his thoughts evolved as he questioned the dogmas, slogans, axioms and rigid theories produced by other American strategists. He was more relaxed than most of them about the Soviet threat. He was a dissenter during the Vietnam war. He was also one of the major critics of the 'New Right' strategic fundamentalists whose ideas were fashionable in the late 1970s. In many of these areas, Ken Booth argues, 'time has vindicated his arguments'.

Brodie's contribution to strategic studies is profound. Students of the subject, Booth argues, have more to learn from 'a silent dialogue with a major thinker of the past', like Brodie, than with 'the loudest talkers of the present'. Although no single author can be an adequate 'guide' to us in our present problems, 'the startling insights that leap up at us from so many pages' of Brodie's work are still applicable to our own times. In Ken Booth's view 'there has been no one to match him since'.

The second chapter focuses on Albert Wohlstetter who, Richard Rosecrance believes, had more direct influence on American nuclear policy in the 1950s and 1960s than any other strategist. Wohlstetter, he admits, was not the only critic of the 'massive retaliation' doctrine, nor the originator of the requirements of stable nuclear deterrence. Nor was he the first to recognize the need for limited-war options and damage-limitation strategies. Nevertheless, his work contains a breadth of conception which is found in few other strategic analyses. According to Richard Rosecrance, his thought represents 'both the most consistent and the most general writings on strategy in the post-World War Two era'.

Wohlstetter's claim to strategic influence rests on two main pillars. The first is the well-known 'Bases Study' which he began at the RAND Corporation in 1951. This study, focusing on the vulnerability of the Strategic Air Command (SAC) to surprise attack, had a major influence on the Gaither Report entitled 'Deterrence and Survival in the Nuclear Age' which was produced in 1957. In turn the Gaither Report had an important impact on American nuclear policy in the late 1950s and 1960s.

Richard Rosecrance shows that Wohlstetter's distinctive contribution came from the methodology he used. He adopted a 'systems analysis' approach to demonstrate quantitatively and authoratively, that SAC forces were incapable of withstanding a well-executed surprise attack by the Soviet Union. He discovered that the SAC had concentrated on 'The Sunday Punch' against Soviet targets but had ignored the vulnerability of its own bases. Using the same rigorous scientific techniques, Wohlstetter set about considering antidotes to SAC vulnerability. Many of his ideas, including the dispersal of bombers and the hardening of bases, were subsequently to be taken up by the Air Force.

Rosecrance argues that 'the base study and its successors were among the most significant analyses ever done at the RAND Corporation'. They established not only the tradition of systems analysis but of 'opposed systems design'. These early Wohlstetter investigations laid foundations for the kind of strategic analysis which has underpinned the procurement of new weapon systems ever since.

Albert Wohlstetter's second claim to fame rests on his conception of deterrence, which 'differed a great deal from that of other influential scientists, public officials and laymen'. For the proponents of Mutual Assured Destruction (MAD) the mere possession of retaliatory forces capable of destroying enemy cities after absorbing a first strike was sufficient to deter. Wohlstetter, however, made it clear that capabilities alone do not deter. There must also be a good chance that they will be used if aggression takes place. Wohlstetter pointed out that *credibility* was as important as *capability*, and this meant that deterrence and 'feasible strategic use' could not be separated. A potential aggressor had to be made to believe that retaliation was likely as well as possible and this could only be done through the possession of credible warfighting capabilities. Deterrence depended not on empty threats but on rational strategies which demonstrated the probability that nuclear weapons will be used.

As Richard Rosecrance shows, Wohlstetter's conception of deterrence owes a great deal to his wife Roberta's brilliant study of Pearl Harbor. It was the lessons of Pearl Harbor which gave rise to his notion of 'alternative risks'. For the Japanese the risk of *not* attacking was greater than the risk of striking the American fleet. Japan therefore could only have been deterred by telling her leaders in advance that prompt retaliation would take place if they attacked. Wohlstetter recognized that if a potential aggressor's international position was deteriorating he might be prepared to take greater risks than other states whose peacetime position was more favourable. In such situations deterrence had to be able to cope with these added incentives for aggression and this, Wohlstetter believed, was not easy to achieve.

The idea of 'alternative risks' was an important part of Wohlstetter's argument in 'The Delicate Balance of Terror' written in 1959. In this justly celebrated article, he argued that deterrent forces had to surmount a number of major hurdles if they were to be effective. For example, they had to be able to survive an attack; they had to be able to receive communications from the national command authorities; retaliatory systems had to reach enemy targets; strategic forces had to be able to penetrate the enemy's active defences; and finally, missiles had to penetrate the enemy's passive defences, including fall-out shelters. Wohlstetter argued that this was a more complex and difficult task than most people realized.

The importance of these requirements led Wohlstetter and some of his colleagues at RAND to devise the notions of 'damage limitation' and 'assured destruction'. Both of these ideas were to be embraced later by Robert McNamara when he became secretary of defence in the Kennedy administration. Richard Rosecrance, however, argues that these notions were somewhat contradictory. He suggests that the problem of maintaining a long-term 'damage limiting' or 'coercive capability' was that it effectively denied 'assured destruction' capabilities to the Soviet Union. As a result it helped to trigger the build-up of Soviet nuclear forces which took place in the mid-to-late 1960s. When McNamara realized this towards the end of his term in office he put less emphasis on the 'damage limiting' task. This led to a parting of intellectual company between Wohlstetter and McNamara.

Wohlstetter's continuing justification of 'damage limitation', and later of ABM systems and SDI, derived from his notion of 'cost-exchange ratios'. For Wohlstetter the standard against which new American strategic systems should be measured was whether the Soviet Union could offset them at a lower cost. Richard Rosecrance acknowledges the point but notes that defence systems ought to be measured not only against what the enemy spends but also 'against what we have given up at home as a result of them'. Too great an emphasis upon the first component may well undermine the second. This means that American strategists should have been just as concerned with lessening the domestic military burden as with offsetting the military preparations of the Soviet Union. Wohlstetter was too preoccupied with rearmament at the expense of a healthy American economy.

Rosecrance concludes his chapter by arguing that despite Wohlstetter's considerable influence over American nuclear policy he failed to make the best use of his ideas about 'alternative risks'. A more subtle use of the notions of 'alternative risks', designed to reassure Soviet leaders about their long-term security, would have been more likely to encourage them to scale down significantly their military expenditure.

If Albert Wohlstetter was one of the most influential of the early nuclear strategists, Herman Kahn was certainly one of the most well known and controversial. In Chapter Three John Garnett attempts to assess the contribution which this 'flamboyant, egotistical figure — this "enfant terrible" of the strategic community — had on strategic thinking in the late 1950s and early 1960s.' Despite certain weaknesses in Kahn's approach, his influence was considerable. After the publication of his book *On Thermonuclear War* in 1960, strategy was never quite the same again.

John Garnett shows that much of the controversy surrounding Kahn's thinking centred largely on his uncompromising style and approach. He was determined to 'think about the unthinkable' and to confront directly the grim realities of nuclear war. For the layman, however, this cold objectivity about the horrors of nuclear war and its chilling 'flavour of amorality' was horrifying and unacceptable.

Despite public revulsion, perhaps even because of it, one of Kahn's greatest achievements was to stimulate widespread discussion about the great strategic issues of the nuclear age. Since nuclear weapons could not be disinvented, Kahn argued that the basic problem of the nuclear age was how to live with such terrible weapons and how to devise policies which could accommodate them and even turn them into instruments of statecraft. This led Kahn to try and provide answers to three basic questions: first, how can states avoid nuclear war?; second, if they cannot avoid it, how can they survive it?; and third, how can they conduct war in the nuclear age without destroying themselves in the process? For Kahn, as for the other nuclear strategists, the primary objective of military forces in the nuclear age was to deter war. Inevitably therefore the concept of deterrence was central to his thought. John Garnett describes the important contribution to deterrence theory which Kahn made by focusing on his categorization of three types of deterrence. Type I deterrence involved the ability to deter a direct attack on one's own country. Type II deterrence involved the ability to deter very provocative acts (such as a Soviet invasion of Western Europe). And type III deterrence involved the ability to deter limited aggressions or provocations of a relatively minor nature. Effective deterrence, according to Kahn, required the ability to deter all three types of provocative behaviour. Like Wohlstetter, he believed that deterrence was rather complicated. It had to work 'on bad days as well as good' — not only when there are minimum incentives for aggression but also when an opponent is in 'a hostile, risk-taking mood, as well'. Deterrence therefore required a mix of defensive and offensive capabilities. The main thrust of Kahn's approach to deterrence is the argument that by making nuclear war marginally more likely in a serious crisis, all forms of war, including nuclear war, are made less likely.

One area of Kahn's work which is often neglected is his concern to reduce overly provocative behaviour by the Great Powers. John Garnett shows that despite his tough-minded reputation, he emphasized the importance of reassurance in East–West relations through intelligent arms control measures. Such measures, he believed, were of significance in maintaining the stability of deterrence, which he considered of crucial importance. Perhaps surprisingly he was also one of the early proponents of 'a no-first-use strategy' for NATO (providing conventional forces could be improved).

Despite the value of deterrence and arms control in keeping the peace Kahn recognized that deterrence might fail and that war was still a possibility. Consequently he argued that it was important to try to discover what thermonuclear war would be like. In his investigation he came to two rather controversial conclusions: it was survivable and that the scale of catastrophe depended on the preparations made to mitigate it. John Garnett is rather critical of Kahn's approach to the question of how to survive a nuclear war. He points out, as others have done, that the hard data used to back Kahn's analysis is actually rather flimsy and provides a 'hopelessly inadequate basis from which to draw the conclusions Kahn drew'. Kahn's methodology 'is not scientifically rigorous. It is based on pure guess-work.'

Because of his interest in surviving nuclear war, Kahn devoted a good deal of attention to the conduct of war. This led him to the idea of limited war and in particular to the concept of 'escalation'. In this area he made a significant contribution to the literature. Building on Thomas Schelling's view of war as a bargaining process, he invented the concept of 'escalation dominance' which subsequently had a major impact on American and NATO strategy. John Garnett argues that Kahn's creative notion of an escalation ladder was 'to become part of the language of strategy, and a major tool for helping us to understand the complexities of conflict and war'. The concept of the escalation ladder was illuminating and useful, especially for those interested in crisis management. However, like all metaphors, it needs to be handled with care since there are aspects of it which are misleading. In particular, the idea of a ladder with equal rungs does not take account of the different levels of crises which can occur in international relations. 'Some thresholds', John Garnett argues, 'are easier to cross than others.'

In his assessment of Kahn's overall contribution to strategic thinking John Garnett admits that there were weaknesses in Kahn's writing. In particular, Kahn lacked the qualities of political and historical judgement which are so important in strategic analysis. Garnett describes him as 'a flawed realist' whose ideas were not sufficiently anchored in an understanding of philosophy or history to give him the kind of deep insights into the human predicament which characterized the work of writers like Morgenthau and Niebuhr. Despite the titles of his books *On Escalation* and *On Thermonuclear War*, he was not a twentieth-century equivalent of Clausewitz. His work contained few 'timeless truths and brilliant insights'. Nevertheless, Kahn's work is an important milestone in the history of nuclear thought for two reasons. 'First, because it challenged some conventional assumptions; and second, because it contained arguments, which, even if they were mistaken, were thought-provoking and interesting.'

In Chapter Four Lawrence Freedman provides a generally negative critical assessment of the work of Henry Kissinger. The thrust of his argument is that Kissinger was a man who swam with the currents and whose work was essentially derivative. He was not responsible, Lawrence Freedman argues, for creating any of the major concepts of nuclear strategy and his prescriptions have tended to be short-lived. As a result, apart from a brief period when he was in office, it is doubtful if Kissinger had a significant influence on the making of strategic policy.

He is most interesting, according to Freedman, as a consumer rather than a maker of nuclear strategy. Freedman argues that Kissinger was a consumer in three senses: First, as a policymaker when he commissioned studies from those in the armed forces and bureaucracy responsible for devising nuclear strategy; second, in a literal sense, as he constantly drew on the ideas of those around him in producing his own work; and third, because his main interest was in foreign policy, he was continuously searching for nuclear strategies which would reinforce American great-power diplomacy.

The search for a credible military policy was at the heart of Kissinger's writing in the 1950s and 1960s. Freedman describes his book on *Nuclear Weapons and Foreign Policy*, written in 1957, as his first and last substantial excursion into nuclear strategy. In this book Kissinger argued (like others at the time) that the current strategic doctrine of 'massive retaliation' was deficient because it failed to translate power into policy. Since all-out-war was too horrendous to contemplate, the Soviet

Union was able to pursue its objectives through more limited and indirect means without much fear of punishment. Apart from the continuing need to deter all-out-war, the United States required the capability to fight limited wars, and, if need be, limited nuclear wars. To fight such wars, Kissinger argued, new revolutionary tactics based on small, highly mobile, self-contained units were required.

Freedman provides a detailed critique of the ideas contained in *Nuclear Weapons and Foreign Policy*, arguing that Kissinger was let down by his inadequate grasp of military strategy. The main problem, he suggests, was that Kissinger had a very narrow understanding of land warfare and was overly influenced by the ill-conceived and unrealistic 'Pentomic' experiment which was fashionable at the time. The 'Pentomic' division had been proposed by a number of military leaders as a way of integrating small nuclear weapons, which in the 1950s were becoming available, into army planning. Little work, however, had been done on the tactical implications of this 'cockeyed technological fix' and it was soon discarded. The problem was compounded, Freedman argues, because Kissinger had no experience of operational analysis, and in some areas he did not really understand the material with which he was dealing. As a result, his broader thesis about limited nuclear war was flawed.

By 1961, when he wrote *Necessity for Choice*, Kissinger's ideas had been modified to take account of some of the criticisms of his earlier work on limited nuclear war. He now recognized that an overemphasis on the destructiveness of nuclear weapons might paralyse the will to respond. On the other hand, too great a concern with developing a flexible strategy for the conduct of war might reduce the risks to an aggressor to such a degree that he might be encouraged. In wrestling with this central dilemma of deterrence theory, Kissinger continued to believe in the need for some capacity to fight limited nuclear wars, but he was now concerned to put more emphasis on conventional capabilities. In this respect, Freedman points out, his ideas were not new; they reflected the growing consensus which had already emerged within the American strategic community in the early 1960s.

In the early 1970s, when he became the Special Assistant for National Security Affairs, Kissinger could make some claims to be a maker of nuclear strategy. Freedman argues that when he arrived in the White House, he lacked any clear agenda for nuclear policy. Nevertheless, his approach to nuclear issues was consistent with the general lines of his thinking since the early 1960s. He remained worried by the way in which the tremendous increase in nuclear power had eroded the traditional relationship of military power to foreign policy. He also sought arms control agreements to stabilize the strategic arms race and free resources for building up American conventional regional forces. The major problem he wrestled with, however, was translating doctrinal innovations into operational plans. A good example of this, discussed by Freedman, is the adoption of the NSDM 242 document by the American government in 1973. Kissinger favoured the idea of a more flexible nuclear posture, but he remained unimpressed by the kind of options contained in NSDM 242. It was the secretary of defense, James Schlesinger, who eventually pushed through the changes in American nuclear targeting policy in 1973 while Kissinger continued to drag his feet on the matter. Freedman argues that the NSDM 242 episode shows that while he was in office Kissinger remained a dissatisfied customer of nuclear strategy 'continually frustrated in his search for strategic concepts that could inject credibility into American foreign policy'.

Kissinger continued to move with the times and the strategic fashions when he left office in 1977. While he was in office in the early 1970s, he had advocated strategic sufficiency. By the late 1970s and early 1980s, however, he was echoing the ideas of the 'New Right' about the dangers of the 'window of vulnerability' without subjecting such ideas to the critical analysis they deserved. Freedman suggests that his change of heart had more to do with political opportunism than intellectual evolution.

The overall assessment of Henry Kissinger's contribution to strategic thought presented in the chapter is rather negative. He is commended for being one of the first to identify the contradictions at the heart of nuclear deterrence, but Freedman insists that Kissinger's work was flawed because it reflected his difficulty in coming to terms with the uncertainties produced by the contradictions of deterrence and his failure to find a means of resolving them.

In Chapter Five Phil Williams focuses on the 'immense and unique' contribution which Thomas Schelling made to nuclear strategy. His assessment of Schelling's work is organized into three main sections: the first considers the assumptions which underpinned Schelling's analysis; the second elucidates some of the key themes which characterized his approach to nuclear strategy and arms control; and the third provides a critique and evaluation of his ideas.

Williams argues that Schelling was a theoretical rather than an empirical strategist. His background in economics led him to try and develop a formal theory of conflict that was all-embracing. Central to his theorizing was the assumption that conflict is both endemic and pervasive in all social relationships. This meant that he was less concerned with trying to abolish conflict than with identifying the kinds of tactics that would lead to successful outcomes in conflict situations.

Another major working assumption at the heart of Schelling's theorizing was that protagonists in a conflict would behave in a rational manner. Williams points out that the notion of rational behaviour is a central feature of game theory which greatly attracted Schelling. In his main theoretical work, *The Strategy of Conflict*, he was concerned with games of strategy and particularly with variable sum games. Most conflicts, he argued, were variable sum games in which adversaries were engaged in both coercion and accommodation: Williams tells us that it was in this area that Schelling made one of his most distinctive contributions to strategic theory. He recognized that in conflict situations characterized by both hostility and cooperation, coercive bargaining was of central importance. Despite common interests in reaching a solution, the side which manipulated the risks most effectively would be likely to emerge more successfully from the conflict. This led Schelling to identify and elucidate what he described as 'the strategic basis for certain paradoxical tactics'.

Although Schelling was one of the pioneers in the use of game theory for enhancing an understanding of international conflict, Williams shows that he was not slavish or uncritical in his approach. He recognized the limitations as well as the insights. Williams argues that 'game theory may have provided the intellectual basis for some of Schelling's ideas, but it was his awareness of its limits and the skill and imagination with which he drew out the implications of the limits that provided such a distinctive and important contribution to strategic analysis'.

In the second section of the chapter Williams considers the way Schelling applied his theoretical insights to the field of nuclear strategy. He argues that Schelling made his most distinctive contribution in three main areas: deterrence, limited war and arms control.

Schelling argued that nuclear weapons enhanced 'the importance of war and threats of war as techniques of influence, not of destruction; or coercion and deterrence, not of conquest and defence; of bargaining and intimidation'. Williams shows that the idea of coercive diplomacy is one of the major themes in Schelling's writing. In particular he stresses Schelling's fascination with one of the central paradoxes of the nuclear age: that in situations where both sides could be severely damaged in a conflict, 'there were all sorts of bargaining advantages to be gained from being able to appear relatively impervious to dangers, risks or potential costs'. His analysis of this paradox led Schelling to produce important insights into 'the art of commitment', the differences between deterrent and compellent threats and risk manipulation through 'threats that leave something to chance'.

Williams goes on to demonstrate that despite Schelling's concern with coercive diplomacy, he was also interested in ways in which conflict could be limited or mitigated. This led him to analyse the nature of limited war. Schelling stressed the importance of limiting conflict in the nuclear age by emphasizing 'salient focal points', 'conventional stopping places or dividing lines'. He was particularly concerned with the psychological importance of the threshold between conventional and nuclear war and attempted to analyse the rules and conventions which might help conflicts from escalating from one to the other.

As Williams points out, Schelling was also a major proponent of arms control. Indeed his work with Morton Halperin helped to establish the basic philosophy of arms control which guided the thinking of strategists from the 1960s onwards. In tune with the rest of his thinking Schelling emphasized the mutual interests which even antagonists have in 'inducing and reciprocating restraint and making sure that force postures do not exacerbate underlying conflict'. For Schelling, however, arms control had more to do with military strategy than with disarmament. What mattered most was stability rather than reducing numbers of weapons. Williams shows that it was this concern with stability rather than numbers which led to Schelling's criticism of the arms control process in the 1970s.

In his assessment of Schelling's work in the third section of his chapter, Williams argues that the skill and rigour as well as the novelty and originality with which he developed his arguments set new standards for strategic thinking. He is, nevertheless, critical of some of Schelling's ideas and arguments. He makes four main criticisms.

First, he notes that Schelling has been subjected to some of the same allegations which have been directed against Herman Kahn; namely that he was insensitive to ethical considerations and advocated policies which bordered on genocide. He argues that although such charges are largely inappropriate there is 'a sense in which Schelling did allow his fascination with games of strategy and with the logic of winning to lead him into areas that could not be treated simply as games'.

His second criticism is that as an economist Schelling lacked the deep historical knowledge of, say, Bernard Brodie. As a result tactics he recommended in the realm of coercive diplomacy had very little appeal in practice for policymakers who were rather more aware of the considerable risks associated with making 'irrevocable commitments' and 'threats that leave something to chance' in crisis situations.

A third, related criticism is that although Schelling was aware of the risks inherent in his tactics, he remained more concerned with maximizing the coercive impact of actions rather than risk reduction. Williams argues that 'the attractions of manipulation invariably outweighed the dictates of prudence'. Consequently, he suggests, if decisionmakers had acted on Schelling's precepts, the Cold War would have been even more dangerous than it was.

The final criticism concerns Schelling's underlying assumptions. A major problem, Williams argues, is that Schelling's work is populated by an artificial 'strategic man' concerned with maximizing his gains through coercion, compellence and the like. Yet 'strategic man' is as much an unrealistic abstraction as is an 'economic man' concerned only with maximizing profits. The difficulty arises because of Schelling's tendency to ignore bureaucratic bargaining processes and broader public pressures and to treat governments as though they were rational monolithic actors.

Williams concludes by arguing that although these are important shortcomings there is no denying 'the sheer intellectual virtuosity and breathtaking brilliance' of Schelling's analysis. He contends that his ideas on deterrence, arms control and stability are of enduring relevance and very real value. Williams' view is that Schelling 'left a rich vein of highly sophisticated argument and subtle analysis which cannot be ignored'.

Chapters Six and Seven shift the focus from American strategists to two important British thinkers. In Chapter Six John Baylis looks at the contribution made to strategic thought by Anthony Buzzard. Buzzard was widely respected in Britain in the 1950s for his critique of 'massive retaliation' and his enunciation of an alternative doctrine of 'graduated deterrence.' He was also admired as a devout Christian who, somewhat unusually for the period, wrestled with the issues of morality in the nuclear age. Baylis argues that his naval experience, together with his later work for the British and World Council of Churches meant that Buzzard was uniquely placed to provide a link between the strategists and churchmen who met at the Brighton Conference in January 1957 to set up the Institute for Strategic Studies.

Although most of the strategists dealt with in this volume were critics of the 'massive retaliation' strategy, Buzzard's critique was one of the first, coming as it did in the early 1950s when he served as Director of Naval Intelligence. The Global Strategy Paper, produced by the British Chiefs of Staff in 1952, argued that greater priority should be given to deterrence through the threat of mass destruction. Buzzard was sceptical of this new emphasis in British strategic doctrine and produced a major 'in-house' critique of it in July 1953. In his view a mass destruction strategy was dangerous because it would increase the incentive for states to strike first if war broke out, and it would make the limitation of war very difficult to achieve. It would be better, he argued, for nuclear weapons to be used in a more discriminating way against military targets rather than against cities. Cities, Buzzard believed, should only be attacked with mass destruction weapons in retaliation. Hence, in 1953, Buzzard was advocating ideas about limited war and 'counterforce targeting' which were to be at the heart of Western debates about nuclear strategy in the late 1950s and early 1960s.

Baylis shows, however, that these ideas had very little influence on the defence establishment in Britain. As a result, Buzzard retired from the navy in 1954 and pursued a more public campaign against the prevailing strategic ideas. He believed that 'massive retaliation' was wholly inadequate in dealing with the most likely threats of subversion and indirect probing. To threaten the destruction of civilization in the event of limited aggression clearly lacked credibility. What was needed was an intermediate capability to deal with local aggression.

The emphasis on intermediate capabilities which Buzzard favoured was based on a combination of moral, political and military considerations. In moral terms, Buzzard argued that limitations were essential in war because the West should never cause or threaten to cause more destruction than was necessary to deter or repel aggression. Strategy had to combine expediency and moral principle. In political terms, 'graduated deterrence' was superior to 'massive retaliation' because it was less frightening and intimidating. As a result it would help to build up trust and reduce tension between East and West. Security, Buzzard argued, had to be thought of in political terms. He supported the idea of arms control and what we would now describe as 'confidence building measures' as important elements of security policy. In military terms he saw 'graduated deterrence' as benefiting the West because agreed limitations would exclude attacks not only on cities but also on ports which are so important for reinforcing Western Europe in the event of war.

Buzzard was not without his critics. Sir John Slessor, the former chief of the air staff, who had been responsible for the Global Strategy Paper, argued in private and in public against Buzzard's ideas of limiting the use of hydrogen weapons which he believed would undermine deterrence. Such limitations, Slessor argued, were impractical and inadequate in dealing with Soviet conventional superiority. These criticisms were rejected by Buzzard who thought 'graduated deterrence' was more credible than 'massive retaliation', and despite the practical difficulties of limiting war, he argued that both sides would have every incentive to limit a conflict if it broke out.

Baylis contends that Buzzard's notion of 'graduated deterrence' represents 'one of the most influential alternative strategies of the late 1950s' and that his ideas have had 'a profound influence on strategic thought down to the present day'. He indicates that Buzzard's papers reveal the extent of this influence through his wide-ranging correspondence with American strategists including Kissinger, Wohlstetter, Nitze and Schelling as well as many influential figures in Britain. In the end his ideas also surfaced in the realm of policy. In Baylis's words 'graduated deterrence' was 'the true precursor of the concept of flexible response.'

In his assessment of Buzzard, John Baylis points out that his ideas remained inflexible. Furthermore he was overly optimistic about the chances of preventing limited war from escalating. Nevertheless, Buzzard presented a well thought out and coherent alternative strategy at a very early stage of the debate about deterrence in the West. He also helped to create a climate of debate as a result of which major changes occurred in Western strategic policies. Buzzard's contribution to strategic thought has been rather neglected by those who have emphasized the role of American strategists, but according to Baylis, Buzzard thoroughly deserves his place as an important thinker about nuclear strategy.

Chapter Seven deals with another British thinker whose work deserves more recognition; Michael Howard looks at the contribution of P. M. S. Blackett and argues that he was not only one of the most brilliant physicists of this century but also one of the most important strategic thinkers of his day.

According to Michael Howard two particular characteristics set Blackett apart from the other strategic thinkers of his time: one was that he was the only atomic scientist to have been a professional fighting man; the other was that he was rather radical in his political judgements and had a passion for social justice. His personal experience of war together with 'an abrasive independence of mind, gave him a healthy scepticism of all theories based on unstated or unverifiable hypotheses'. Blackett's distinctive contribution to strategic thinking, in Howard's view, derived from his scepticism of fashionable American strategic analysis.

It might have been expected that a man who encouraged numerical analysis and was a pioneer of operational research would have favoured the rigorous scientific methodology of writers like Wohlstetter and Schelling. In practice, as Howard shows, Blackett did not. Elegant American strategic theories affronted the pragmatic instincts Blackett had developed in his long experience with the armed services. In 1961, he wrote a major critique of 'The Delicate Balance of Terror', an article which typified Wohlstetter's distinctive mixture of numerical analysis and tough common sense. In particular Blackett attacked the political assumptions which underpinned Wohlstetter's analysis. He argued that it was unrealistic to assume, as Wohlstetter did, that any government would launch a surprise attack if it knew that it would be destroyed in return. He also argued that the scale of forces advocated by Wohlstetter to overcome the vulnerability of American strategic forces would be interpreted by the Soviet Union as a pre-emptive force. If implemented, Wohlstetter's recommendations would have led to a worsening of the international climate.

Although Blackett agreed with many of the contemporary criticisms of 'massive retaliation', he was very sceptical about the deterrence ideas put forward by the

American strategists generally. In his view atomic and hydrogen weapons had virtually abolished total war. Strategists therefore had to concentrate on working out how *few* were needed for deterrence. In a sense, Blackett was an early advocate of what McGeorge Bundy was later to call 'existential deterrence'. Sophisticated scenarios of nuclear warfighting like those put forward by Wohlstetter were not necessary. It was the prospect of nuclear war itself which deterred. The crucial requirement of minimum deterrence was simply the preservation of a stable second-strike capability.

Howard shares some of Blackett's concerns about the methodology used by some of the American strategists. He also accepts that in terms of political realities Blackett's views were highly persuasive. The main problem, he suggests, is that however politically realistic, such ideas are militarily inadequate. He points out that although 'politicians may prefer not to peer beyond the curtain of the first dreadful nuclear exchange', strategists have a professional obligation to think about the unthinkable. They have to think about the implications of initiating a nuclear strike, the targets against which it would be directed and the responses it would be likely to evoke. Howard does, however, admit that the consequences of such thinking were just as Blackett foretold — an endless arms race and complications for arms control.

Howard concludes his chapter by arguing that although Blackett did not produce any specific theories or any original insights into the new problems of the nuclear age, he nevertheless made a significant contribution to strategic thought in the 1950s and 1960s through the sheer quality of intellect which he brought to bear on the prevailing strategic ideas of others. There were a number of influential thinkers in Britain at the time, among them Buzzard, Buchan and Liddell Hart, but Howard argues that Blackett was the most important. It was 'his experience and incisiveness that largely dominated their thinking and it is his work that best bears re-reading'. Similarly, set in the context of the more influential American strategists, he argues that Blackett still stands out. His vigorous scientific approach combined with common sense and an understanding of both war and politics was rare among 'his fluent and sophisticated contemporaries'. In Michael Howard's view the only figure of comparable quality was Bernard Brodie.

Chapter Eight focuses on one of the major French strategists of the era, André Beaufré. In his chapter, François de Rose looks at Beaufré's distinctively French contribution to strategic thought which, although derived from a combination of wide-ranging military experience and an acute intellect, was grounded in an extensive knowledge of the past. He describes Beaufré as a man 'equally gifted for imagination and reflection — both analytic and synthetic', with a lucid understanding of the present and sound intuition about the future.

One of the main themes of de Rose's chapter is a consideration of Beaufré's conception of strategy. For Beaufré, strategy was not a doctrine but 'a method of thinking'. It was an unreasonable emphasis on what was commonly regarded as an infallible strategy in the inter-war period which resulted in France's defeat in 1940. Circumstances change, and strategy has to be flexible enough to accommodate these changes. This was particularly the case, Beaufré argued, in an age of total war when strategy had to be conducted on a number of different planes — political, economic, diplomatic and military. Following Clausewitz, he argued that although strategy was 'the art of making force contribute to achieving the goals of politics', force included not just military might but all the factors involved in the confrontation between protagonists. Victory involved imposing one's will on an adversary not simply defeating him in battle. As a result strategic reasoning 'must combine the psycho-

logical and material elements of the situation by an abstract, rational operation of the
mind involving analysis and synthesis'.

De Rose shows how Beaufré brought this form of strategic reasoning to bear on
three main areas of strategy: conventional military strategy, nuclear strategy and
indirect strategy. In the field of conventional strategy Beaufré stressed the difficulties
created by the variability of war. All routine, he said, is condemned in advance to
failure. One of the crucial elements of success in warfare, therefore, is the need to
understand, more rapidly than one's adversary, the changes taking place in the nature
of warfare and in the relationship of the elements on which victory in battle depends.
For Beaufré, the ability to transform and adapt operational strategy is the key to a
successful conventional military strategy.

De Rose goes on to show that Beaufré's emphasis on the importance of the
combination of material realities and psychological factors was also crucial to his
analysis of nuclear strategy. The power of nuclear weapons meant that the aim of
nuclear strategy had to be deterrence rather than military victory. And for deterrence
to work effectively the credibility of the threat was of major importance. Like most of
the nuclear strategists considered in this volume, Beaufré was critical of 'massive
retaliation' because it rested on an incredible threat of reciprocal suicide. However,
the concept of limited counterforce options, put forward by American strategists to
improve the credibility of deterrence and provide protection for the European allies,
was also unconvincing to Beaufré. He rejected the argument put forward by
McNamara that independent deterrents were incredible and unnecessary. For Beaufré, third-country nuclear forces were useful partly because they complicated the task
of a possible aggressor and helped deter actions in areas which were marginal for other
allies.

De Rose concluded that Beaufré's treatment of independent deterrents was one area
in which he made a distinctive contribution to strategic thought. While not accepting
the thesis put forward by another French strategist, Pierre Gallois, that nuclear
weapons had an 'equalizing power', he did nevertheless argue that independent
deterrents had an important role to play within an alliance context. Independent
forces, Beaufré stressed, had to be allied but not integrated. They had to be part of a
whole 'while remaining independent'. Consultation and coordination were important
in the context of the alliance, but there must be 'no abdication of the responsibility of
decision-making or any right of veto'. It is this view of 'independence in alliance'
which has characterized French nuclear strategy since the mid-1960s.

De Rose shows that Beaufré's analysis of nuclear deterrence led him to stress the
importance of the concept of 'indirect strategy'. Because the risk of nuclear war
excludes direct confrontation, there is a need to gain the upper hand by manoeuvring
rather than fighting. In Beaufré's view the more nuclear strategy succeeds in
strengthening overall deterrence, the greater the use that will be made of indirect
strategy. Hence, in the new age of nuclear weapons, there was a need for the West to
develop a total strategy which combined deterrence with an indirect strategy. Beaufré
believed that although military power would not disappear, the paralysis created by
nuclear weapons meant that other factors would play an essential part in a total
strategy. He believed that 'a total strategy in the indirect mode was likely to be the
strategy of the future'.

It is de Rose's contention that Beaufré's stress on the primacy of the mind
characterizes his most significant contribution to strategic thought. Unlike his British
and American counterparts, his approach centred much less on the immediate and
tangible aspects of the Soviet threat and rather more on the need to master 'the rules
of the new era'. Instead of concentrating on strategies designed specifically to counter

Soviet nuclear and conventional forces and doctrines, Beaufré's main concern was 'to fathom the depths of the new ocean of problems' facing the West in the nuclear age. It was this unique emphasis on how to think about strategy which made Beaufré one of the most original strategists of his generation.

The final chapter deals with strategic thinking in the Soviet Union. Neil MacFarlane discusses the contribution of Marshal V. D. Sokolovskii to the debates about nuclear weapons in the Soviet Union, and assesses the impact of the volume he edited on *Military Strategy* on the development of Soviet strategy.

MacFarlane points out that Sokolovskii's contribution to strategic thought was rather different from the contributions made by other strategists discussed in this book. He was head of a collegium of authors who were responsible for the three editions of *Military Strategy* between 1962 and 1968. As such, the views expressed in the edited volume were not those of Sokolovskii alone. *Military Strategy* does, however, represent the first systematic attempt by a number of prominent Soviet military theorists to develop a coherent body of strategic principles on how to fight a war in the nuclear age. The Sokolovskii volumes deserve attention, MacFarlane argues, not only because of their impact on Soviet policy but also because of their influence on Western perceptions of the Soviet threat.

MacFarlane discusses *Military Strategy* under three main headings: first, the historical and political context in which it was written; second, the substance of the work and the changing emphasis of the three volumes; and finally, the developments which have taken place in Soviet strategic thinking and practice since the last edition of the book was published.

In terms of the context in which *Military Strategy* was written, MacFarlane emphasizes the internal debates about strategy and defence budgets which took place in the Soviet Union after the death of Stalin. He shows how military thought was 'de-Stalinized' as Khrushchev attempted to shift the emphasis in Soviet defence policy towards nuclear weapons. These events, together with American debates about flexible response and the difficulties in East–West relations associated with the U2 incident and the Berlin crisis, prompted a major debate in the Soviet Union about the nature of nuclear deterrence. MacFarlane shows that the 1962 edition of *Military Strategy* was an attempt to develop a coherent general statement on Soviet strategy in the context of changing internal and external conditions. He suggests, however, that given the nature of the on-going, unfinished debate in the Soviet Union, the book was something of a compromise, embodying 'the lowest common denominator' on which all the authors could agree. Numerous critical issues were left unresolved and important contradictions remained. Although the authors accepted that nuclear weapons had fundamentally altered the character of war, they still believed that large land forces would continue to play their traditional role.

The view of war presented in the first edition of *Military Strategy* was that it would be unlimited, global and inevitably nuclear. The authors were sceptical about Western ideas of 'limited war', arguing that the aim of Soviet forces would be to defeat the enemy armed forces and devastate his cities. This would necessitate simultaneous 'counterforce' and 'countervalue' strikes. The thrust of the argument was that although nuclear war was not inevitable, it was necessary to develop a strategy which defined how to fight such a war if it occurred. Such a strategy would involve combined arms operations using all of the services and both conventional and nuclear weapons.

MacFarlane argues that this strategy for fighting and winning a nuclear war was deeply rooted both in the historical development of Soviet military thought and in Marxist–Leninist theory. It was based on a view of nuclear weapons and the relationship between war and politics which was distinctively Soviet. MacFarlane shows that these ideas differed from American strategic thinking in three very important respects. First, Sokolovskii and his colleagues rejected the notion that the nuclear era was different from previous eras in military history in the sense that nuclear weapons could not be used as rational instruments of policy. Second, they rejected the idea that the security of the state could, or should, be based on a mutual hostage relationship. Third, they did not believe that there could be a significant conventional phase in major war. As a result, they gave no serious thought to many of the ideas which were discussed in Western strategic debates — ideas about firebreaks and thresholds, tacit or explicit communication in war, limited nuclear war and intra-war deterrence. Instead they emphasized the massive and indiscriminate use of strategic nuclear weapons at the start of any major war.

Despite what he calls 'the clear and substantial differences' between this body of strategic theory and contemporary American doctrine, MacFarlane argues that the view, held by some in the West, that the Soviet Union actually believed it could fight and win a nuclear war, is incorrect. Although the rhetoric talked about victory, he suggests that Soviet strategists like Sokolovskii knew that the strategic balance was unfavourable to them and that the Soviet Union might not win a major war. The aim was superiority, but this objective was by no means assured. The purpose of elaborating ideas of victory and warfighting was to deter the West and, if deterrence broke down, to provide the Soviet Union with various strategic options to fight any conflict which might occur.

MacFarlane discusses the impact which the Sokolovskii volumes had on both Western and Soviet strategy. In terms of the American reaction, he believes that the emphasis on warfighting and the importance of military superiority had a major effect on American doctrine and procurement in the late 1970s and early 1980s. American notions of a 'countervailing strategy' and the development of credible capabilities to fight and 'prevail' in a nuclear war with the Soviet Union reflect the kind of ideas put forward by Sokolovskii and his colleagues. The United States felt obliged to adopt these ideas in order to produce a credible deterrent posture which the Soviet Union would understand.

As far as the impact of Sokolovskii on the Soviet Union itself is concerned, MacFarlane contends that the developments in strategic policy in the mid- and late 1960s indicated a desire to produce the kind of capabilities recommended in *Military Strategy*. At the same time, the failure of the book to resolve the contradiction between the nuclear revolution and traditional military theories helped to fuel a continuing debate about strategy from the late 1960s onwards. For some critics the book went too far in focusing on strategic nuclear forces. For other, more radical critics, the volume failed to appreciate the fundamental significance of the nuclear era. For them, traditional ideas of war as a continuation of politics were obsolete.

MacFarlane concludes by showing how the radical critics generally became more influential, especially following Brezhnev's Tula Speech in 1977 and a growing appreciation of the mutuality of security and strategic stability under Gorbachev. As a result, he suggests that Sokolovskii's ideas about military strategy are less relevant than they once were. The era of *glasnost* has opened up new debates in the Soviet Union. At the moment there is no settled Soviet doctrine on nuclear weapons. A new Sokolovskii is badly needed to make sense of Soviet military policy in a radically changed world.

Notes

1. B. H. Liddell Hart. *Deterrent or Defence*, London: Stevens, 1960, p. 66.

1 BERNARD BRODIE

Ken Booth

Bernard Brodie was the quintessential strategist of the first generation of the nuclear age. He was among the very first pioneers of *The New Strategy*[1], and his subsequent career reflected most aspects of the new profession that developed out of it. But Brodie was more than simply a man of his time, professionally speaking. Above all he was concerned to nurture the roots of strategic thinking. These, he believed, had been most comprehensively expressed by Carl von Clausewitz, the great nineteenth-century German thinker on war. Brodie attempted to develop Clausewitz's legacy for the first nuclear generation. He explained the novel and frequently paradoxical interrelationships between war, politics and strategy.

Brodie has been somewhat overshadowed in fame by more prolific, protagonistic and precocious members of his profession. He failed to have Albert Wohlstetter's direct influence on policy; he never displayed Herman Kahn's inflated virtuosity; he did not exhibit Thomas Schelling's formal reasoning; and he lacked Henry Kissinger's experience in the practice as well as the theory of great power. Even so, Bernard Brodie's reputation has been secure in the minds of the most distinguished of his profession. Michael Howard has described him as 'quite the wisest strategic thinker of our generation' while Thomas Schelling called him the 'first — both in time and in distinction' among those whose profession was to think about the unthinkable.[2] Brodie's work will be read long after that of most of his contemporaries has been forgotten. He was a strategist's strategist, who insisted on thinking about first principles. Strategic history will acclaim Brodie as the Clausewitz of the age of nuclear deterrence.

Bernard Brodie, who was born in 1910, had an exemplary career as a student.[3] He had the knack of being in the right place at the right time, and he made good use of his early opportunities. After excelling as a student of philosophy at the University of Chicago in the mid-1930s, he was drawn into the young subject of international relations by his interest in military affairs and the gathering storm clouds over Europe and the Far East. Brodie stayed at Chicago and, in the graduate school, studied under Quincy Wright, whose own work was making him one of the unquestioned masters of his subject. Wright was then approaching the end of his mammoth project, *The Study of War*.[4] Brodie also greatly benefited from Jacob Viner, a member of the economics department. Viner was an impressive thinker about international relations and in time became an early and original contributor to thinking about the atomic bomb.[5] He had a significant influence on Brodie during his graduate years and later when he became a junior professor. Brodie's graduate dissertation was on the impact of naval technology on diplomacy in the nineteenth century; he finished it in 1940.

Following Brodie's auspicious beginnings at Chicago he went to Princeton where he took up a research fellowship, helped by Wright's contact with Edward Meade Earle.[6] Like Wright, Earle was at the forefront of his field and was overseeing a book, *The Makers of Modern Strategy*, which would become a milestone. Through its numerous reprintings, it became the only volume on strategic history that would be read over the next thirty years by most of the new breed of civilian strategists.[7] For Brodie, in contrast, strategic history was already an open book.

As a junior academic at Princeton Brodie adapted his dissertation into his own first book, *Sea Power in the Machine Age*. Meanwhile, as the war spread in Europe, and then the Pacific, his interest in military affairs grew. He was also learning that the strategic theorist might be valued by the practitioner, since the US Navy bought his book in large numbers. Following this success, Princeton University Press commissioned him to write another, again on sea power. He completed it quickly, and in 1942 *A Layman's Guide To Naval Strategy* was published. This book was also a success, though more so with professionals than laymen, once the term 'Layman's' had been dropped from the title.[8] It appeared that civilian theorists could be appreciated by military professionals; later, Brodie learned that this was the exception rather than the rule.

After being a successful student, junior academic and author, Brodie — now in his early thirties — moved from Princeton to Dartmouth College. There he organized a course called 'Modern War, Strategy and National Policies'.[9] With lecture titles such as 'Pressures Short of War', 'War as a Continuation of Politics', and 'The Quest for National Security', the syllabus he taught has a remarkably contemporary ring. It has a claim to be the first modern course in what later became strategic studies. In defining his syllabus Brodie also set down a significant part of his professional agenda for the next thirty years.

Brodie discovered at Dartmouth that energy and ability do not always lead to success in academic life. His achievements failed to earn him the support of some of his immediate colleagues, and his contract was not renewed. He was seen to be 'too much of a specialist' and 'too big a man' in his field.[10] He left academic life, and for the last two years of the war worked in various departments of the United States' Navy. Among his tasks, he wrote speeches for the chief of naval operations and propaganda for broadcasting to German U-boats.[11] This interruption to his academic career proved to be a positive twist of fate since it gave Brodie first-hand experience of government in Washington and contact with the military establishment at a high level. He soon began to learn that the relationship between civilian experts and the military could be unsatisfactory, as well as important.

Brodie did not sever his academic contacts during this period, and towards the end of the war his work impressed some members of the Institute of International Studies at Yale. Among the latter were some of the key figures (notably Frederick Dunn, W. T. R. Fox and Arnold Wolfers) in the development of 'realist' thinking about international relations. Brodie accepted their invitation to join the Institute. He planned to develop his interest in naval matters and began working on the future of the battleship.[12] Events quickly changed the direction of his study just as they changed the future of the battleship.

On 7 August 1945, the day after the city of Hiroshima had been destroyed by a single atomic bomb dropped from a single B-29 bomber, Brodie bought a newspaper at a pharmacy. After looking at the main news report he told his wife Fawn that all his previous work on the effect of technology on war was now obsolete.[13] The ruins of Hiroshima were a turning-point in strategic history, but Brodie had not been present at the destruction. Unlike most great strategists of the past, he was a civilian rather than a soldier, and he did not experience great military events at close quarters. It was a fitting start for what was to be the new era of long-distance terror weapons and academic experts: the man who became the absolute strategist of his generation first became aware of the impact of the atomic age in his home town, from a newspaper, before going to his office.

One bomb from one bomber could now leave a city in ruins. What could many such bombs do, from many more bombers — not to mention long-distance rockets? Such questions re-directed Brodie's interests and energy, and through his contacts and the force of his argument he became prominent among those who tried to comprehend the implications of the new weapons. While some argued that the atomic bomb was just a more destructive weapon to be added to the armoury of strategic bombing,[14] Brodie put forward the proposition that it had changed the basic character of strategy. His initial thoughts were expressed in an essay published in November 1945.[15] From henceforth, he argued, the nature of war had changed. The strategic situation would be dominated by the offence, and cities would be the most valuable and vulnerable targets. In such circumstances, constant readiness was essential. This might provoke tension and preventive war; alternatively, it might produce stability through mutual fear. He had not yet decided which way the balance would tip.

In order to carry the debate forward, Brodie and his colleagues at Yale decided to write a book. In part it was their aim to counter what they believed to be the excessive idealism then being expressed in some groups about the prospects for the international control of atomic power. The originators of the book were Dunn and Fox; Brodie was chosen to be the editor. Percy Corbett and Arnold Wolfers were also contributors. The title, a phrase of Fox's, was chosen by Brodie.[16] *The Absolute Weapon* was written and published scarcely half a year after the dropping of the first atomic bombs. It was, and remains, an extraordinary achievement.

The Absolute Weapon (subtitled *Atomic Power and World Order*) was a landmark in the story of thinking about nuclear weapons. This is not to say that it was an influential or widely read book. Like several of the key works in strategic history, it has been referred to more frequently than actually read, and in hindsight its reputation has become more significant than in the late 1940s.[17] Even today it is unlikely that most members of the strategic profession know more about it than a couple of much-repeated quotations. Nevertheless, it deserves a place in the history of strategic thought. It was the first comprehensive exposition of American strategy for the age of nuclear deterrence.

The Absolute Weapon was a remarkable book. Quickly produced, not only was it the first volume on deterrence in the atomic age, it was also a work of exceptional quality. It was a book of considerable analytical clarity and technical expertise; it represented a sophisticated application of the ideas of political realism; and it also exhibited extraordinary prescience. There were no comparable works for over ten years. Brodie, who a few years earlier had devised and taught the first modern strategic studies course, had now edited the first book on nuclear strategy, the issue that would dominate the subject when it became established a decade later. The first step down the road of new strategic theory had been made by civilians rather than from within the military profession, the traditional source of what passed for strategic thinking. So it would remain. The authors of *The Absolute Weapon* were also American; this too would be a dominating feature in strategic theorizing over the following decades.

When people talk about *The Absolute Weapon* Brodie attracts almost all the attention; indeed, not a few people imagine that he wrote the whole book. It was however a cooperative effort, qualitatively and philosophically. Each of the five contributors wrote one chapter apart from Brodie himself, who wrote two. Brodie's contribution cannot be separated from the school of thought represented by his colleagues, not to mention the continuing influence of Viner, Wright and Earle. Lack of space precludes an analysis of the chapters by Corbett, Dunn, Fox and Wolfers, but it should be noted that they exhibited a marked coherence of style and approach. They expected that the main problem in the years ahead would be how to live with the bomb rather than how to eliminate it; they believed that the international system bred suspicion, which limited the value of treaties and international agencies on security questions; they proposed that equality in deterrent power would be a better guarantee of peace than the international control of atomic weapons; they argued that world government was not within the world's grasp; they assumed that the mutual threat of the destruction of cities was not an absolute guarantee against war; they forecast that the key problem would be Soviet–American relations, not out of any anti-communist beliefs on their part but because of the realist expectation of irreducible suspicion between two powers able to lay each other's cities to waste; they expected stumbling into war to be a greater risk than direct aggression, and in such circumstances they did not believe that peace would be served by a United States paralysed by fear. Above all, each believed that the new imbalance between defensive possibilities and destructive certainties meant that national security now depended not on national strength but on mutual restraint in the presence of an awesome threat. The era of security interdependence had arrived — if not yet in practice, at least in theory.

Brodie's two chapters, 'War in the Atomic Age' and 'Implications For Military Policy' were a development of the ideas published in his essay of the previous November. They elaborated his view that the destructiveness of the bomb had fundamentally changed the character of war: 'the atomic bomb seems so far to overshadow any military invention of the past to render comparisons ridiculous'.[18]

The bulk of Brodie's first chapter consisted of a discussion of eight conclusions which he believed to be 'inescapable'.[19]

I The power of the present bomb is such that any city in the world can be effectively destroyed by one to ten bombs.

II No adequate defence against the bomb exists, and the possibilities of its existence in the future are exceedingly remote.

III The atomic bomb not only places an extraordinary military premium upon the development of new types of carriers, but also greatly extends the destructive range of existing carriers.

IV Superiority in air forces, though a more effective safeguard in itself than superiority in naval or land forces, nevertheless fails to guarantee security.

V Superiority in numbers of bombs is not in itself a guarantee of strategic superiority in atomic bomb warfare.

VI The new potentialities which the atomic bomb gives to sabotage must not be overrated.

VII In relation to the destructive powers of the bomb, world resources in raw materials for its production must be considered abundant.

VIII Regardless of American decisions concerning retention of its present secrets, other powers besides Britain and Canada will possess the ability to produce the bombs in quantity within a period of five to ten years hence.

These conclusions, generated within weeks of the destruction of Hiroshima, have stood the test of time. At their root was Brodie's recognition of the revolutionary destructiveness of the new weapon. Even with the aircraft then available, he contended that a state possessing atomic bombs could destroy most of the cities of any other power, though this might involve one-way missions.[20] Nevertheless — one of his major arguments — the increased effectiveness of bombing would not result in 'the apotheosis of aggressive instruments'.[21] This was because atomic aggression would be deterred — a word Brodie used from the beginning — as long as the potential attacker believed that there was a good chance of retaliation. Here, in this first major exposition of strategy for the atomic age, Brodie was expressing the importance of what would later be called a 'secure second-strike capability'. To Brodie, in 1945–6, this meant that a deterrent force of bombers should be protected from enemy surprise attack by dispersal and underground storage.[22]

In his essay of the previous November, as Kaplan has pointed out, Brodie had been 'tentative' on the question of whether the atomic bomb would deter or provoke tension. In the intervening months Jacob Viner had helped him make up his mind; he came to accept Viner's argument that the bomb would be stabilizing since no promise of victory would be worth the price if devastating retaliation was certain.[23] Brodie was greatly impressed by the revolutionary character of the new weapon. Consequently, in one of the most quoted sentences of the book, he wrote: 'Everything about the atomic bomb is overshadowed by the twin facts that it exists and that its destructive power is fantastically great.'[24] Believing that there was little likelihood that the weapon could be abolished, or that an effective defence could protect a country's major cities, Brodie concluded that the weapon would be a 'powerful inhibitor to aggression'. In asserting that the bomb's existence and destructiveness overshadowed all else, Brodie was anticipating the notion of 'existential deterrence', coined by McGeorge Bundy three decades later.[25]

Despite his tilt towards stable deterrence, Brodie did not believe that the absolute weapon had made war absolutely impossible (he believed that it would be difficult to deter 'madmen' for example).[26] Atomic wars were possible, he argued, and even major wars without the use of atomic weapons. What he could not conceive was the idea of a war in which atomic bombs would be used in only a limited way.[27] The latter was an issue that would trouble him throughout the rest of his career.

Brodie not only opened the debate and set down the agenda for deterrence — the pre-occupation of the new strategists for the decades ahead — but he also offered opinions on a range of subsidiary issues. He discussed, for example, the need to have forces to carry on the fight after one's cities had been destroyed or for participation in a long war of attrition if atomic weapons were not used. Even in the atomic age he believed that ground must eventually be occupied, and so there was a need for invasion and counter-invasion forces to bring war to a conclusion.[28] Here Brodie was pre-empting discussion of 'broken-backed warfare', a topic which would preoccupy naval circles in the 1950s. Somewhat at odds with this possibility was his discussion of the prospect of rapid wars of atomic destruction. These implied that old-style modes of mobilization would no longer be satisfactory, certainly with regard to front-line forces. For such contingencies the United States would have to fight with the forces it had ready when war broke out. Brodie recognized that the major powers were moving into an era of 'go-as-you-are' warfare. He also saw no reason why other countries should not join the atomic bomb club.[29] Proliferation thus reared its head for the first time.

Brodie's comments on these and other issues were scattered. He was obviously feeling his way. The primacy which Brodie gave to deterrence through retaliation, for example, led to what all commentators have subsequently picked out as Brodie's most prophetic statement: yet it was tucked away on page seventy-six. These words of Brodie, taken from a paper he wrote in 1945, became a compulsory quotation for the age of nuclear deterrence (as did Clausewitz's famous aphorism about war as a continuation of politics for the age of the classical European states' system):

Thus, the first and most vital step in any American security program for the age of atomic bombs is to take measures to guarantee to ourselves in case of attack the possibility of retaliation in kind. The writer in making that statement is not for the moment concerned about who will *win* the next war in which atomic bombs are used. Thus far the chief purpose of our military establishment has been to win wars. From now on its chief purpose must be to avert them. It can have almost no other useful purpose.

It is hardly an exaggeration to say that other nuclear strategists, in the years following, have simply written footnotes — long and short, spare and rococo — to these five sentences written in the shadow of the first mushroom cloud.

Brodie himself, with no false modesty, wrote many years later that much of the debate in the intervening years had revolved around these early thoughts.[30] He was right; but this does not mean that those who addressed themselves to his words were merely disciples. Indeed, his ideas also signalled other directions that might be followed. Gregg Herken has noted that the last of Brodie's famous five sentences contained an important qualifier. After the argument that the 'chief purpose' of the military establishment was to avert war, Brodie had added that it can have '*almost* no other useful purpose' (Herken's emphasis). Whether nuclear weapons can have any other useful purpose apart from basic deterrence proved to be a focus of contention for strategists over the next forty years. As it happened the opening shots in the debate were fired almost immediately, and on Brodie's own doorstep. William Borden, also at Yale in 1946 and a lawyer unusually interested in military matters, published *There Will Be No Time* soon after *The Absolute Weapon*. His main theme was that atomic weapons were just bigger weapons and should be conceived in traditional ways, for example by giving primacy at the outset of war to eliminating the enemy's offensive potential.[31] The positions adopted by Brodie and Borden in 1946 later became labelled the 'deterrent' and 'warfighting' schools respectively. The debate was still reverberating at the time of Brodie's death over thirty years later, but whereas he had made regular contributions to it, Borden made just one. Particularly in the early days, when destructive power was still somewhat limited, there was more common ground between the protagonists than some have suggested. As is evident from *The Absolute Weapon*, for example, Brodie believed that effective deterrence depended upon a state having the weapons and doctrines to conduct effective offensive and defensive operations, that is, an operational warfighting strategy. The key, in Brodie's mind, was one of priorities. His eventual position was that an effective policy of deterrence should not be undermined in order to gain marginal advantages in fighting a nuclear war.[32]

Brodie's contribution to *The Absolute Weapon* was of exceptional authority. He was occasionally cautious, as was appropriate, but he did not avoid drawing conclusions; and these were vindicated. He recognized that fundamental changes had taken place in the traditional role of force between the major powers and in doing so he opened the debate and gave guidance on so many new issues: the primacy of deterrence, the danger of surprise attack, the reduced utility of strategic superiority, the supremacy of the offence, the limited prospect for strategic defence, the possibility of nuclear proliferation, the advent of existential deterrence, the emptiness of the notion of victory in atomic war, the significance of the security of retaliatory forces, the problems of broken-backed war and the changed nature and utility of war between nuclear powers. Together with his co-writers, Brodie was clearing his mind about the absolute weapon; but in so doing he set down the agenda for a generation of strategists.

While some in the United States were arguing that the new weapon was simply a bigger bomb to be fitted into existing plans, and others were asserting that everything had changed and that world government was the only answer, the Yale group chose a different path. They believed that the bomb was revolutionary but that states would not put their security in the hands of an international organization. As a result, the great powers could not return to old-style wars, but neither could they move forward to world government. They therefore had to learn to live with the bomb but without war; this meant living in a world of competitive arms building and deterrence.[33] So it was that the 'reality' of the postwar strategic confrontation was in part created out of the realist images of the Yale group and other early contributors to the atomic debate.

In the years immediately following his success with *The Absolute Weapon* Brodie's career became dominated by atomic issues. In words which Herman Kahn was later to echo and make famous, Brodie summed up the task of the new strategists as follows: 'War is unthinkable but not impossible, and therefore we must think about it'.[34] *Thinking About the Unthinkable* (the title of Kahn's 1962 book) is what Brodie did in the late 1940s, and he communicated his ideas by means of regular lectures to the American military and a steady output of publications.

Notable among his early articles was 'Strategy as Science', published in *World Politics* in 1949.[35] Here Brodie challenged the traditional hegemony in military life of principles, maxims and slogans (such as 'don't divide the fleet'). Instead, he insisted upon rational analysis and decisionmaking, and suggested the introduction into strategy of concepts from economics such as 'marginal utility' and 'opportunity costs'. In this and other early writing Brodie was helping to create that stock of literature on which strategic studies later developed. But Brodie soon lost whatever aspirations he had for making strategy a 'science'. He remained sensitive to the importance of economic considerations, but he became a strong critic of those who fostered the illusion that laws of war existed which were equivalent to scientific laws.

Brodie's growing reputation as a strategist in the late 1940s led him to leave Yale and work again for the government. This was a natural and welcome step, since both his early mentors and his own predisposition had made him keen to be an insider; he looked forward to the opportunity to turn sophisticated theory into improved national strategy. But his ambition was never fulfilled. To his regret he never became a 'maker' of nuclear strategy. Instead, he remained on the sidelines, helping to set the agenda, write the literature, and stimulate the thinking of 'the new strategy'. But all this was yet to be decided.

Among the issues which Brodie addressed in the late 1940s, strategic bombing and particularly the problem of target selection was dominant. He had studied the data on the effects of strategic bombing in World War II, and while he was convinced about its importance, he did not believe that victory was synonymous with simply wasting cities. A city-busting campaign on the lines of the recent war, but with atomic bombs, would be 'pure terrorist destruction' and thus both a moral and material failure. Careful target selection, in Brodie's mind, was a priority, and particularly while the number of bombs was relatively limited. These views were propounded in an article in *The Reporter*, 15 August 1950, entitled 'Strategic Bombing: What It Can Do'. In the short term what the article did was to bring Brodie's name to the attention of General Hoyt Vandenberg and General Lauris Norstad, the chief and vice chief of staff of the air force. These men did not share their service's faith in the utility of city busting, and so they asked Brodie to work as a consultant to the air staff on targeting plans.[36] Brodie went hopefully to Washington to turn his theory of the new strategy into practice.

In the event, Brodie's career with the air force proved to be brief. The service was passing through troubled times. It had no shortage of resources, but in rapid succession it had to try to adjust to the atomic bomb, the cold war, the explosion of the Soviet atomic bomb and the war in Korea.[37] It was a difficult period for the air force, and, as it proved, for Brodie as well. But he learned a great deal. Above all, he discovered the primitive thinking of many air force planners.

The issue of target selection preoccupied Brodie. In contrast, the air force planners did not think it a complex problem. In their view the A-bomb had reduced target selection to the practical problem of carrying out an 'atomic blitz' on the Soviet Union. Such an attack, they believed, would automatically lead to victory for the United States. This thinking was simply a continuation of World War II city busting with an admixture of atomic means. During the war, targets had frequently been chosen not because of their inherent value but because allied air power could destroy them. The air war over Japan in 1945, in particular, was not so much a matter of discriminate target selection, but more a case of rationalizing what could be flattened; and with the air superiority that the United States enjoyed at the time that meant a great deal. Even when the results of the bombing accumulated, they were not used as the basis for more sophisticated target selection.[38] The success of American air power in intimidation and destruction pushed aside, then and later, the prospect of a truly Clausewitzian air strategy. To the air force, the city busting they believed had brought success in the hot war was good enough for the cold war that followed. In contrast, Brodie believed that if bombing was to be truly strategic, then intelligent target selection was the key. In the atomic age this meant that there had to be 'sample attacks', with cities kept as hostages. A city actually destroyed was a threat lost.

The Strategic Air Command (SAC) continued to demand that victory would be the child of city busting. The air staff was less sure; it found Brodie's discriminating attacks more congenial. Brodie continued to emphasize that instead of an all-out blow, it was possible by avoiding the destruction of Soviet cities to gain what he called 'strategic leverage'. These city-hostages would, if all went well, encourage the Soviet leaders to stop fighting for fear that matters might get disastrously out of hand. But if SAC was allowed to waste cities, as it planned, there would be no incentive for Soviet restraint. If Brodie was not the first he was one of the first to advocate limitation in atomic war by avoiding cities;[39] this later came to be a prominent theme in strategic literature under the label 'intra-war deterrence'.[40] If Clausewitzian thinking was to inform the conduct of atomic war, diplomacy and bargaining would be at their very toughest. But absolute atomic war was absolutely un-Clausewitzian. In Brodie's mind there was more to making war than making urban deserts.

Brodie told the air force staff about his misgivings about target selection.[41] Not surprisingly he received somewhat more sympathy there than from the SAC, whose commander-in-chief was General Curtis LeMay. LeMay had commanded the city-busting attacks on Japan at the end of the war, and he did not take to Brodie or his recommendations. He dismissed Brodie's idea of restraint as being contrary to the principles of war, and neither he nor his staff would discuss Brodie's arguments with him at length. The report Brodie wrote on target selection — which he later described as his best and most important work — was lost or destroyed.[42] LeMay favoured the blitz, whether in war or bureaucracy. He had the 'right stuff' to lead men into battle but the wrong stuff to oversee the integration of strategy and policy. But the world war was a recent event, and famous fighters exercised enormous authority. Civilian academics like Brodie possessed little. As a result of this opposition from SAC,[43] and the moving on of his mentors, Norstad and Vandenberg, Brodie had also to move on. He never forgot these early experiences of the military mind at the highest level.

Brodie's departure from the air force marked a turning-point in his career. His twenties and thirties had been years of professional promise and progress, but his forties had started with difficulty and so they continued. For the moment, though, the initial prospects looked bright. He did not want to return to university life, and he did not need to. In 1951 he was offered a post at one of the frontiers of his subject, the recently opened, air force-sponsored RAND Corporation at Santa Monica, California. Through the 1950s and 1960s RAND came to make an enormous and sometimes controversial contribution to the development of American-style deterrence theory.[44] Brodie, who remained a senior staff member until 1966, was an important participant in a remarkable team.

When he went to RAND Brodie planned to write a history of strategic air warfare; within two years the strategic landscape was overturned by the detonation of an H-bomb by the United States and, soon after, by the Soviet Union. This new magnitude of destructive power finished Brodie's work on strategic air warfare almost as decisively as the first atom bomb had sunk his work on the battleship a few years earlier. But he found some historical continuity at the level of ideas. In the course of studying strategic bombing Brodie had become interested in the work of the Italian Guilio Douhet, whose writings in the inter-war years had helped to establish the idea that air power had revolutionized warfare. He had argued that there was no defence against a properly planned bomber attack and that air power would make the difference between a good victory and a bad defeat. With the coming of the H-bomb, Douhet's vision of instant wars of annihilation seemed to have materialized.[45]

For nearly a decade after Hiroshima Brodie had hoped that some restraint might be exercised if atomic war were to break out. As the mid-1950s approached, and stockpiles grew from relative scarcity to plenty, he became increasingly pessimistic about the prospects for restraint. At the start of 1954 he pointed out in a *Foreign Affairs* article 'Nuclear Weapons: Strategic or Tactical?', that the new weapons of mass destruction were neither in short supply, nor exceedingly costly, nor too bulky.[46] Despite the growing challenges to restraint he continued to criticize SAC's city-busting approach. He told the air force that their approach was not so much a war plan as a 'war spasm'. In using this phrase Brodie may have triggered in his colleague Herman Kahn's mind the notion of 'wargasm', a typically flip but psychologically revealing Kahnian metaphor.[47] Brodie later criticized Kahn's coinage for its 'levity'.[48] To Brodie war in the H-bomb era had become far too serious. In one technological bound the H-bomb had outflanked the 'absolute weapon' of 1945 and had undermined the 'political philosophy of war'[49] which Brodie had inherited from Clausewitz. These devices of mass destruction did not fit into the traditional framework of thinking about war and politics nor could their destructiveness be accommodated within the traditional notions of instrumentality implied by such words as 'weapon' and 'strategy'. Even so, strategists like Brodie who intended to stay within the confines of the policy-relevant debate believed that they had no alternative but to rationalize the paradoxes of the nuclear predicament.

The new dilemmas that now confronted Brodie the strategic analyst interacted with Brodie the human being. The 1950s proved to be personally and professionally difficult. As he agonized about the implications for strategy of the growing numbers of tactical and strategic nuclear weapons, his relations became strained with a number of his colleagues. He suffered from insomnia, he struggled with writer's block, he underwent psychoanalysis and he was eventually rebuffed by the Washington policy-making machine he wanted to join.[50] Out of these difficulties the involvement with psychoanalysis proved the most positive; it became a subject that continued to fascinate Brodie for the rest of his life and to the enrichment of his writing. Despite everything, his published output during these difficult years suffered little. Most of his profession would have been more than satisfied with the productivity he did achieve, not to mention its quality.

It would be a mistake to interpret the inner turmoil in Brodie's work and character in any sense as a weakness. It was possible to think about the unthinkable in a variety of ways. It could be done with a certain grim levity, in the manner of Herman Kahn. Or the predicament could be made more manageable by turning it into an exercise in systems analysis, as was done by Albert Wohlstetter. And in all societies there are ostriches, who face the future with their heads in the sand. Or there was Brodie's way. In the late 1950s his mind and body reacted to the hellish possibilities opened up by the new weapons of mass destruction. Neither the mind nor the body of this humane and imaginative strategist could easily adjust to the new situation.

Strategic developments in the mid- and late 1950s introduced a new tone of uncertainty and occasional pessimism into Brodie's discussion of man's strategic predicament. From this time onwards strategic rationality was something Brodie hoped for but no longer assumed, just as restraint in war was something he argued for but seemed unsure of achieving. These attitudes were reflected in his major work of the decade, *Strategy in the Missile Age*, which will be discussed later. Lawrence Freedman has described it as a 'gloomy' book because of its 'awareness that there is no escape from the possibility of war nor from horrific levels of destruction should worst fears be realised'.[51] It was gloomy. But what other mood was appropriate for the superpower nuclear spiral in the second half of the 1950s?

Brodie agonized over the impact of the H-bomb, but he never opposed it. Instead, within a short time, he simply announced that the world had come to the end of strategy as it had been known. By the mid-1950s he was writing that many of the interpretations made 'at the dawn of the atomic age' had since been shown to be 'too conservative'; and in 1954 he expressed the belief that it had become clear that 'strategy' and 'unlimited war' were simply incompatible concepts in a world of H-bombs. Albeit in private, he expressed a 'certain contempt' for his fellow strategists who seemed oblivious to the changes that nuclear weapons had brought about.[52] Herman Kahn later said that the H-bomb 'sort of swamped Brodie'.[53] But Kahn was wrong. What really happened was that the H-bomb had 'sort of swamped' the traditional notion of strategy. While Brodie was trying to understand this historic change, and yet stay within the bounds of policy relevance, many of his colleagues attempted to conventionalize nuclear devices by surrounding them with the scaffolding of traditional thinking.

While trying to comprehend the implications of the thermonuclear revolution, Brodie was not so 'swamped' that he ignored the debate about limited war that followed the prolonged and frustrating conflict in Korea. This debate was part of the growing opposition to the Dulles–Eisenhower posture of 'massive retaliation'. Although massive retaliation was never as simple or extreme as its critics asserted, it was highly controversial. Brodie was one of its heavyweight opponents, and an early one. His article 'Nuclear Weapons: Strategic or Tactical?' appeared in the same month as Dulles's famous massive retaliation speech and addressed some of the same issues. Brodie, like the other major critics, argued that in so far as massive retaliation represented a threat to expand a local war into a superpower homeland-to-homeland war, it would lose 'all credibility' in the face of the increasing vulnerability of the United States.[54] Because Western Europe was an area vital to American interests, however, he believed that in this case massive retaliation did represent a credible threat.[55] The leading critics of massive retaliation — Brodie, Henry Kissinger, William W. Kaufmann and others — together helped to fuse a critical mass of interest in strategic matters in the United States, and in so doing helped to create the academic subject of strategic studies as it is understood today. By virtue of his courses at Dartmouth, his writing on the atomic bomb at Yale, his targeting ideas as an air force insider, his think-tank activity at RAND and his extensive writing on nuclear issues and limited war, Bernard Brodie had established himself by the late 1950s as the quintessential civilian strategist of the nuclear age.

In parallel with massive retaliation the growing body of civilian strategists had become concerned with the problem of defending American interests in the grey areas of the superpower confrontation. The Korean War had hoisted the warning flag, and it inevitably became the case study on which theorizing, both good and bad, was based. The notion of 'limited war' did not fit comfortably within the outlook of the American Way of War as it had developed in the 1940s, with its predeliction for total solutions, offensive action and decisive results. But explaining the requirements of limited war was a task for which the new strategists were well suited, and Brodie was drawn into the limited war debate, at the classified level, as early as 1952. His subsequent thinking was made public in a series of articles, and was later synthesized in *Strategy in The Missile Age*.[56] Brodie was not the first[57] or most prominent contributor to the debate, but he was one of the most down to earth. His basic theme was that if certain conflicts could not be avoided, they had to be consciously controlled.[58]

The context for modern limited-war thinking was in Brodie's opinion the realization that a large-scale mutual exchange of nuclear weapons on cities had reduced war to 'a suicidal absurdity'. Victory had lost its former meaning, therefore limited war was necessary. The United States had been unprepared for Korea, he commented: 'If our behaviour was in general correct, it is a credit to our intelligence even in confusion and not to our foresight.'

The essence of limited war was 'deliberate restraint', which Brodie said must be 'massive'. Despite this, he still suggested that such a war 'might conceivably' include strategic bombing carried on in a limited manner, such as nuclear attacks on airfields. But while the degree of restraint within the theatre of war was open for discussion, strategic bombing between the superpowers was definitely ruled out. This would constitute a 'deliberate hobbling of a tremendous power'. The latter would nevertheless remain highly mobilized in order to induce the enemy 'to hobble himself to a like degree'. A separate limited-war capability was necessary, he insisted, since the manner of intervention should not prevent the achievement of the objective. War must be kept limited, he kept reminding his readers, because total war in the age of nuclear plenty was 'simply too unthinkable, too irrational to be borne'. How much restraint and what kind would depend on the objectives, which must be limited: 'We cannot have limited war without settling for limited objectives, which in practice is likely to mean a negotiated peace based on compromise.' Brodie believed that many in the United States needed educating into viewing war in this way. It was a 'curious and interesting' fact, he noted, that there was no consensus in the United States behind the idea that limited war was preferable to total war.

The Korean experience had not been positive for many Americans; they believed that too much restraint had been shown. Brodie disagreed. But he did argue that mistakes had been made, particularly the 'cardinal error' of halting the 1951 offensive. This missed opportunity had resulted in long negotiations, unsatisfactory terms, disillusionments and distaste for limited war. Against the insistence of 'high officials and military officers' that if the response to aggression was to be limited geographically, at least it must be atomic, Brodie believed that the non-use of nuclear weapons had been justified. The 'major question', he said, was 'How large can a war get and still remain limited?' This was still unclear, but the larger it was, he believed, the more pressure there must be for abandoning limitations. Consequently, the United States had to remember that the chief problem was not 'how to fight it conveniently', or how to achieve a 'decisive local victory', but rather 'how to make sure that it stays limited'. Brodie knew that nuclear weapons would complicate the limitation process, since between their use and non-use existed 'a vast watershed of difference and distinction' that ought not to be 'cavalierly thrown away'. For this reason he was sceptical about demonstration shots and he warned against the 'erroneous' belief that there were 'marked intrinsic differences' between tactical and strategic nuclear weapons. Even so, he did not rule out the use of nuclear weapons on principle, he only argued that their use would be far from being 'unequivocally right'. Somewhat fatalistically he said: 'Perhaps they will have to be used in some situations [but] . . . The conclusion that nuclear weapons *must* be used in limited wars has been reached by too many people, too quickly, on the basis of far too little analysis of the problem'.

Brodie considered Europe to be a special case for limited war. He believed it difficult 'at present' to imagine that a war could be fought in that theatre without resort to nuclear weapons, 'tactically, even if strategic bombing could somehow be avoided'. An alternative to total war was necessary: 'we ought to be interested in developing a real NATO limited war capability'. Under existing arrangements, nuclear weapons would be necessary to stop a Soviet attack, but that 'can hardly be a sufficient reason for using them' since the Soviet Union would reply and what chance would there be of keeping a nuclear war in Europe limited 'for more than a few hours'. A massive Soviet invasion was unlikely, he believed, without a Soviet decision to fight a total war. For this the United States 'seems to be committed to retaliate massively'. A NATO limited war force would have little to do with that kind of war, but it would be useful for dealing with border probings, tests of will and accidents — the 'fuzzy' issues he thought the most likely causes of war.

The proponents of massive retaliation argued that the willingness of the United States to limit its response to any aggression must tend to encourage aggression. Brodie admitted an element of truth in the argument but stressed that the main aim was to avoid total war. In this respect he identified two prevalent ideas which would make limitation 'extremely difficult, if not impossible'. One was that limited wars would inevitably become total; the other was that total war had been abolished so that all effort should be directed towards limited wars. The latter idea was the more dangerous in Brodie's opinion since it encouraged a neglect of 'the basic precautions enjoined by the danger of total war' and at the same time 'a recklessness about the handling of limited wars that will make it more likely they will erupt into unlimited ones'.

As tactical nuclear weapons arrived in growing numbers in Europe in the mid-1950s, Brodie supported their controlled use in the event of war. His basic assumption was simple: controlled (selective) use is better than an uncontrolled (spasm) attack. Just as limited war was preferable to total war, so limited nuclear war was preferable to all-out nuclear war. This was a far from unanimous opinion in American political and military circles and Brodie needed to educate them. He was troubled by the 'completely accepted axiom . . . that all modern war must be total war' and the 'fantasies of total war which have the United States doing all the hitting while receiving few if any nuclear bombs in return'.[59] Since total war was irrational but not impossible, control was essential, and that meant the use of tactical nuclear weapons. For this to have some hope of coming about in practice, it first had to be developed in theory. This was also the view, for a time, of Henry Kissinger. Kissinger's views on this perplexing issue fluctuated, drawing the ironical fire of some of his colleagues,[60] but he did eventually achieve high office. Brodie, whose views were more stable, also drew critical fire but no government pay cheques.

Brodie's early public ideas on tactical nuclear weapons had been expressed in his 1954 article 'Nuclear Weapons: Strategic or Tactical?' There he had argued that since mutual strategic bombardment using nuclear weapons would be the equivalent to national suicide, there was no alternative to the controlled use of battlefield nuclear weapons. Later writing filled out his argument.[61] He did not think that a Soviet attack could be held without the use of tactical nuclear weapons, in view of Soviet conventional superiority; these weapons were an area of relative NATO technological advantage and they would save money. He did not give much credit to the role of NATO forces as a trip-wire.[62] To activate such a mechanism would require either 'incredible Soviet recklessness or stupidity'. Either they would be deterred by the threat of massive retaliation or they would strike at the United States first. They would not first signal their intentions by activating a trip wire. Brodie favoured conventional forces in Europe to deal with probes and tests of will, but he continued to argue (throughout his career) that larger ground forces were not necessary. Like all arguments about war in Europe in the age of nuclear plenty, Brodie's contained contradictions and paradoxes. He appreciated this. He also became less hopeful about the prospects for maintaining limitations if nuclear weapons were used. By the late 1950s he defined the difference between limited nuclear war and total war as 'a few hours'.[63] As early as 1955 he saw 'the same kind of nihilistic result' in unrestricted tactical warfare as in unrestricted strategic warfare.[64] He commented ironically: 'a people "saved" by us through the free use of nuclear weapons over their territories would probably be the last that would ask us to help them'.[65]

Despite the problems of tactical nuclear weapons Brodie adhered to them as a 'second line of insurance': they added something, however inadequate, to the credibility of the deterrent threat of massive retaliation and the controllability of terribly destructive wars. Brodie did not consider that tactical nuclear war was a desirable or particularly realistic option: he simply saw it as the least worst of a number of terrifying alternatives. His continued support of it was more the result of his own strategic rigour than the notion's inherent validity.[66] There was a pragmatic necessity to offer some sort of coherent operational strategy, since the risks of war were finite and there should be an alternative to 'all-or-nothing'. It was professional pride rather than a belief that tactical nuclear war would 'work' that led Brodie to offer a strategy for all scenarios.

Brodie's intuition about the difficulty of controlling atomic war had been revealed early. In *The Absolute Weapon* he had written that wars between atomic powers might avoid atomic weapons or be terribly destructive: what was least likely was the limited use of weapons of mass destruction. He believed that any nuclear use would add to the difficulties of restraint. Even so, he argued that controlled tactical nuclear use might in some circumstances be the least worst action. In the 1950s a strategy of controlled nuclear use appeared to Brodie as the only rational posture: throwing his hands up in resignation, abolishing from his calculations the prospect of total war, advocating nuclear pacifism, prescribing the non-acquisition of tactical nuclear systems, or supporting city busting SAC-style — these alternatives were all unacceptable. They were rejected either because they were unstrategic or because they would have placed Brodie outside the circle of policy-relevant cold war advisers. And Brodie never wanted to be considered either unstrategic or irrelevant.

Though Brodie continued to hold severe reservations about the controllability of limited nuclear war, the dissonance in his mind was checked by his growing conviction that the probability of an American–Soviet war was very low. Although in the late 1950s he endorsed the fashionable view that the balance of terror was 'delicate', there is no sense of war urgency in his writings at the time. Here, as elsewhere, Brodie's approach echoes that of Clausewitz. In this case it is an echo of the Clausewitzian dialectic between war 'on paper', which tended to the extreme, and 'real' war, where politics might limit the scope of violence (which meant, in the age of nuclear deterrence, not letting it break out in the first place).

Paper was, and has remained, the battlefield of the nuclear strategists. Brodie's position on theatre nuclear war led him into conflict with the big battalions at RAND as well as scrapes with like-minded people such as William Kaufmann.[67] At RAND Brodie became an increasingly isolated figure in the second half of the 1950s, as strong rivalries developed, and some became more than professional. A now well-known antagonism developed between Brodie and Albert Wohlstetter, who was best known for his work in systems analysis, and who became the central figure of a group which was increasingly in the ascendant at RAND.[68] Brodie's more traditional approach was scornfully dismissed by Wohlstetter as being in 'the essay tradition'.[69] The systems analysts were riding an intellectual wave on the West Coast, and Brodie felt and was made to feel out of it. He saw some merits in systems analysis, but he was also critical of the narrowness of approach that it could engender. In an article published many years later, Brodie unburdened himself, in a controlled but clearly angry fashion, of some of his feelings towards his former RAND critics.[70] He had just cause: after all, the one great 'discovery' of the systems analysts — the need for a secure retaliatory force — had been identified by Brodie in *The Absolute Weapon* over a decade earlier.[71]

A long career is bound to generate personality clashes and professional rivalries, especially when strong characters interact in an organizational hothouse. In the particular environment of think-tank politics, victory in the short term went to the systems analysts. Wohlstetter's school not only became the dominant force at RAND but also went on to provide a number of officials in the Pentagon Robert McNamara organized following John Kennedy's election in 1960. Brodie was marginalized at RAND and was not invited to serve in Washington. Negative feelings had developed towards him among the systems analysts at RAND who advised McNamara on recruitment.[72] Brodie was not the only prominent academic strategist to be left aside, for Henry Kissinger was also not invited to join the whizz kids. But whereas Kissinger's time for office did come, Brodie's did not. So, in 1961, he lost his best chance to fulfil his ambition to become a true maker of modern strategy. Despite this, intellectual victory in the longer term went to Brodie. With the passage of time it is evident that Brodie's position is secure as one of the formative thinkers of the first generation of the nuclear age; the systems analysts, on the other hand, proved to be an important but transitory fashion. In the history of strategic thought Brodie will stand ahead of Wohlstetter just as Clausewitz came to stand ahead of Jomini. Those with political savvy will always outlive those with only formal reasoning power, however impressive.

Despite his problems in the second half of the 1950s, private and professional, Brodie did manage to write *Strategy In The Missile Age*, as was mentioned earlier. It was published in 1959 and quickly became established as one of the key statements of the so-called golden age of contemporary strategic thinking — that period between the late 1950s and mid-1960s which was so creative and productive in American defence circles.[73] Facing the title page Brodie inserted two quotations which reflect continuing themes in his writings: the need for political sense to control war and the importance of being able to meet the ultimate pragmatic test. The first quotation was by Clausewitz, to the effect that in great things as well as small, man usually acts 'more on particular prevailing ideas and emotions than according to strictly logical conclusions, [and] is hardly conscious of his confusion, one-sidedness, and inconsistency'. The second quotation was Plato's question: 'And is anything more important than that the work of the soldier should be well done?' In the book that followed Brodie tried to rectify some of the problems in strategic behaviour identified by Clausewitz, and in so doing ensure that Plato's question was well answered.

Strategy In The Missile Age was a big book which brought together a discussion of many of the problems that had been troubling Brodie over the previous few years. In particular, he grappled with the interplay between old and new forces, when the latter were truly revolutionary:[74]

It is our major dilemma in thinking about war and peace today that we do so within an intellectual and emotional framework largely molded in the past. Our images, slogans, ideas and attitudes, on the subject of war, some of which are buttressed by the most powerful cultural sanctions, are transmitted to us from times when war was, characteristically, with a few historical exceptions, a limited-liability operation.

The chief problem confronting us he wrote, was the 'ever-widening disparity in accomplishment between man's military inventions and his social adaption to them'.[75] As a result, over a quarter of the book is devoted to strategy in the pre-missile age. It is a rich discussion, with insights that stay with the careful reader.

Brodie stressed that strategy was an 'Intellectual No-Man's Land' in the United States, falling between the stools of the politician and the soldier. This had led to a tendency to grasp principles and axioms; costly mistakes had resulted. Sophisticated strategic theory was necessary to overcome this, since 'there is no other science where judgements are tested in blood and answered in the servitude of the defeated'.[76] Throughout the book Brodie exhibited his 'deep-seated impulse' to shy at maxims. He was also critical of the dominance of offensive thinking in military life, since it had sometimes resulted in the neglect of the idea that war should project national policy.[77] Brodie praised Clausewitz's work, though he noted that the latter had often been misinterpreted, and his idea about the relationship between war and politics had never appeared on lists of the principles of war. The most ominous lesson of the 'purposeless war' of 1914–18 was that the vast advance in the technology of war had been attended by *'suppression of rational concern with the political aims of war'*.[78]

Brodie proceeded to 'The Heritage of Douhet'. He spent much time discussing Douhet's 'demonstrable errors', yet declared him to have possessed the 'largest and most original mind' among the air-power theorists. He admired his independent mind, his 'over-all vision', his criticism of principles and his creation of a framework for understanding air power which was 'peculiarly pertinent to any general war in the nuclear age'.[79] If the nuclear age posthumously vindicated Douhet, his own era did not. Brodie argued that World War II had been a fair test for Douhet's ideas, but that he had been proven wrong on almost every salient point.[80]

Brodie's verdict on strategic bombing in World War II must be seen within his recognition of it having been an almost totally new experiment. Even so, there were still 'many critical (and perhaps unnecessary) errors'.[81] The most important had been poor target selection against the German war economy, the lack of tangible battlefield results, and the great waste of effort involved in area bombing, which 'must be set down unequivocally as a failure'. Overall, it was 'neither proved nor provable' that the air war against Germany could have been decisive 'even in the absence of ground

operations'.[82] These doubts did not pertain to the war against Japan: 'It is unequivocally to the credit of the strategic bombing offensive that it secured all the objectives
of the planned invasion before the latter could be mounted.'[83] In achieving this
outcome, Brodie placed relatively little weight on the dropping of the two atomic
bombs.

With the advent of nuclear weapons, Brodie argued that strategic bombing had
become 'incontrovertibly' the dominant form of war. Differences in targeting were
still possible, but only if planners took deliberate measures to refrain from hitting
cities. 'Overkilling' (a word Brodie may have coined) was cheap, and the strategy of
'broken-backed war' was based on dubious assumptions.[84] His opinion that 'the
intensely conservative among the military are always proved wrong'[85] led him to
criticize those who still talked of strategic bombing as if it would be like World War II.
The casualties would represent 'a catastrophe for which it is impossible to set upper
limits very far short of the entire population of a nation'.[86] He expressed amazement at
those leaders who placed nearly exclusive dependence on thermonuclear weapons for
security, but who at the same time rejected the most obvious consequences of their
use against the United States.[87] This led directly to the question: 'Is There A
Defense?'. Brodie's arguments about defence constituted one of the gloomiest
sections of the book. His prognosis was not good; minimum expected fatalities in a
strategic-bombing attack could be reckoned in terms of millions, while the old adage
that every offensive development inevitably provoked a defensive one 'is hard to
justify historically, and it is certainly excessively optimistic in the nuclear era'.[88]
Furthermore, the chances were high that the United States would receive rather than
deliver the first blow. He considered people to be an 'end value';[89] they are precious
'regardless of how many or how few survive' Nevertheless his chief practical
prescription was the 'absolute' need to protect the American retaliatory forces. If
enemy planners came to believe that they might be able to paralyze the American
response, it might make the difference between a 'go' or 'no-go' decision. It was
therefore 'necessary to do all we can to prevent such a conviction from taking hold in
the enemy camp'.[90] In short, Brodie was arguing that people could be saved only by
deterrence, and that effective deterrence rested on the adversary's perception of one's
own assured retaliatory capability.

Brodie rejected 'The Wish For Total Solutions' (preventive war, pre-emptive attack
and massive retaliation) which he believed to have had influence in military circles
since the start of the atomic era. He strongly opposed preventive war: it would be
'presumptious and reckless in the extreme', he wrote, 'to base so cataclysmic an action
on the thesis that total nuclear war is inevitable or nearly so'.[91] After noting that
recorded civilization was 5–6,000 years old, he said he thought it difficult to conceive
the human race continuing for a comparable period 'without once pulling the stops on
the kind of destructive orgy' which nuclear weapons make possible.[92] But if we could
defer total war for fifty years, 'it would surely be worthwhile to do so even if we were
only deferring the inevitable'. Preventive war led Brodie to discuss the moral issue. To
deny the relevance of moral issues, he said, 'is to plunge ourselves immediately into
absurdities, for example the absurdity of holding that the lives of any number of
foreigners are as nothing compared to the freedom-from-fear of a single American'.[93]
This throws important light on Brodie's sensibilities, and one does not see similar
points made by many other nuclear strategists of the time. In his opinion,
'sophisticated people nowadays become embarassed at the intrusion of explicit
reference to moral issues in debates on national policy, especially strategic policy'. He
believed that moral values did have a role and that they were a 'powerful and rigid
barrier' to American planning of preventive war.[94]

Brodie was also sceptical about pre-emptive attack as a realistic option, though it did not present the same moral qualms.[95] He considered pre-emption to be theoretically feasible, but believed it would be foolish to rely on it as if it were a good possibility; nevertheless, he warned that such reliance is what the United States appeared to be doing. Brodie reserved much greater criticism for massive retaliation.[96] He commented that the idea appealed 'to certain characteristically military ideas or doctrines', but that it lacked credibility. He suggested that American civilian leaders had over-estimated their own readiness to resort to this 'dread sanction' if the moment for decision actually came. Despite its problems, Brodie noted that there was 'no great inclination' within NATO to relinquish massive retaliation in the event of an attack. In Europe he believed the retaliatory force had credibility. None the less, he thought that American readiness to defend Europe by massive retaliation 'may be called into question sooner or later', though he considered the challenge would come 'sooner' in areas beyond Europe. But this was where credibility was an issue: 'Where our interests are not vital, how can a general threat of this kind be believed?'[97] Massive retaliation was only acceptable as a last resort. Despite this, he warned that in the late 1950s American force structures had increased rather than lessened their dependence on massive retaliation. In the short run at least, organizational inertia was proving more powerful than the massive retaliation of the civilian strategists against American policy.

In the pro-deterrence hubris of the 1960s it was not sufficiently recognized that Brodie, one of the earliest exponents of deterrence theory, had by the late 1950s come to be rather anxious about several dimensions of it. This was well reflected in his comments on the psychology of deterrence. He wrote that 'apparently it is not hope but delirium that springs eternal in the human breast', and that 'the one great area' in public affairs where romanticism had survived was that of national defence policy.[98] In further comments on the psychology of war he came close to arguing that strategic logic was little more than the rationalization of national prejudice. He explained the problems in nuclear deterrence arising from military ways of thought, particularly the preference for seizing the initiative and carrying the war to the enemy. The military had what he called an 'abiding faith in the ritual of liquidation', but deterrence and limited war involved conceptions of national security that were 'fundamentally opposed' to such ideas.[99]

Continuing his theme of emphasizing the problems of deterrence, rather than celebrating it, Brodie warned that deterrents ('even what sometimes looked like superior force') had often failed to deter in the past. The situation looked different today, since deterrence 'uses the kind of threat which we feel must be absolutely effective, allowing for no breakdowns ever. The sanction is, to say the least, not designed for repeating action. One use of it will be fatally too many.' Nevertheless, the success of deterrence could not be guaranteed, and so the American retaliatory force had always to be 'ready to spring while going permanently unused'. Brodie believed there was 'something almost unreal' in this. Few strategists seem to have agreed, but those who enjoyed *Dr Strangelove* not long afterwards did. Brodie continued to draw attention to the difficulties of nuclear deterrence, particularly those that had their roots in men's minds. As he had done elsewhere, he pointed to the danger of being unable to predict one's own behaviour in a crisis.[100] This might bring about the total war which many people, in his estimation, now believed impossible. Brodie believed this to be a dangerous delusion, since it would encourage the very risky behaviour which in turn might bring about a nuclear war.

Turning to the more technical difficulties of deterrence, Brodie sought to distinguish between 'deterrence' and 'Win-the-War' postures.[101] It was important, he argued, not to confuse them. Returning to one of the themes in *The Absolute Weapon*, he argued that 'deterrence *per se* does not depend on superiority'. This did not mean that the United States could be content with 'minimum deterrence', or that it had no interest in a warfighting capability: 'So long as there is a finite chance of war, we have to be interested in outcomes; and although all outcomes would be bad, some would be very much worse than others.' Outcomes required Brodie to return to his old preoccupation with target selection. He continued to stress that no matter how difficult it was to maintain control, one should never deliberately abandon the attempt. Hitting the enemy's cities, for example, would simply force the destruction of one's own. Nevertheless, for the sake of deterrence 'the enemy must expect us to be vindictive and irrational if he attacks us'. Indeed, he proceeded to argue that in order to maximize the punitive aspect of deterrence, 'we may find a need even for super-dirty bombs'.[102] The contending requirements of deterrence and warfighting have always bedevilled deterrence theorists. Brodie's verdict on the balance of error was given on the final page of *Strategy In The Missile Age*, which will be quoted later.

Because Brodie believed that the chances of deterrence failing were finite, he thought that civil defence should be given more attention,[103] but how much should be spent was not discussed. He was more forthcoming about arms control, which he saw as a significant dimension of deterrence policy, though it had a 'long and dismal history'.[104] He dismissed total nuclear disarmament as a reasonable objective: 'Violation would be too easy for the Communists, and the risks to the non-violator would be enormous.' But he did not think that the kind of 'bitter, relentless race' in nuclear weapons and missiles that had been going on since 1945 was the answer; it had its own 'intrinsic dangers' and posed 'the gravest risks'. The small risks in arms control had to be measured against the latter. The benefits promised included reducing the dangers of surprise attack and ensuring the security of the retaliatory forces of both sides. The objective of arms control should be to enhance stability, which he defined as a situation 'when each nation believes that the strategic advantage of striking first is overshadowed by the tremendous cost of doing so'. Security in the nuclear age could not be unilateral: 'If the opponent feels insecure, we suffer the hazard of his being more trigger-happy.'

Cost always played a big part in Brodie's thinking about strategy.[105] He characterized the contemporary predicament as one in which the United States spent far more on security than ever before but was 'fated' to remain less secure. 'If there is no end to our insecurity', he argued, 'there does have to be an end to our military expenses. Why not, then, end them early rather than late?' In determining how much is enough he was critical of 'official judgements'.[106] They were usually reflections of 'traditional service thinking', and the higher one was in the policymaking structure, the more one tended to be removed 'from the area of careful, dispassionate analysis'. This was not an encouraging ending to a discussion about an area where 'the dollar becomes the instrument by which we measure the wisdom of our choice'.

One theme of *Strategy In The Missile Age* was that there was now 'a special "it-must-not-fail" urgency about deterrence'.[107] But it could fail, and this led Brodie to identify three principles of action for the United States: to cut down drastically the advantages the enemy can derive from striking first; to provide a 'real and substantial' capability to cope with limited and local aggression; and to provide provision for the saving of life 'on a vast scale' in view of the danger of total war being 'real and finite'.[108] Stability was therefore the key.[109] Brodie consequently warned of the danger of provoking the enemy to fear the United States too much. These are words that strike a chord thirty years later, when 'common security' is on the agenda. They were ignored in his own country then as they largely are now. Equally, he warned that if a nuclear war could not be stopped quickly 'what follows is not strategy but grandiose, wanton destruction'.[110] Nuclear war was not strategy. Another three decades of nuclear theorizing have not altered the wisdom of Brodie's words or reversed the pro-nuclear orientation of the American defence posture.

Brodie ended *Strategy In The Missile Age* with a suitably cautious section entitled 'The Unpredictability of the Outcome'. He warned that, historically, pre-hostilities' calculations had generally been proved wrong,[111] yet each generation of military planners was certain that it would not make the same mistakes as its predecessors. Brodie emphasized that experience should warn us to appreciate 'how imperfect is even the best we can do'. Strategists were faced by an utterly unprecedented rate of change in weapons innovation, but they remained immersed in old biases. Compared with the arrogance of many fellow strategists, who gave the impression that their generation had solved the fundamental problems of peace and war, Brodie warned that: 'we have been, and therefore may yet be, entirely wrong on fundamentals in our official policies'. Following Thucydides, Brodie expressed the belief that peace is better than war 'not only in being more agreeable but also in being very much more predictable'. Consequently, in a classic contribution of the 'deterrence' versus 'warfighting' debate, he wrote: 'A plan and policy which offers a good promise of deterring war is therefore by orders of magnitude better in every way than one which depreciates the objective of deterrence in order to improve somewhat the chances of winning.'

Finally, glimpsing the environmental concerns of a later decade he wrote that one part of the world faced the threat of disaster from uncontrolled population growth, while another faced the threat of nuclear bombs: 'The two parts of the world share in common the fact that the chief menace facing each of them is man-made. Do they also share in common a bemused helplessness before the fate which each of them seems to be facing?'

The book thus closes with a question mark. What other objective ending could there have been to an analysis written on the brink of strategy in the missile age?

Strategy In The Missile Age was a landmark in the growth of Brodie's pessimism about the use of force in the modern world. This is more evident in hindsight than it was at the time, since contemporary readers were more interested in what Brodie had to say about the doctrinal issues of the day rather than in his comments (almost asides) about the cosmic predicament. Most readers probably skipped as decoration, for example the first pages of the book, which relate the story of the war in heaven between the rebel and loyal angels[112] (as in Milton's *Paradise Lost*). The angel Raphael had said, 'War seemed a civil game to this uproar.' Now, it was not strategy, it was unrestrained violence: it could not be stopped by the participants, only by divine intervention. To Brodie this mythology dramatized the chief dilemma confronting modern man, namely the disparity between military inventions and his social adaptation to them. The missile age promised to be no better than the past in this respect: only the consequences of error were so much more catastrophic. Brodie was not confident about the rationality of decisionmakers. Irrational propensities and professional predispositions, together with technological innovations, threatened to increase the violence in war. These, together with his attack on total solutions and maxims were major themes in the book, paralleling his explanation of the primacy of deterrence and the requirements of stability.

Brodie's later comments on his book, written in the Preface to the paperback edition in 1965, were not as gloomy as the original. His main contribution, he believed, had been in the development of thinking about limited war. At that time, he noted, his ideas had been advanced against much opposition; now the problem was the 'possible over-emphasis of what is basically a good and necessary idea'. This was a prescient verdict on limited-war theory in the year of the Gulf of Tonkin incident. The other main change he thought had been the growth of 'immeasurably more stability'. This had been the result of the diminished incentives for a first strike as a result of the increased invulnerability of retaliatory forces, a major theme of Brodie's ever since 1945. He remarked upon the continuing supremacy of offensive forces and the lack of civil defence. The latter, he said, was the result of the unwillingness of people to contemplate the consequences of the failure of deterrence. This has remained the case within the strategic community down to the present day.

Strategy In The Missile Age was and is a major book, both as a snapshot of golden age thinking at its brightest and for its many insights of lasting relevance. It became a standard text for the burgeoning study of strategy. Despite this success, as was mentioned earlier, Brodie did not get a call to Washington following the election of John F. Kennedy in 1960. He was ignored and felt it deeply. He later expressed his regret in the course of rebutting a charge that civilian strategists were 'overimpressed' with the 'potential transferability' of theory to the world of action.[113] Brodie sprang back:

> What, pray, could their theory possibly be for if it were not meant to be transferable to precisely that world. The theory of strategy is a theory for action . . . People like in general to be more, rather than less, useful, and as one who was not invited into the McNamara circle I am bound to say I would not have felt sullied if I had been.

It was not Brodie but the 'scientific strategists' from RAND who were invited to Washington and who came to dominate its corridors of power, just as they had back at Santa Monica. The fact that it was the disciples of Wohlstetter who had the ear of princes destabilized the already delicate balance of the Brodie–Wohlstetter relationship. Brodie felt scorned professionally and, according to Kaplan, 'would frequently take one side of an argument just because Wohlstetter had taken the other'.[114]

Brodie's marginalization had been sealed by Kennedy's choice of Robert S. McNamara as his secretary of defense. A 'whizz kid' from industry, and a former statistician, McNamara found himself comfortable with the systems analysts from RAND, and it was inevitable that he invited them to fill important positions at the Pentagon. Brodie accepted that systems analysts were clever and that their techniques were useful for dealing with certain military problems; but he did not think that they had that Clausewitzian understanding of war and politics which he believed to be the essence of strategy.[115] Just as Brodie had found SAC commanders like LeMay to have had 'the right stuff' to have led men into battle, but to be unsuited to the task of devising sophisticated war plans, so he saw the systems analysts as the right staff to solve problems of weapons procurement, but to be lacking the political and historical judgement to give the best advice on using those weapons.

In the early 1960s McNamara built up a team of advisers from RAND and elsewhere who would, within a few years, participate in an adventure that brought widespread death, destruction and deforestation to south-east Asia, but no positive political benefit to the United States. Meanwhile, disappointed at being shunned, but with the luxury of being an outsider, Brodie underwent an intellectual greening. Now in his early fifties, with a strong reputation but no direct influence, he used the opportunity to take a step back and to think and write more widely about strategy.

Brodie's work now more frequently took up positions that were uncongenial to successive American administrations and the military establishment; he also exhibited more scepticism towards some of the ideas of the 'strategic community', for whom success and expansion had led to a certain hardening of the intellectual arteries. The changes that took place in Brodie's thinking at this time marked a significant stage in his evolution as a strategist. It is rather belittling of Kaplan, therefore, to describe Brodie's development simply as a 'series of flip-flops' which 'suddenly puzzled' those who had known him for years.[116] As the nuclear confrontation and the cold war were coming to be seen with more perspective, Brodie became more questioning. From the day after the first atomic bomb had destroyed a complete city Brodie had, intellectually speaking, been riding an exciting roller-coaster. Fifteen years later he recognized that the mainstream strategist's world view — which had partly been created by himself — was limited. New ideas and experiences, the evolution of international politics and the new freedom from institutional pressures changed Brodie. Some of his colleagues may have been puzzled, but what is more puzzling, with hindsight, was their failure to be as open to change.

Brodie was not a prolific author in the 1960s, but his previous output had already secured for him a distinguished reputation among the growing number of people who were starting either to teach or read strategic studies at university. He produced two books during this decade. The first, aimed at a more 'popular' audience than usual, was *From Crossbow to H-bomb* in 1962. This book provided a basic introduction to the history of weapons' innovation, and as such it helped to service some of the new courses in strategic affairs.[117] From his early days Brodie had been technically literate; *The Absolute Weapon* had shown his ability to assimilate large amounts of information about hardware, and for all his emphasis on history he obviously found this a source of fascination (though less so as he grew older). Nevertheless, he never failed to impress on his readers that thinking about the sharp end of war is not the same as thinking about the ultimate end. Appropriately, *From Crossbow to H-bomb* closes with a reminder that the marvels of technology and the discipline of cost are not the essence of the strategic problem: 'Naturally', he wrote, 'an even more basic question is the purpose or necessity for any given military posture, let alone any proposed military action'.[118] Brodie co-authored this book with his wife Fawn, a historian and distinguished biographer. All who knew the Brodies attest to her importance in his life. If strategic thinking is to have a human face, its practitioners need daily reminders that there are other than strategic and masculine ways of thinking.

Partly encouraged by his biographer wife's interest in psychology, Brodie continued to manifest his own belief in its importance in strategy. His interest in the human mind and in the caprice of history led him to think about the unconscious motives for action and the role of chance. This interest may have been strengthened by an unconscious motive on his own part, namely a desire to separate himself as far as possible from the 'technical' or 'scientific' strategists who had usurped his place in Camelot. But if the scientific strategists were not expert in the politics of strategy, the politics of strategy did not ignore them: in Vietnam they connived in their country's major foreign policy tragedy in two hundred years.

Until the early 1960s, when he spent a year in France,[119] Brodie had little direct contact with the world outside his own country. It proved to be an important life experience, not least because it was a time of ferment in French thinking about nuclear strategy and international affairs. The value of NATO and the credibility of the American nuclear guarantee were being questioned, while France struggled to create its own independent *force de frappe*. As the 1960s progressed, French assertiveness made Washington hot under the collar. McNamara pressed the allies to strengthen their conventional defence capabilities and was scathing about so-called independent nuclear deterrents; he described them as 'dangerous', 'expensive', 'prone to obsolescence' and 'lacking in credibility'.[120] Brodie witnessed some of *le grand debat* at first hand and was impressed by its leading exponents, particularly Aron, Beaufré and Gallois.[121] As the debate continued through the first half of the 1960s, Brodie found himself drawn to the French position rather than to that of the Pentagon that had ignored him. But there was nothing in Brodie's developing ideas that was not already rooted in his theories: the fresh air from France simply cleared away some intellectual cobwebs and gave his ideas room to grow.[122]

As a result of his experiences in France, Brodie came better to understand what he already knew intellectually: that strategic reality is in the eye of national beholders. As he had written earlier, 'bad anthropology contributed to bad strategy'.[123] Unusually for an American strategist of that period, he became sympathetic to several arguments advanced by French strategists, including the idea that NATO had become overblown. While accepting the need for a Western alliance, he later criticized the 'etiquette and mythology' surrounding NATO's huge bureaucracy and described it as 'useless, costly and obnoxious'. The last adjective was included to refer to NATO's role in relation to the coup by the Greek colonels in 1967.[124] Brodie came to believe that there was too much permanence built into the NATO infrastructure. He became sceptical about the constant and virtually unanimous calls of the Anglo–American strategic community for its strengthening. While Brodie was in Europe, the debate about the size and role of NATO's conventional forces was being given one of its periodic airings. He played a prominent role in this debate, and his position was at variance with that of the United States' government. In contrast to the prevailing pro-conventional forces wisdom in Washington (a position somewhat belied by the continued expansion of American tactical nuclear weapons in Western Europe), Brodie strongly argued the case against creating a comprehensive and potentially effective flexible response strategy; that is, he rejected the idea of so strengthening the alliance's conventional forces that it would be able to meet the Warsaw Treaty powers at whatever the level of conventional attack. As a result of this stand, Brodie became even more of an outsider in the McNamara Pentagon.

Brodie's ideas about the problems of NATO strategy in a condition of superpower parity evolved during the early 1960s and were published in various forms; they were eventually summed up in a short book, *Escalation and the Nuclear Option*, which was published in 1966.[125] Fred Kaplan has suggested that the source of Brodie's dissent lay largely in events in his personal life — his break with RAND and his rejection by the Pentagon — rather than 'objective ruminations on strategy'.[126] Leaving aside the false assumption that there can be 'objective ruminations' about human behaviour, the more immediate point is that what emerged in Brodie's book was the logical outcome of previous positions. There is no doubt that his personal life gave his argument a sharper edge, but this was not simply a case of a strategic theory being a rationalization of an individual's professional disappointments.

The essence of *Escalation and the Nuclear Option* can be stated simply. It lay in Brodie's belief that while some conventional options were necessary for NATO (as he had made clear in *Strategy In The Missile Age*), under McNamara and his supporters the idea was being pushed too far and risked being both wasteful and counter-productive. The arguments on which this conclusion was based had been advanced by Brodie over the previous years: the requirements of deterrence should have primacy over the needs of defence; nuclear deterrence had worked and was working; the main firebreak should be between peace and war, not between different levels within war; the presence of nuclear weapons was of unprecedented importance in shaping the consideration whether or not a country would go to war; deterrence would continue to work if the Soviet leaders feared nuclear retaliation against a conventional attack; within NATO the political costs of changing existing arrangements outweighed any theoretical military advantages involved in a substantial increase in conventional forces; the European allies of the United States did not wish to face the costs of deploying more conventional forces nor the risks of having a major conventional war fought across their territory; Soviet military doctrine did not accept that limited nuclear wars could be fought in Europe without rapid and devastating escalation; tactical nuclear weapons were an area of relative NATO superiority which enabled the West to have smaller armed forces; and tactical nuclear weapons favoured the defender. In sum, Brodie's attitude to NATO strategy was, in American vernacular: 'if it ain't broke, don't fix it.'

Instead of building up conventional forces, Brodie favoured extracting the maximum amount of deterrence utility from tactical nuclear weapons. He did not regard the latter as useful instruments for advancing political interests in war, but he did believe them to be of pragmatic deterrent value. Intellectually, he realized that a 'strategy' was needed, in case deterrence failed, and that the strategy adopted should involve less than all-out strategic bombing but more than surrender. Tactical nuclear weapons were therefore the least worse alternative.

Brodie's position on tactical nuclear weapons is vulnerable to several criticisms. The two most urgent relate to early use and the fallacy of the last move. First, Brodie did not favour early nuclear use, but this was the practical implication of his ideas since he placed more emphasis on tactical nuclear weapons than upon the acquisition of more robust conventional forces. Second, his argument was short-sighted in two respects; it assumed that NATO's tactical nuclear superiority would remain (although the Soviet Union was bound to try and catch up) and that escalation to the nuclear level might be a useful tactic (although the enemy might well retaliate, thus leaving everybody worse off). Brodie's ideas about escalation and the nuclear option had problems, but he believed that the conventional option of McNamara and his supporters had even more. In the event, his rationalization of what was the existing compromise strategy won the day. His campaign against the danger of proliferating options continued into the late 1970s.[127]

A year after Brodie's new book had been published, NATO did in fact adopt a 'flexible response' strategy. But it was not McNamara's original conception, with a real battle-winning conventional option. Instead, it was what has more felicitously been called a strategy of 'flexible escalation', the outcome of many political and military compromises. Despite its inadequacies, flexible escalation has been the posture that NATO has maintained down to the present day. The posture accepted in 1967 and put into practice for the next twenty and more years was more along the lines advocated by Brodie than along those advocated by McNamara and Brodie's former RAND colleagues. This outcome was not the result of Brodie winning the debate in an intellectual sense. The explanation was more prosaic, as he himself recognized. The 1967 compromise was largely the result of the attitudes and inertia of the Western European allies, and particularly their unwillingness to spend the enormous quantities of money believed to be needed to build an effective conventional defence. The Pentagon's pro-conventional forces logic failed because, in Brodie's words, the Western Europeans went on 'sit-down strike'.[128]

Brodie's experience in France may well have strengthened his tendency at that time to adopt a more relaxed attitude to the Soviet threat. Like the other American 'makers' of nuclear strategy — be they theorists or practitioners — Brodie did not have any particular expertise in Soviet affairs. Indeed, it has justifiably been argued that one of the tragedies of the first generation of nuclear strategy was the fact that nuclear deterrence theory developed in the United States with virtually no input from Soviet specialists.[129] This had several deleterious effects. It led to the accumulation of 'overkill'; it produced deterrence theories that were too abstract; it exacerbated American–Soviet relations as well as induced caution; it contributed to the institutionalization of the cold war; and it helped ensure that the mathematics of the nuclear balance came to have a wholly disproportionate importance in the evolution of East–West affairs.

Brodie was never a cold war warrior who made his living out of exaggerating the Soviet Union's expansionism nor the danger of communist ideology. As revealed in his published writing as early as 1946, he was a political realist. He believed that mutual suspicion, political interests and military posturing were inherent in a situation where two superpowers existed who were capable of inflicting the severest damage on each other. This had been the position of the co-authors of *The Absolute Weapon*. Brodie's work never revealed the visceral anti-Sovietism that animated so many of his countrymen. During his time at RAND Brodie learned about the Soviet Union through some of the area specialists there, notably Nathan Leites; he came to appreciate that Soviet behaviour was neither irrational nor imprudent.[130] As a result of this, and his French experience, he became significantly more relaxed about the Soviet threat than other prominent members of the American strategic community, most of whom preferred to imbibe cold war Sovietology neat and unshaken. All this gave him the confidence in the 1970s to challenge the fashionable anti-Sovietism associated with the Committee for the Present Danger, whose rising influence contributed to the breakdown of American–Soviet *détente*. Brodie now argued that a Soviet attack on the West in the late 1940s had been 'simply inconceivable', and he challenged the Committee's assertions with facts. He reminded them, for example, that nobody who had witnessed the American strategic build-up in the early Kennedy years could properly describe the Soviet arms build-up in the 1970s as 'unprecedented'.[131]

European security problems and nuclear strategy were not the only issues on which Brodie diverged from the administration in the 1960s and 1970s. He was also a dissenter on the most tragic issue of the period, the American practice of limited war in south-east Asia. The Vietnam War was the cause of the internal and external struggles by all Americans remotely interested in military affairs and Brodie was no exception. At first, in 1965, he publicly defended the American bombing of North Vietnam as 'warranted and effective',[132] but his opinion changed as American involvement grew. He was by no means the first to defect from his government's position, but he was among the first in the strategic profession.[133] Brodie's opposition to the war was not based on anti-war principles, like that of many peace activists, but rather on those strategic principles that had informed his thinking for many years, notably the essential unity of war and politics. He later summarized his position as follows:

the main reason we failed in Vietnam was also the reason why it was impossible from the beginning to succeed. We were supporting a government that not only did not deserve that support but which could not benefit from it. It could only be kept in place for as long as we were there in force. Nor was this an insight available only after the fact of failure.[134]

Brodie cannot reasonably be criticized for having failed to reach this verdict at the very outset of the American involvement. He was not an area specialist and he was not involved in policymaking. As an outsider his position evolved as he learned more about the situation. The tragedy for the United States, and for Vietnam as well, was that several administrations half slid and half jumped into the cockpit of south-east Asia without knowing or looking where they were going.

The responsibility for this ignorance, in Brodie's opinion, was widely shared; systems analysts and other civilian strategists, political scientists, the military and the political leadership had all played a part. He wrote: 'Our failures have been at least 95 percent due to our incomprehension and inability to cope with the political dimensions of the problem . . . If we have understood these problems we should certainly not have gone in.[135]

The major military error, he argued, was failure to anticipate the importance of giving the enemy a sanctuary; this was the result of 'misreading the lessons of Korea'. But this disaster 'pales in comparison' with the political error, 'our willfull blindness' in trying to shore up 'a corrupt, inefficient, and thoroughly unpopular regime. We had no business trying, and we could not succeed.'[136]

Brodie suggested that a 'reasonable' criterion for judging people on Vietnam was the timing of their second thoughts. The record of the civilian strategists, he thought, was 'quite mixed'. He identified some notable defectors from the official position and recorded that, like Alain Enthoven, his own position changed when the troop levels began to climb towards 200,000 men. Brodie was extremely critical of those who did not change position. In 1973 he wrote:

But to the best of my knowledge some of the civilian strategists . . . either fell off very late or are still hanging on, loyal to the last — to what?, What notions now lie behind words like credibility or 'honor' to defend a policy which has become too patently absurd for any rational defense, and indeed on the part of the Administration, with its pretenses to 'Vietnamization', quite phony?[137]

Like most Americans, Brodie had been tempted into supporting the war at the outset; but he came, reasonably early, to believe that it was a bad war. He summarized its lessons as follows:

We are learning to be mistrustful of political dogmas, and less diffident about confronting military dogmas. We certainly need to stress the superior importance of the political side of strategy to the simple technical and technological side. Preserve and cherish the systems analysts, but avoid the genuflections. The same goes for the soldiers, who are of course not threatened with extinction.[138]

There is a long way to go, he wrote, but much distance has already been travelled: 'When we recall how we discussed methods for demonstrating "our superior resolve" without ever questioning whether we would indeed have or deserve to have superiority in that commodity, we realize how puerile was our whole approach to our art'.

In the article from which these quotations about Vietnam have been taken, Brodie exposed his heart, as well as his mind, as had Clausewitz in his brief essay, 'I Believe and Profess', written in condemnation of the Franco–Prussian Treaty of 1812.[139] Both strategists were united in believing, in words as relevant in 1973 as when Clausewitz wrote them in 1812: 'the time is yours; what its fulfilment will be, depends upon you'.

The experience and the agonies of the Vietnam War were the background against which Brodie wrote his last book, *War & Politics*, which was published in 1973. It proved to be a flawed book in several respects. It is badly organized; some parts do not hang well together; and there are altogether too many words in some chapters. In places it could have done with rather more thorough editorial work (in these respects there are again echoes of Clausewitz, whose own *On War* was in need of revision).

Despite its weaknesses, *War & Politics* remains an important book both for understanding the evolution of Brodie's thinking and the strategic times in which it was written. It was largely ignored by the studies of Kaplan and Herken which have done so much to draw attention to Brodie's work. It has also generally been ignored by the strategic community, perhaps because of the relatively small attention it pays to those nuclear matters which have remained the professional preoccupation. But *War & Politics* should not be ignored. It repays careful reading and its arguments would surprise people who have only read the early Brodie, or who have only read him superficially. The book is also a rebuke to those with a stereotyped image of 'defence intellectuals' and 'academic strategists'. It reveals some of the experience and wisdom of a man whose career as a strategist spanned the nuclear revolution, who tasted life as an 'insider', who worked at RAND during its most creative period, who taught and researched at universities and who saw during the Vietnam era the hubris of both his country and his profession and the sorry aftermath.

As should be evident from its title, *War & Politics*, Brodie's intention was to emphasize that the use and threat of force should be considered as a branch of politics. (To Brodie the latter included domestic politics, a dimension of the strategic *problematique* that almost all the other nuclear theorists disregarded.) As has been suggested several times, Brodie throughout his professional career carried out a time-transcending dialogue with Clausewitz about the relationship between war and politics. This reached its culminating point — to borrow a Clausewitzian expression — in this last book. Its themes echoed those of the great Prussian thinker, though the book also showed the imprint of Brodie's own times, thought and experience.

The book begins with Clausewitz's famous sentence that 'war has its own language' (the means or methods of warfare) 'but not its own logic' (that is, purposes). Clausewitz was here expressing, in Brodie's words, 'the single most important idea in all strategy'. It is the idea, he went on, 'expressed in the question that Marshal Ferdinand Foch used to ask, *De quoi s'agit-il?* — 'What is it all about?'[140] 'De quoi s'agit-il?' was in fact the title of the first chapter, and in it, and throughout the rest of Part I, Brodie showed that men have too often paid lip-service to Clausewitz but have not integrated his philosophy into their outlook. At one point Brodie quotes Marshal de Saxe, Louis XV's leading soldier, as saying that 'very few men occupy themselves with the higher problems of war'.[141] Brodie suggested that matters have changed remarkably little in the intervening two hundred years, and he provided historical illustrations to support his case. He was particularly critical of what he believed to be the obsession of military establishments with victory for its own sake.

One of the ideas most closely associated with Clausewitz's philosophy is the notion of the inherent uncertainty of war. Figuring prominently in this is the concept of 'friction', which explains why plans fall short of the mark. Brodie, more than any other of the first generation of nuclear strategists — and certainly more than the bunker of nuclear warfighters who achieved prominence shortly after his death — stressed the potential uncontrollability of military action. Brodie pointed out how the best-laid plans of military staffs can go wrong and the familiar inability of nations to stop senseless wars.[142] 'The first casualty in war is not truth but reason,' he wrote.

Related to the idea of friction was the interest he shared with Clausewitz in the psychological dimensions of war.[143] Unlike those of the behavioural school who tried

— unsuccessfully — to make strategy a science, Brodie's emphasis on war as being a clash of violence resulted in more sophisticated strategic analysis. Brodie underlined the importance in military affairs of passion, faith, unconscious motives and feelings. He argued from his own experience with the military establishment that there was a connection between deep-seated neuroses and particularly rigid attitudes towards strategic problems. 'Man is deeply emotional,' he stressed, and because this is not sufficiently recognized, governments sometimes fail to predict their own behaviour. This was particularly important in crisis management. Against those who exaggerated the 'science' of crisis management and the primacy of prudence, Brodie reminded them that when they think about the future rather few men ask how they will *feel*.[144] In the academic world, Brodie wrote, computers are 'in' and psycho-pathology is 'out': but this fashion did not reflect their relative value in understanding the real world.[145] Brodie pointed out that governments are not black-boxes and that personalities can be decisive. *War & Politics* contains interesting comments on the likes of Generals MacArthur and LeMay, and Presidents Johnson and Kennedy.[146] He argued that the course of the Vietnam War would have been different had Kennedy lived. Even had the president been dragged further into the war during 1965, Brodie did not think that he would have 'stubbornly' escalated the commitment thereafter, as its 'bankruptcy' and 'failure' became evident, nor would he have tolerated the 'unvarying optimistic reports' and 'constantly disproved predictions' of General Westmoreland or the 'uniformly biased reports' monitored by Walt Rostow; nor could Brodie imagine Kennedy 'long outlasting in hawkishness' a Bundy or a McNamara.[147] Brodie was not impressed by the militarized mind, whether it belonged to a civilian or a soldier.

The war in Vietnam was driven by cold war dogmas (such as the 'domino theory') and fuelled by a hot war economy. Another of Brodie's Clausewitzian themes was his constant criticism of dogmas, slogans, axioms and rigid theories in strategy. Just as Clausewitz had tried to overthrow the rule-bound thinking that had characterized warfare in the eighteenth century, so Brodie railed against those in the second half of the twentieth century who seemed to believe that strategy could be learned by rote. For thirty years of his professional life he stressed that rigid principles undermine effective practice.[148]

Brodie always took seriously the idea of strategy as a 'theory of action' and the academic strategist as a potential policy adviser. 'Who are the experts?' was a question that troubled him not only because it was a logical one but also because of his unfortunate first-hand experience with military planners and the costly monuments wrought by the American military mind during his lifetime. His criticisms of the makers of modern strategy in *War & Politics* were not particularly original, but what he said is important because it was Bernard Brodie — the 'dean' of the first wave of nuclear strategists[149] — who said it.

Brodie had doubts about everybody's capacity to grasp the nuclear dilemma; he considered it too serious to be left to any single group. But he was particularly wary of military professionals, the ostensible experts. The idea that the military knew best when it came to making strategic decisions was one which attracted Brodie's scorn, and *War & Politics* contains several bitter attacks on the military way of thinking. He argued that the American military was insensitive to the profounder issues of war, that their professional training was not relevant to higher strategic thinking, and that the nation could better rely upon them if they had more imagination and more objectivity. Their ideas were stimulated more by emotion than by reason, he asserted, and if the arguments of the military establishment proved to be correct, then it was an accident.[150] The practical implication of all this was pure Clausewitzian: it all pointed, Brodie said, to the importance of civilian control over the military. He gave this belief the prominence of the very last sentence of the book: 'The civil hand must never relax, and it must without one hint of apology hold the control that has always belonged to it by right.'[151] For Brodie, as for Clausewitz nearly a century-and-a-half earlier, experience and logic permitted no other conclusion.

While stressing the rightful supremacy of the 'civil hand', Brodie was far from uncritical of its actual performance. He castigated civilian leaders when they were unduly deferential to those in uniform, and he expressed disapproval of their frequent lack of strategic expertise.[152] Deference was not just an individual problem, he warned, it was society-wide. Repeating, consciously or not, President Eisenhower's famous warning in his Farewell Address, Brodie expressed concern about the militarization of thinking throughout the United States.[153] He identified the problem as 'military-orientated civilians'. Civilian leaders were not only deferential, in his opinion, they also failed to receive the wisest strategic counsel. Brodie thought that this was in part because of the influence of the scientific strategists. It was disappointing to Brodie that political scientists and area specialists had failed to get a hearing in Washington while those whose views were fashionable had neither the qualifications nor the experience to advise on political matters. There could be no more damaging criticism, given the Clausewitzian theme of *War & Politics*. That Brodie believed it necessary to comment on civil-military relations is noteworthy, since this issue was not a characteristic concern of most nuclear strategists. The game theorists and former natural scientists who came into the strategic field, and indeed those historians and political scientists who should have known better, tended to conceive strategy simply as an outward-orientated activity, a virtual global chess game. Brodie understood that strategy began at home. This was evident not only in *War & Politics*; it had been clear in his stress in *Strategy In The Missile Age* and other writings that 'Strategy Wears a Dollar Sign'.[154] Brodie saw no virtue in ostentatious military spending for its own sake, resulting in tax-payer's money being wasted to fund a militaristic potlach. He did not subscribe to the norm of the strategic community that when it comes to defence spending, nothing impresses like excess.

In *War & Politics*, written against the background of the Vietnam War, it was the political rather than the economic dimension of domestic affairs that most concerned Brodie. He was critical of Henry Kissinger, President Nixon and others for their complete conviction regarding the primacy of foreign over domestic affairs.[155] These criticisms came out forcibly in his discussion of American thinking about limited war generally but especially the war in Vietnam. It is not surprising that those American leaders who failed to give due weight to their own society when thinking about war should have adopted an attitude of ethnocentric arrogance towards those they were fighting.

Brodie was very critical of American behaviour in south-east Asia.[156] Since the early 1950s he had argued that the United States needed a limited war strategy, but by the late 1960s he had decided that the theory had become over-complex and the practice indiscriminate. Brodie criticized the idea that 'options', one of the buzz-words of the McNamara Pentagon, were necessarily desirable. This was heresy to the RANDites. Options were fine in theory, he argued, but it was sometimes preferable not to possess some capabilities, since they could lead a country into trouble. Brodie's worry about the dangers that might come from proliferating limited war options also shaped his thinking about the dangers to nuclear deterrence that might result from proliferating options for nuclear warfighting. Since the late 1950s his steady advice had been that it was more important not to have a nuclear war than to pursue some marginal advantage in fighting one.

War and not simply strategy was Brodie's concern. Unusually for a 'strategy' book in the nuclear age, Brodie had a section in *War & Politics* which dealt with the causes of war. Brodie, more than any of the first generation of nuclear strategists in the United States (with the exception of Henry Kissinger), was concerned with the context within which the threat and use of force took place.[157] His approach in the 1970s was along the lines he had learned in the 1930s from Quincy Wright and others, namely that war is a multicausal and multifaceted phenomenon. But in the 1970s, unlike the 1930s, real realism suggested that significant changes were taking place in the institution of war. In discussing this Brodie demonstrated a breadth of knowledge and interest that was wider than that of the typical 'defence intellectual' of his day.[158] To them 'war' was a given, like having an enemy. The cold war witnessed the intellectual hegemony of high Hobbesianism. The 'realism' which informed Brodie's outlook was partly empirical, partly the result of his academic socialization and partly the result of the place and era in which he lived. But his philosophy was also related to and tempered by his study of history and the sociology of international relations. In contrast, the 'realism' of those strategists with other temperaments and from different intellectual backgrounds — Wohlstetter from mathematics or Kahn from physics for example — was intuitive, ideological and unadulterated. Because Brodie's realism was not doctrinaire,[159] he was more open than many of his colleagues to other ideas or evidence of change in world politics. In one of the most-quoted sentences of his 1946 book he noted (long before Thomas Schelling wrote about the 'Diplomacy of Violence')[160] that the task of the military in future would not be to fight but to avert war. In his last book, a quarter of a century later, he concluded a long chapter on changing attitudes to war by suggesting that the international system no longer conformed to the simple Hobbesian pattern assumed by traditional realism:

> We can predict over the longer term a much lesser inclination than in times past to take for granted the periodic recurrence of war, certainly the recurrence of large-scale warfare. We can predict also much greater earnestness about searching for alternatives to war . . . that violence should continue indefinitely to take that specific institutional form known as war . . . is now decidedly questionable. This could be wishful thinking, but we are not obliged to deny important visible changes simply because they happen to be in a direction we like.[161]

If one believes that the utility of war *as an institution* is changing, it is natural to give less attention to the details of strategy. Had Brodie lived longer it is reasonable to suppose that he would have spent less time thinking about strategy and more time searching, with what he called 'greater earnestness', for 'alternatives to war'. His later work thus begins to hint at the convergence of the concerns of strategic studies and peace research that took some shape in the 1980s.

With the passage of time, Brodie expressed greater sensitivity than many of his colleagues to the character of the societies between which the business of strategy was conducted. His knowledge of history was a help, as was his understanding of Clausewitz, who had written about the necessary interrelationship between societies and their war-making character. Because one detects behind Brodie the strategic analyst a man who agonized and possessed wide sympathies, it is not surprising that he brought moral issues into his discussion of strategy. He did not write much about this, and the additional spur of the war in Vietnam came relatively late in his career, but in *War & Politics* he dismissed as 'absurd' the idea that moral considerations should be expunged. Indeed the realist in him proceeded to argue that policies which are immoral are likely to be quite inexpedient and ultimately self-defeating.[162]

Despite his changing opinions, Brodie was not an 'anti-war' thinker. He recognized the troubled history of the world, accepted that turmoil would persist and believed that wars could be fought for noble reasons as well as senselessly. He argued, for example, that the decision to drop the A-bomb had been justified, since it had saved lives in a war he believed to have been just.[163] However, he also argued that political leaders were trustees for others, *including the enemy*. He criticized the callousness and ignorance of his fellow countrymen towards the Vietnamese, and the infliction of what he believed to have been needless suffering.[164] Such expressions of concern were unusual among the US nationalists who dominated strategic thinking during the first generation of the nuclear age: while claiming to be objective, and purporting to explain the world 'as it is', the writing of most nuclear strategists was shot through with an implicit assumption that the United States had the unquestionable right to threaten and if necessary obliterate large tracts of the earth — ultimately civilization in the northern hemisphere — in order to pursue the United States' 'national interest'. This unstated moral position was at the very core of their strategic thinking; everything else was technique. Those who have been identified as belonging to the radical wing of the arms debate (peace researchers for example) have often been criticized for their transparently normative approach. But there is no value-free strategic thinking. Subject and object, and image and reality have an inevitable and dynamic interrelationship in the study of human behaviour. Is it therefore worse, academically speaking, to wear one's heart on one's sleeve, like a Rapoport, or to conceal the nationalist fire in one's belly like a Kahn?

War & Politics contained a great deal about the nature of war and about the major wars of the period (notably Korea and Vietnam). There were few references in the book to nuclear matters. This emphasis reflected Brodie's growing belief that nuclear war was politically unthinkable while nuclear strategy had reached a dead end; 'existential deterrence' was a fact of life. This emphasis may also have reflected his feelings about the gap that had opened between what Clausewitz had called 'war on paper' and 'real war'. Brodie had spent much of his professional career thinking about the former, at the highest levels of violence; towards the end of his life he was agonizing about the latter, at somewhat lower levels. Perhaps what he deeply feared was that all the human faults revealed by the latter might one day manifest themselves in catastrophic practice at the higher levels. This, at least, is the sub-text of his book.

Brodie's distate for war grew. The impact of Vietnam undoubtedly crystallized his emotions on this score. In *War & Politics* he criticized the descriptions of battlefields in strategy books for rarely having the smell of death[165] and was bitter towards those leaders who possessed limited analytical powers yet sent men to fight and bleed for 'values held too sacred to question yet in fact juvenile'.[166] His conclusion was that 'on the whole nations have been too ready to fight. Wars avoided are sometimes totally avoided, and that's almost always a good thing.'[167] This judgement, written when he was in his early sixties, summarizes his longest and most personal statement about the inter-relationship between war and politics.

Though unsatisfactory in some respects, *War & Politics* remains an important and impressive book by a man who will continue to be regarded as one of the most eminent strategists of the twentieth century and the absolute strategist of the first thirty years of the nuclear age. After the book's publication in 1973, Brodie lived for another five years. He ended his professional life, as he had begun it, in a university environment. He had left RAND in 1966 but had stayed on the West Coast, at the University of California, Los Angeles. He does not seem to have re-settled easily to the life of an academic. And he was certainly a discontented strategist. Kaplan has recorded that Brodie participated in discussions about strategy in his later years, but that his friends noticed that he quickly faded out of them, 'from gloom or boredom', when the conversation left the matter of first principles.[168]

Brodie's published work during these final years was small in quantity, but as ever pertinent and important. As was appropriate, in the age of SALT, he wrote an article on arms control, and as was typical of Brodie, he attempted to bring the subject back to first principles, by clarifying its objectives.[169] His thesis was controversial. He argued that in a pragmatic approach to arms control saving money deserved a superior rating to saving the world. This conclusion derived from his belief in the extremely low probability of war between the superpowers and his conviction that arms control had little impact on that probability. Even more fittingly, he contributed extensively to the editorial and commentry on the most comprehensive edition of Clausewitz's work yet published.[170] Finally, in his last published article, in 1978, he wrote a general essay, 'The Development of Nuclear Strategy'.[171] In this he chided some of the increasingly fashionable ideas of the time being propounded by those New Right strategic fundamentalists in the United States who were increasingly laying down the strategic agenda for their own country and the world. He rejected the idea that the balance of terror had ever been delicate, dismissed the notion of a war-winning nuclear strategy, criticized the Richard Pipes' argument about Soviet thinking in this regard, dismissed the growing belief that the Soviet strategic buildup in the 1970s was unprecedented (with a reminder about that of the United States in the 1960s) and he expressed his disquiet about cruise missiles and the Schlesinger doctrine with the argument that one way to keep out of trouble is to deny oneself the means of getting into trouble. Paradoxically, he also argued in favour of tactical nuclear weapons (including the neutron bomb). An important theme of his argument was that the rigidity in strategy was not in the thinking but in the situation: to suggest otherwise and to devise alternatives was merely to play with words. In the course of making his case Brodie criticized the coming wave of thinkers in Washington from a historical and philosophical perspective; and time has vindicated his arguments.

Bernard Brodie died in 1978. The legacy he left was greater than his words, as prolific and full of insight as they were. The shadow of his professional life, as it still casts along the corridors of power, research institutions and universities, probably tells us more than that of any other single individual about the effort of intellectuals to comprehend the early history of the nuclear age. In addition, we are fortunate that the first major exponent of nuclear strategy was a man who believed in first principles and who was able to integrate into his approach to the subject an understanding of philosophy, history, technology and international relations. As a result, Brodie helped set high standards in this new field of enquiry. Those standards have not always been matched, but they will always remain for that minority of strategists who believe that there is more to learn from a silent dialogue with a major thinker of the past than with the loudest talkers of the present.

While it is always difficult to attach the label of 'originality' to individual writers, Brodie surely has some claim to be an original thinker. The collegial atmosphere at Yale and at RAND undoubtedly fertilized his thoughts, but what he said, and the way he put ideas together, marks him out. He was far-sighted and an originator of critical aspects of the stock of ideas that have contributed to our thinking about strategy in the nuclear age: the primacy of deterrence, the declining usability of force at the highest levels, the need for invulnerable retaliatory forces, the importance of target selection and restraint, limited war and so on. Naturally there were mistakes, omissions and inconsistencies in a long and productive professional life during an era of change. This was inevitable, as were the loose ends. There is no alternative to paradox if one commits one's self to the logic of nuclear strategy. But the body of Brodie's work stands firm for its integrity, coherence and comprehensiveness. Of all the early nuclear strategists discussed in this book Brodie was transcendant both in terms of the length of his career and the breadth of his interests.

As was evident from the first course he taught at Dartmouth, to his last piece of writing, Brodie insisted on thinking about first principles. But he always railed against maxims for conduct in strategy; it was an area of human conflict that did not permit reduction to a set of rules. This had also been Clausewitz's view in a different era. In this and other respects Brodie attempted to reinterpret Clausewitz for his own country and own times. By insisting upon the centrality of politics in strategy, he tried to ensure that the study of war and the threat of war had a human face. He insisted on rigorous thinking but showed why strategy could never fully become a true 'science'. But if it was an art rather than a science it was a truly practical art. In Brodie's mind strategic thinking was never to be a pastime exclusively for the ivory tower: because it involved judgements 'tested in blood', it was the ultimate pragmatic activity.

The first principles in Brodie's outlook were established by the doctrine of political realism. Brodie the student and junior academic had been professionally socialized within that school of thought. By the late 1940s the assumptions of this school seemed to offer an accurate representation of international reality, with Hitler in the immediate background and the cold war very much in the foreground. The realists won the intellectual battle with those at the time looking forward to security through law and idealism (and in some cases American isolationism). With hindsight, though, the realists learned their lessons too well; as a result, their work exaggerated the role of nuclear weapons and gave too much prominence to the military dimension of containment. At worst, the American realists become the 'mindguards' of the cold war, just like their conservative counterparts in Moscow.[172] The realist mindset and the world it helped to create through innumerable small decisions has proved difficult to dismantle. To his credit, Brodie recognized the need in the second half of his professional life to mitigate some of the misjudgements of the first. He remained, however, a critic of nuclear strategy from the inside; he showed no inclination to try to transcend the hegemonial strategic outlook. To the end he believed that it had been right to drop the atomic bomb in 1945 and that nuclear deterrence was helping to rid the world of the scourge of war.[173]

Brodie was a 'realist', but he was neither complacent nor doctrinaire. He did not have a static view of international politics, as is shown by his comments on the institution of war and his shifts of opinion in the 1960s. It is often assumed that people become more conservative with age; Brodie belonged to that category that become less satisfied. From being the bright power-political strategist who interpreted the dawn of the atomic age, he grew into a wise sceptic about some of the strategic fashions of the day and about the persistence of old thinking about war. He did not become as radical as some of the other political realists of the 1940s, notably Hans J. Morgenthau and George F. Kennan, but he probably did move further than any other major figure in the strategic profession. One can only speculate about where his ideas might have taken him had he lived longer. There seems little doubt that he would have spoken out against the excess and simple-mindedness of the Reaganites. It is also likely that he would have paid more attention to the alternatives to force as instruments of national policy.

At several important points in his career Brodie was a dissident, and it is to his credit as a professional and a human being. He did not avoid professional discomfort; he was always learning; and he did not think it threatening to change his mind. He did not defer to the authority of air force commanders when he believed them wrong; he was not tempted by the social science hubris of the late 1950s and 1960s; he was not pulled along by the strategic fashions of the day; he did not believe that his colleagues at RAND had discovered timeless truths about strategy; he challenged the conventional wisdom about options and flexibility; and, most unusual of all for an American strategist of his day, he did not believe that his own country was always right. He was an early critic of the Vietnam War. Brodie became discontented by the power of his colleagues' arrogance and by the arrogance of his country's power. If part of the strategist's calling is to 'speak truth to power',[174] then Brodie was an exemplar.

In the light of the above it is not surprising that Brodie's direct influence on the making of American strategy from the mid-1940s until the late 1970s was limited. But does influence matter? Who now worries whether Clausewitz had any influence on those around him? What counts is the enduring worth of what he wrote. In any case, those who have 'influence' in a direct sense tend to be simply those whose ideas happen to be congenial to the national policymakers of the day. The influence Brodie wielded was indirect rather than direct and philosophical rather than technical. His writing and teaching helped to shape the sensibilities of numerous individual strategists, including some who never knew him. He was not a 'maker' of modern strategy in a direct sense, like von Schlieffen in Germany before 1914; he was influential in a more general and indirect sense, like Clausewitz.

Rationality naturally became the highest value in the strategic profession in the nuclear age. But with many strategists rationality became a fact, not a value: the 'ought' of rationality became 'is', and then 'will be'. Brodie the historian, psychologist and philosopher of war knew better. Unlike so many of his contemporaries, and others who took up the subject later, he appreciated the role of chance in human affairs, the unpredictability of plans, the influence of emotions, the propensity of irrationality in human behaviour and the dangerous millstone of old ideas. In his books, more so than any other of his contemporaries, one sees a mind grappling at the potentially world-shattering interface of the old world of the sovereign state and nationalist emotions and the new technology of nuclear weapons and their paradoxical logic.

On this last point, as on so many others, the affinity between Brodie and Clausewitz is unerring. When one goes back and reads Brodie one is occasionally struck by how familiar, even banal, some of his ideas now seem. The same thought also occurs when reading Clausewitz: after all, did not Clausewitz earn an enormous reputation for elaborating the hardly novel idea that war is a continuation of politics with an admixture of other means? The reason for such a sense of familiarity with these mens' ideas is simple. We should remember the old lady who saw Shakespeare's 'Hamlet' for the first time.The play had been very nice, she said, but then added that the dialogue had been full of clichés. Other influential and lasting writers can have the same effect. In their own field Clausewitz and Brodie also invented our clichés. The familiarity of their ideas is a testament to their importance. Clausewitz helped coin our clichés for the age when wars were rational, national and instrumental.[175] Bernard Brodie helped coin our clichés for the age of nuclear deterrence, when the threat and use of force as an instrument of statecraft for the great powers became increasingly more problematic, and when general war became functionally (though not practically) obsolete.

Clausewitz did not give those who followed him direct answers to their problems, but, to those who read him properly, he gave sharpened receptivity, profound insights and a deepening sensibility. Brodie once described Clausewitz as a

deeply emotional man who . . . knew very well the worth of his own ideas. He knew well enough that war was a deadly serious matter, not a game to be played for the sake of winning. Although no single author could be an adequate 'guide' to us in our present problems . . . the startling insights that leap up at us from so many pages of his great work are still often directly applicable to our own times. There has been no one to match him since.[176]

Among the first generation of nuclear strategists, these words could be Brodie's own epitaph.

Notes

1. *The New Strategy* is the title of the massive but regrettably unfinished manuscript of the late James E. King.
2. Michael Howard, 'Empathy with the enemy', *Times Literary Supplement*, 13 June 1980; Thomas Schelling, 'Bernard Brodie (1910–1978)', *International Security*, Winter 1978, pp. 2–3.
3. The outlines of Brodie's career were not well known until the publication of Fred Kaplan, *The Wizards of Armageddon* New York, Simon & Schuster, 1983 and Gregg Herken, *Counsels of War*, New York, Alfred A. Knopf, 1985. The present chapter, which offers an interpretation of Brodie's published strategic thought, is indebted to these sources for basic information about his life.
4. See 'Quincy Wright (1890–1970). Beyond the Study of War' in Kenneth W. Thompson, *Masters of International Thought*, Baton Rouge, Louisiana State University Press, 1980 pp. 182–201.
5. J. Viner, 'The Implications of the Atomic Bomb for International Relations', *Proceedings of the American Philosophical Society*, **90**, No. 1, January 1946, pp. 53–8.
6. Kaplan, op. cit., p. 16.
7. Edward Mead Earle (ed.), *Makers of Modern Strategy. Military thought from Machiavelli to Hitler*, Princeton, Princeton University Press, 1941. A new edition, edited by Peter Paret, was published in 1986.
8. Herken, op. cit., p. 7.
9. Kaplan, op. cit., pp. 17–18.
10. Ibid.
11. Ibid., pp. 18–19.
12. Ibid., p. 19.
13. Ibid., pp. 8–9.
14. See Harken, op. cit., p. 346, note 8; and Lawrence Freedman, *The Evolution of Nuclear Strategy*, London, Macmillan, 1981, ch. 1–3.
15. Bernard Brodie, *The Atomic Bomb and American Security*, Yale Institute of International Studies, Memorandum No. 18, 1 November 1945.
16. Kaplan, op. cit., pp. 28–9. Fox wrote: 'When dealing with the absolute weapon, arguments based on relative advantage lose their point'. See p. 181 in Bernard Brodie (ed.), *The Absolute Weapon: Atomic Power and World Order*, New York, Harcourt, Brace, And Co., 1946.
17. This book's landmark status when it was first published is exaggerated by Herken and Kaplan. Freedman's verdict (op. cit., p. 30) is correct,: the book stands out only in retrospect. It was 'peripheral' to the main professional concerns of the late 1940s, the implications of atomic bombs for strategic bombardment.
18. *The Absolute Weapon*, p. 34.
19. Ibid., p. 24ff.
20. Ibid., pp.40–6.
21. Ibid., pp.72, 87ff.
22. Ibid., p. 91. He also recommended the decentralized command of atomic weapons. This did

not survive his later thinking about safety in the nuclear age, when the United States no longer had a monopoly of the weapons.

23. Kaplan, op. cit., p. 27. See also Freedman, op. cit., pp. 43-4.
24. *The Absolute Weapon*, p. 52.
25. McGeorge Bundy, 'Existential Deterrence and its Consequences', pp. 3-13 in Douglas Maclean (ed.), *The Security Gamble*, Totowa, NJ, Rowman and Allan Head, 1984. The comparison is made by Robert E. Osgood, *The Nuclear Dilemma in American Strategic Thought*, Boulder, Westview Press, 1988, p. 121, note 15.
26. *The Absolute Weapon*, p. 15.
27. Ibid., p. 88.
28. Ibid., pp.88-91, 94ff.
29. Ibid., p. 63.
30. *War and Politics*, pp. 377-8.
31. For Herken's comments on Borden see Herken, op. cit., pp. 10-14, 34-45, 341-2, and 'The Not-Quite Absolute Weapon: Deterrence and the Legacy of Bernard Brodie', *The Journal of Strategic Studies*, **9** 4, December 1986, pp. 15-24. All further references to Herken are to *Counsels of War*. Also see Freedman, op. cit., pp. 43ff.
32. This argument was best and most prominently displayed on the last page of Bernard Brodie, *Strategy In The Missile Age*, Princeton, NJ, Princeton University Press, 1959, reprinted 1965, p. 409.
33. See Dunn's comments, *The Absolute Weapon*, p. 90.
34. Quoted by Kaplan, op. cit., p. 34.
35. Bernard Brodie, 'Strategy as a Science', *World Politics*, **1**, 4, July 1949, pp. 467-88. See Brodie's own comments, *War and Politics*, p. 474.
36. Brodie's problems with the air staff are discussed in Kaplan, op. cit., pp. 34-40, 45-9 and Herken, op. cit., pp. 34-8.
37. Kaplan, op. cit., pp. 33-40.
38. Michael S. Sherry, *The Rise of American Air Power. The Creation of Armageddon*, New Haven, Yale University Press, 1987.
39. Kaplan suggests Brodie was the first, op. cit., p. 222.
40. See Brodie's discussion of target selection in *Strategy in the Missile Age*, pp. 152-60. Brodie did not rule out the utility of attacking Soviet cities, for example, as a way of impeding a Soviet invasion of Western Europe: see his 'The Atom Bomb as Policy Maker', *Foreign Affairs*, **27** 1, October 1948, p. 30.
41. Kaplan, op. cit., pp. 45-6.
42. Ibid., p. 48.
43. Earle, a former wartime aide on targeting issues, also broke with Brodie over this matter: Ibid., p. 49.
44. See, *inter alia*, Bruce, I. R. Smith, *The RAND Corporation: Case-Study of a Non-profit Advisory Corporation*, Cambridge, Mass., Harvard University Press, 1966); Colin S. Gray, 'Think Tanks' and Public Policy', *International Journal*, **33**, 1, Winter 1977-8, pp. 177-94.
45. G. Douhet, *Command of the Air*, translated by Dino Ferrairi, London, Faber, 1943. Brodie's assessment of Douhet is in *Strategy in the Missile Age*, pp. 71-106.
46. Bernard Brodie, 'Nuclear Weapons: Strategic or Tactical?', *Foreign Affairs*, **32**, 2, January 1954, pp. 217-29 and 'Strategy Hits a Dead End', *Harpers*, October 1955, pp. 33-7.
47. Norman Moss, *Men Who Play God*, Harmondsworth, Penguin Books, 1970, pp. 263-86; Herken, op. cit., p. 37; Kaplan, op. cit., pp. 222-3 gives a different interpretation of the origin of Kahn's remark, but Brodie again was the trigger.
48. Moss, op. cit., p. 124; Herken, op. cit., p. 206.
49. For this characterization of Clausewitz's work see Anatol Rapoport, 'Introduction', in his edited volume, *Clausewitz, On War*, Harmondsworth, Penguin books, 1968.
50. Herken, op. cit., pp. 382 note 5, and below.
51. Freedman, op. cit., p. 133. Freedman's own book might be said to be 'gloomy' for similar reasons.
52. 'Strategy Hits a Dead End' and Herken op. cit., p. 38.
53. Quoted by Herken, op. cit., p. 35.

54. 'Nuclear Weapons: Strategic or Tactical?', pp. 227–8.
55. Among his own contributions to the debate about limited war, Brodie thought particularly highly of his article 'Unlimited Weapons and Limited War', *The Reporter*, 18 November 1954, pp. 16ff. See *Strategy In The Missile Age*, p. 309.
56. See *Strategy In The Missile Age*, chapter 9; 'Nuclear Weapons: Strategic or Tactical?'; and 'Unlimited Weapons and Limited War'. Brodie surveyed the 'more important and original' literature in a review article 'More About Limited War' in *World Politics*, 1 **X**, October 1957, pp. 112–22.
57. Brodie acknowledged a debt to Liddell Hart, going back to 1952: Freedman, op. cit., p. 100.
58. *Strategy In The Missile Age*, chapter 9.
59. *Strategy In The Missile Age*, pp. vi, 314.
60. They sang, 'I wonder who's Kissinger now', Moss, op. cit., p. 251.
61. In the 1950s, notably in 'Strategy Hits A Dead End' and *Strategy In The Missile Age*.
62. *Strategy In The Missile Age*, p. 339.
63. Ibid., p. 341.
64. 'Strategy Hits A Dead End'.
65. *Strategy In The Missile Age*, p. 324–5.
66. Kahn said that 'Brodie — like everybody else in our circle — was very hostile to the use of tactical nuclear weapons. However, he was prompted to pursue the idea out of a "kind of intellectual integrity", this led him to adopt a devil's advocate position'. Herken, op. cit., p. 87. See Herken's own comments in *The Not-Quite Absolute Weapon*, p. 13; and Kaplan, op. cit., pp. 193–4.
67. On Brodie's isolation and the personality clashes see Herken op. cit., pp. 100–1; Kaplan, op. cit., pp. 76–7, 253.
68. Kaplan, op. cit., pp. 76–7, 337–9.
69. Herken, p. 100.
70. Bernard Brodie, 'Why Were We So (Strategically) Wrong?', *Foreign Policy*, 5, Winter 1971–2, pp. 151–61.
71. *The Absolute Weapon*, pp. 75–6.
72. Gray, op. cit., p. 211, note 20.
73. See Ken Booth, 'The Evolution of Strategic Thinking' especially pp. 46–53 in John Baylis *et al.*, *Contemporary Strategy*, vol. I, New York, Holmes and Meier, 1987.
74. *Strategy In The Missile Age*, p. 391.
75. Ibid., pp. 5–7.
76. Ibid., p. 21.
77. Ibid., pp. 20–7.
78. Ibid., pp. 50ff.
79. Ibid., p. 106.
80. Ibid., pp. 101–5.
81. Ibid., p. 115.
82. Ibid., p. 129.
83. Ibid., p. 144.
84. Ibid., pp. 165, 172. 'Overkilling' appears on p. 159.
85. Ibid., p. 167.
86. Ibid., p. 172.
87. Ibid., p. 221.
88. Ibid., p. 205.
89. Ibid., p. 222.
90. Ibid., pp. 227–9.
91. Ibid., p. 232.
92. Ibid., pp. 232–5.
93. Ibid., p. 235.
94. Ibid., pp. 237.
95. Ibid., pp. 241–8.
96. Ibid., pp. 248–63.
97. Ibid., p. 254–5.

98. Ibid., pp. 264-6.
99. Ibid., pp. 268-9.
100. Ibid., pp. 274.
101. Ibid., pp. 274-81.
102. Ibid., pp. 289-95.
103. Ibid., pp. 295-9.
104. Ibid., pp. 299-303.
105. Ibid., pp. 358-60.
106. Ibid., pp. 388-9.
107. Ibid., p. 392.
108. Ibid., p. 394-7.
109. Ibid., pp. 397-9.
110. Ibid., pp. 401-4.
111. Ibid., pp. 406-9.
112. Ibid., pp. 3-5.
113. The criticism came from Colin Gray. See 'Why Were We So (Strategically) Wrong', p. 152.
114. Kaplan, op. cit., p. 339. In *Strategy In The Missile Age* (p. 128). Brodie described Wohlstetter's famous 'The Delicate Balance of Terror' article as 'incisive and well-informed'. He later repudiated the idea that the balance had ever been delicate: Bernard Brodie, 'The Development of Nuclear Strategy', *International Security*, **II**, 4, Spring 1978, p. 68. Brodie was not only repudiating Wohlstetter; he was also repudiating his own warnings about the dangers of war.
115. Brodie, 'Why Were We So (Strategically) Wrong'.
116. Kaplan, op. cit., p. 339.
117. Bernard and Fawn M. Brodie, *From Crossbow to H-bomb. The Evolution of the Weapons and Tactics of Warfare*, Bloomington, Indiana University Press, 1973. First published 1962.
118. Ibid., p. 308.
119. Kaplan, op. cit., p. 358.
120. Quoted in Henry A. Kissinger (ed.), *Problem of National Strategy*, New York, Praeger, 1965, p. 12.
121. Kaplan, op. cit., p. 338.
122. Kaplan is for once mistaken (p. 338) when he suggests that Brodie went to France as a 'firm believer' in the strategy of conventional limited war but went home 'siding with his French friends'. The confusion arises out of the different possible locations of a limited war. Brodie argued the case for limited conventional war outside Europe, but believed Europe to be a special case in which war could not be kept limited for long, and so required only a limited conventional capability. He argued this before going to France: see *Strategy In The Missile Age*, pp. 335-42.
123. *Strategy In The Missile Age*, p. 52.
124. *War And Politics*, pp. 370-4.
125. *Escalation and the Nuclear Option*. See also 'What price Conventional Capabilities in Europe', *The Reporter*, 23 May 1963, reprinted in Kissinger, op. cit.; and 'The McNamara Phenomenon', *World Politics*, **XVII**, 4, July 1965.
126. Kaplan, op. cit., p. 340.
127. 'The Development of Nuclear Strategy', pp. 78-83.
128. 'Why Were We So (Strategically) Wrong?', p. 154.
129. Michael MccGwire, 'The Insidious Dogma of Deterrence', *Bulletin of the Atomic Scientists*, **2**, 10 December 1986, pp. 24-9.
130. Kaplan, op. cit., p. 338. With Leites, the author of an important psychological study of Soviet behaviour, Brodie wrote a psychological study of his strategic *bête noire*, Curtis LeMay. It was not published.
131. *War & Politics*, p. 393 (see also pp. 331, 386, 415ff.); and Bernard Brodie, 'The Development of Nuclear Strategy', *International Security*, **II**, 4, Spring 1978, pp. 65-83.
132. Herken, op. cit., p. 210.
133. Ibid., and p. 368, note 17.

134. *War & Politics*, p. 173.
135. 'Why Were We So (Strategically) Wrong?', p. 173.
136. Ibid., p. 157.
137. Ibid., p. 160.
138. Ibid., p. 161.
139. Karl Von Clausewitz, 'I Believe and Profess', pp. 301–4 in Karl Von Clausewitz, *War, Politics & Power*, translated and edited by Edward M. Collins, Chicago, Henry Regnery Co., 1962.
140. *War & Politics*, p. 1.
141. Ibid., p. 433.
142. Ibid., chapter 4.
143. Ibid., pp. 17, 60, 115–7, 120, 209, 302ff, 389–90.
144. See also Bernard Brodie, 'The Impact of Technological Change on the International System: Reflections on Prediction', *Journal of International Affairs*, **2**, 1971, pp. 209–23.
145. *War & Politics*, pp. 314–5.
146. Ibid., pp. 107, 126ff, 132ff, 191–2, 477.
147. Ibid., pp. 132ff.
148. Ibid., pp. 447, 450ff.
149. Herken, *Counsels of War*, p. 341.
150. *War & Politics*, pp. 79, 381, 479, 413, 433ff, 440, 472, 486, 492, 495.
151. Ibid., p. 496; see also pp. 464, 471.
152. Ibid., chapter 10 'Strategic Thinkers, Planners, Decision-Makers'.
153. Ibid., pp. 459–62, 460, 473ff.
154. *Strategy In The Missile Age*, chapter 10.
155. *War & Politics*, p. 200.
156. Ibid., chapter 4, 'Vietnam: How We Became Involved' and chapter 5, 'Vietnam: Why We Failed'.
157. Kissinger, it might be argued, was not primarily a strategist. A major non-American exception was Raymond Aron: see his *Peace and War: A Theory of International Relations*, Garden City, Doubleday, 1966.
158. See *War & Politics*, chapter 6, 'Changing Attitudes Toward War' and 'Some Theories on the Causes of War'.
159. The distinction between 'doctrinaire' and 'empirical' realists is made by W. T. R. Fox, 'E. H. Carr and Political Realism: Vision and Revision', *Review of International Studies*, **11**, 1, January 1985, p. 13.
160. Thomas C. Schelling, *Arms and Influence*, chapter 1.
161. *War & Politics*, pp. 274–5.
162. Ibid., pp. 365, 369, 374 (see also *Strategy In The Missile Age*, pp. 235ff).
163. Ibid., pp. 55–6.
164. Ibid., pp. 170ff.
165. Ibid., pp. 7–8.
166. Ibid., p. 3.
167. Ibid., p. 148.
168. Kaplan, op. cit., p. 341–2; Herken, op. cit., p. 341.
169. Bernard Brodie, 'On The Objectives Of Arms Control', *International Security*, **1**, 1, Summer 1976, pp. 17–36.
170. Karl Von Clausewitz, *On War*, edited and translated by Michael Howard and Peter Paret, Princeton, Princeton University Press, 1976.
171. 'The Development of Nuclear Strategy', p. 75.
172. The concept of 'mindguards' is from Irving L. Janis, *Victims of Groupthink*, Boston, Houghton Mifflin Co., 1972.
173. *War & Politics*, p. 490.
174. See Gray, op. cit., p. 193.
175. This formulation is from Rapoport (op. cit), 'Introduction'.
176. *War & Politics*, p. 446.

2 ALBERT WOHLSTETTER

Richard Rosecrance

Probably no civilian strategic analyst has had more influence in the nuclear age than Albert Wohlstetter. This is not to say that he was the innovator of most, or even many new doctrines.[1] In the days before and after Hiroshima, he was not the first to recognize the need for a 'retaliatory' nuclear capability; (he was not even doing strategic analysis at the time) he was not the only originator of 'counterforce' and 'city avoidance' options and he was among several who propounded 'damage limitation' strategies. He was not the only critic of 'massive retaliation' doctrines, nor was he the first to discuss the need for 'limited war' options in the open literature. He did not originate the requirements of 'nuclear deterrence'.[2] Yet with all of the accomplishments he shared or left to others, his thought and work perhaps represent both the most consistent and the most general writings on strategy in the post-World War II era. Wohlstetter's notions of deterring an opponent who faces 'alternative risks' display a breadth of conception found in few other strategic analyses. Thomas Schelling's bargaining theories perhaps contribute a dimension that is underdeveloped in Wohlstetter's corpus, but even there, the latter's doctrines are eclectic enough to accommodate them.[3]

Given these strengths, one still finds it difficult to account entirely for the great influence that Wohlstetter has had. His work, of course, typifies both the positive and negative features of the quantitative tradition of 'systems analysis', which abstracts from history and yields useful results only so far as its assumptions and data are valid.[4] Yet on critical issues, like the potential or actual vulnerability of the United States Strategic Air Command (SAC), Wohlstetter and his associates were able to show, quantitatively, that SAC-programmed systems were at various past periods inadequate to withstand a well-designed and executed surprise attack. To be sure, such analyses rest their case on an assessment of capabilities, not intentions. It may well be that the marshals of the Soviet Union never considered making a strike on a vulnerable SAC, just as American leaders never planned a strategic attack on the Soviet target system when the latter either possessed no atomic bombs or were confined to extremely limited retaliatory capabilities. As the Israelis found out to their dismay in the October 1973 Yom Kippur War, however, a nation cannot rely wholly upon purported enemy intentions. The assessment of capabilities is an essential part of any realistic analysis of probable opponent behavior.

In Wohlstetter's case, the claim to strategic influence and originality rests on two important pillars: first is the well-known 'base study' performed in several versions at the RAND Corporation beginning in 1951. Wohlstetter and his group devised the distinction between a first-strike and a second-strike capability when they examined the vulnerability of SAC bases to strategic attack in the early 1950s, their weakness and inadequacy in light of the development of the Soviet long-range bomber force in 1956 and afterward, and finally the vulnerability of American strategic forces to attack by Soviet intercontinental ballistic missiles (quaintly called IBMs)[5] in 1960 and the years following. This continuing effort took many classified forms, anticipated and

strongly influenced the conclusions of the famous Gaither Report on 'Deterrence and
Survival in the Nuclear Age' in 1957 and later found public expression in a seminal
article, 'The Delicate Balance of Terror' published in the January 1959 issue of the
journal, *Foreign Affairs*.

His second claim to influence and originality rests on his conception of deterrence,
which has differed greatly from that of influential scientists, public officials and
laymen. Many devotees of mutual assured destruction capabilities believe that the
mere possession of a retaliatory force capable of devastating enemy cities after
absorbing an attack assures deterrence. In contrast, Wohlstetter has always insisted
that capabilities alone do not deter: there must also be some reasonable prospect that
they would be used in response to an assault. 'Credibility' is as important as
'capability'. Of course, many have recognized this as a truism of the nuclear age, but
not all have understood its full implications. After an enemy attack on Europe or one
directed at American strategic bases, policymakers would scarcely want to launch
their missiles on innocent Soviet civilians. This would only imperil American cities
without limiting Soviet capabilities to damage them. Thus Wohlstetter has always
rejected the idea that 'deterrence' and feasible 'strategic use' are separable elements of
a strategic posture. Unless an opponent believes that his potential victim might
actually respond and has a credible option of in fact doing so, deterrence cannot be
guaranteed.

From this standpoint, Wohlstetter criticized the Catholic Bishops who in their
Pastoral Letter in 1983 claimed that strategic nuclear weapons should be retained,
presumably because of their deterrent value, but that in no circumstances should they
ever be used.[6] He also differs from French thinkers who believe that 'deterrence'
inheres in the very possession of a small number of strategic weapons. No plans have
to be made actually to employ such weapons. 'Strategy' is separate from 'dissuasion'.
Rejecting these conceptions, Wohlstetter has nevertheless abjured the conventional
wisdom that declares that the response to attack must be massive and nuclear. In the
future, he points out, increasingly accurate conventional weapons might destroy
military targets that in the past could only have been hit by nuclear weapons. But
there must be some credible threat of riposte, or an aggressor can thrust without his
victim even drawing a sword.

Since he rejected 'massive retaliation', some have accused him of favouring
'warfighting' capacities which increase the likelihood of war and reduce deterrent
sanctions. Neither is the case. If the probability of employment of a very severe
sanction (massive retaliation or mutual assured destruction) is zero, then the product
of deterrent capability and credibility is still nil. More limited and discriminating
responses might reduce the weight of response, but their deterrent product will be far
higher than that based on an empty threat to destroy the enemy and the world.

This is not to say that there might not still be a small though not entirely negligible
benefit to be derived from the outside chance that major escalation could result from
aggressive action, even though it might be unplanned and not in the interest of the
deterrer to carry out. Some believe, wrongly, that any use of nuclear weapons is
bound to degenerate into all-out use. Even if this were true, however, a rationally
calculating defender still cannot entirely exclude the possibility that he or his
opponent might escalate *in extremis*. Thus the aggressor cannot ignore such an
eventuality in planning an attack.[7] Chance may determine the outcome, and this has
led Thomas Schelling to depict a retaliatory threat in such circumstances as 'the
threat which leaves something to chance'.[8] The French have sometimes referred to
this slender probability of massive use as 'the shadow of incertitude' which hangs over
an aggressor and (in their view) ultimately deters him. This possibility also remains a

background threat in nuclear strategies of finite deterrence or of mutual assured destruction.

Wohlstetter, however, would not rest deterrence on such essentially 'irrational' possibilities and shaky foundations. In his view, deterrence depends on rational strategies, and if retaliation is 'irrational', the threat to retaliate cannot deter. *Ex ante* threats have to have some correspondence with *ex post* incentives.[9]

The base study and its successors

In 1951 Wohlstetter began work on a RAND project dealing with the selection and use of strategic bases.[10] He rapidly discovered that SAC had focused on the means of delivering a devastating 'Sunday Punch' against the Soviet target system, but had spent virtually no time examining the vulnerability of American strategic bases to a Soviet attack. Since most of the bases from which SAC planned to operate were overseas (and plans involved moving bombers and support equipment to such bases prior to an attack), they were in easy range of Soviet bombers, carrying perhaps 150 bombs of 40 kilotons each. Wohlstetter also pointed out that bases in the United States were vulnerable to one-way missions carried out by the Soviet Tu-4 (the Russian copy of the B-29). Most of the American bases were within 200 miles of the border and would receive very little warning; in any event, SAC had not provided for a rapid response or dispersal capability upon tactical warning. Rather, General LeMay and other SAC leaders counted on receiving reliable strategic warning of attack, as much as weeks in advance. Wohlstetter and his associates considered a variety of antidotes to SAC vulnerability and recommended a number of them in the next few years, including use of overseas bases for refuelling only, dispersal of SAC bombers within the United States and shelters for the bombers against attack. Even as early as 1951 it was obvious to Wohlstetter, Henry Rowen and others that two functions were involved in carrying out the strategic mission: (1) solving the vulnerability problem (that is, surviving a Soviet first strike) and (2) executing an attack on the Soviet target system (that is, delivering the second strike). In this way, the distinction between first-strike and second-strike capabilities was born.[11]

When the study was relayed to officers of the air force, beginning in 1953, they were told: 'The presently planned base system will be extremely vulnerable in 1956.'[12] Expanding upon this theme, Wohlstetter stated: 'In a strike using only a fraction of the capability we assign them in 1956, the Soviets would destroy 90 percent of our bombers and tankers based in the United States. If the remaining few planes went overseas, as they would according to our mobility plan, they would be flying from the frying pan into the fire.'[13] The briefing concluded that SAC vulnerability could be reduced by 'measures enabling evacuation in the United States and measures reducing and making irregular the time spent on bases overseas'.[14] The latter meant that overseas bases would be confined to ground refuelling at irregularly spaced intervals. The Soviet Union would not want to use its then limited bomb stockpile on such targets unless it was sure that bombers would be stationed on them.

A year later, SAC had taken some measures to reduce vulnerability: specifically, new overseas bases were being built for ground refuelling, and a programme of hardening bases to withstand atomic attack had been initiated. Neither of these, however, considered the effect of large future quantities of Soviet H-bombs which would render all overseas bases vulnerable. SAC thus had to turn to aerial not ground refuelling overseas.

The advent of the intercontinental ballistic missile also changed the calculations. Programmed defences would not protect SAC against an ICBM attack delivered with essentially no warning. Only a system of hardened shelters for aircraft (which would exploit ICBM inaccuracies) would be expected to protect the capability to strike back in the 1960s. Wohlstetter and Fred Hoffman wrote in February, 1954:

> If the IBM is a probable threat, and we cannot protect our strategic force against it, then our advertised capability for retaliation will be fictitious. We could not expect to hurt the Russians very much, unless we could be sure to strike the first blows. This should make us rather trigger happy, particularly if we were to couple this fragile strategic capability with an announced policy of relying mainly on a threat of major strategic atomic attack to deter even minor war. It would appear also to make the Russians equally trigger happy. Because in this case striking the first blow is the only means of defense, any delay in striking the first blow by either side risks the chance that the enemy will be the one to have this prerogative. With a defense of SAC against the IBM and any other likely menace, on the other hand, we can assure ourselves and Russia that whether we strike first or second we can lay waste a large proportion of the Russian economy and the Russian population. This will make a decision to strike a first blow extremely unpleasant for the decision-maker as well as for the recipient of the blow.[15]

After the 1960s, however, shelter and dispersal would no longer protect bombers or American ICBMs against attack. 'The missile might improve drastically in accuracy and payload. However, the date at which the Russians will have a missile capable of carrying at 25 MT bomb with a 1500 foot CEP appears sufficiently far removed to make the defense good, let's say until the end of the Sixties.'[16] In this study Wohlstetter and Hoffman anticipated some of the early versions of counterforce targeting. As ICBM accuracies increased, it would be possible to hit strategic force targets in the Soviet Union; these in turn would 'become increasingly worthy as the Russian stockpile increases'.[17]

In 1956 the Wohlstetter team extended their analysis to consider not only ICBM attacks but also strikes by the new and longer-range Soviet bombers, the Bison and the Bear. The latter would make it possible to outflank American continental radars by a refuelled surprise attack through the Caribbean. Soviet ICBMs would continue to accentuate vulnerability problems and could only be countered by increased shelter and dispersal of bomber aircraft. SAC readiness to respond had to be greatly increased. The September 1956 RAND report recommended: extending the continental early-warning line to the south and locating all SAC bases within its perimeters; increasing crew and aircraft readiness; sheltering aircraft and bombs against ICBM attacks.[18] All these measures were shown to be more effective than increasing the number of SAC bombers or adding active defences to protect them.

The base study and its successors were among the most significant analyses ever done at the RAND Corporation. They established not only the tradition of 'systems analysis' but of 'opposed systems design', where it is assumed that an enemy takes countermeasures to offset one's efforts to protect the strategic force. Only when those responses were not cost-effective could it be assumed that they would be overcome. In this way the early Wohlstetter investigations laid the foundation of the strategic analysis which today underpins new weapons systems and calculates the balance of deterrence with the Soviet Union.

The delicate balance of terror and the Ellsberg model

Wohlstetter consistently maintained that deterrent sanctions (comprised of credibility and capability) would have to overcome the rational or conceivably even the irrational incentive that an enemy might have to strike. His wife Roberta Wohlstetter's brilliant study of the Japanese attack on Pearl Harbor and America's failure to interpret the intelligence warnings which the breaking of Japanese codes provided in 1941,[19] made it clear that 'a bolt from the blue' could not be dismissed as a possibility in the nuclear age. Japan had struck not because she was sure she would win the Pacific War; in fact on balance she thought she would lose. It was because her risks of not striking (Wohlstetter's 'alternative risks') were so unfavourable. If she attacked America, her probability of success could be rated at much less than fifty percent. If she did not strike and gained no additional oil supply, her position in China and as a military nation was doomed. Admiral Nagano pointed out that:

> The current relations between Japan and the United States might be compared to an illness in which a decision was necessary on whether to perform an operation. Avoiding surgery would contain the threat of a gradual wasting away of the patient. Great danger would attend the operation, but it could not be said that surgery offered no hope of saving the patient's life.[20]

Her only hope was that America, like Russia in 1904–5, would accept a compromise peace after early Japanese successes. How could Japan have been deterred? Only by understanding in advance that America would devastate her in prompt retaliation for her attack on Pearl Harbor. America's response not only had to be powerful, but the capability of administering it had to be in hand and the Japanese fully cognizant of it. Since aggressors whose international position is deteriorating may be much more willing to take military risks than nations whose peacetime situation is less unfavourable, deterrent restraints have to cope with such added aggressive incentives.

Wohlstetter's 'Delicate Balance of Terror' article in 1959 made it clear that surviving an attack and retaliating was no mean feat.[21] Six hurdles had to be surmounted:

(1) Deterrent forces had to be capable of being sustained on a steady-state, peacetime basis within feasible budgets;
(2) They had to be able to survive an attack (this depended in turn on the amount of warning, the reaction time of particular forces, the dispersal of targets, the size of the target, the degree of mobility and the amount of protection the target could be given);
(3) They had to be able to receive a communication from national command authorities to retaliate. Here dispersed or mobile systems posed problems. 'Long distance communications may be jammed and, most important, communications centers may be destroyed.'[22]
(4) Retaliatory systems had to possess the ability to reach enemy territory with fuel enough to complete the mission (bombers dependent on pre-target refuelling from tankers based near the Soviet Union could face extreme hazards on this score);
(5) American strategic forces had to be able to penetrate the enemy's active defences. This might require an ability to ward off air and missile defences with penetration aids. Missiles with limited payload might not be able to carry the needed equipment.

(6) Finally, the incoming warheads would have to penetrate the enemy's passive defences, including blast and fall-out shelters.

Wohlstetter pointed out that rewards were given not to systems which got over a few of the hurdles but only to those which surmounted all six. That was a much more complex and demanding task than the influential public generally realized. In 'the Delicate Balance' Wohlstetter was not drawing attention to the 'missile gap', (the respective pre-strike numbers of American and Soviet ICBMs) but rather to the 'deterrence gap', which focused on how many American retaliatory weapons would be left after a well-designed and executed Soviet first strike, and on how many of those could in fact carry out their second-strike mission. Wohlstetter stressed that, under plausible circumstances, America's ability to retaliate might be so disabled by a Soviet strike that it would do less damage to the Soviet Union than it had endured in World War II.

> On the other hand, the risks of not striking might at some juncture appear very great to the Soviets, involving, for example, disastrous defeat in peripheral war, loss of key satellites with danger of revolt spreading—possibly to Russia itself — or fear of an attack by ourselves. Then, striking first, by surprise, would be the sensible choice for them, and from their point of view the smaller risk.[23]

In his submissions to the Gaither Committee and also in 'The Delicate Balance' Wohlstetter worried about premature attempts to fill what was then believed to be the missile gap by basing intermediate-range ballistic missiles in Europe. Such weapons might reassure the public, but they would be very vulnerable to Soviet attack, nearly as vulnerable as European bomber bases had been. They might add to American first-strike capabilities but would contribute very little to the American second-strike mission.

At this time, Daniel Ellsberg, then a young systems analyst at the RAND Corporation, wrote an extremely interesting paper titled 'The Crude Analysis of Strategic Choices'. Among other objectives, Ellsberg sought 'to formalize some of the propositions in Wohlstetter's discussion in 'The Delicate Balance'.[24] In particular Ellsberg provided a mathematical representation of Wohlstetter's doctrine of 'alternative risks' by comparing the utility of first-strike and second-strike outcomes with that of non-war outcomes (Wohlstetter's utility of 'not striking'). It should be stressed, without in any way detracting from Ellsberg's deductive elaboration, that the notions in his paper express in the abstract terms of numerical utilities the comparisons that Wohlstetter had in mind in his doctrine of 'alternative risks' and that in broader terms, aggressors have had to make throughout history.

It follows from both Wohlstetter's and Ellsberg's analysis that any decline in the utility of the non-war outcome as perceived by an aggressive power reduces the stability of deterrence. As a result, the utility of the first-strike outcome becomes relatively more attractive, even though it may not have increased absolutely. Such comparisons were made by Japanese leaders as they deliberated on whether to attack Pearl Harbor (see Butow quote in footnote above). Ellsberg's utilities were as follows:

Soviet Union		United States
V_{11}	utility payoffs for non-war	U_{11}
V_{21}	utility payoffs for first strike	U_{21}
V_{12}	utility payoffs for second strike	U_{12}
q	subjective estimate of the probability of an opponent first strike	p

For deterrence (of the Soviet Union):

The Soviet utility attached to waiting had to be greater than the Soviet utility attached to striking, or:

$$V(WAIT) - V(STRIKE) > 0$$

The Soviet value of WAIT = $(1-q)V_{11} + q.V_{12}$

The Soviet value of STRIKE = V_{21}

Hence: $(1-q)V_{11} + qV_{12} - V_{21} > 0$

Ellsberg explained that deterrence would be less stable if there were:

(a) a drop in the 'no all-out War' outcome V_{11} (due to Soviet losses or expectation of losses in a limited war, shifts in prestige, influence or alliances, 'cold war' failures, domestic set-backs or uprisings, political rivalries with third parties); (b) a drop in the Soviet 'strike second' outcome V_{12} (due to increased U.S. force size or ability to exploit weaknesses in Soviet warning systems or defenses, or prospect of U.S. 'annihilation tactics' in a U.S. first strike); a rise in the Soviet 'strike first' outcome V_{21} (a reduction in U.S. 'strike second' or retaliatory capability, due to changes either in U.S. or in Soviet posture, procedures, tactics).'[25]

The larger the interval between V(WAIT) and V(STRIKE), the greater the disturbance needed to destabilize deterrence. Thus Ellsberg provides an index of the reliability or stability of deterrence.

Applying the model to the basing of IRBMs in Europe, Ellsberg points out that the Soviet first-strike utility, V_{21}, might be expected to decline, though only marginally because European-based IRBMS offer such tempting and vulnerable targets. Much more important, there would be a sharp decrease in V_{12}, the Soviet second-strike outcome and a sharp increase in U_{21}, the American first-strike outcome, reducing deterrent stability and making the Soviets less willing to WAIT.

There are other implications of the Wohlstetter–Ellsberg notions as well. Any increase in V_{11} would also increase the value of WAIT, thereby making it more attractive relative to the value of STRIKE. This provides another policy implication that is embedded in Wohlstetter's analysis: if a decline in V_{11} or an increase in the adversary's 'alternative risks' occurs, he becomes more willing to STRIKE. If his alternative risks decline (and V_{11} increases), the deterrent situation becomes more stable.

Thus, there are two ways to overcome the problem of alternative risks: one involves buttressing the deterror's retaliatory capability; the other lessening the adversary's fears, so long as any such action does not simultaneously reduce the deterror's own position and attachment to general peace. British Prime Minister Neville Chamberlain failed to find a way of making Nazi Germany a stronger adherent of the status quo, and his concessions to Hitler only served to undermine Britain's own non-war utilities. On the other hand, if such policies had been tried by Austria, Germany, Russia and England in 1914, they probably would have worked.

In agreement with the conclusions of this model Secretary of Defense Robert McNamara acknowledged in 1963 that an improvement in the Soviet second-strike capabilities would not unsettle deterrence; it would in fact enhance it. If the Soviet second-strike outcome had improved, the Soviet interval between Waiting and Striking would have increased and the Soviet Union would have become less ready to strike first.[26]

Wohlstetter has seldom discussed these particular implications of his strategic notions, but they flow just as naturally from his doctrine of 'alternative risks' as does the more straightforward conclusion that a decline in the enemy's political and military position may tempt it to act aggressively.

Damage limitation, counterforce, and city avoidance

Wohlstetter was among several at RAND who devised the notions of 'damage limitation' and 'assured destruction' in the late 1950s which were later embraced by Defense Secretary Robert McNamara in the Kennedy administration. McNamara had been convinced of their worth by William Kaufmann, a former RAND staff member then at MIT, and the doctrines were strongly reinforced by former RAND analysts, Alain Enthoven and Henry Rowen, who joined the defence department in 1961. Wohlstetter declined a job in the Pentagon, preferring to remain with his work at RAND. All four insisted that the United States had two strategic tasks: the first to deter a Soviet attack through possession of a powerful second-strike capability; second, to limit damage to itself and allies should an attack none the less occur. The 'assured destruction' task of maintaining a retaliatory force which could devastate one-fifth to one-third of the Soviet population and one-half to two-thirds of its industrial capability was not a supremely difficult one in those days, especially when it was revealed that Soviet ICBM capabilities were extremely limited, and SAC bombers had been protected in various ways. Much more rigorous was the task of 'limiting damage' should the Soviets strike. Wohlstetter insisted that 'damage limitation' was a worthy effort even if the United States had to respond to a strike directed at American missile and bomber bases. In those circumstances the Soviets would withhold forces for later attack on American cities, hoping to prevent an immediate American retaliation on Soviet urban areas. If the United States then succumbed to the temptation to launch an all-out response, it would insure the destruction of its own cities. Much preferable was an American counter-attack on Soviet military targets: missile reload, bomber capabilities and submarine bases, diminishing the Soviet ability to do damage to the American and Western urban populations. If the Soviet Union then attacked cities, it would be sacrificing its own citizens in the process.

Retaliatory damage limitation strategies could inflict hardship on the Soviet strategic force, but they would not be likely, as Soviet systems grew in number and sophistication, to deny them Soviet 'assured destruction' capabilities against American cities. In the early 1960s, however, 'damage limitation' might not be confined to retaliation after a Soviet strategic strike. In response to a massive ground attack on the North Atlantic Alliance, the West might have launched a strategic counterattack on Soviet ICBM, bomber and submarine bases. Under the circumstances prevailing at the time, the Soviet retaliatory force might have been reduced to a small fraction of its pre-war size, 'limiting the damage' that it could do to Western populations. At RAND, prospective American fatalities were plotted against Soviet delivered bombs, and the resulting curve demonstrated that if Soviet capabilities could be significantly diminished by a counterforce strike, the damage to the United States might in some degree be 'acceptable'. Thus the United States might force a Soviet capitulation.

The United States Air Force developed a doctrine of 'coercion' that was based on abilities to limit damage. The American counterforce strike would be so powerful that Soviet leaders would face the choice of a ragged attack on American cities, thereby bringing on their own destruction or not retaliating at all.

The problem involved in maintaining a long-term 'damage limiting' or 'coercive' capability of this sort was that it effectively denied 'assured destruction' capabilities to the Soviet Union. It was not surprising that the Soviet buildup of the mid-to-late 1960s was often linked to McNamara's 'counterforce' and 'damage limitation' doctrines of 1962 — doctrines which seemed to demand continuing American and Western strategic superiority.[27] McNamara himself realized this and played down the 'damage limiting' task after his first two years as American secretary of defence. Wohlstetter, however, continued to stress 'damage limitation' and 'counterforce' so long as the Soviets would be forced to spend more to offset our counterforce and anti-ballistic missile deployments than they cost themselves. In this way he parted intellectual company with McNamara during the latter years of his tenure as secretary of defense.

Perhaps neither strategist fully took account of the doctrines of Assistant Secretary John McNaughton, revealed at a speech at Ann Arbor in December 1962, which sought to limit damage in a strategic conflict without forcing the Soviet Union to give up.[28] Wohlstetter's conceptions strove to limit damage by influencing the enemy's *capability*. McNaughton's, perhaps drawing upon Schelling, aimed to limit damage by influencing the enemy's *will*. He held out the possibility through 'city avoidance' of a 'mutual improvement of security'. Physical 'damage limitation' involved hitting as much of an enemy's strategic force as possible before it could be used to attack cities. Volitional 'damage limitation' involved sparing Soviet cities even if in the process some Soviet strategic capabilities were allowed to remain intact. Under the physical approach to damage limitation, if the Soviets hesitated, the United States would make an additional attack on their strategic force. Under the volitional approach, Soviet restraint would be followed by American restraint. The war would wind down without massive attacks on cities even though the Soviets had not been forced to surrender.

Many criticized such notions because, it was said, they would not deter, and in any event the Soviets would not abide by them. Soviet anticipation of major attacks on their strategic forces would not prevent them from launching an invasion of Europe. Again the greater credibility of such responses more than compensated for any reduction in the weight of attack. Deterrence would thus increase not decline. Soviet doctrines, first elaborated by Marshal V. D. Sokolovskii, however, stressed mixed attacks on civilian and military targets without restraint. Since, however, it was in the Soviet interest to advocate such approaches, *ex ante*, denying the possibility of 'city avoidance' and making their sanction appear as large as it could possibly be, no one could know how seriously they would take the new doctrines, *ex post*. Wohlstetter himself stressed that it would be in the Soviet interest to show the same restraint as the United States.

In the late 1960s Wohlstetter became involved in the ABM controversy, supporting both Sentinel and Safeguard systems, the first a light area defence against China, the second a hard-point defence (with some area coverage) of Minutemen designed to work against the Soviet Union.[29] While others argued that the Soviet Union would not be able to knock out an appreciable number of Minuteman silos and hence there was no need for ABM protection, Wohlstetter rejoined that the accuracies assumed for Soviet re-entry vehicles in the mid-1970s were no better than we projected for our own strategic forces. He also pointed out that ABM defence of Minuteman was a good investment in terms of cost effectiveness.

> For adversaries with roughly the same resources, the practical question has to do with how much extra the offense must pay to overcome a given amount of defense and how this compares with the cost of defense itself. The answer in the case of Safeguard defense of Minuteman is that it would cost the Russians more than twice as much to add offense as it would cost us to add an offsetting number of Sprint missiles with their fair share of the missile site radar expense.[30]

The fears for the longer-term vulnerability of Minuteman turned out to be prophetic when the mid-1970s arrived. Calculations then showed that the Soviets did have the accuracies to destroy all but about 5 percent of Minuteman.[31] Only 'launch under attack' scenarios seemed to make them survivable.[32] (See recommendations of the Scowcroft Commission.) Some of those who inveighed against ABM to protect silos in the late 1960s favoured Minuteman protection in the mid-1970s.[33]

The debate on the utility of ABM continued into the 1980s with the announcement of President Reagan's Strategic Defense Initiative. Wohlstetter was cautious but he did agree with the conclusions of the Hoffman report which stated:

> Deployment of defensive systems can increase stability, but to attain this goal we must design our offensive and defensive forces properly; especially, we must not allow them to be vulnerable. In combination with other measures, defenses can contribute to reducing the prelaunch vulnerability of our offensive forces. To increase stability, defenses must themselves avoid high vulnerability, must be robust in the face of enemy technical or tactical countermeasures, and must compete favorably in cost with expansion of the Soviet offensive force.[34]

It might well be that SDI would be cost-effective for protection of offensive forces, but not cost-effective for protection of cities. Conclusions, on this score, however, would await the results of further research and testing. Each layer of the system would have to be justified in terms of its ability to withstand Soviet countermeasures and to be procured at costs lower than those the Soviets would incur to offset it.

Other strategic issues

Wohlstetter wrote persuasively of the credibility of the American deterrent and the nuclear guarantee to Europe as compared with that of nuclear sharing schemes or small individual nuclear forces.[35] He also stressed that nuclear proliferation posed difficulties for the two major nuclear powers as well as failing to solve the problems of fledgling nuclear states, who might be better advised to seek security links with an established nuclear power. For the superpowers, there was the danger that small, highly nationalistic, and possibly unstable nuclear states might use their capacities more readily than the two central powers. While any use of nuclear weapons did not entail widespread or central use, it certainly increased the risks of superpower involvement. For small powers, the acquisition of nuclear weapons would not necessarily produce deterrence because those systems might be vulnerable to enemy attack.

Wohlstetter was always aware that there was a tension involved in designing a system which would both guarantee to respond and also guarantee not to cause accidental war. The more emphasis placed on automaticity of response, the greater the danger of nuclear accident. The more carefully one designed a stable steady-state system immune to spoofs and accidents, the less responsive it would be in a real contingency. It was desirable to protect strategic bombers by putting them in the air on receipt of warning, but it was not desirable to have them execute their mission without positive instructions and control.

Wohlstetter helped design the Fail-Safe system by which American bombers proceed to preset locations but do not (and cannot) continue their mission without receiving arming and release signals from Washington. He also was an author of the Bomb Alarm System in which the detonation of a nuclear weapon upon one target immediately alerts others.

Commentary and conclusions

Wohlstetter was not particularly worried about arms race interactions between the superpowers because in terms of new strategic launchers the United States was much less engaged in the arms race from the mid-1960s to the mid-1970s than was the Soviet Union.[36] He constantly stressed that the standard against which new American strategic systems should be measured was whether the Soviets could offset them at lesser costs. If they could not, the United States might proceed. As we have seen, some damage limiting notions do permit 'mutual security' in the avoidance of attacks upon cities and do not involve one-sided advantages. However, there has frequently been a tension between American–Soviet relations (which probably must rest upon long-term possession on both sides of assured destruction capabilities) and American–European relations (which assume that the United States will take the strategic initiative in response to a massive Soviet attack upon Europe). America could be expected to do this only if it could limit the damage of a Soviet counterstrike — which would normally mean that the Soviet Union did not possess a fully developed retaliatory capability. Reassurance for Europe thus strikes terror into the hearts of the Soviets. Wohlstetter's 'damage-limiting' notions, founded as they were upon heavy attacks on the Soviet force structure, did not seem to reduce this tension. Continued American attempts to acquire a unilateral damage-limiting capability could only be expected to call forth Soviet responses leading to a further round in the arms race.

This is not to say that Wohlstetter did not suggest ways out of the dilemma such as an increase in Western conventional forces so that there would be no need to escalate in response to a massive Soviet conventional attack, but it is not clear that his strategic recommendations fully take account of probable action–reaction effects.

A second issue involves the extension of cost-exchange calculations via the economic doctrine of 'opportunity costs.' Cost-exchange ratios inquire into how much the enemy pays to offset our systems as compared to the cost of the systems themselves. Yet our defence systems need to be measured not only against enemy expenditures but against what we have given up at home as a result of them. There are two components of national strength: one consists of mobilized military forces, forces in being; the second comprises the underlying strength of the mobilization base, the economy upon which all military procurement rests. Too great an emphasis upon the first component may well undermine the second. In the case of the United States, economic growth rates have declined even though the military burden as a fraction of GNP has not secularly increased. It is still much higher than that of our principal economic competitors who have continued to grow at rates well in excess of our own. Greater military spending, like other national expenditure, increases the government deficit, bids up interest rates and forestalls investment in new plant and equipment. Higher interest rates may increase the value of the currency, bringing foreign investment into the United States. That liability can only be carried and discharged by American exports, but exports in return require higher civilian research and development and investment in order to keep up with competitors and creditors. Excessive military spending undercuts our ability to pay — domestically and internationally. As the United States begins its third century of existence it may well wish to contemplate the fates of early modern Spain, seventeenth-century Holland, and nineteenth century Britain — all of whom encountered economic decline as their military commitments and obligations increased. The same outcome may well await the United States in the twenty-first century. Under these circumstances, an American strategic analyst should be as concerned with mitigating the military burden domestically as offsetting the military preparations of the Soviet Union. From the record, however, it appears that Albert Wohlstetter mainly decried American failure to rearm, not the reverse.

Notes

1. His most important theoretical innovation was the derivation of the distinction between a first-strike and a second-strike capability.
2. Some of these contributions were owed to Bernard Brodie and William Kaufmann together with Wohlstetter's collaborators: Henry Rowen and Fred Hoffman.
3. See Schelling, *The Strategy of Conflict*, London: Oxford University Press, 1960, chapters 2–3 and *Arms and Influence* New Haven: Yale University Press, 1966, chapter 3.
4. See particularly, Wohlstetter, 'Analysis and Design of Conflict Systems', chapter 7 in E. S. Quade (ed), *Analysis for Military Decisions*, Chicago, Rand McNally and Co, 1964.
5. The nomenclature was changed after 1954 presumably to reflect the fact that there is only one *IBM*.
6. See Wohlstetter, 'Bishops, Statesmen, and Other Strategists on the bombing of Innocents', *Commentary*, June, 1983, pp. 15–16.
7. M. Pierre Hassner opts for such an alternative in responding to Wohlstetter, 'Morality and Deterrence' *Commentary*, December 1983, p. 8.
8. T. C. Schelling, *Strategy of Conflict*, chapter 8.
9. On the distinction between *ex ante* and *ex post* incentives, see Rosecrance, 'Deterrence in Multipolar and Bipolar Environments' in Rosecrance (ed.) *The Future of the International Strategic System*, 1972.
10. The earliest record of Wohlstetter's work is in: 'Economic and Strategic Considerations in Air Base Location: A Preliminary Review' (with H. S. Rowen), RAND Corp. D-1114, 29 December 1951.
11. See the account in Fred Kaplan, *The Wizards of Armageddon*, New York, Simon and Schuster, 1983, pp. 97–101 and Gregg Herken, *Counsels of War*, New York: Alfred Knopf, 1985, pp. 88–92.
12. *Special Staff Report: The Selection of Strategic Air Bases*, R-244-S, RAND Corp, 1 March, 1953, p. 3.
13. Quoted in Herken, op. cit., p. 91.
14. R-244-S, p. 27.

15. A. Wohlstetter and F. Hoffman, 'Defending A Strategic Force after 1960', 1 February 1954, RAND Corp, D-2270, p. 3.
16. Ibid., p. 19.
17. Ibid., p. 18.
18. *Staff Report: Protecting US Power to Strike Back in the 1950's and 1960's*, RAND Corp. R-290, 1 September, 1956, p. 95.
19. R. Wohlstetter, *Pearl Harbor: Warning and Decision*, Stanford: Stanford University Press, 1962.
20. In *Tojo and the Coming of the War*, Stanford, Stanford University Press, 1961, p. 255.
21. A. Wohlstetter, 'The Delicate Balance of Terror', *Foreign Affairs*, **37**, no. 2, January 1959.
22. p. 220.
23. p. 222.
24. Ellsberg, 'The Crude Analysis of Strategic Choices', RAND Corp., P-2183, December 1960, p. 6.
25. p. 5-6.
26. See William Kaufmann, *The McNamara Strategy*, New York, Harper and Row, 1964, p. 148.
27. See the account in Kaufmann, pp. 116-17.
28. Ibid., pp. 145-7.
29. See 'Good Guys, Bad Guys and the ABM', *Los Angeles Times*, 3-4 August, 1969.
30. Ibid.
31. Paul Nitze, 'Assuring Strategic Stability in an Era of Detente', *Foreign Affairs*, **54**, no. 2, January 1976.
32. *Report of the President's Commission on Strategic Forces*, April 1983.
33. Richard L. Garwin, 'Effective Military Technology for the 1980s', *International Security*, **1**, no. 2, Fall, 1976.
34. Fred Hoffman, Study Director, *Ballistic Missile Defenses and U.S. National Security*, prepared for the Future Security Strategy Study, October 1983, p. 3.
35. 'Nuclear Sharing: NATO and the N+1 Country', *Foreign Affairs*, **39**, no. 2, April, 1961.
36. 'Rivals But No Race', Albert Wohlstetter, *Foreign Policy*, **16**, no. 16, Fall 1974, pp. 48-81.
37. See Rosecrance, *The Rise of the Trading State: Commerce and Conquest in the Modern World*, New York, Basic Books, 1986.

3 HERMAN KAHN

J. C. Garnett

Herman Kahn was a remarkable man and he said some remarkable things. Of all the nuclear strategists described in this book he is the only one — with the possible exception of Henry Kissinger — who genuinely captured the layman's imagination and became a public, controversial figure — the *enfant terrible* of the strategic community. James Newman, in a devastating review of Kahn's major book, described him as 'Genghis Kahn, a monster who had written an insane, pornographic book, a moral tract of mass murder: how to plan it, how to commit it, how to get away with it, how to justify it'.[1] Many believed that Kahn was the model for the fictional Dr. Strangelove, and even those who were not outraged by his ideas were usually disconcerted by them.

Part of the reason for his notoriety lay in his public personality. He was a flamboyant, egotistical figure, a performer with a grim sense of humour and a sense of the dramatic. It was typical of him to claim, 'I believe that I can change the present course of world history.'[2] He liked to shock, and his mammoth lecture presentations usually left audiences stunned. I vividly remember listening to him at the London School of Economics in 1960, and like most of the academics present I was both fascinated and repelled by his performance. But a more persuasive explanation for the powerful emotions which he generated is to be found in the subject matter which he espoused and the manner in which he espoused it. Anyone who talks about modern war is almost bound to shock. It is a ghastly subject. Kahn, quite uncompromisingly, stared right down the throat of thermonuclear war without flinching. What is more, he was the first person to do it, and when a totally unprepared public was suddenly confronted by his findings they reacted with a mixture of fear, horror and amazement. Even today, when we have all been anaesthetized to the horrors of nuclear war by films like *The War Game* and *The Day After*, and a spate of apocalyptic strategic fiction,[3] it is still shocking to read about wars where casualties are measured in tens, even hundreds, of millions and postwar conditions where the survivors may envy the dead. But in the relative innocence of the early 1960s Kahn's detailed, 650-page presentation of the deadly statistics of thermonuclear war was simply mind boggling.[4]

For years, ordinary people had comforted themselves with the thought that 'it will never happen'. As Norman Moss has pointed out, 'underlying most talk of nuclear war is the phenomenon that Raymond Aron calls "nuclear incredulity". To most people, nuclear war does not seem to belong to the world of things that can really happen, like business troubles or school exams or next summer's holiday'.[5] Even the professional strategists had, through their advocacy of policies of deterrence and arms control, directed their attention towards *avoiding* war rather than facing up to its consequences. Kahn changed all that. Now, suddenly, war seemed more real and more possible. It was not that Kahn was against arms control or deterrence; indeed, as we shall see, he was in favour of both, but he reminded everyone in the most dramatic terms that thermonuclear war was a real possibility. By making us confront the simple question, 'What happens if the enemy hits us?'[6] Kahn stripped away much of the complacency of the first fifteen years of the nuclear age. After *On Thermonuclear War*, strategy was never quite the same again.

But, as we have already hinted, it was not just the substance of Kahn's work which jolted peoples' sensibilities. As much as anything it was the *style* in which he couched his analysis which inflamed his critics. First, there was the peculiar jocularity about the way in which he examined the grisly details of human calamity. Bernard Brodie once objected to the way in which Kahn used the term 'wargasm' to describe all-out nuclear war. 'So grim a subject does not exclude an appropriate kind of humor used very sparingly — but levity is never legitimate.'[7] Walter Marseille made a similar point: 'Funeral directors are not supposed to gambol or frolic in public. Kahn does not violate these tactics, but his very readable prose deals so enthusiastically with the grimmest problems that the reader cannot help expecting him to do so at any time.'[8] One cannot help feeling that there were occasions when Kahn enjoyed rubbing our noses in the grim realities of nuclear war, and that is something which many readers found offensive. To appreciate the human predicament is one thing; to take a mischievious delight in it is quite another.

The second feature of Kahn's style which his critics found objectionable was the inelegance of his style and the ominous jargon in which he couched his thoughts. He seemed to live in a world of 'megadeaths', 'nuclear blackmail', 'spasm' wars, 'doomsday machines'. Even the metaphors which he developed for thinking about international politics had a knack of trivializing the subject. To compare East–West relations with the 'game of chicken', to talk about escalation in terms of 'ladders' or wars in terms of 'labor strikes' may have exposed the logic of these matters in an illuminating way, but it has the unfortunate (though unintended effect) of making world-shaking events seem ordinary and normal.

No one could describe Kahn's literary style as elegant or his jargon as attractive. Much of his writing would have benefited from ruthless editing, and at least one book, *On Thermonuclear War*, needed to be rewritten. But for all his literary vices, Kahn was invariably interesting, arresting and clear. He had an excellent analytical mind and some important things to say about strategy in the nuclear age.

Some critics were also upset by Kahn's 'what if. . .' style of argument, a technique which led him to develop imaginary international scenarios, of varying plausibility, in order to think through the strategic implications. What if the United States is subjected to an attack 'out of the blue'? What if an intense crisis erupted into a nuclear war? What if the United States struck first in order to defend Western Europe? What if another Napoleon or Hitler should come to power in the Soviet Union?

This kind of speculation occurs throughout Kahn's work. It was one of his favourite techniques for exposing the strategic logic behind American policy, and in his final book, published posthumously, he described these kinds of questions as *Gedanken* (thought) experiments.[9] 'Let us assume that the president of the United States has just been informed that a multi-megaton bomb has been dropped on New York City. What do you think he would do?'[10] Suppose 'the Soviets destroy five capital cities in Western Europe — London, Paris, Rome, Stockholm, and Bonn, just to show that they can get away with it.' What then?[11]

In another, more plausible, Gedanken experiment, Kahn speculated as follows. Assume he said, that

the Soviets believe they have a historic mission to further the transition to world socialism; they also believe that this final transition may very well be preceded by a last desperate attempt on the part of the capitalist world to preserve its existence by launching an attack on the Soviet Union; they feel they can win such a war but despite their rhetoric, they are not certain; on the other hand, a *temporary* 'window of opportunity' has opened up which might make possible a much earlier and safer transition to a world socialist state.

Assume further, said Kahn, 'that the Soviet Union could destroy virtually all the U.S. land-based ICBM force, . . . disrupt or destroy a very large portion of the U.S. bomber force, and reduce the capabilities of U.S. strategic submarines by some uncertain amount.'[12] In this situation, would the Soviet Union launch a first strike?

The heuristic value of this kind of analysis is undeniable, but, in so far as it raises awkward questions and alerts us to painful possibilities, most people are psychologically uncomfortable with it. It is as if articulating unpleasant possibilities makes them more likely. There is a bit of an ostrich in all of us, and we do not like being reminded of stark possibilities even if the purpose of the exercise is merely to stimulate our thinking.

But perhaps the most shocking quality of Kahn's style was the matter of fact, unemotional, detached way in which he considered the horrors of war. Instead of righteous indignation, condemnation and despair at the folly of war, there was, in his writing, a clinical acceptance of thermonuclear war as a fact of life like other facts of life. Whereas most people have a mental block when it comes to nuclear war, Kahn didn't, and the fact that he didn't gave his writing a chilling flavour of amorality. James Newman described *On Thermonuclear War* as follows: 'This evil and tenebrous book, with its loose-lipped pieties and its hayfoot – strawfoot logic, is permeated with a bloodthirsty irrationality such as I have not seen in my years of reading.'[13] Anatol Rapoport felt much the same way. He has spoken eloquently and passionately about the 'moral blindness' of those strategists whose pursuit of academic detachment 'blinds them to the enormity of the evil associated with being positively and "creatively" involved in a "game" in which the suffering and death of untold millions of innocent human beings are the payoffs'.[14] In a nutshell, what is missing from Kahn — and strategic thinking generally — is 'conscience'. Strategic thinking is 'psychopathic', that is, thinking utterly devoid of 'moral sense'.[15]

According to Rapoport, strategic thinkers like Herman Kahn suffer from a functional deafness which prevents them from listening to moral argument. 'Someone with a facile knowledge of weaponry and logistics has an excellent chance of catching the strategists ear. Someone moved by a passionate concern for human values but with no understanding of the intricate strategic issues and their highly proliferated ramifications may as well be speaking a dead language.'[16] There is, according to Rapoport, a sharp distinction to be drawn between 'strategic' and 'human' ways of thinking, and those, like Kahn, who practice the former at the expense of the latter are dangerous and misguided.[17]

Instinctively we can all sympathize with the revulsion of Newman and Rapoport and the many who think like them. Should anyone be intellectually detached when millions of lives are at stake? Can we afford the luxury of academic objectivity in such desperate times? Despite our uneasiness, we must surely answer in the affirmative. When the issues are important detachment is not a luxury; it is a necessity. We need *more*, not *less*, objectivity if we are to survive. Rapoport treads a dangerous path when he argues that, 'while detachment is a source of supreme strength in the investigation of nature, it may be debilitating if it is carried over from natural science to areas purporting to deal with human behavior'.[18]

Kahn defended himself vigorously against those who attacked his hard-headed, rational approach to strategic questions. He pointed out to those who argued that thinking about nuclear war bred callousness and indifference that we have no alternative. Nuclear weapons cannot be 'uninvented'; responsible statesmen, therefore, have an obligation to consider their implications dispassionately and factually. 'Emotionalism and sentimentality, as opposed to morality and concern, only confuse debates.'[19] Decisionmakers and researchers 'cannot afford the luxury of denying the existence of agonizing questions. The public, whose lives and freedom are at stake, expects them to face such questions squarely.'[20]

To those who argued that it is useless to apply rationality and calculation in any area dominated by irrational decisionmakers, Kahn pointed out that there is no reason at all why rational discussions of war and peace should not 'include the possibility of irrational behavior'.[21] When critics referred to the 'icy rationality' of the Hudson Institute or the RAND Corporation, Kahn remarked, 'I'm always tempted to ask in reply, "Would you prefer a warm, human error? Do you feel better with a nice emotional mistake?" We cannot expect good discussion of security problems if we are going to label every attempt at detachment as callous, every attempt at objectivity as immoral.'[22]

Though Kahn's interests spanned almost the entire field of strategic studies, it is in the field of nuclear strategy that he made his mark. For him, and, indeed, for most of the post-war strategic thinkers, the central question had been posed by the development of nuclear and thermonuclear weapons. Since they could not be 'uninvented', the problem was how to live with these new, terrible devices: in particular, how to devise policies which could accommodate them and turn them into useful instruments of statecraft.

Even in the narrow field of nuclear strategy, it is not easy to categorize Kahn's thought. He overflowed with unfinished ideas on almost every subject which caught his attention, and he wrote articles on topics as diverse as NATO policy, the ABM debate, nuclear proliferation, the Vietnam war. But it is probably fair to say that the main thrust of his work sought to provide answers to three basic questions: first, how can we avoid modern war? second, if we cannot avoid it, how can we survive it? and, third, how can we conduct war without destroying ourselves in the process? For years Kahn had wrestled with these problems at the RAND Corporation, but it was not until the publication of his first book in 1960 that the general public was exposed to his thoughts.

It is impossible to summarize *On Thermonuclear War*. Though it bristles with ideas, some good, some bad, it remains a poorly structured, clumsily written, repetitive book which reflected the wide-ranging, rambling lecture presentations from which it originated. As F. Kaplan has commented, 'It was a massive, sweeping, disorganized volume, presented as if a giant vacuum cleaner had swept through the corridors of RAND, sucking up every idea, concept, metaphor and calculation that anyone in the strategic community had conjured up over the previous decade.'[23] One of the reasons Kahn's contribution to strategic thought is so difficult to evaluate is that many of his ideas originated in that whirlpool of intellectual energy which characterized RAND in the late 1950s. Much of what he wrote reflected ideas and concepts whose origins are difficult to trace but which had fermented in the RAND hothouse. What Kahn did in *On Thermonuclear War* was to systemize those ideas, push them a little further than his colleagues had done and, for the first time, give them an airing in the public domain.

Throughout his career he unashamedly 'borrowed' ideas from his friends and colleagues, sometimes with, and sometimes without, acknowledgment. 'Working with Herman,' said one of his Hudson colleagues William Pfaff,[24] 'is like having a kleptomaniac for a roommate.' Undoubtedly part of this problem lies in the collaborative nature of 'think-tank' research. For example, a glance at the RAND papers clearly indicates that the civil defence research, on which Kahn relied so heavily in many of his publications, was a team effort. Kahn may have had overall responsibility for the project, but much of the research was done by others.

Many of the ideas which Kahn developed (but did not necessarily invent) have now been absorbed into the literature of strategic analysis, and they are now so commonplace that it is difficult to imagine that they were once novel and exciting; but others have simply sunk without trace, curiosities with no practical application in the final quarter of the twentieth century.

How to avoid war

A good deal of Kahn's thought was devoted to this subject. Like most strategists of his day, Kahn agreed that 'the primary objective of our military forces is to deter war'.[25] But Kahn, like Albert Wohlstetter and others, was at pains to point out that the goal of deterrence was not nearly so easy to achieve as some of the simple-minded 'minimum' deterrence theorists had claimed.[26] In particular, Kahn emphasized that the popular notion that no state whose decisionmakers were sane would attack another state with nuclear weapons at its disposal needed considerable refinement.[27]

He pointed out that if it was to have an effective deterrent, a state needed to be able to deter at least three kinds of provocative behaviour. First — and most important — it needed to be able to deter a direct attack on its territory. As Wohlstetter had already demonstrated,[28] even this kind of 'passive' or 'finite' deterrence (described by Kahn as 'Type-I Deterrence') was not easy to achieve. Kahn described the problems faced by governments seeking to guarantee the survival of their retaliatory systems in terms of 'an expensive combination of *alert, hardness, dispersal*, and *concealment*'.[29] And he explained the further difficulties encountered in seeking to penetrate Soviet territory and punish its people in circumstances where the Soviet government had taken elaborate air defence and civil defence measures.

Kahn also noted that ideally a state needed the sort of deterrent which can deter an enemy no matter what mood he is in. It is fairly easy to deter an enemy when he has minimum incentives for aggression — 'even a frown might do that';[30] but a good deterrent must be able to deter the same enemy when he is in a hostile, risk-taking mood as well. Kahn put the point thus: when an engineer puts up a structure designed to last twenty years or so, 'he does not ask, "Will it stand up on a pleasant June day?" He asks how it performs under stress, under hurricane, earthquake, snow load, fire, flood, thieves, fools and vandals.'[31]

A reliable deterrent has to deter enemies on bad days as well as good days, and one cannot automatically assume that a deterrent which appears to have worked in a period of *détente* is going to withstand the strains of crisis and cold war. Of course, even very conservative engineers do not plan on 'worst case' analysis without taking into account the *likelihood* of the 'worst case' occurring. No one wants to pay a huge premium to insure against a very unlikely (but possible) contingency. But, equally, no one can afford to ignore the possibility of such contigencies just because they seem unlikely.

The second kind of aggression that a state needed to be able to deter was described by Kahn as 'very provocative acts'. A good example of a 'very provocative act' for Kahn would have been a Warsaw Pact invasion of Western Europe. To deter this kind of behaviour Kahn recommended his 'Type-II Deterrent'. Finally, Kahn pointed out that in order to maintain a full spectrum of deterrent capability, a state would need to be able to deter *limited* aggressions or provocations of a relatively minor nature. An example of a minor provocation would have been Soviet intervention in Africa or the Middle East. To deter this kind of threat Kahn recommended his 'Type-III Deterrent'.[32]

Emphasizing the importance of these three kinds of deterrence was a valuable corrective to those crude theorists who, during the 1950s, had thought almost entirely in terms of Type-I Deterrence — deterrence of a Soviet attack on the United States' homeland. While he admitted the primary importance of this kind of deterrence, Kahn argued that the other sorts of deterrent were very important and, arguably, even more difficult to achieve. For the rest of his life Kahn used the typology which he had invented to explain the complicated kind of military posture which he believed the United States needed to aim for. To meet its Type-I Deterrent requirement, the United States needed to be able to convince the Soviet Union of Washington's capacity to retaliate and punish after a Soviet surprise attack. To possess Type-II Deterrence, Kahn argued that the United States needed what he called 'a credible first strike capacity'. Now that suggestion was both novel and controversial. It directly contradicted the conventional wisdom which assumed that the United States, (being a virtuous power), would *never* strike first. Kahn developed his argument out of the following familiar scenario.

Suppose for a moment that the relationship between the United States and the Soviet Union is one of mutual — but only finite (Type-I) deterrence. Suppose further that the Soviet Union threatened to bomb several European cities, but made it absolutely clear that it had no plans to attack the United States. How would the United States' government deter such an attack? It could, of course, threaten to use its Type-I Deterrent to attack the Soviet Union; but to carry out that threat would almost certainly provoke a retaliatory strike which would probably kill millions of American citizens. In short, the administration would be in the unhappy position of having to trade American lives for the sake of Europe. And, according to Kahn, no American president would do that. In his words,

I am not saying that the United States would stand idly by. We would clearly declare war on the Soviets. We would make all kinds of *limited* military moves. We would go into a crash mobilization on at least the hundred-billion-dollars-a-year level. But there is one thing that we would almost certainly not do. *We would not launch an all out attack on Soviet cities*[33] (my italics).

Clearly, if the Americans themselves, (to say nothing of the highly cynical Europeans) interpreted the situation in this way, it is only reasonable to suppose that the Soviets would reach a similar conclusion and would discount the American threats — perhaps not completely but certainly substantially. How then is this sort of very provocative behaviour to be discouraged? Simply, says Kahn, by the possession of 'a credible first strike capability'.

Now we need to be clear about what 'credible first strike capability' means. And a modern reader needs to be reminded that it does not, as he might have supposed, mean the ability to launch a *disarming* strike against the Soviet Union. Credible first-strike capability does not even refer to an *improved* capacity to hurt the Soviet Union in a first strike. *Credible* first strike capability 'depends on being willing to accept the other side's retaliatory blow. It depends on the harm he can do, not on the harm *we* can do. It depends as much on *air defense* and *civil defense* as on *air offense*.'[34]

In short, credible first-strike capability simply means acquiring sufficient capability (both offensive and defensive) to raise the probability that when the Soviet government asks itself, 'If we try this provoking act, will the United States strike us'?,[35] they will answer in the affirmative. And Kahn goes on to point out that even if they do not answer this question affirmatively, 'if we have a credible first strike capability, a capacity for deliberately initiating a war, then even if the Soviets doubt that we would have the resolve to use our S.A.C. they must have some doubts about their doubts'.[36] And that, said Kahn, is probably enough to deter the Soviets from very provocative acts.

Now it might be thought that if the United States possessed both Type-I and Type-II Deterrence, then this would automatically imply that the Soviet Union did not. 'One side's Type I Deterrence is measured by the inadequacy of the other side's Type II Deterrence.'[37] Putting it crudely, if one side can threaten unacceptable punishment then the other cannot have a credible first-strike posture. Nevertheless, Kahn believed that it was possible for two opponents to possess, simultaneously, reasonably satisfactory levels of Type-I and Type-II Deterrence. His reasoning was sophisticated and complex. What he aimed at was a situation in which each side was generally deterred from attacking its opponent by the fear of retaliation, but not absolutely deterred. By acquiring a sophisticated mix of 'retaliatory' and 'limited first-strike' capability, Kahn argued that both sides could, at the same time, feel sufficiently protected against a surprise attack, sufficiently confident of the advantage of striking first to be able to deter very provocative behaviour and yet sufficiently afraid of punishment to be reluctant to strike first except in the most threatening circumstances.

The following table lists the factors involved in this *symmetrical multi-stable deterrence* relationship.[38]

(1) Both sides have a significant first-strike advantage (Type-II Deterrence);
(2) Both sides have sufficient second-strike capability (Type-I Deterrence);
(3) Thus neither side wants war, but if war is 'inevitable' they must prefer going first;
(4) If war isn't inevitable, then threat of (3) above is enough to deter extreme crisis, without being very destabilizing in ordinary crisis.
(5) Thus pre-emptive or other war might or might not be more likely while there was an extreme crisis, but extreme crises are less likely and more easily resolved. This last, on balance, probably improves stability. Either a one-sided or mutual recognition of this could further reduce the probability of pre-emptive war.

Symmetrical multi-stable deterrence mutually deters various forms of war and extreme provocation by relying on what appears to be a paradoxical formulation: by making nuclear war marginally more likely in a serious crisis, one actually makes all forms of war — including nuclear war -- less likely. The key to understanding this formulation lies in the following chain of reasoning:

(1) Symmetrical multi-stable deterrent forces produce a reciprocal fear of surprise attack in a crisis;
(2) This fear is intentional — by design, not by accident;
(3) As a result, extreme provocations will be less, not more, frequent;
(4) Since nuclear wars are most likely to start as a result of extreme provocation (rather than out of the blue), they are less likely if such provocation is deterred.[39]

This is an interesting argument, but the idea of any first-strike capability horrified the laymen and did not convince the professionals.

To acquire Type-III Deterrence, Kahn believed that the United States needed to be able to increase its strength 'very rapidly whenever the other side provokes us'.[40] It needed to have 'credible and explicit plans to initiate crash programs for civil defense and limited war capabilities'.[41] More specifically, Type-III Deterrence deters provocations 'by making the potential aggressor afraid that the defender or others will then take limited actions, military or non-military, which will make the aggression unprofitable'.[42]

Kahn used the examples of the Korean war and an imaginary Berlin crisis to develop his argument. What is it, he asked, that deters the Soviet Union from a series of Korea-type aggressions? 'It is probably less the fear of a direct U.S. attack than the probability that in response to such crises the U.S. and its allies will greatly increase both their military strength and their resolve.'[43] When the Korean War broke out, Congress increased the American defence budget by a factor of four.' 'No matter what success the Communist cause had in Korea, that authorization represents an enormous military defeat for the Soviets, since after the authorization, the Soviets came at length to face a very impressive military power.'[44] If the Russians know that deterioration in international relations will push us into a crash defense program, they may be much less willing to let international relations deteriorate.'[45]

In the case of Berlin, Kahn reminded his readers of Western impotence. 'If we send soldiers, they [the Russians] say they will kill them; if we send tanks, they will burn them; if we send bombers, they will destroy our cities.'[46] What, in the face of an assault on Berlin, should the United States do? It could attack, but 'it is much more likely that it would authorize enormous defense budgets — to buy large limited-war forces and such things as civil defense and the corresponding military forces that would give us a credible capability for initiating a war at some appropriate level of violence if a humiliating crisis should be repeated.'[47] Then, even if we lost Berlin in the military sense, the Soviets would have lost much more. Henceforth, they would have to face a vastly strengthened enemy. A clear ability to engage in this kind of crash rearmament and mobilization programme would, Kahn thought, be a successful deterrent to minor provocations.

Again, the argument is an interesting one. It reflects an early response to the 'suicide or surrender' dilemma which has worried successive generations of American presidents. But it is significant that no administration has found it persuasive. From J. F. Kennedy onwards, every president has preferred to acquire the appropriate military capability to deal with limited provocations rather than to rely upon explicit plans to acquire that capability. 'Flexible response', rather than ambitious plans to expand military strength at short notice, has been the route chosen. Nevertheless, to the end of his life Kahn emphasized the importance of mobilization capability as a deterrent. A strong mobilization base would require plans for rapidly reorientating peacetime industry, avoiding 'bottlenecks' in supplies, changing designs and showing flexibility in production techniques and materials. One of the advantages of a mobilization programme is that 'it can provide a much more acceptable bridge between current force levels and those that might be necessary to meet a serious crisis or conflict with the Soviet Union'.[48]

To help us think our way through the logic of deterrence, Kahn invented two conceptualized devices — the 'Doomsday Machine' and its more sophisticated offshoot, the 'Doomsday-in-a-Hurry Machine'.[49] Kahn's simple doomsday machine was essentially a super 'dirty' bomb capable of destroying the planet. Assume that the device is protected from enemy action 'and then connected to a computer which is in turn connected, by a reliable communication system, to hundreds of sensory devices all over the United States. The computer would then be programmed so that if, say, five nuclear bombs exploded over the United States, the device would be triggered and the earth destroyed.'[50] In essence, the doomsday machine provides the perfect Type-I Deterrent.

The doomsday-in-a-hurry machine was basically the same as the doomsday machine, but its computer was given all the facilities it would need to be 'well informed' about world affairs. 'We would then unilaterally legislate into existence a *Soviet* (or *Chinese*) *Criminal Code*. This would list in great detail all the acts which the Soviets were not allowed to commit. The Soviets would then be informed that if the computer detects them in any violations it will blow up the world.'[51] With a bit of luck this machine should be able to take care of Type-II and even Type-III Deterrence as well. After all, as Kahn pointed out, doomsday machines possess many of the necessary qualities of a perfect deterrent. They are frightening; indeed, they are as frightening as anything that can be devised. They are much more inexorable and persuasive than currently available deterrent systems. They can probably be made non-accident prone, and they might even be relatively cheap.

The leader of a deterrent power possessing a doomsday machine does not have to worry about whether his retaliatory systems will survive the enemy's first strike or whether he will be able to take and communicate the decision to retaliate. Nor does he have to worry about whether his missiles are able to penetrate enemy air defences or punish his enemy despite whatever 'passive' defence measures he may have taken.

But whatever their theoretical virtues, doomsday machines were firmly rejected by Kahn, largely because, once primed, they are fundamentally beyond human control. Any failure kills too many people and kills them too automatically. 'There is no chance of human intervention, control, and final decision.'[52] The value of the doomsday-machine concept lies solely in the graphic way in which it clarifies our thoughts about the requirements of a successful deterrent. It provides a typical example of the way in which Kahn was able to use a novel, startling idea to illuminate real world problems. In passing, it is perhaps worth noting that Kahn's fertile brain dreamed up another hypothetical deterrent, a doomsday variant which he called a 'Homicide Pact Machine'. This weapon reflected an attempt to make the failure of Type-I Deterrence mean simple mutual homicide *for the belligerents only*. And it was typical of Kahn that he would defend such a machine on the humanitarian grounds that it spared neutrals.[53]

Though 'deterrence' was a major plank in his thought, Kahn did not regard it as a panacea for peace. Throughout *On Thermonuclear War*, and his later work, he showed an acute awareness that strategies of deterrence were fallible. Properly pursued they might dramatically reduce the probability of war, but they could never reduce it to zero. Kahn developed his thoughts in an essay entitled, *The Arms Race and Some of its Hazards*,[54] where he reminded us of two things: first, that since threats of punishment may fail to deter, even *premeditated* war is possible between states pursuing strategies of deterrence; and second, that since strategies of deterrence are only useful against a calculating enemy, they make no contribution at all to the elimination of *accidental* or *irrational* wars.

Kahn described in some detail how, as a result of irrationality, inadvertance, human error, mechanical failures in weapon systems, false alarms, mischief making and 'escalation', the superpowers could become embroiled in thermonuclear war. In 1960 Kahn believed that 'the probability of unpremeditated war is low',[55] but he was perceptive enough to see that as the number of buttons increased the problem would intensify. The main point of this analysis of the various ways in which war could start was to dent the complacency of those simple deterrent theorists who seemed to identify mutual deterrence with permanent peace.

Arms control

Though he was an enthusiastic supporter of the strategy of deterrence, Kahn recognized that 'purely military solutions to our security problems are likely to be grossly inadequate in the long run, and may prove to be so in the short run'.[56] Hence, we needed 'extensive arms control measures in addition to unilateral security measures'.[57] Those who regard Kahn as an archetypal militarist, in favour of ever-expanding defence budgets, do him a serious injustice. It is true that he was not a disarmer, either temperamentally or intellectually, but he saw very clearly that arms control had a critical role to play in modern defence planning. The days when those who favoured disarmament and arms control were regarded as being on the opposite side of the fence to the military strategists were over. By the late 1950s, security policy reflected a seamless web in which deterrence, arms control and warfighting were all inextricably entwined. Kahn recognized that, and the various discussions on arms control which are woven into his work reveal a sophisticated grasp of contemporary arms control literature.

Kahn was particularly worried by two problems in this field: first, the problem caused by rapid technological changes in weaponry: and second, the problem of horizontal nuclear proliferation. Significantly both problems are still with us, and Kahn's reflections are as relevant today as they were over a quarter of a century ago.

In the context of technological innovation in weaponry, Kahn argued that we are having a complete technological revolution in the art of war approximately every five years.[58] As a result, he said, 'we are now [1961] three technological revolutions away from World War II. Any attempts to apply the concepts and rules of common sense derived from that experience run the grave risk of being as outmoded as some American Civil War concepts would have been in World War II.'[59] The problem of revising and developing strategic doctrines to accommodate new weaponry is a very familiar one to those who have wrestled with the strategic implications of Emergent Technology (ET) at the conventional level and 'ballistic missile defence' at the strategic level. Kahn identified the problem though he almost certainly overestimated the pace of technological change.

Writing in 1961, admittedly with some 'judicious exaggeration' to make allowances for the 'unexpected', Kahn thought the following might give a reasonable feel for the technology of 1970:

cheap simple bombs; cheap simple missiles; cheap satellites; controlled thermo-nuclear reaction; other sources of cheap neutrons; other sources of nuclear fuels; californium bullets; ground-effect machines: reliable sensors; super calculators; cheap calories; medical progress; advanced materials; cheap, fast-transportation (for limited wars) reliable command and control; Doomsday machines; and disguised warfare.[60]

Kahn also predicted 'clean' nuclear bombs, nuclear-powered aircraft and climatological and environmental weapons. For a scholar who later pioneered several studies in 'Futurology',[61] he showed little early aptitude for it. Even thirty years after his prediction, much of this technology seems as far away as ever. But even though the timescale was wrong, there were some good guesses among the wilder ones. Kahn recognized that reliable sensors using advanced computers to identify and track hostile objects might make it possible to destroy ICBMs. He also recognized that this might revolutionize the 'offence/defence' balance by pushing us towards a situation in which defensive technology might have the edge.[62] Kahn also predicted a situation in which satellites might make both the United States and the Soviet Union 'open books from the sky'.[63] In addition, he foresaw the time when new anti-tank weapons might 'enable relatively lightly trained, immobile, but determined, citizen divisions to hold ground against attacks by mechanized divisions'.[64]

Kahn recognized that technology, because of its 'decentralized' nature, was largely out of control, but he believed that measures of arms control might have a contribution to make in controlling the research and preliminary development phase of new weapons. He was aware of the difficulties of drawing a meaningful distinction between civilian and military research[65] but believed that it might be possible to control military activities in space, limit nuclear-testing etc.

On the subject of his second major arms control concern — nuclear proliferation — Kahn was convinced that nuclear weapons would give small powers, *vis-à-vis* one another, 'greater opportunities for blackmail and mischiefmaking; greater likelihood of an accidental triggering of weapons; an increased possibility of a 'local' Munich, a Pearl Harbor, and blitzkriegs.[66] He admitted that the possession of nuclear capability might induce a degree of political responsibility in a leader, and he believed that the ability of small nuclear powers to trigger a superpower war had been exaggerated; but, overall, the problems caused by the spread of nuclear weapons were deadly serious. 'The diffusion of nuclear weapons may or may not increase the number of crises, but it will almost undoubtedly tend to increase the seriousness and the grim potentialities of any crisis or even the misunderstandings that do occur, besides increasing enormously the importance of having responsible and competent governments everywhere.'[67] Kahn's vision of uncontrolled proliferation leading to a world in which private citizens, rebels and nationalists, to say nothing of irrational statesmen, gangsters and dilettantes, are able to buy nuclear bombs on the black market remains a nightmare for all of us.

Kahn argued that a sudden, explosive diffusion of nuclear weapons would be particularly dangerous since the world would not have time to adjust to a multiplicity of new, inexperienced and uneducated centres of nuclear decisionmaking. If proliferation is inevitable, there was, he thought, something to be said for trying to make sure it happens gradually. Kahn suggested that with gradual proliferation and only an occasional use of nuclear weapons, 'reliable conventions might be established', and 'nations might learn the utility and disutility of the weapons, thus becoming skilful, and perhaps prudent, in their threat and use'.[68]

In order to prevent the nightmare of general proliferation from becoming reality, Kahn thought it might be useful for the superpowers to do all they could to maintain the 'ban' on nuclear use which has prevailed since the end of World War II. The psychological significance of a 'no nuclear use' convention which has lasted for so many years cannot be overestimated. Kahn hoped that if potential nuclear powers could be convinced of both the 'unusability' of nuclear weapons and the feelings of revulsion which they generate, then some of them would be deterred from acquiring them. Bolstering this point, he even suggested that military defeats suffered by the United States might at least have the good effect of 'showing that the mere possession of nuclear weapons is far from solving a nation's problems'.[69]

Kahn noted that the emergence of a 'multipolar' world, containing a multiplicity of both great and small nuclear powers, would almost certainly increase the need for strategic defences. 'Most of the Great Powers would not wish to be starkly (and unnecessarily) vulnerable to an attack by a two-bit nuclear power.'[70]

In general terms, Kahn believed that intelligent arms control proposals can do three things. First, they can 'reduce the probability of events, both international (tensions and crises) and technical (accidents, false alarms and misunderstandings), that could give rise to war'. Second, they can 'reduce the probability that a war-causing type of event would actually cause a war'. Third, they can 'reduce the damage done if a war actually occurs'. They can do this not only by abolishing the use of certain weapons and controlling the use of others but by facilitating ahead of time the machinery by which wars are ended before they become overly destructive.

Kahn regarded all of these tasks as important — so important in fact that he was reluctant to link them with other, more trivial, issues in East–West relations. He recognized that no government can afford to ignore the general East–West political climate in formulating its arms control policies, but Kahn was convinced that there was nothing to be gained from tying arms control measures to progress on such issues as human rights, improved trade relationships etc.[71] He was, therefore, against the idea of 'linkage' which became fashionable during the Carter administration.

Kahn recognized that both the United States and the Soviet Union shared common interests on which measures of arms control could be built. 'Neither the United States nor the Soviet Union wants a war that would annihilate us both — neither side wants the cost of the arms competition to become more onerous; neither side wants to permit lax operational practices for nuclear forces.'[72] It was the existence of these common interests which made arms control a practical proposition. And Kahn realized that useful arms control measures can be instituted without formal negotiation. In 1962 it made very good sense for the United States to encourage the Soviet Union to 'accident proof' its nuclear weapons and to explain how this could best be done. It was equally sensible from the point of view of their mutual security for both sides to improve their 'fail-safe' devices and their 'command and control' systems.[73]

Kahn was conscious of the need not to look too dangerous or provocative to the enemy nor too dangerous to neutrals or allies.[74] He believed that security depended on satisfying the enemy that the policies being pursued were, up to a point, reassuring, and that one of the best ways of reassuring both friends and enemies was by intelligent arms control. For example, if it was clear that both superpowers were pursuing mutual deterrence, then an American policy of 'hardening' retaliatory systems and limiting 'soft' 'first-strike' systems would have a wholly desirable effect of reassuring everyone that the United States believed in stable deterrence. (It is true, as we saw earlier that Kahn believed that the United States should acquire *some* first strike capability, but in the interests of 'stability' he was anxious that this should be *non-alert*, credible first-strike capability.) Another measure of arms control which Kahn thought would contribute to stability by reducing the chances of accidental war, human error and miscalculation was the introduction of proper communications — a 'hot line' — between the superpowers.

As a contribution towards reducing the ferocity of war itself, Kahn believed that NATO should consider the possibility of unilaterally declaring that after a certain date it would not be the first to use atomic weapons ('except possibly in air defense and naval warfare'). In a remarkably modern sounding passage in *On Thermonuclear War*, he recommended a 'No First Nuclear Use' strategy on condition that the Russians reciprocated.[75] He did, of course, recognize, as do most current believers in a 'no first-use' strategy, that before such a policy could be implemented, NATO would have to make good the various gaps and omissions in its conventional forces.

By 1983 Kahn was even more committed to a 'no first-use' strategy. 'I am very strongly in favor of the United States issuing two basic statements: first, we will not be the first to use nuclear weapons against a nonnuclear power. Second, sometime between 1985 and 1990 we will adopt a full no-first use policy — that is, we will not be the first to use nuclear weapons under any circumstances (we might well include in this statement bacteriological and perhaps chemical weapons.)'[76]

Though he could appreciate the many possibilities inherent in measures of arms control, Kahn was well aware of the obstacles in the way of successful negotiation. He warned against the danger of being more afraid of the arms race than the Russians. This skewed fear, he believed, had in the past led the United States to be so anxious for arms control agreements that its negotiators displayed far too great a willingness to make concessions.[77] He was particularly aware of the possibility of 'cheating', the difficulties connected with 'verification' and the weaknesses of the sanctions which could be brought to bear against those caught breaking the rules.

Kahn reminded us that the 'evader' 'had an almost incredible advantage *vis-à-vis* the overt and official system . . . He can use all his ingenuity and expertise to devise methods for evading a fixed control system . . . and *he may have years to work out the method*, having almost complete flexibility in choosing his means. The would-be arms controllers, on the other hand, are attempting to set limits on the ingenuity and cleverness of man for years in advance. They are trying to protect against all possible ways of cheating.'[78]

Kahn suspected that violations might not be clear cut, and subsequent history has proved him right by providing a good deal of evidence of 'ambiguity' in the context of arms control violations. The problem of 'verification', which has been with us throughout the history of disarmament negotiations, was always in Kahn's mind; and he had some interesting points to make about 'risk taking' in this context. Speaking of the dangers of signing a Test Ban Treaty to which compliance could not be reliably verified, he had this to say, 'I think it may still be worthwhile under some conditions to enter agreements which involve some moderate risks.'[79] His point was that in strategy there is no such thing as a risk-free policy. Policies which ignore arms control may be just as risky as those which embrace it. For policymakers it is a matter of comparing the risks involved in signing a treaty which may be evaded with the risks of continuing the arms race and not having any treaty at all. That is an important point which is often forgotten, even today, by those who insist on foolproof systems of inspection.

The problems involved in monitoring arms control agreements and detecting violations are compounded by the difficulty of applying any serious sanctions against those who cheat. Kahn knew this; he was particularly conscious of the difficulty of imposing sanctions against superpower cheats. But, in the case of minor powers, Kahn argued in favour of monitoring arms control agreements even against the will of violators, if necessary by the use of military force. 'One simply cannot allow any and every nation to decide at times of its own choosing whether or not it will agree to accept regulation.'[80] Even superpower cheats could reasonably expect to suffer the hostility of world opinion. In so far as states value their reputation as law-abiding members of the international community the prospect of a hostile press is hardly likely to be welcomed. Second, any state violating a treaty obligation could reasonably expect the arms race to return with a vengeance. Its outraged enemy would probably pursue crash rearmament programmes. That prospect may in itself be a deterrent to cheating in all circumstances short of those where cheating brings a decisive advantage. Third, a cheating state could expect to have to pay a political price for its evasion in terms of a deteriorating international situation.[81]

Surviving war

Despite strategies of deterrence and policies of arms control, Kahn knew that war was possible, and since, at any given moment, there was a finite but unmeasurable chance of it occurring, it was important to know what it would be like. That thought was the starting point for his investigation into the phenomenon of thermonuclear war. It led him to examine, as scientifically as he knew how, the nature and consequences of a thermonuclear attack in which as much as 20,000 megatons of explosive power would be delivered upon the United States.

Kahn examined the effects of massive strikes on the United States. He tried to quantify the physical destruction, the fall-out problems, the social effects and the economic effects of large-scale thermonuclear war. He produced tables of statistics purporting to show the genetic damage caused by radiation, the 'life-shortening' effects of different kinds of radiation — particularly Strontium-90 and Carbon-14, the survival potential of American industry, the extent of destruction to 'standard metropolitan areas'. And the most important conclusion which emerged from the evidence he collected was that thermonuclear war was not synonomous with Armageddon! Now that conclusion conflicted sharply with the accepted wisdom of the day. Bombarded with ideas about 'mutual annihilation', and impressed by poorly researched but sensational novels like On the Beach, the man in the street (and others) had come to believe that nuclear war was unsurvivable. Kahn was challenging some deeply entrenched opinions. Now one might, perhaps, have expected Kahn's optimistic conclusion to be greeted with relief. For the human race to be told that even something as horrible as thermonuclear war did not, after all, mean the end of the world, ought, surely, to have lifted the human spirit somewhat. But that was not the reaction. Kahn's findings were instantly challenged and his integrity impugned.

Perhaps Kahn ought not to have been surprised at the opposition which he generated. He had already pointed out that there is something curiously comforting about the idea of mutual homicide. It is comforting, first, because if it is true we can expect statesmen to refrain from bringing it about, and, second, because it relieves everyone of the responsibility of taking expensive precautions to reduce war casualties, lessen damage and facilitate post-war recuperation. The proposition that thermonuclear war, though bad, was survivable raised some awkward questions which, until that moment, everyone had been able to sidestep. Kahn could hardly have expected the public to thank him for destroying one of their most comfortable assumptions.

A second conclusion which Kahn drew from his study of the nature of thermonuclear war was that the magnitude of the catastrophe was 'closely dependent on what kinds of preparations have been made, and on how the war is started and fought'.[82] If we are careful and plan properly, said Kahn, we may be able 'to cope with all of the effects of a thermonuclear war, in the sense of saving most people and restoring something close to the prewar standard of living in a relatively short time.'[83] Proper planning, he argued, might make the difference 'between a country which survives a war with say, 150 million people and a gross national product (GNP) of $300 billion a year, and a nation which emerges with only 50 million people and a GNP of $10 billion'.[84]

Again one might have expected people to react with relief to the discovery that by their own efforts they could mitigate the disasters of nuclear war. But again that was not their reaction. When told that '. . . objective studies indicate that even though the amount of human tragedy will be greatly increased in the post-war world, the increase would not preclude normal and happy lives for the majority of the survivors and their descendents,[85] most people reacted with a mixture of outrage and incredulity. More than anything else in On Thermonuclear War it was this remarkable conclusion which caused the fur to fly among the critics. It is, therefore, important to understand how Kahn reached it.

Kahn argued that 'proper planning' for thermonuclear war required two sorts of preparation. First, it required a military strategy which would limit the effectiveness of the enemy's attack and encourage him to behave reasonably during the conduct of the war. Second, it required elaborate civil defence arrangements to limit the damage which the enemy could cause. In a chapter entitled 'Additional Remarks on Military Problems',[86] Kahn spelt out the military requirements — a 'preattack mobilization base' which could be rapidly expanded, air defence systems properly hardened, dispersed or mobile retaliatory systems, centralized and effective decisionmaking and communication systems and a flexible mixture of 'counterforce' and 'counter value' targeting capability for intra-war bargaining purposes.

In other parts of the book Kahn described the civil defence requirements — fall-out shelters, a trained pool of skilled manpower, adequate food supplies, manuals and instructors to aid adjustment to the new conditions of life, up to a quarter of a million trained semi-military cadres, and adequate supplies of radiation meters. Radiation meters were particularly important, and Kahn, quoting his earlier RAND study, recommended the immediate purchase of about 100-million dollars' worth. Meters were important because they could maintain 'the morale and the risk-taking capacity of the cadres who would be exposed to radiation'.[87] Kahn's defence of radiation meters is worth quoting in full if only because this passage typifies his terrifying style:

> The radiation from fallout has curious and frightening effects. Most people already know, or will know in a postattack world, that if you get a fatal dose of radiation the sequence of events is about like this: first you become nauseated, then sick; you seem to recover; then in two or three weeks you really get sick and die.
>
> Now just imagine yourself in the post-war situation. Everybody will have been subjected to extremes of anxiety, unfamiliar environment, strange foods, minimum toilet facilities, inadequate shelters and the like. Under these conditions some high percentage of the population is going to become nauseated, and nausea is very catching. If one man vomits, everybody vomits. Almost everyone is likely to think he has received too much radiation. Morale may be so affected that many survivors may refuse to participate in constructive activities, but would content themselves with sitting down and waiting to die — some may even become violent and destructive.
>
> However, the situation would be quite different if radiation meters were distributed. Assume now that a man gets sick from a cause other than radiation. Not believing this, his morale begins to drop. You look at his meter and say, 'You have received only ten roentgens, why are you vomiting? Pull yourself together and get to work'.[88]

Kahn knew that radiation poisoning was a real bogey in the public mind. If he was to convince people that nuclear wars were survivable, he had to dispel the myths surrounding the subject of radiation. He attempted to prove that although radiation is invariably injurious to human life, a proper civil defence programme could reduce radiation dosages to levels which society could deal with. Again Kahn's argument is instructive. Even if we assume, he said, that many people will receive doses which will shorten their lives by ten years, this will only restore the life expectancy of American citizens to what it was in 1900.[89] If it is possible to regard the increased life expectancy which Americans have enjoyed since the beginning of this century as a sort of bonus, then, in a peculiar sense, nuclear war merely returns the situation to normal.

Kahn paid particular attention to the effects of Strontium-90. Strontium-90, if ingested, eventually gets into the bones where it causes bone cancer, leukemia and stunts growth. A massive thermonuclear strike would almost certainly contaminate large areas of farmland for many generations, and would cause severe shortages of healthy food. But, said Kahn, the problem could be dealt with if we were prepared to relax our peaceful standards of acceptable risk by eating some, but not excessive, quantities of contaminated food. Needless to say, Kahn had a plan for reorganizing our eating habits. He suggested that Strontium-90-contaminated food should be classified into five grades, A,B,C,D, and E, each grade more lethal than its predecessors.

The A food would be restricted to children and to pregnant women. The B food would be high-priced food available to everybody. The C food would be a low-priced food also available to everybody. Finally, the D food would be restricted to people over age forty or fifty. Even though this food would be unacceptable for children it probably would be acceptable for those past middle age, partly because their bones are already formed so that they do not pick up anywhere near as much strontium as the young, and partly because at these low levels of contamination it generally takes some decades for cancer to develop. Most of these people would die of other causes before they got cancer. Finally, there would be an E food restricted to the feeding of animals whose resulting use (meat, draft animals, leather, wool and so on) would not cause an increase in the human burden of Sr-90.[90]

Kahn also tackled the problem of long-term genetic damage caused by radiation. Making what he regarded as fairly plausible assumptions, he calculated that in the aftermath of a thermonuclear war the number of live but seriously defective children might increase worldwide to about 25 per cent above the normal rate and a similar though smaller price would have to be paid for many generations.[91] But he pointed out that 'while four chances in a thousand is a high price to pay for the use of radiation, it is not obviously excessive, especially when one considers that it is only a 10 percent increase in the natural rate of 4 percent'.[92] Even a very much higher level of genetic damage would not threaten the viability of society, and, oddly enough, the fact that the damage is spread over thirty or forty generations, makes it easier, not harder, for society to deal with it. 'In other words, if you can spread the genetic damage over tens of thousands of years you have done something very useful.'[93] That argument may be morally repellent but it has a certain persuasiveness.

It is difficult to know what to make of this analysis, but one thing is clear. The hard data used as the basis for his argument was very flimsy and seems a hopelessly inadequate basis from which to draw firm conclusions of the sort which Kahn drew. Philip Green is only one of many critics who has pointed to both the *paucity* of the hard evidence used by Kahn, and the *misuse* to which he puts it in his analysis. Green's book, *Deadly Logic: the Theory of Nuclear Deterrence,*[94] contains a devastating hatchet job on Kahn's pseudo-scientific methodology. Step-by-step he effectively demonstrates that whether Kahn is talking about the effects of fallout or the recuperative potential of American society, his conclusions have only a very fragile connection with the data with which he was working.

Green reminds us of the table on p. 20, and repeated on p. 34 of *On Thermonuclear War* (see p 86). It is preceded by the sentence: 'here again is a summary of the situation.' In other words, the table is referred to as if it contained factual information; but as Green points out, it contains no facts at all. The whole table is a purely speculative concoction. Nowhere in the book does Kahn provide his readers with any reason for believing that a particular number of dead is related to a particular rate of economic recovery. The table, despite its scientific form, contains no scientific information; the figures in it are pure guesswork on Kahn's part.[95]

J. C. Garnett

TRAGIC BUT DISTINGUISHABLE
POSTWAR STATES

Dead	Economic Recuperation
2,000,000	1 year
5,000,000	2 years
10,000,000	5 years
20,000,000	10 years
40,000,000	20 years
80,000,000	50 years
160,000,000	100 years

Will the survivors envy the dead?

Of course, Green cannot prove that Kahn's conclusions are wrong — though he certainly believes they are — but he is able to show that there is nothing scientifically rigorous about the way they were reached. If they are right, they are right only because Kahn had a sophisticated, intuitive feel for what would happen in a nuclear war. If they are wrong, (and I believe they are), they are wrong because Kahn lacked the qualities of political judgment necessary for reflecting wisely on this sort of problem.

A further example of Kahn's flawed analysis is to be found in the casual way in which he builds a number of highly contentious assumptions into his examination of the way in which American society might recover from the effects of thermonuclear war. He assumes, for example, that 'bourgeois values' will continue to prevail in a post-attack environment; that people will rally round and give credit to the government for its foresight in providing a proper civil defence organization; that they will dedicate themselves to the job of recuperation by working hard; that they will accept 'workable', ie dangerous, safety standards in order to get the economy moving.[96] All of these propositions are tendentious, and yet Kahn provides no real evidence for any of them. They are simply accepted as a matter of faith and then built into the foundations of the analysis.

But Kahn was surely right about some things. He was right to castigate those anti-nuclear activists like the Physicians for Social Responsibility who claim that nuclear war will lead either to the destruction of the created order and/or the destruction of all human life. Even though the nuclear arsenals of the superpowers have grown enormously since the time when he first examined the possibility of civil defence at RAND in the later 1950s, Kahn continued to insist that (in 1983) 'there are no respectable objective analyses or calculations to indicate that either of these [outcomes] is likely'.[97] Of course, everyone knows that it is virtually impossible to defend against a massive, malevolent surprise attack against population centres, but as Kahn frequently pointed out, such an attack is 'one of the least likely possibilities'.[98] It is irresponsible, therefore, to *assume* that kind of attack and to oppose civil defence measures which may save millions of lives in other, more probable, circumstances. It is a curious fact that those who complain bitterly about the strategist's penchant for assuming the 'worst case' when considering the Soviet threat often commit precisely the same sin when they contemplate the consequences of nuclear war.

Kahn was particularly hard on those 'gloom and doom' merchants who deliberately distort the scientific evidence in order to exaggerate the horrors of war. In a critical review of Jonathan Schell's book, *The Fate of the Earth*,[99] Kahn took him to task both for nuclear alarmism and for misusing his source materials by quoting 'only that which supports his vision of global holocaust'.[100] Schell, he believed, 'by increasing the fears of war to an intolerable degree, while offering no guide to policy, *increases* the probability of nuclear war'.[101]

To the end of his life Kahn remained a keen advocate of civil defence. Most of the available evidence, he believed, indicated 'that the United States or Soviet Union could survive and recover from even a fairly massive nuclear war'.[102] What is more, 'in the event of a war, civil defense measures could not only save millions of lives but could also prove critical to the continued survival in the world of Western ideals and institutions'.[103] Therefore, said Kahn, 'we have a compelling obligation, at once moral and political, to examine and implement the kinds of steps that might greatly reduce war-related deaths, destruction and human suffering — whether or not we can rely on such steps completely.'[104]

Most of Kahn's critics attacked his civil defence proposals on the grounds that they would be hopelessly ineffective, but some took the opposite line — that they would be *too* effective. Here, the argument was that the Russians would react in two ways. First, they might come to believe the United States was contemplating a first strike because its improved civil defences would enable it to survive a retaliatory blow. Second, they would respond by building more and bigger weapons capable of cancelling out American civil defence measures. Kahn recognized the dangers; that is why he advocated only a modest civil defence programme, one which would reassure the American people and save millions of lives, but one which would not seriously undermine the deterrent capability of the Soviet Union.

Even if the United States' government implemented the programme which he advocated, the Soviet Union would, according to Kahn, still be able to kill tens of millions of American citizens in a retaliatory strike. Knowing that they still had this capability should, said Kahn, encourage the Russians not to engage in a crash missile programme and, further, should reassure them that the United States was not preparing to attack first. 'No country is going to go lightly to war simply because by doing so it could reduce its own fatalities from 60 million in a *possible* future war to, say 20 million, in an immediate war.'[105]

This analysis suggests another of Kahn's strengths — his ability to see the connections between the various aspects of contemporary strategy. 'Civil Defence' was not something to be considered in isolation from deterrence and warfighting, or deterrence and warfighting in isolation from arms control. All of these subjects were interrelated in the sense that policies in one area inevitably spilled over into other areas. A *rational* strategy was a *coherent* strategy, an overall strategy with as few inconsistencies as possible. Hence, there was no point in considering any problem in isolation. Kahn was good at pointing out the connections and reminding us of the wider ramifications of particular policies.

Warfighting

It was probably inevitable that someone interested in surviving nuclear war should also interest himself in the conduct of war itself. Indeed, Kahn was quick to point out the connection between the two subjects. Survival conditions, he noted, depended, to a large extent, on the circumstances in which the war was terminated — and the way it was terminated depended, to a large extent, on the way it was fought. Kahn's reflections on 'warfighting' are to be found mainly in a series of essays reproduced in *Thinking about the Unthinkable* and in his book *On Escalation*.

Like most of the strategists of his day Kahn had absorbed the ideas of T. C. Schelling;[106] in particular, he had grasped the significance of Schelling's notion of war as a 'bargaining process'. He had also read F. Ikle (who had been at RAND)[107] on the subject of diplomatic bargaining, and the central ideas of both men were woven into his thinking. Kahn defined 'bargaining' as 'the attempt by one side in a controversy to convince the other that a given solution is in both their interests'.[108] He identified a series of ploys or arguments which statesmen frequently employed, in one form or another, to apply pressure on their opponents in order to strike a satisfactory bargain. Some of the tactics were characterized as follows:

(1) *'It is in your interest.'* The gist of this tactic is to try to persuade the enemy that the solution suggested is in his interest, that it represents a reasonable compromise and that he should be realistic and settle for it.
(2) *'Somebody has to be reasonable.'* Those who use this argument try to suggest that they are implacable, incapable of making concessions and either unable or unwilling to listen to reason. That being so, it is the other side that must yield and compromise if further trouble and violence is to be avoided.
(3) *'My partner won't let me.'* The thrust of this argument is to say, 'I would love to be reasonable, but my colleagues/allies won't let me. Therefore, since I cannot give in, you must.'
(4) *'This is my last demand.'* This technique, somewhat discredited since Adolf Hitler, suggests that if only the enemy will settle on this issue, then all will be well in the future.[109]

All of these tactics refer to verbal bargaining between adversaries, but Kahn (like Schelling) was also interested in the diplomacy of violence itself. Kahn recognized that every state is able to apply physical pressure to bring its opponent to agreement, and this can happen not just in peaceful negotiations but also during the conduct of war itself. He also observed a tendency in bargaining situations 'for each side to counter the other's pressure with a somewhat stronger one of its own'.[110] Kahn called this increasing pressure, step by step, 'escalation', and although he neither invented the phrase nor was the first to use it in this context, he, more than anyone else, demonstrated its applicability to the field of international relations.

It is important to distinguish Kahn's view of escalation as a deliberate act of coercion, part of what Schelling calls a 'competition in risk taking', from an earlier tradition of thinking which regarded 'escalation' as an unwanted consequence of mistakes or misunderstandings. Kahn recognized the possibility of accidental escalation; but in the context of bargaining, he was interested in the way in which those involved in a conflict could consciously increase the pressure on their enemy in order to gain some advantage. He argued that a state could deliberately escalate a conflict in three ways: first, by increasing the *intensity* of a crisis or war; second, by *widening* its area; and, third, by creating a *compound* escalation. By this Kahn meant precipitating a new crisis or conflict in some new geographic area.[111]

Kahn recognized that in any typical conflict it is possible for one side to win by escalating to the point where the other side is intimidated and gives up. Of course, the escalation tactic is not without risk because, instead of giving up, the other side may overreact and shift the entire conflict to a higher and more dangerous level. When that happens, both sides are involved in a 'competition in risk taking'. In order to

explore this complicated bargaining situation, Kahn invented the concept of 'escalation dominance' — a phrase which he used to describe the superior power of a state
which dominates the conflict at a given level of violence. 'Escalation dominance' goes
to the side which either has least to lose by escalation or fears escalation the least.[112] A
version of this concept of 'escalation dominance' has been adopted and developed by
various American officials seeking to justify the acquisition of new weapons in terms
of the bargaining power which they would give to the United States.

To explain the possibilities inherent in the tactic of deliberate 'escalation' and
'escalation dominance', Kahn developed the idea of an 'escalation ladder'. His
elaboration of a sixteen-rung ladder in *Thinking about the Unthinkable* and a forty-four-
rung ladder in *On Escalation* provide us with a detailed and sophisticated body of
thought which has now become part of the language of strategy and a major tool for
helping us to understand the complexities of conflict and war.[113]

An 'escalation ladder', Kahn explains, is 'a linear arrangement of roughly
increasing levels of intensity of crisis. Such a ladder exhibits a progression of steps in
what amounts to, roughly speaking, an ascending order of intensity through which a
given crisis may progress.'[114] Kahn's forty-four-rung ladder leads in progressive steps
from a state of 'Disagreement – Cold War' at the bottom, to what he calls, 'Aftermath'
— the consequences of unrestricted thermonuclear war — at the top. Each rung on
the ladder represents a particular, identifiable level of violence, and the ladder leads,
step by step, first through various levels of crisis, then through conventional and
tactical nuclear wars and finally through strategic wars in which some targets are
spared to 'spasm' wars in which no one is spared.

Between the various rungs of the ladder are barriers which Kahn describes as
'thresholds'.[115] Crossing any threshold inevitably involves escalation, but it is clear
that some thresholds are more important than others. Kahn identifies six basic
thresholds at which very sharp changes in the character of the conflict take place. To
cross one of these 'firebreaks' is to take a particularly serious step; it demonstrates a
willingness to accept much greater risks and much greater violence.

The most important threshold of all is clearly the 'nuclear use' threshold. Below it,
the war, however violent, does not involve the use of nuclear weapons — though if
the 'nuclear war is unthinkable' threshold has been crossed, then the belligerents will
have contemplated their use. Above it, the war is nuclear — with all of the violence
and danger that implies. But although the salience of the nuclear threshold is
unquestioned, there are, as Kahn indicated, important thresholds beyond it. In
particular, the *no homelands* threshold, which distinguishes wars in which the
territory of the superpowers is attacked from those in which it is not and the *no cities*
threshold which separates wars in which cities are targeted from those in which they
are spared are important break points in any escalation ladder.

But as Kahn says, 'it remains true that once war has started no other line of
demarcation is at once so clear, so sanctified by convention, so ratified by emotion, so
low on the scale of violence, and — perhaps most important of all — so easily defined
and understood as the line between not using and using nuclear weapons'.[116]

Kahn admitted that in certain situations there may be pressures to cross the nuclear
threshold. He recognized that a state might decide to use nuclear weapons either to
counteract its conventional weakness or to improve its credibility as an ally. He was
also conscious of the illogicality of forbidding the use of even very small nuclear
weapons while permitting the use of very large chemical explosives. But Kahn was
even more impressed by the dangers inherent in breaking this well-established taboo
— particularly the risk that nuclear war, once unleashed, would turn out to be
uncontrollable and the remaining thresholds quickly violated.[117]

And yet despite his nervousness about crossing the nuclear firebreak, Kahn was keen to explore the possibility that even strategic war between the superpowers could be limited. Though the upper end of his escalation ladder contained some bizarre possibilities, Kahn was optimistic that both the 'no homelands' threshold and the 'no cities' threshold could, in certain circumstances, be made to stick.[118] He pointed out in an essay entitled 'Some Comments on Controlled War' that when the alternative is *total* destruction, limited strategic war looks like a good option.[119] 'If the only alternatives are between the all-out mutually homicidal war and the city exchange, bizarre and destructive as the city exchange is, it is not as bizarre and destructive as mutual homicide.'[120] And even at this highly dangerous level of warfare Kahn believed that 'bargaining' was still possible by the selective use of controlled counter-force strikes, 'tit-for-tat' counter city exchanges and complicated mixtures of both.[121]

To those who argued that this kind of bargaining, particularly at the upper end of the ladder, implied a degree of cool rationality which was unlikely to be present in real world situations, Kahn responded as follows: 'Researchers who study these problems do not really assume that decision-makers are wholly rational, but rather that they are not totally irrational — which is quite different from the assumption of rationality.'[122] Kahn believed that in the case of the United States there was 'a premium on cool conduct, a pattern of expectations built up to influence decision-makers in times of nuclear crisis',[123] and in the case of the Soviet Union, with its tradition of using force cynically and instrumentally, he believed their political leaders were 'unlikely to behave emotionally in making crisis decisions'.[124]

Perhaps the best way of thinking about Kahn's escalation ladder is to consider it as a rule book both for limiting conflicts and wars, and for exploiting them. What Kahn was trying to do was to build a series of 'stops' or limitations into the conflict spectrum so that the belligerents could, if they so wished, either keep to particular levels of violence or exceed them by escalating to new, higher levels.

The concept of an escalation 'ladder' is illuminating for those interested in managing conflicts, crises and wars. It outlines the options and possibilities available to the participants in a conflict, and it helps us to order our thoughts about them. But, like all metaphors, it needs to be handled with care, since there are aspects of it which are misleading. For example, the idea of a 'ladder' inevitably suggests that the rungs are evenly spaced, equally important and equally difficult to climb. However, in international relations some levels of crisis are more important than others, some thresholds are easier to cross than others and the rungs are at irregular intervals.

Kahn was aware of these problems, and he was also aware of the fact that although real ladders are equally easy to ascend or descend, this might not be the case with 'escalation' ladders.[125] Kahn believed that 'in many ways escalation is an irreversible process', and that a 'de-escalation ladder' would not necessarily be an escalation ladder in reverse. But perhaps the main weakness of the ladder metaphor is that it may encourage people to believe that the parties to a conflict will share the same ladder. Kahn, always aware of the importance of national perceptions, knew that this was unlikely, and that in the case of American–Soviet relations, it would be very dangerous to assume that the Soviets shared the American rule book. Since the Soviets have repeatedly insisted that they neither believe in the possibility of 'controlled escalation' nor accept the existence of 'thresholds', it is very difficult to envisage the kind of bargaining which Kahn has described. Kahn recognized the difficulty. 'I have committed the besetting sin of most US analysts and have attributed to the Soviets a kind of military behavior that may in fact be appropriate only to US analysts — and not at all relevant to Soviet conditions and attitudes'.[126] In *On Escalation*, Kahn made an imaginative attempt to construct a plausible Soviet ladder.

Interestingly enough, there were some similarities with its 'American' equivalent. Perhaps the degree of overlap suggests that the intrinsic logic of East–West relations is so compelling that both sides will appreciate it in roughly the same way and will draw roughly similar rules for both containing war and waging it.

The flawed realist

If, as the title *On Thermonuclear War* implies, Kahn sought to write the twentieth-century equivalent of Clausewitz's classic, then he failed. There is nothing in *On Thermonuclear War* which compares in profundity with some of the ideas in *On War*. It contains no timeless truths, no brilliant insights or concepts to which successive generations will return for inspiration. And yet it is a very significant milestone in the history of nuclear thought for two reasons: first, because it challenged some conventional assumptions; and, second, because it contained arguments which, even if they were mistaken, were thought-provoking and interesting. Kahn had an unconventional, original mind. He was less inhibited than most of his professional colleagues, and he had ideas which simply did not occur to more disciplined thinkers. What he wrote was different, less scholarly perhaps, and certainly more polemical; but perhaps because of this he reached an audience denied to his more academic fellow strategists. Arguably, one of his greatest achievements was in stimulating discussion about the great strategic issues of the nuclear age among educated laymen who had hitherto regarded strategy as a highly specialized, esoteric subject.

Another of Kahn's strengths (or weaknesses) was that he never abandoned an argument just because he did not like where it was going. In that sense he was a remarkably objective thinker who did not seem to care where the argument led. In general, his technique was to voice the argument, and then leave it to others to evaluate. This approach sometimes left the reader with a feeling that Kahn either lacked common sense or was unable to tell the difference between a good argument and a bad one. But it is quite unfair to Kahn to argue that he approved of all the arguments, hypotheses and possible policies which abound in his work. Though it is true that there are many policy recommendations mixed up with the analysis, throughout his writing Kahn's main objective was to stretch his readers' minds by articulating all the contradictory arguments, implications and possibilities surrounding any possible courses of action. A good example of his technique is to be found in the final chapter of *Thinking about the Unthinkable* where he identifies fourteen alternative strategies which the United States could adopt — ranging from a unilateral renunciation of the use of force to a preventive war against the Soviet Union. Kahn commented critically on all fourteen possibilities, but it is left to the reader to make up his mind about their relative merits.[127]

Kahn, a physicist by training, had no background in either political science or history. It was a weakness which surfaced in his writing wherever political judgments were called for. The breathless urgency with which he regarded all our nuclear problems probably had something to do with his lack of historical perspective: 'I think that the decade of the sixties will be the turning point of the twentieth century.'[128] And, writing in 1960, he commented that our problem lies 'in three parts: that of satisfactorily reaching 1961, of reaching 1965, and finally, of reaching 1975'.[129] No one with any kind of perspective on human affairs could write in that vein. After all, there was nothing special about the human predicament in the 1960s; and 1961, 1965 and 1975 came and went without a hint of serious disaster. But since Kahn was unable to fit the issues he confronted into any historical context, he was unable to see them in a balanced way. In a sense, he was overwhelmed by the problem of survival. Martin Wight once warned us of that provincial spirit

which is constantly assuring us that we are the summit of human achievement, that we stand on the edge of unprecedented prosperity or unparalleled catastrophe, that the next summit conference is going to be the most fateful in history. It is a liberation of the spirit to acquire perspective to recognize that every generation is confronted by problems of the utmost subjective urgency, but that an objective grading is probably impossible; to learn that the same moral predicaments and the same ideas have been explored before.[130]

Wight might have been writing about Herman Kahn.

Like most strategists, Kahn can most easily be accommodated in the 'Realist' tradition of thinking about international politics. Consciously or unconsciously, he had absorbed a body of ideas which emphasized the importance of power and *realpolitik* in state behaviour, which stressed a pessimistic view of human nature and which contained a good deal of scepticism about the possibility of radically transforming the human condition. Kahn knew that political realities are power realities; that power must be countered with power and that self interest is the driving force in statesmanship.

And yet in some respects Kahn was a flawed 'Realist'. He lacked the philosophical profundity which characterizes the sophisticated Realist. His views were not sufficiently anchored in history or philosophy to give him the kind of deep insights into the human predicament which we associate with writers like Hans Morgenthau or R. Niebuhr.

Like all Realists Kahn was cautious in his estimate of what is possible in politics. He did not believe that a disarmed world was an achievable goal. Hopefully, military power could be successfully managed in such a way that wars would become both less likely and less destructive; but military power could not be abolished. And yet Kahn's conservatism in terms of practical politics did not prevent him from flirting with the radical idea of world government. In 1960 he spoke sympathetically of the book by Clark and Sohn[131] in which they spelt out some possible constitutions for a new world order. He said, 'I do not believe that the twentieth century will see a disarmed world, but it may see a world government or the equivalent.'[132] In *Thinking about the Unthinkable* he wrote: 'We probably must accept the notion that the world as we know it is passing from the stage of history, and that attempts to preserve this 500-year-old nation-state system would probably be as futile as the earlier attempts of some of the small German or Italian states to stave off the unification of their countries.'[133]

Considered as a piece of very long-term speculation this is acceptable enough, but as a piece of analysis relating to the forseeable future it is absurd, and by 1963 Kahn had already begun to change his mind. He became convinced that a world government could not be brought about peacefully in the forseeable future, and if it came about as a result of crisis or war, he believed we might not like it. 'It looks very unpleasant as far as I can see . . . There are many kinds of plausible world governments that could be worse than many kinds of plausible thermonuclear wars.' Kahn became very much aware of the possibility that a world government 'could become oppressive, or could be taken over by an oppressive group'.[134]

Elements of ambiguity and inconsistency remained a feature of Kahn's thinking about world government. During the early 1960s he still seemed to believe that democratic world government was a worthy objective, however difficult it might be to achieve. Raymond Aron was moved to comment in his introduction to *Thinking about the Unthinkable*, 'Herman Kahn, with all his scientific studies, all his subtle analysis, all his hypothetical experiments, *remains a reformer*[135] (my italics), and a universal state under the rule of law was his preferred vision even if it was not the most plausible one.

It was a curiously simple view for someone with such a tough-minded reputation, and twenty years later he had virtually abandoned it. At the end of his life he described the creation of a world government as a 'non-issue' — 'basically irrelevant, impractical, inaccurate or foolish'.[136] He saw no prospect of bringing it about and felt compelled to comment very scornfully on Jonathan Schell's utopian vision of some kind of world government to which sovereign states had ceded their political authority and military power. 'How we get to there from here is one of the many "awesome, urgent tasks" — "the political work of our age" — that Schell says he has "left to others".'[137]

Kahn was not a pacifist, but he was fairly sensitive to the moral issues raised by his thoughts on peace and war, and he was much more sensitive to such issues than his critics acknowledged. Unfortunately, it is very difficult to deduce from his writing what his precise moral position was. My impression is that his morality was built on relatively simple assumptions. First, he was convinced that there was nothing immoral about self defence. 'It is immoral from almost any point of view to refuse to defend yourself and others from very grave and terrible threats . . .'[138] It followed from this that although 'peace' was a very important value it was not 'an overwhelming value'. Kahn believed that there were circumstances in which both the threat of war, even the conduct of war itself, was morally justifiable.

Furthermore, he argued that there were circumstances in which both the threat and use of nuclear weapons was morally acceptable. 'Nuclear weapons are intrinsically neither moral nor immoral, though they are more prone to immoral use than most weapons. But they can be used to accomplish moral objectives and can do this in ways that are morally acceptable.'[139] Kahn believed that the avoidance of war by the strategy of deterrence was a perfectly moral use of nuclear capability, and he also maintained that the *controlled* use of nuclear weapons with the objective of limiting pain and damage was morally justifiable. 'I would judge them [nuclear weapons] as moral when used solely to balance, deter, or correct for the possession or use of nuclear weapons by others.'[140]

Since the use of nuclear weapons was morally permissable, the problem for Kahn was largely one of imposing restraints on their use, and in this context he seemed to accept the validity of some of the principles of the Just War doctrine. In particular, he stressed the significance of 'proportionality' and the distinction between 'military' and 'civilian' targets. 'The benefits of violence must be "proportionate" to the human and other costs, and one must be able to discriminate between actions against an aggressor (which are justified) and those that hurt noncombatants (which are not).'[141]

It was the principle of 'proportionality' which led Kahn to reject entirely the use of nuclear weapons against non-nuclear enemies, and to favour the adoption of a 'No first-use' doctrine against nuclear opponents. And the same principle led him to reject 'massive retaliation' and 'uncontrolled war' in favour of measured responses and 'tit-for-tat' exchanges which were related to the initial aggression. He acknowledged the moral problem attached to the talionic law of 'an-eye-for-an-eye' — particularly when the city attacked in retaliation 'is inhabited by persons with no specific responsibility for the initial nuclear attack.'[142] But he was not prepared to relinquish the option out of hand.

Throughout his career Kahn was anxious to strengthen the distinction between 'military' and 'civilian' targets. One of the most important ways of 'humanizing' the barbaric business of war is to discriminate between targets in such a way that loss of life and destructiveness can be minimized. Kahn recognized the difficulties of target discrimination, but nevertheless advocated strategic ideas which put a premium on 'city avoidance' and encouraged the enemy to do likewise. He believed 'that civilians are not an appropriate routine target, enemy weapons *should* be targets and the system must be designed for the task'.[143] It was his concern for the civilian population which led Kahn to couch some of his arguments for civil defence in moral terms: 'If there is a reasonable possibility for the survival of society after a nuclear war, we have a moral obligation to prepare in advance'.[144]

And yet, as we have seen, Kahn was not willing to *completely* renounce city targeting, although he was willing to renounce it 'except as a last resort or in very special circumstances.'[145] But if a powerful enemy destroyed an American city 'just to teach us some kind of lesson', he wanted the option to retaliate in kind to be available.

In effect, what this implies is that Kahn was not prepared to rule out *any* strategic option as a matter of principle, except perhaps that of a massive, indiscriminate, uncontrolled, 'spasm' retaliation which could serve no political purpose whatsoever. But that should not be taken to mean that he contemplated nuclear war with equanimity or that he was anxious to use any very destructive options. The entire thrust of his thought was directed towards the preservation of human life. 'The principal moral obligation of a government in the nuclear age is to make every effort to enforce deterrence or, should deterrence fail, to limit as much as possible the damage to its citizens and its economy and to enhance the prospects for postwar recovery.'[146]

The trouble with this statement of Kahn's position is that the word 'moral' in it is really irrelevant. The obligation which he regards as his guiding light is essentially a *prudential, political* obligation — not a moral one at all. What Kahn offers in his strategic thought is a sophisticated approach to the problem of survival in the nuclear age — how to avoid war, and if that proves impossible, how to survive war. Almost every policy calculated to promote these goals is regarded as moral. The security of the state and the survival of its people is an end which seems to Kahn to justify the use of almost any means — including, in certain circumstances, large-scale thermonuclear war. Why this is so is never fully explained.

And Kahn never agonized about what to do when the price of survival becomes very high. Sacrificing one million people may be alright, but what about ten million or two hundred million? When is it time to say 'enough is enough'? Apart from commenting at one point that 'almost nobody wants to go down in history as the first person to kill 100,000,000 people',[147] there is no evidence that Kahn ever considered the question of whether there is a level of violence for which no moral defence is possible.

Notes

1. J. Newman, Review of H. Kahn, 'On Thermonuclear War', *Scientific American*, **204**, no. 3, 1961, p. 197.

2. See H. Kahn, 'Refusing to Think About the Unthinkable', *Fortune*, 28 June 1982.

3. See for example, E. L. Burdick and H. Wheeler, *Fail Safe*, London, Hutchinson, 1963; N. Shute, *On the Beach*, London, Heinemann, 1966; P. George, *Red Alert*, London, Ace Books, 1958; A. Gray, *The Penetrators*, London, Souvenir Press, 1965; C. Pincher, *The Penthouse Conspirators*, London, Michael Joseph, 1970; Sir J. Hackett, *The Third World War*, London, Sidgwick and Jackson, 1978.

4. H. Kahn, *On Thermonuclear War*, Princeton, NJ, Princeton University Press, 1960.
5. N. Moss, *Men Who Play God: The Story of the Hydrogen Bomb*, London, Victor Gollancz, 1968, p. 205.
6. Kahn, 1960, op. cit., p. 625.
7. Quoted by G. Herken, *Counsels of War*, New York, Alfred A. Knopf, p. 206.
8. Quoted by Moss, 1968, op. cit., p. 244.
9. H. Kahn, *Thinking about the Unthinkable in the 1980s*, New York, Simon and Schuster, 1984, p. 58.
10. Ibid., p. 59.
11. Ibid., p. 67.
12. Ibid., pp. 73–4.
13. Newman, 1961, op. cit., p. 200.
14. A. Rapoport, *Strategy and Conscience*, New York, Evanston and London, Harper and Row, 1964, p. 199.
15. Ibid., pp. 139–40.
16. Ibid., p. 194.
17. Ibid., pp. 175–95.
18. Ibid., p. 109.
19. H. Kahn, *Thinking about the Unthinkable*, London, Weidenfeld and Nicolson, 1962, p. 37.
20. Ibid.
21. Ibid., p. 30.
22. Ibid., p. 35.
23. F. M. Kaplan, *The Wizards of Armageddon*, New York, Simon and Schuster, 1983, p. 227.
24. This feeling was shared by many of Kahn's RAND colleagues.
25. Kahn, 1960, op. cit., p. 96.
26. A. Wohlstetter, 'The Delicate Balance of Terror', *Foreign Affairs*, January 1959, **37**, pp. 211–34.
27. Kahn, 1960, op. cit., pp. 8–13.
28. Wohlstetter, 1959, op. cit., particularly pp. 219–22.
29. Kahn, 1960, op. cit., p. 533.
30. Ibid., p. 138.
31. Ibid.
32. See ibid., p. 126 for short definitions and chapters IV and V for a detailed exposition of the main ideas and a recapitulation in chapter XI.
33. Ibid., pp. 2–9.
34. Ibid., p. 32.
35. Ibid., p. 36.
36. Ibid., p. 217.
37. Kahn, 1984, op. cit., p. 117.
38. Ibid., p. 119.
39. Ibid., pp. 119–20.
40. Kahn, 1960, op. cit., p. 219.
41. Ibid., pp. 220–1.
42. Ibid., pp. 126.
43. Ibid., p. 219.
44. Ibid.
45. Ibid., p. 220.
46. Ibid., p. 221.
47. Ibid., p. 222.
48. Kahn, 1984, op. cit., p. 172.
49. Kahn, 1960, op. cit., p. 145.
50. Ibid.
51. Ibid., pp. 145–6.
52. Ibid., p. 147.
53. Ibid., pp. 152–3 and a further discussion in H. Kahn, 'The Arms Race and Some of Its

Hazards' in D. G. Brennan (ed.), *Arms Control and Disarmament*, London, Jonathan Cape, 1961, p. 108.
54. Ibid., p. 108.
55. Ibid., p. 93.
56. Kahn, 1960, op. cit., p. 224.
57. Ibid.
58. Kahn, in Brennan (ed.), 1961, op. cit., p. 109.
59. Ibid.
60. Ibid., p. 117.
61. See for example H. Kahn and B. Bruce-Briggs, *Things To Come: Thinking About the Seventies and Eighties*, New York, Macmillan, 1972; H. Kahn, W. Brown and L. Martel, *The Next 200 Years: A Scenario for America and the World*, London, Associated Business Programmes, 1977; H. Kahn and A. J. Wiener, *The Year 2000: A Framework for Speculation on the Next Thirty-Three Years*, London, Macmillan, 1967.
62. Kahn, 1960, op. cit., p. 495.
63. Ibid., p. 499.
64. Ibid., p. 498.
65. Ibid., p. 234.
66. Kahn in Brennan (ed.), 1961, op. cit., p. 119.
67. Ibid., p. 120.
68. H. Kahn, *On Escalation: Metaphors and Scenarios*, London, Pall Mall Press, 1965, p. 131.
69. Ibid., p. 129.
70. Kahn, 1984, op. cit., p. 203.
71. Ibid., p. 190.
72. Ibid., p. 192.
73. Ibid., p. 193.
74. Kahn, 1960, op. cit., pp. 155–60.
75. Ibid., p. 241.
76. Kahn, 1984, op. cit., p. 218.
77. Ibid., p. 196.
78. Kahn, 1960, op. cit., p. 246–7.
79. Ibid., p. 251.
80. Ibid.
81. Ibid., pp. 248–50.
82. Ibid., p. 11.
83. Ibid., p. 71.
84. Ibid., p. 19.
85. Ibid., p. 21.
86. Ibid., pp. 256–308.
87. Ibid., p. 85.
88. Ibid., pp. 85–6.
89. Ibid., pp. 59–60.
90. Ibid., pp. 66–7.
91. Ibid., p. 46.
92. Ibid., p. 45.
93. Ibid., p. 48.
94. See P. Green, *Deadly Logic: The Theory of Nuclear Deterrence*, Ohio, Ohio State University Press, 1966, particularly pp. 15–92.
95. Ibid., pp. 55–6.
96. Kahn, 1960, op. cit., pp. 74–95.
97. Kahn, 1984, op. cit., p. 30.
98. Ibid., p. 176.
99. J. Schell, *The Fate of the Earth*, London, Picador in association with Jonathan Cape, 1982.
100. See H. Kahn, 'Refusing to Think About the Unthinkable', *Fortune*, 28 June 1982.
101. Ibid.
102. Kahn, 1984, op. cit., p. 182.

103. Ibid., p. 189.
104. Ibid., p. 175.
105. Kahn, 1962, op. cit., pp. 94–5.
106. See pp. 120–35 for some details of Schelling's thought.
107. See in particular F. C. Ikle, *How Nations Negotiate*, New York and Evanston, Harper and Row, 1964.
108. Kahn, 1962, op. cit., p. 178.
109. Ibid., pp. 178–80.
110. Ibid., p. 185.
111. Kahn, 1965, op. cit., p. 4.
112. Ibid., p. 290.
113. See Kahn, 1962, op. cit., pp. 185–203, and Kahn, 1965, op. cit., pp. 37–51.
114. Kahn, 1965, op. cit., p. 38.
115. Ibid., pp. 30, 51.
116. Ibid., p. 95.
117. Ibid., pp. 109–13.
118. Ibid., pp. 142–3, and pp. 167–95.
119. H. Kahn, 'Some Comments on Controlled War' in K. Knorr and T. Read (eds.) *Limited Strategic War*, London and Dunmow, Pall Mall Press, 1962, p. 43.
120. Ibid., p. 43.
121. Ibid., pp. 47–66.
122. Kahn, 1965, op. cit., p. 220–1.
123. Ibid., p. 221.
124. Ibid.
125. Ibid., pp. 230–1.
126. Ibid., p. 218.
127. Kahn, 1962, op. cit., pp. 233–54.
128. Ibid., p. 225.
129. Kahn, 1960, op. cit., p. 575.
130. Quoted by the author in *Commonsense and the Theory of International Politics*, London, Macmillan, 1984, p. 140.
131. G. Clark and L. B. Sohn, *World Peace Through World Law*, Cambridge, Mass., Harvard University Press, 1958.
132. Kahn, 1960, op. cit., p. 494.
133. Kahn, 1962, op. cit., pp. 230–1.
134. Kahn, 1984, op. cit., p. 87.
135. See Kahn, 1962, op. cit., p. 12.
136. Kahn, 1984, op. cit., p. 23.
137. Ibid., p. 208.
138. Ibid., p. 31.
139. Ibid.
140. Ibid.
141. Ibid., p. 46.
142. Ibid., pp. 222–3.
143. Ibid., p. 215.
144. Ibid., p. 189.
145. Ibid., p. 214.
146. Ibid., p. 211.
147. Kahn, 1962, op. cit., p. 171.

4 HENRY KISSINGER

Lawrence Freedman

It is doubtful that Henry Kissinger really deserves the title 'Maker of Nuclear Strategy'. His main claim is that he wrote the first 'best seller of the nuclear age', *Nuclear Weapons and Foreign Policy*. Although the basic ideas behind this book were not new, this was an unusually forceful and systematic presentation of the main lines of criticism of the policy of 'massive retaliation' that had been adopted by the Eisenhower administration in 1954. As such it repays reading. However its most original feature — the proposal to prepare to fight a limited nuclear war — was unconvincing. Three years later the author also declared himself unconvinced and proposed more emphasis on conventional deterrence.

This conversion earned him the reputation of a man who swam with the currents. In the area of nuclear strategy that remained true because his work was essentially derivative. He was never a full-blooded nuclear strategist. His strength was more in great-power diplomacy. On this he wrote with more insight and independence.

There seems little point in adding in this chapter to the general literature on Kissinger as a person or Kissinger as a diplomat. The concern here is with Kissinger the theorist. Even with this focus it is possible to touch only fleetingly on his grand designs in order to concentrate on nuclear matters. I shall argue that Kissinger is most interesting as a dissatisfied consumer of nuclear strategy, continually frustrated in his search for strategic concepts that could inject credibility into American foreign policy.

There is no shortage of material on Henry Kissinger. A complex personality, who operated in mysterious ways while exercising enormous influence over the policies of the world's most powerful state, inevitably excites curiosity. Given that he had written extensively prior to taking office on both the substance and process of American foreign policy there is a natural inclination to relate the early theories to the later practice. As a controversial figure he has stimulated works of virtual hagiography as well as of bitter denunciation. Thus a 1983 book, which considered among other things whether Kissinger exhibited the patterns of behaviour typical of a depressive personality and whether this helped explain his policies, listed in its bibliography some twenty-four books and thirty-eight articles concerned in some way with the man and his policies. This was in addition to ten books, thirty-two articles and a Bachelor's thesis written by Kissinger.[1] There has been more since.

The items in this extensive literature do not tend to be distinguished by their brevity. Kissinger himself has a verbose style and is not afraid of length. Until the author's later notoriety, one of his major claims to fame was that his undergraduate thesis on *The Meaning of History: Reflections on Spengler, Toynbee and Kant* was so long at 350 pages that it resulted in the school setting a limit of 150 pages on all future undergraduate theses. His two volumes of *mémoires* on his period in office, up to Nixon's resignation in August 1974, are 1,521 and 1,283 pages respectively. This is more than a page for every day in office.[2] The same tendency appears to afflict his critics. Seymour Hersh's examination of Kissinger's record in office runs to 698 pages.[3]

A further problem is that Kissinger has taken more than a passing interest in what has been written about him and has an instinct for self-promotion. The brothers Kalb open their generally laudatory biography with thanks to 'Henry A. Kissinger, who, as an historian as well as a statesman, understands the critical importance of primary sourcing'.[4] Kissinger is reported to have taken great efforts to ensure that John Newhouse's detailed description of the first SALT negotiations reflected well on his efforts, including encouraging his staff to provide Newhouse with briefings based on classified material.[5]

Because Kissinger is one of the few scholars to have successfully made the transition to statesman, much of the literature that assesses his academic work does so in order to obtain an insight into his later diplomatic practice. One author, having taken the trouble to examine Kissinger's undergraduate thesis, has even gone so far as to suggest that 'much of Kissinger's intellectual development as a scholar and a statesman can be seen as a secret dialogue' with the philosopher Kant. One clue: the word 'imperative' kept appearing in Kissinger's speeches.[6] More common has been to compare the analysis of diplomacy found in Kissinger's doctoral thesis, eventually published as *The World Restored*,[7] with his approach in government. This soon reveals a fascination with the relationship between international order and revolutionary process, problems of legitimacy, the need for creativity in statesmen as they face the limits of power.[8] On the nuclear side there is less, perhaps because Kissinger's excursions into nuclear strategy in government attracted far less attention than his broader foreign policy, and his early writings on nuclear strategy soon became rather dated.

Kissinger was not responsible for developing any of the major concepts of nuclear strategy, and his prescriptions have tended to have a short shelf-life. The prescriptions contained in *Nuclear Weapons and Foreign Policy*, which certainly helped Kissinger make his reputation, were unconvincing, and he himself jettisoned them within a few years. As both an academic and a practitioner he demonstrated considerable skill in providing frameworks through which the more pressing problems of the day could be analysed — if not solved. In terms of nuclear strategy what is interesting about Kissinger is his continuing effort to devise, out of the ideas circulating around him at any given time, a strategy relevant to the underlying requirements of great-power politics.

My contention is that Kissinger is much more interesting as a *consumer* than as a *maker* of nuclear strategy. He has been a consumer in three senses; first, in the practical sense that as a policymaker he commissioned and received studies from those in the armed services and the bureaucracy responsible for devising nuclear strategy; second, he has been a consumer in a literal sense in that he has drawn liberally on other peoples' work in developing his own ideas. His first two works in this area — *Nuclear Weapons and Foreign Policy* and *The Necessity for Choice* — were linked to study groups populated by the great and the good. The influence at different times of General James Gavin, Albert Wohlstetter and Tom Schelling among others is quite visible.

Third, he has been a consumer because his main interest has been in foreign policy. He has sought a nuclear strategy that could back up America's great-power diplomacy. While there has been little consistency in his own strategic prescriptions, there has been great consistency in his definition of the problem that these prescriptions should solve. At stake has been the integrity of American foreign policy which he has argued must be matched by a credible military policy. To inject this credibility he has explored limited nuclear war, counterforce, selective strikes and arms control with varying degrees of enthusiasm and circumspection. The unsatisfactory nature of these various explorations leaves a large question mark against the ability of the United States to sustain the foreign-policy commitments that it took on in simpler times when it believed in the durability of nuclear superiority.

The biography can be brief. Alfred Heinz was born to Louis Kissinger, a high school teacher, and his wife Paula in Furth in Germany in May 1923. Kissinger had a younger brother and was brought up as an orthodox Jew in a reasonably comfortable household until the Nuremberg Laws of 1935 deprived his father of a job as a government employee.[9]

In 1938 the Kissingers managed to emigrate to the United States and Heinz became Henry. At George Washington High School in New York City he began to shine academically. On graduating he began to study accounting but in 1943 was drafted and sent into the Army. Here he found some of his early intellectual contacts and the sort of responsibility that comes to young men with special talents in a war.

In September 1946 he entered Harvard, to major in philosophy. After graduating *summa cum laude* in 1950, he joined the government department as a graduate. He got his Master's degree in 1952 and a doctorate in 1954. The thesis was a study of the Congress of Vienna and is a work of significant scholarship. It was published in 1957 as *The World Restored*. It is a natural source for anyone interested in Kissinger's sense of the challenge for statesmanship in a revolutionary age.

Our main interest is in his next major undertaking, *Nuclear Weapons and Foreign Policy*. In 1954 the Council on Foreign Relations, the meeting place for the eastern establishment, set up a study group on nuclear weapons policy. Kissinger had been invited to the Council to discuss his possible appointment as editor of its journal, *Foreign Affairs*. He was not considered suitable for this post but did seem appropriate to serve as rapporteur for the nuclear weapons policy study group. Although most of the study group's work had been completed by the time he arrived, Kissinger set about the task of writing it up with great enthusiasm and to considerable effect. *Nuclear Weapons and Foreign Policy* was an immediate success and extremely influential. It was in the best-seller lists for fourteen weeks.

While still working for the Council on Foreign Relations, he became director of the security panel of the Rockefeller Brothers' Fund and helped write an influential report which appeared in 1958.[10] This was the start of his acquaintance with Nelson Rockefeller. Over the next ten years Kissinger's star did not exactly fade but he failed to sustain his early promise. His next major book, *The Necessity for Choice*[11] reversed some of the most interesting ideas of *Nuclear Weapons and Foreign Policy*. Later in the 1960s, *The Troubled Partnership*, which was in some ways his most intelligent contribution to discussion of contemporary foreign policy, made only a slight impact. Perhaps this was because its sensitivity to the complexities of America's relationship with its major allies meant that it lacked the self-confident certainties of his earlier work.[12]

While he was also writing interesting things during this period on the relationship between intellectuals and the foreign policy bureaucracy,[13] his own attempts to manage that relationship had not been a resounding success. A spell as a consultant in the Kennedy administration was neither happy nor productive. Politically his attachment to Nelson Rockefeller made any hope of a high-level post apparently dependent upon Rockefeller's (failing) presidential aspirations.

Unexpectedly in 1968 the call came when the newly elected President Nixon appointed him special assistant for national security affairs. He stayed until 1973 and was then promoted to secretary of state, a position he held under President Ford. At a time when America was having to come to terms with the Vietnam débâcle and the loss of the last vestiges of nuclear superiority, Kissinger was responsible for an

unusually creative, though at times cynical, diplomacy. He improved relations with
the traditional adversaries of the Soviet Union and China, with the Arab world and
helped extricate the country from Indo-China. So it was as a practitioner of great-
power diplomacy that he eventually made his name.

During this period Kissinger also could make some claims to being a maker of
nuclear strategy. The first SALT (Strategic Arms Limitation Talks) agreements signed
in May 1972 represented an attempt to consolidate whatever stability the superpower
strategic relationship had then reached. He also set in motion a shift in American
strategic thinking which sought to escape from the apparent implications of this
stability. Out of office since 1977 he has continued to move with the times. Much of
his writing appears to have been written with a view to facilitating his return to office.
It has not been successful and has mainly encouraged an image of inconsistency and
opportunism.[14]

Nuclear Weapons and Foreign Policy was Kissinger's first and last substantial
excursion into nuclear strategy. It reveals to the full his strengths and weaknesses in
this area and for that reason is worth examining in some detail. Central to the book is
the sense of living in a revolutionary time, both in political and military terms.
Politically the United States had now to confront a communist challenge of global
dimensions, unambiguously directed towards undermining the established order.
Unfortunately the revolution in military technology meant that the tools had yet to be
found to meet this challenge. The problem was not so much that new capabilities were
irrelevant but that they had not been fashioned with these challenges sufficiently in
mind. This in turn reflected a more general lack of understanding of the relationship
between force and diplomacy.

Kissinger confronted what he took to be the traditional American tendency to see
war and peace in absolute terms and in quite separate compartments. War meant the
exercise of maximum force to defeat the enemy; peace required the use of diplomacy
through legal process to support the international order. For Kissinger peace needed
to be backed by force just as war did not preclude diplomacy. If the United States
allowed itself to get into the mental state whereby force was confined to war, and force
in war was assumed to be all out, then its diplomacy would be inhibited. This would be
especially true in the nuclear age when all-out war was so dangerous and repugnant.
The incentive would be to expand the terms of peace even though this could reward
irresponsibility.

Diplomacy had to be backed up by force — 'the penalty for intransigence'.[15]
Continued failure to back American diplomacy by force would encourage the Soviet
Union to take greater risks. 'Until power is used, it is what people think it is.'[16] If
American power could not be used, then it would undermine policy. The task of
strategic doctrine was to translate power into policy. Current doctrine failed to do
this; the task was to develop a new doctrine appropriate to the changed circumstances.

The atomic bomb had naturally come to be understood in terms of a 'concept of
warfare which knew no goal save total victory, and no mode of war except all-out
war'.[17] Under the existing concept the United States had assumed that war would only
come about through aggression and that it would be decided through attrition. By dint
of its industrial and economic resources the United States was well placed to prevail in
such a war. American forces only needed to be powerful enough to gain sufficient time
for the country to mobilize its industrial potential.[18]

All-out war was becoming too horrendous for any state to initiate without complete
confidence of success. The Soviet Union would be content to pursue its objectives
through subversion and limited moves, and in each case the United States, without
the means to meet these challenges on their own terms, would be forced to question

whether they were 'worth' all-out war. By threatening all-out war (through the doctrine of massive retaliation which sought 'to limit aggression at its source by the threat of general war'),[19] the United States had made itself appear bellicose without forcing the Soviet Union to hesitate.

Kissinger suggested that the moral repugnance surrounding nuclear use, encouraged by the Soviet Union, imposed inhibitions even during the period of atomic superiority. Now the inhibitions had been compounded by mutual vulnerability. The winner of an all-out war could not be judged in terms of 'relative damage'; an inferior level might still have drained it of its 'national substance'.[20] Nor was he likely to retain sufficient physical resources to impose his will on the other's society.[21]

The declining utility of all-out war did not mean that this sort of warfare could be ignored. It was no good maintaining a token force and then building up in response to overt aggression. There must be sufficient forces-in-being to survive a surprise attack. The surprise attack option was not available to the United States. Conceding the first blow as a matter of principle, the United States in effect conceded 'the margin required to impose its will'. It was also forced to plan to absorb a first blow for an indefinite future. An aggressor without fear of a first blow could devote all its resources to planning its own.[22] It was necessary to preserve what would later be described as an 'assured destruction' capability: 'to prevent a situation arising in which the USSR can calculate that it possesses a sufficient margin of certainty to make a surprise attack on the US worthwhile'.[23]

As to whether or not this would be difficult in the future, Kissinger was not wholly clear. In the near term he argued, correctly, on the basis of an analysis of actual and projected capabilities, the Soviet Union would *not* be in a position to launch a surprise attack.[24]

So there was no need to be 'panicked' by Soviet nuclear blackmail. When discussing matters at a more abstract level he suggested that technology's future impact on military strategy will be largely incremental without the drama of the discovery of nuclear weapons. But he then moved on to inject drama by describing a much more delicate balance, fuelled by an offence–defence duel.

> At the current level of technological change the side which has conceded the first blow to its enemy [ie the United States] will always live on the verge of catastrophe, for an adverse technological breakthrough is always possible. Thus the stalemate for all-out war is inherently precarious. It will imply a continuous race between offense and defense, and it will require a tremendous effort on our part simply to stay even.[25]

Developing air defences would at best reduce the level of damage and at least force the enemy to spend excessive resources on offensive forces.[26]

The defence, bolstered by guided missiles, could be expected to gain over the offensive bomber during the coming decade. But soon the offence would be getting its own missiles — ICBMs. Through protection, mobility and dispersal they should be able to survive a surprise attack. The United States could further reduce its vulnerability to surprise attack through dispersal of the Strategic Air Command bases, improving anti-submarine warfare capabilities and reversing the neglect of civil defences. Kissinger saw civil defences as an obvious way of compensating for the deficiencies in active defences. 'A power whose population is protected to some degree by a deep shelter program can run greater risks than an enemy whose people are totally exposed to attack.'[27]

Although all-out war was the only type for which the United States had a doctrine it was now the least likely. Americans had to disabuse themselves of the idea that limited war was an aberration and all-out war the norm or that the real alternatives were either total war or total peace. In practice there were many intermediate stages and it was necessary to be able to operate at each stage. It was no good saying that all-out war could deter all conflicts: 'A deterrent which one is afraid to implement when it is challenged ceases to be a deterrent'.[28] Admittedly what one *might* do could prove as deterring as what one *will* do, but to rely on this would be 'risky and demoralizing' for it requires the enemy to take words more seriously than deeds.[29] In his later works he would take appearances more seriously.

Limited War could take many forms with the limitations deriving from a variety of moral, political and strategic restraints. Physical and geographical restraints, such as those on supply, were being eroded. So were political restraints. Hence, limited wars could proceed as a form of dispute settlement within an agreed international framework; this was less possible in a revolutionary period when the basis of international order was under challenge. It was the fear of all-out war that had put it back on the agenda. Total objectives could still lead to total war, so limited war required limited objectives. Military and political objectives had to be harmonized.[30]

Kissinger's concept of limited war was highly political. He did not discuss it simply in terms of meeting a communist challenge at the level at which it was posed. His concept envisaged the United States upping the ante. Nor was it wholly reactive; it was intended to support political initiatives. He sought power sufficient to defeat the enemy militarily, both in terms of thwarting an assault in Europe and even effecting fundamental strategic change in a favourable direction. However, the basic idea was to increase pressures to punish intransigence: 'In a limited war the problem is to apply graduated amounts of destruction for limited objectives and also to permit the necessary breathing spaces for political contacts.'[31]

Politically it was therefore necessary to create a climate in which survival was not seen to be at stake with each issue and public opinion was prepared for the frustrations and diplomatic activity of limited war. In military terms it was necessary to keep the challenge to the opposition below the threshold which would unleash all-out war. Here was a tension with the suggestion that the application of pressure should be in a sense *disproportionate* to the objectives being pursued in the dispute in order to force a favourable settlement[32] — which at some point must raise the risk of all-out war. Indeed in a passage which anticipates later discussions by such figures as Kahn and Schelling on 'escalation and the manipulation of risk', he writes:

The key problem of present-day strategy is to devise a spectrum of capabilities with which to resist Soviet challenges. These capabilities should enable us to confront the opponent with contingencies from which he can extricate himself *only* by all-out war, while deterring him from this step by a superior retaliatory capacity. Since the most difficult decision for a statesman is whether to risk the national substance by unleashing an all-out war, the psychological advantage will always be on the side of the power which can shift to its opponent the decision to initiate all-out war.[33]

There could be no limited war capability without the threat of massive retaliation. Moreover, the logic of this argument was that the United States needed a palpable *superiority* in limited war capabilities.

Hence the attraction of limited nuclear war for Kissinger. He considered this to be a type of warfare in which the United States would enjoy considerable advantages. He was well aware that it might be easier to draw a line between conventional and nuclear warfare. But conventional war might itself become nuclear (for example with nuclear-tipped air defence missiles); or if the United States was unprepared, the Soviet Union could decide to take the fateful decision. The worst situation would be one in which nuclear weapons were introduced suddenly without prior doctrinal preparations. What he was proposing could not be improvised.

Because limited nuclear warfare would lack the integrity of all-out war American strengths in industrial potential, technological sophistication and general adaptability could be brought to bear. The Soviet advantage in massed manpower would be of less value. He conceded that the army argued that in a nuclear war of battlefield attrition more rather than fewer troops might be needed, but he argued that the Soviet troops would lack the innovativeness and technical competence needed for the sort of limited nuclear warfare that he had in mind.

Certainly limited nuclear warfare as described by Kissinger was complex. He proposed a revolution in tactics to complement the revolution in technology. The leap in thinking required was to understand it in terms of naval rather than traditional land warfare. It would be based on 'small, highly mobile, self-contained units, relying largely on air transport even within the combat zone'. To the extent that the combat units would themselves be small, only small nuclear weapons would be needed to attack them. They would be mobile in order to survive attack and self-contained in order to avoid dependence on supply lines.[34]

This independence from supply lines was critical because it rendered interdiction fruitless. The role of cities as centres of military communications would decline and with it their attraction as military targets. Given the consequences of initiating attacks on cities, they might now be spared completely, so truly limiting the war. The other obvious large targets — air bases — would also become irrelevant as tactical air power became based on vertical take-off aircraft and missiles of ever increasing range.

It would be necessary to establish conventions if wars were to be fought in this way. The Soviet Union should be made to understand that aggression would be met with nuclear weapons if necessary, but unless the level was raised by the Soviet Union these weapons would be of yields of no more than 500 kilotons and would be 'clean' with minimum fallout. Enemy retaliatory forces or cities would not be attacked so long as they were located more than a certain distance behind the battle zone or the initial line of demarcation (say 500 miles). Within that zone cities would still be spared so long as they were declared open and so verified by inspection. The inspectors would be obliged to stay in the zone even during the war to verify compliance.[35]

To gain agreement on such rules to mitigate the horror of war should be the task of negotiators rather than to fret unduly about surprise attack. Kissinger was generally sceptical of arms negotiations but felt that in this case there was a common lack of interest in an all-out war.[36] The allies too would need some persuading, given a tendency to 'identify any explosion of a nuclear weapon with the outbreak of an all-out war'.[37] So completely had they accepted the doctrine of all-out war that they were either busy duplicating American capabilities to fight such a war (as was Britain) or else believed themselves so protected by American nuclear capability that they did not need to do much at all.

Could they be persuaded that limited nuclear war would be a reasonable option? It seemed odd that allies would tolerate preparations for all-out war but not limited war. None the less he recognized that Carte Blanche, the unfortunately named NATO exercise which simulated 'tactical' nuclear use of a sort that would have caused millions of casualties, had created an unfortunate impression that limited nuclear warfare would be total in its implications for Europe yet when threatened would not deter so effectively as all-out war.

The answer was that a nuclear war fought to an appropriate doctrine would not require 300 detonations in 48 hours. The concept of operations would not be to attack every communication centre. What then was the objective? To deny political control by forcing dispersal of forces. Dispersed forces could not establish effective control of another's territory, but if they concentrated in order to control then they would be highly vulnerable. Tactically it might therefore be sufficient to enforce dispersal, but should it be possible to enforce concentration then it became possible to envisage victory.[38]

Kissinger appeared to be arguing for something more than limited nuclear war as an effective defence against Soviet aggression. In his general argument for limited war capabilities as a means of supporting a campaign of pressure and in his occasional descriptions of the strategy of limited nuclear war he suggested that it could support a more assertive approach. A gradual loss of political control would push enemy units back into fixed points where they would become vulnerable. Then the Soviet Union would face the choice between local adjustments and all-out war.

When published, Kissinger's book was largely appreciated as an unusually forceful presentation of the case against dependence on the deterrent threat of massive retaliation. Nobody pretended that it was an easy read — 'a good deal of it is turgid in style and repetitive in content' commented Michael Howard in a generally favourable review.[39] It was appreciated for its comprehensiveness, with informative chapters on the development of NATO's military policies and its strategic thought, and Kissinger's capacity to relate each of the West's dilemmas to each other.

It was written in a combatitive style designed more than most books, even in this generally policy-orientated area, to influence elite thinking. Michael Howard expressed his impatience with Kissinger's 'somewhat naive distress at the clumsy and illogical way in which high policy is formulated and the affairs of the world are run', but that was part of the method. Another part was not to canvass a broad range of alternative options or to be anything less than definite when proposing a course of action. Not surprisingly, given its origins, *Nuclear Weapons and Foreign Policy* was a work of advocacy.

To produce this work Kissinger had managed to assimilate most of the important ideas then developing in the strategic studies community, hinting at some of the concepts (such as the manipulation of risk) that were soon to become central to strategic theory. As a result not all were generous with regard to the praise that Kissinger appeared to be obtaining for their ideas. Bernard Brodie believed Kissinger to have had 'deliberate and petty motives' for not acknowledging Brodie as the source of his ideas.[40] Reviews by other specialists in nuclear strategy were generally critical.[41]

The problem, as noted by Philip Windsor, was that Kissinger was really a generalist yet made his reputation as an expert.[42] Kissinger had no history in operational analysis; his background was philosophy and diplomatic history. His source materials were standard, but in some cases dated (for example, the Symington Hearings of 1955 on air power). In other areas he clearly did not understand the material, and elsewhere there were curious lapses. His material on the effects of nuclear weapons was confined to those in the megaton range and seemed designed to demonstrate the horror of all-out war. However, given the critical importance of limited nuclear operations to his argument the absence of material on weapons in the kiloton range, notably in the low-kiloton range is decidedly odd (500 kilotons is a curiously high yield for weapons to be used for limited operations.) Elsewhere, he was premature with some technological developments — for example vertical take-off aircraft — and then exaggerated their consequences. It has to be said in some areas where he was criticized, for example for being too sanguine over the prospects for a Soviet surprise attack capability, he was correct. However, as we have seen, he was ambiguous on the impact of technological change and in later years he tended to a more alarmist interpretation.

Kissinger was let down by his grasp of military strategy. If he looked to naval weapons as his inspiration for limited nuclear warfare, then this could only be because of a very narrow understanding of land warfare as dominated by static fronts. More seriously, he never really demonstrated how limited nuclear warfare would be conducted in practice.

Kissinger had started off with an interest in foreign policy and nuclear strategy. His first critique of 'massive retaliation', published in 1955, did not involve proposals for limited nuclear war.[43] These ideas developed during the course of the Council working group and were influenced by developing views in the United States' army on this sort of warfare, and in particular by General James Gavin who, in the army with General Maxwell Taylor, was a leading opponent of massive retaliation. Gavin, along with Generals Lemnitzer and Andrew O'Meara and Lieutenant-Colonel William Kintner, was on the Council on Foreign Relations panel.

The army was enthusiastic about the integration of small nuclear weapons into its plans but was still uncertain about their tactical implications. Attempting to operate with static fortified defences seemed foolhardy in the nuclear age as well as debilitating. Gavin stated the challenge to be: 'learning how to control the amorphous mass of men who must be dispersed over an entire zone, an entire tract of land, dispersed thinly enough not to invite bomb blast, yet strongly enough to tackle the enemy.'

The keywords were 'dispersion, flexibility, mobility', but as Bacevich has pointed out, these words took 'on the semblance of mantras, chanted again and again, cherished for their simplicity; but in the end they obscured as much as they enlightened . . . moving from the abstract to the concrete would prove much more elusive'.[44]

Gavin had told the Council Working Group that atomic combat units should be like 'an amorphous biological cell' so that even damage to one part of a division composed of many cellular components would not preclude the rest from fighting on. The existing military organization had to be devolved down to 'the size of units you are not afraid of losing to one (nuclear) blast'.

The army attempted to follow these ideas, developing the Pentomic Division, new weapons such as the *Honest John* and *Corporal*, and even conducted tests, such as *Task Force Razor* in 1955 when American troops opened fire with tank cannon and machine guns half a minute after a 30-kiloton explosion. But this was a demonstration rather than a genuine exercise in which the units involved had adopted positions which would have been wholly impractical in actual combat. As the studies developed, the basic problem that soon emerged was that of combining dispersion with the need to muster sufficient forces to stop an attacker. The solution was to situate battle groups on key terrain, charged with defending it on an essentially independent basis. The objective was to make it impossible for the enemy to control territory by keeping his lines of supply hopelessly vulnerable. The future battle units would be moved backwards while others moved forward, intermingling with enemy units. These ideas were vague as to how much territory would none the less be conceded to the enemy and about the logistic support of one's own units.

By the end of the decade the army had reorganized itself and many of the 'tactical' nuclear weapons had come into service, but the appropriate tactics had not been developed. The evidence of exercises suggested that the units would be hard to sustain in nuclear conditions, with casualties high and morale low, leaders lost and vital supplies contaminated.[45] The Pentomic concept overestimated the potential for mobility and underestimated the requirement for logistical depth. It was soon discarded. Bacevich's comment is harsh:

> Service leaders fashioned a critique of strategic nuclear weapons that was thorough, cogent, and wise. Convinced, nevertheless, that tactical variants of nuclear weapons would be helpful in preserving the Army's legitimacy, these same soldiers rebuilt the Service around missiles and low-yield nuclear weapons and plunged into the ill-conceived, unrealistic Pentomic experiment . . . Service leaders had been stampeded into accepting a cockeyed technological fix without grasping its implications.[46]

This is unfortunately a reasonable criticism of Kissinger's own approach which was very much influenced by these same soldiers. His description of the conduct of a limited nuclear war was not a personal fantasy, but a reflection of army planning. Kissinger's stark presentation of these plans captured their flavour and exposed, unwittingly, the deficiencies which the army was addressing but failed to solve.

There were three obvious objections to a strategy of limited nuclear war. First, the assumption that the combat would predominantly involve nuclear units ignored the obvious possibilities for effective conventional operations against the nuclear units. Second, conventional forces of any strength would need logistic support, and the presumption that the nuclear units could be effectively self-contained and self-sufficient was quite unfounded. Once supply lines had to be established then these lines themselves would become targets. The war would soon spread into the communications networks and cities of the society hosting the battle and become in this way inseparable from all-out war. Third, the picture of nuclear operations as controlled and purposive with their own rules and conventions was wholly unrealistic. Even if there were no supply line to interdict, commanders would not be economical with their nuclear munitions. If the price of failure would be to suffer a nuclear attack from the enemy unit then the pressure would be to ensure that sufficient weapons were used to destroy the target. As Kaufmann caustically noted of Kissinger: 'In his version of warfare, airmen do not get panicky and jettison their bombs, or hit the wrong targets, missiles do not go astray, and heavily populated areas — whether rural or urban — do not suffer thereby. Surely this is wishful thinking.[47]

Kissinger did not retreat immediately from his wishful thinking. In the report he did for the Rockefeller Brothers in 1958 he conveyed the same message of the inadequacy of massive retaliation, the need to prepare for limited nuclear war as well as advocacy of a major programme of civil defence. This was then the fashion and a proposal strongly supported by Nelson Rockefeller. Along with his earlier book there was little evidence of serious consideration of the problems of conventional war, though apparently there had been serious discussion of this issue in the panels.[48]

It was in *Necessity for Choice*, published in 1961, that Kissinger acknowledged the force of many of the criticisms and backed away from his ideas on limited nuclear war.[49] This book was written in the typically gloomy Kissinger style. His starting point (which makes strange reading for those who are now told by Kissinger himself that the 1950s were years of American strength and certainty) was that the previous fifteen years had been years of decline. There was no sense of a let-up in the cold war nor of the weaknesses on the Soviet side such as the developing split with China.

None the less there was a greater tolerance towards allies, the attitude towards arms control was moderating and he now saw a need for negotiations to 'reduce the tensions inherent in an unchecked arms race'.[50] The reasons for this more conciliatory attitude was a respect for the strategic power of the Soviet Union. In one of those embarrassing passages that are shown to be wrong just as they are published, Kissinger took the existence of the 'missile gap' for granted.

The 'missile gap' described the fear, which developed after the Soviet success with Sputnik and early ICBM tests in 1957 and which Khrushchev did very little to discourage, that the Soviet Union was surging ahead in missile production and deployment.[51] Kissinger wrote, as the new Kennedy administration was beginning to make clear that the 'gap' did not exist, that 'there is no dispute about the missile gap as such. It is generally admitted that from 1961 until at least the end of 1964 the Soviet Union will possess more missiles than the United States.'[52] In fact, by late 1961 it was apparent that if there was a missile gap, at least in strategic nuclear forces, it favoured the United States. Kissinger's pessimism influenced the overall tone of the book. The missile gap confirmed to him the declining utility of all-out war as an instrument of policy and encouraged the developing pre-occupation with issues related to stability.

The critical question was whether the missile gap would turn into a 'deterrent gap'. This depended as much on how matters appeared to the Soviet Union as on any evaluation of comparative capabilities. He described deterrence at one point as depending on a 'combination of power, the will to use it, and assessment of these by the potential aggressor'. However, he was now giving most weight to the 'state of mind of the potential aggressor' which meant that in the end it was 'psychological criteria' that were most important. Such was his understanding of the cold war that he suggested that a shift in the understanding of the military relationship could soon undermine deterrence: 'if the gains of aggression *appear* to outweigh the penalties even *once*, deterrence will fail'. Perhaps the Soviet threshold for unacceptable damage would be higher than that for the United States. A status quo power would not take advantage of its strategic superiority, but for a power opposed to the status quo the pressure to take advantage of superiority could be overwhelming. Moreover, perceptions are volatile because technology is so volatile, . . . the 'truths of one year become the perils of another'.[53]

Kissinger now accepted the view that had been most publicly developed by Albert Wohlstetter: that the balance of terror was 'delicate'.[54] He confessed that he had been too complacent in his earlier writings with regard to strategic nuclear stalemate. He had previously assumed that stalemate would result naturally from an age of nuclear plenty and had not forseen that 'for an interim period at least, the strategic advantage' would be with the 'offensive'.[55] Stability would have to be achieved through 'invulnerability not numbers'.

The missile gap meant that the Soviet Union would be best able to take advantage of this new technology. The resultant vulnerability might paralyse the United States. In this way the missile gap could turn into a deterrent gap in that the United States would no longer be able to deter the threat of all-out war from the Soviet Union. At best, the United States could no longer use the threat of all-out war to deter more limited forms of Soviet aggression.[56]

Ideally, the status quo power would be invulnerable and the potential aggressor vulnerable. To accept a condition of mutual invulnerability (in strategic retaliatory forces) would be to ease the calculations of a potential aggressor. He saw problems with policies based on either counterforce or finite deterrence:

A counterforce strategy is nearly impossible technically and equally complex psychologically. On the other hand, finite deterrence as a deliberate military policy may be an invitation to local pressures. If not coupled with a dramatic build-up of local forces, it will expose the free world to constant pressure and blackmail.

The awkward compromise was for a retaliatory force that retained some counter-force capacity. If nothing else this might suffice to deter a campaign of attrition against the retaliatory force itself.

What then of Kissinger's previous proposals for solving the dilemma by preparing for limited nuclear war? He still believed in the validity of limited-war theory, and indeed the bulk of the relevant chapter of *Necessity for Choice* is a vigorous defence of this theory. Limited war might pose less of a threat to an aggressor than all-out war, but any loss in deterrent effect was compensated for by the certainty of the response. There was a risk of 'escalation' — 'the adding of increments of power until limited war insensibly merges into all-out war'.[57] The challenge for a strategy of limited war was to provide 'an opportunity for a settlement before the automatism of the retaliatory forces takes over'.[58] Precisely because of the danger of escalation, limited war might succeed. Both sides would be aware of the dangers of employing all the uncommitted military resources at their disposal.

The criteria for limited-war capabilities must be that they could prevent the aggressor from achieving a *fait accompli*, create a risk but not the inevitability of all-out war and be coupled with a diplomacy that allowed for a settlement short of unconditional surrender.[59] Borrowing explicitly from Tom Schelling, Kissinger suggested that the problem was one of ensuring that the limitations were well understood by both sides and could stick.

Would it be possible to fight a limited war with nuclear weapons and still meet these objectives? The spectre of nuclear war was now with us and would inevitably influence military planning in some ways. Furthermore, the choice as to whether or not to go nuclear was no longer simply up to the United States. There remained powerful arguments in favour of a nuclear strategy: nuclear weapons were still the West's 'best weapons' and could serve as a substitute for the levels of manpower which the East enjoyed but the West could not afford; they would force an aggressor to disperse his forces and introduce complexity and uncertainty into all his calculations; by relying on small, self-contained military units of high mobility (of the sort he had advocated in 1957) damage need not be excessive.[60]

Against this, proponents of conventional strategy insisted that any use of nuclear weapons would lead to the 'desolation of the combat zone and the decimation of the population'. There could be no restraints. The attempts to distinguish between different types of nuclear explosives, for example on the basis of yield, would be extraordinarily difficult. He summarized the arguments used against his own proposals of a few years earlier. There would still be an advantage in strong conventional forces — to harrass and raid the nuclear units and to cope with the high rates of attrition. Furthermore, because superior industrial capacity need not in the end manifest itself in superior nuclear capability, it was not self-evident that such a strategy would favour the West. A conventional strategy would allow the West to exploit fully its industrial capacity, hold a line against aggression and put the onus for any resort to nuclear weapons on the communist states.[61]

Kissinger questioned the dogmatism with which these arguments were put but also noted that, from the different perspectives, both sides might be right. The question was which should be stressed:

deterrence or the strategy for fighting a war. Obviously an overemphasis on destructiveness may paralyze the will. But an overconcern with developing a tolerable strategy for the conduct of war may reduce the risks of aggression to such a degree that it will be encouraged. While the deterrent threat must be credible, the quest for credibility must not lower the penalties to a point where they are no

Lawrence Freedman

longer unacceptable. A course of action that increases the opponent's uncertainties about the nature of the conflict will generally discourage aggression. If war should break out, however, through accident or miscalculation, it may make limitation extremely difficult.[62]

This is a concise statement of the dilemmas that became familiar to all students of alliance strategy over the coming decades.

Kissinger now decided that the balance had to swing away from the nuclear towards the conventional. He was discouraged by the marked lack of consensus within the American military establishment and in the alliance with regard to nuclear strategy. It was clear that limitations would be far harder to establish with nuclear weapons than with conventional weapons: the dividing line between conventional and nuclear was understood and therefore possible to maintain; that would be far harder with any distinction along the spectrum of nuclear weapons. For better or worse, nuclear weapons had now been stigmatized in arms-control negotiations and that would reinforce the reluctance to make them a centrepiece of strategy. Long-range missiles were further complicating the calculations; they could influence the outcome of hostilities within the combat zone yet could not be neutralized except by extending the combat zone. There were no technical reasons why conventional forces could not be built up to cope with those of the Soviet Union.[63]

It would still be necessary to maintain some capacity to fight limited nuclear war if only because the Soviet Union might attempt to fight in that manner. Nor would it be wise to move to a declared no-first-use of nuclear weapon's policy as this would ease the aggressor's calculations excessively. But a readiness to prepare for conventional war had important implications for military planning. It would not be possible to rely on the mobilization of industry once war had started to build up conventional forces: it would be necessary to maintain higher levels of conventional forces. The nuclear components of the force structure should be clearly distinguished from the conventional. If the forces were dual purpose then it would prove impossible to sustain any limitations. If nuclear weapons were to be weapons of last resort, then the definition of what constitutes the last resort should be the responsibility of a centralized command. If the military establishment accepted that it would no longer be built around nuclear weapons, then the current arms control themes could be reinforced. It was however now necessary to 'accept the paradox that the best road to nuclear arms control may be conventional rearmament'.[64]

While this may have been the developing consensus among the American strategic studies' community at the start of the 1960s it was not the consensus within the alliance. The arguments within NATO over the proper balance between conventional and nuclear forces became as dogmatic as he feared, and the resultant doctrine as confused. Kissinger's interest in trying to provide a coherent strategy dwindled as he became increasingly aware of the practical and political difficulties facing any attempt to gain agreement. By 1965, in *The Troubled Partnership*, he was noting the tension between an American approach based on technical competence and analytical precision and European judgements based on politics and psychology.[65] The Europeans saw the American military establishment on the continent in political terms, as a symbol of commitment, while the Americans still wrestled with its military utility. His own discussion of the problem is much more politically sensitive than previously. There is greater emphasis on the problems of the control of nuclear weapons in crisis and war and how this can effect the sensibilities of allies. Of course, it would have been surprising if Kissinger had not addressed these issues as they had been so central to the NATO debates: however, unlike many of his American colleagues he understood the European concerns.

He now put even more emphasis on the psychological aspects of deterrence: 'It depends on the aggressor's assessment of risks, not the defender's. A threat meant as a bluff but taken seriously is more useful for purposes of deterrence than a "genuine" threat interpreted as a bluff.'[66]

Again we find Kissinger accepting the strategic consensus building up around him — this time in relation to the declining value of a counter-force capability. The mobility and hardening of long-range missiles 'magnify the force required for a successful counterforce "disarming" strike'.[67] There was now a substantial force of tactical nuclear weapons based in Europe, that were seen by the Europeans to be politically important even though they lacked a clear military mission. They were also vulnerable to pre-emptive attack. It was clear that NATO would not build up conventional forces sufficient to match those of the Soviet Union, yet the likely resort to tactical nuclear systems in desperate circumstances might only encourage pre-emption. He therefore returned to limited nuclear war. However, he no longer had confidence in the prospect of self-contained units fighting around the combat zone. Now there was to be some uneasy balance: the conventional forces at the front should be organized to cope with a full-scale attack in the hope of holding it back or at least preventing sudden seizures of territory and providing a means of determining the extent and location of the attack. Behind this conventional screen there would be nuclear forces, deployed so as to reduce the incentives for pre-emption. These forces would be linked with the strategic nuclear forces and not separate from it — in the first instance they would try to prevent an initial onslaught succeeding but must then threaten punishment to force the aggressor into negotiations.[68] Kissinger is now caught in all the familiar paradoxes of NATO strategy. He ends up with a slightly more systematic version of flexible response, but the concept is not dissimilar; in operational terms it is no more satisfactory.

His approach to strategy was becoming more jaundiced. He concluded his contribution to the *festchrift* for Basil Liddell Hart, which summarized many of the arguments found in *The Trouble Partnership*, by reviewing the changes of the previous decade:

> when strategy first attracted the attention of academic analysts, the inconsistency between traditional modes of thought and the nature of modern weapons was obvious. As long as an analysis was systematic, it was likely to uncover discrepancies and weaknesses that needed correction.

The trends in strategic analysis during the 1960s had left him unimpressed:

> Skill in quantitative analysis may down-grade those factors which cannot be quantified. A complex strategic theory may be so intellectually satisfying that the difficulties of its employment by human beings in moments of great tension and confusion may be overlooked. It may be tempting to treat allies as factors of a security arrangement and to forget that their ultimate contribution depends on many intangibles of political will.[69]

Like others with a background in philosophy and history, Kissinger was ill at ease with a study of strategy influenced more by economics and engineering. Moreover, with the international system now settling down there was no pressure to come up with new concepts and formulations.

His views on nuclear strategy published on the eve of joining the Nixon administration in 1969 reflect none of the convictions of a decade earlier. The themes were now familiar: the great power of nuclear weapons could not be translated into policy except when it came to preventing direct challenges to survival; the difficulty in establishing a stable balance of power is accentuated by the regular 'five-yearly' upheavals in weapons technology; for political purposes, the meaningful measurement of military strength is the assessment by the other side; these psychological criteria are difficult to meet because of the internal divisiveness of security issues which result in the wrong impression being conveyed; the measures for actually signalling a willingness to use force are limited by both the high state of readiness in which forces are maintained (there is little scope for ostentatious preparations) and the danger of appearing too provocative. The perplexing nature of the strategic position encouraged an interest in arms control, but unless terms like 'superiority' and 'stability' could be given an operational meaning then there would be a lack of criteria by which to judge the progress of negotiations.

Kissinger raised these points in a series of increasingly open-ended questions. If there was no clear relationship between nuclear power and policy, and no operational nuclear strategy could be found which promised a credible reinforcement of diplomatic activity, then that was to suggest the strategic irrelevance of nuclear weapons to everyday diplomacy. But what then of alliance commitments predicated on a willingness to use nuclear weapons on behalf of other countries?[70]

Kissinger lacked any clear agenda for nuclear strategy when he arrived in the White House as Nixon's special assistant for national security affairs. His main preoccupation in this area was the arms control negotiations with the Soviet Union. The SALT negotiations, which began in November 1969, involved him becoming immersed in the details of the weapons inventories of the two sides and making broad judgements with regard to the balance of American strategic interests. However, the value of arms control — as with nuclear strategy — was judged by Kissinger in terms of overall foreign policy objectives, in this case the need to sort out relations with the Soviet Union. Hence the emphasis on 'linkage'. Arms control was part of a much larger game, with the prize as much the extrication of the United States from Vietnam as a stable military balance.

Those who worked on the SALT delegation in the early 1970s have written with some bitterness of Kissinger's insistence on keeping close control of the negotiations, even when it meant keeping responsible officials in the dark, and his occasional incompetence with the details.[71] Because of the focus of this chapter, the intricacies of the negotiations on SALT will be left unexplored. Rather we will concentrate on the influence Kissinger had on nuclear strategy itself during his years in office.

By and large Kissinger's approach in office was consistent with the general lines of his thinking during the 1960s. Although one must treat with care Kissinger's memoirs when describing his views in office, the elements of continuity with his earlier thinking give them a degree of plausibility. In the relevant section in *Years of Upheaval* we find the familiar thought that the 'momentous increase in the element of power' had none the less eroded the traditional relationship of military power to foreign policy because an 'all-out strategic nuclear exchange would risk civilized life as we know it'.

The strategic arsenals of the two sides find their principal purpose in matching and deterring the forces of the opponent and in making certain that third countries perceive no inequality. In no postwar crisis has an American President come close to considering the use of strategic nuclear weapons. There was, in short, no more urgent task for American defense policy than to increase substantially the capacity for local resistance.[72]

'Technology tended toward parity in any case'. Therefore, Kissinger saw benefit if arms control was allowed to 'stabilize the strategic race and free resources for building up our conventional and regional forces, where clear and present imbalances existed'.[73] He claimed at the time of the signing of the SALT I accords in 1972 that this did demonstrate 'a certain commonality of outlook, a sort of interdependence for survival between the two of us . . . both we and the Soviet Union have begun to find that each increment of power does not represent an increment of usable political strength'.[74] One of his most celebrated outbursts — quoted at the start of this essay — 'What in the name of God is superiority?'[75] clearly reflected a consistent impatience with the acquisition of strategic military power for its own sake.

Less often quoted than his rhetorical question on the meaning of superiority were the lines that came after: 'If we have not reached an agreement well before 1977 . . . you will see an explosion of technology and an explosion of numbers . . . a world which will be extraordinarily complex, in which opportunities for warfare exist that were unimaginable 15 years ago.' This concern, along with much of the new thinking on nuclear strategy during the 1970s, was dominated by the impact of multiple, accurate warheads on long-range warheads — the process known as MIRVing. Kissinger quotes in his memoirs a comment made at a meeting of the Verification Panel responsible for the formulation of SALT policy:

> Equal MIRVs with equal numbers would give the first striker a great advantage. It would be only a cosmetic equivalence, not real. It would put a premium on striking first. It may be unavoidable, but if you have five times as many warheads as missiles, and your aiming points are fewer than your missiles, it puts a premium on the first strike. That creates a massive element of instability.[76]

The trouble with this analysis was that it made no allowances for the submarine and bomber forces which would still be able to retaliate even after a first strike against ICBMs. This theme of ICBM vulnerability is one that dominated American strategic debate during the 1970s.[77] Again Kissinger was picking up on ideas that were around him, without subjecting them to the critical analysis they deserved.

His belated recognition of the significance of MIRVing was the occasion for another one of his confessions which came at a press briefing in 1974: 'I would say in retrospect that I wish I had thought about the implications of a MIRVed world more thoughtfully in 1969 and 1974 than I did.'[78] One of the notable failures of SALT I was that it failed to come to terms with MIRVing. This was largely because Kissinger calculated that the American national security apparatus could cope with the loss of anti-ballistic missiles or MIRVs but not both, and ABMs seemed to offer the most fruitful possibilities for useful agreement. It was not the case that Kissinger was unaware of these issues. He had been fully briefed by a group of former academic colleagues who met regularly with him during his early months in the White House and encouraged him to take action on MIRVs.[79] Indeed one of the points he had listed in 1968 as part of the agenda for the nation was 'the implications (both political and military) of new developments such as MIRV . . . and ballistic missile defenses'.[80]

He argued in *Years of Upheaval*, after explaining the limits of military power, that none the less the democracies should have maintained for as long as possible a counterforce capability, that is, a capacity to threaten the Soviet land-based missiles — the backbone of Soviet strategic forces. So long as the Soviets had to fear a counterforce attack in response to local aggression, their inhibition against such adventures would be considerable.[81]

Yet before taking office he had been pessimistic about the prospects for retaining counterforce capabilities and even here acknowledged that the main thrust of his argument supported pessimism. During his period in office he did attempt to find some means of using the new capabilities of nuclear weapons for precision attacks to find some way out of the dilemmas of assured destruction. He described 'Assured Destruction' as 'one of those theories that sound impressive in an academic seminar but are horribly unworkable for a decision-maker in the real world and lead to catastrophe if they are ever implemented'. The description was in some ways curious because he was in his own way one of the first academics to come to terms with the implications of assured destruction for the conduct of foreign policy. What he appears to have been objecting to was the fact that the theory apparently required the United States to welcome its own vulnerability and also that a policy based on the 'mass extermination of individuals' was not one that could be implemented should deterrence fail. If there were limited strikes by the Soviet Union then the American president would be obliged to confront the terrible choice of surrender or upping the ante so much in his retaliation that the result would be suicidal.[82]

The first manifestation of these concerns was a rhetorical question, drafted by Kissinger, and found in President Nixon's first foreign policy report. 'Should a President, in the event of a nuclear attack, be left with the single option of ordering the mass destruction of enemy civilians, in the face of the certainty that it would be followed by the mass slaughter of Americans?'[83]

The question was rhetorical because there was more than one option. Kissinger reports a conversation with Robert McNamara when he entered office. McNamara told him that he had tried for seven years to give the president more options, but then had given up in the face of bureaucratic opposition and decided to improvise. Kissinger was determined to do better, but conceded that his success was partial.[84] He describes opposition from civilian planners worried about the extra forces required for extra options, while the service chiefs were worried about being required to meet requirements established by civilian analysts and 'deeply suspicious of any doctrinal formulation that later might interfere with their procurement decisions'.

However, the problems were not solely bureaucratic. It was also conceptually difficult to formulate options of the sort required. The studies that Kissinger set in motion with his National Security Council staff soon demonstrated that superiority was unobtainable and that a shift away from assured destruction to a defence-dominated assured survival was impractical. He came up with the idea of criteria for 'strategic sufficiency', which he claims related strategic planning to military as well as civilian targets, providing 'at least the theoretical capability to use force for objectives other than the mass extermination of populations'.[85]

It proved difficult to translate the doctrinal innovations into operational plans. In the summer of 1973 the NSC staff took over a study, then virtually complete, which had been underway at the Pentagon, headed by John Foster, director of defense research and engineering. This study was influenced by many of the people who had been working at RAND on counterforce options for some time and had participated in some of the early efforts in McNamara's time to incorporate these options into the SIOP (Single Integrated Operational Plan). The result was National Security Decision Memorandum 242 which was completed in the fall of 1973. NSDM 242 assumed the need for a flexible nuclear posture. In the event of conflict the goal would be to 'seek early war termination on terms acceptable to the United States and its allies, at the lowest level of conflict feasible'. This required a range of employment options to be used in conjunction with other political and military measures to 'control escalation'. They would involve selective strikes against targets such as command and control centres or ICBM silos. The options must enable the United States at the same time to communicate determination to resist aggression as well as a desire to exercise restraint. This could be achieved by: '(a) holding some vital enemy targets hostage to subsequent destruction by survivable nuclear forces, and (b) permitting control over the timing and pace of attack execution, in order to provide the enemy opportunities to reconsider his actions'.[86]

Kissinger and his staff were less than convinced by NSDM 242. However much he accepted the theory, Kissinger remained unimpressed with the options actually available. A case in point was a study required of the joint chiefs of staff in early 1974 of the options the president might utilize in the event of a Soviet invasion of Iran. Option one was to fire 200 nuclear weapons at military targets in the southern region of the Soviet Union. This did not seem very limited to Kissinger and he told the military to come back with something smaller. Option two focused on the two roads linking the Soviet Union with Iran: an atomic demolition mine would be dropped on one, and two nuclear weapons would be fired at the other. This was too limited — the United States would take the terrible risks of going to war and then use only two weapons.[87]

James Schlesinger, who was enthusiastic about NSDM 242 and had participated in the work leading up to its formulation, became secretary of defense in July 1973. In January 1974, irritated by foot-dragging by Kissinger's staff, he went public with the new strategy. On 17 January 1974 Nixon signed NSDM 242.[88] The passages in Kissinger's memoires concerning the attempt to develop a strategy for tactical nuclear weapons convey an even more profound sense of hopelessness when it comes to turning doctrinal innovations into operational policy.[89]

Since leaving office Kissinger has given no evidence that he has successfully resolved the dilemmas with which he has been wrestling since the mid-1950s. He has made many comments on strategic affairs since January 1977, but only two need command our attention. These both received widespread publicity. The first was his testimony during the SALT II hearings of late 1979; the second a talk to a conference on the future of NATO at about the same time.[90]

In his testimony on SALT Kissinger was concerned to explain the new conditions which would allow him to support the ratification of a treaty that he himself had begun to negotiate. His approach was consistent with his long-standing attempts to link arms control with global political developments. It also reflected his long-standing tendency to draw large conclusions from developments within the strategic balance that he did not fully understand.

The key shift in the strategic balance that worried him was the strengthening of Soviet counterforce capabilities while the United States had failed to improve its own comparable capabilities. In a passage reminiscent of his equally confident and equally overstated prediction of 1960 with regard to the missile gap (a time which he now interpreted was one of great strength and confidence), Kissinger warned:

there is now general agreement that their improvements in missile accuracy and warhead technology will put the Soviets in a position to wipe out our land-based forces of Minuteman ICBMs by 1982. Whether this capability is ever exercised or not — and I consider it improbable — it reverses and hence revolutionizes the strategic equation on which our security and that of our friends has depended through most of the postwar period.[91]

His condition therefore for supporting SALT II was the improvement of American counterforce capabilities; then apparently everything would be fine. But if this was not done he predicted something dire. The continuing reassurances demanded by America's allies of an 'undiminished American military commitment' could no longer be sustained: 'if my analysis is correct we must face the fact that it is absurd in the 1980s to base the strategy of the West on the credibility of a threat of mutual suicide'.[92]

Of course in the 1980s matters turned out to be more complex than such simplistic arguments could have ever anticipated. These remarks however, do capture the essence of Kissinger's approach to nuclear strategy. He was one of the first to identify the contradiction at the heart of a strategy of nuclear deterrence. He has continued to argue that this contradiction will have terrible effects on American foreign policy and continued to examine new means of lessening this contradiction. But temporary strategic fashions have never managed to cope with the permanent dilemmas. In the meantime the past three decades have hardly been a calm period in American foreign policy. None the less, it is hard to lay the blame for the problems that have arisen at the feet of nuclear strategy. The prospect of assured destruction has cautioned policymakers without causing them to worry unduly about whether doctrines based on this prospect might turn out in the end to be so much bluff. Those like Kissinger who find it difficult to cope with the uncertainties produced by the contradictions of deterrence have failed to find means of resolving them other than placing less reliance on nuclear deterrence. Fortunately their efforts are less important than they would like to believe. Whatever he may have thought up to 1968, the experience of eight years in office ought to have persuaded Kissinger that the working of the international system involves rather more than the credibility of America's nuclear threats.

Notes

1. Dan Caldwell (ed.), *Henry Kissinger: His Personality and Policies*, Durham, Duke Press Policy Studies, 1983.
2. Henry Kissinger, *The White House Years*, Boston Little Brown & Co, 1979; *Years of Upheaval*, Boston, Little Brown & Co., 1982.
3. Seymour Hersh, *The Price of Power: Kissinger in the Nixon White House*, New York: Summit Books, 1983. Raymond Garthoff's analysis of the rise and fall of *détente* which at times reads like an extended rebuttal of Kissinger's memoirs, though of course it covers much else, weighs in at 1,147 pages. *Detente and Confrontation: American-Soviet Relations from Nixon to Reagan*, Washington DC, Brookings Institution, 1985.
4. Marvin and Bernard Kalb, *Kissinger*, Boston, Little Brown & Co, 1974.
5. John Newhouse, *Cold Dawn: The Story of SALT*, New York, Holt, Rinehart & Winston, 1973. Kissinger's efforts are described in Hersh, op. cit., p. 530.
6. Peter Dickson, *Kissinger and the Meaning of History*, Cambridge, Cambridge University Press, 1978, p. 33. This book contains one of the most alarming footnotes I have ever come across: 'The parallel between Kissinger's anthropocentric philosophy of history and Heidegger's *Existenzphilosophie* is so striking that it would take a separate book to treat the subject properly', (p. 177).
7. The original title of the thesis was 'Peace, Legitimacy, and the Equilibrium: A Study of the Statesmanship of Castlereach and Metternich', submitted to Harvard University, 1954. It was published as, *A World Restored: Castlereach, Metternich, and the Restoration of Peace, 1812-1822*, Boston, Houghton Mifflin, 1957.

8. A good example is found in the second chapter of Robert S. Lutwak, *Detente and the Nixon Doctrine: American Foreign Policy and the Pursuit of Stability, 1969–1976* Cambridge: Cambridge University Press, 1984. See also Bruce Mazlish, *Kissinger: The European Mind in American Policy*. New York Basic Books, 1976; H. Starr, *A World Perceived: Henry Kissinger's Images of International Politics*, Lexington, University of Kentucky Press, 1983; Caldwell, op. cit., footnote 1.

9. For biographical background on Kissinger see David Landau, *Kissinger: The Uses of Power*, New York, Houghton Mifflin, 1972; Bernard and Marvin Kalb, Kissinger, op. cit., Dana Ward, 'Kissinger: A Psychohistory' and other essays in Dan Caldwell, op. cit.

10. Report of the Rockefeller Brothers' Fund Special Studies Project, *Foreign Economic Policy for the Twentieth Century*, New York, Doubleday, 1958.

11. Henry Kissinger, *The Necessity for Choice: Prospects for American Foreign Policy*, New York, Harper & Row, 1961.

12. Henry Kissinger, *The Troubled Partnership: A Reappraisal of the Atlantic Alliance*, New York, McGraw Hill, 1965.

13. For an early exploration of this question see 'The policy maker and the intellectual', *The Reporter*, 5 March 1959. This was republished in *Necessity for Choice*.

14. For a sample see Henry Kissinger, *For the Record: Selected Statements, 1977–1980*, London: Wiedenfeld & Nicholson and Michael Joseph, 1981.

15. *Nuclear Weapons and Foreign Policy*, p. 4.

16. Ibid., p. 7. He attributed this aphorism to Colonel George Lincoln. In later works he used it without attribution.

17. Ibid., p. 12.

18. Ibid., p. 45.

19. Ibid., p. 54.

20. Kissinger's phrase to describe the vital essence of a society that would be put at risk by nuclear bombardment. Ibid., p. 56.

21. Ibid., p. 89.

22. Ibid., p. 143.

23. Ibid., p. 97.

24. Ibid., p. 104.

25. Ibid., p. 129.

26. Ibid., p. 105. But there was no discussion of the relative cost effectiveness of the offence and the defence.

27. Ibid., p. 112.

28. Ibid., p. 134.

29. Ibid., p. 135.

30. Kissinger was one of a group of authors proposing a stress on limited war as an alternative to massive retaliation. This group is discussed in my *Evolution of Nuclear Strategy*, London: Macmillan, 1981, Section 3. The major study of this period was Robert Osgood, *Limited War: The Challenge to American Strategy*, Chicago: University of Chicago Press, 1957. For a review of the literature see Morton Halperin, *Limited War in the Nuclear Age*, New York, John Wiley and Sons, 1963.

31. Ibid., pp. 156–7.

32. The purpose of limited war is to 'inflict losses or pose risks for the enemy out of proportion to the objectives under dispute'. Ibid., p. 145.

33. Ibid., p. 144.

34. Ibid., p. 180.

35. Ibid., p. 231–2.

36. Ibid., p. 205.

37. Ibid., p. 271.

38. Ibid., p. 309.

39. Michael Howard, 'Foreign Policy in the Nuclear Age', *The Listener*, 3 October 1957.

40. Brodie to Max Ascoli, 6 September 1957, Box 1, Bernard Brodie MSS, UCLA, quoted in Gregg Herken, *Counsels of War*, New York, Alfred A. Knopf, 1985. Herken, for some reason,

believes that Kissinger was providing 'an intellectual justification for the Eisenhower Administration's nuclear strategy of massive retaliation' (p. 99). It was the opposite.

41. The most important were Paul Nitze, 'Limited War or Massive Retaliation', *Reporter*, 1 September 1957 (over which, according to Herken, Kissinger was ready to sue); William Kaufmann 'The Crisis in Military Affairs', *World Politics*, July 1958, and James King 'Limited Defense' and 'Limited Annihilation?', *New Republic* July 1957 and 15 July 1957. The annotated bibliography at the end of *Nuclear Weapons and Foreign Policy* tends to condescension.

42. Philip Windsor 'Henry Kissinger's Scholarly Contribution', *British Journal of International Studies*, **1**, 1 April 1975, p. 27.

43. Henry Kissinger, 'Military Policy and Defense of the "Grey Areas",' *Foreign Affairs*, April 1955 pp. 416–28.

44. A. J. Bacevich, *The Pentomic Era: The US Army Between Korea and Vietnam*, Washington DC, National Defense University Press, 1986, p. 70.

45. T. N. Dupuy, 'Can America fight a limited nuclear war', *Orbis*, **1**, Spring 1961.

46. Bacevich, op. cit., p. 150.

47. Kaufmann, op. cit., p. 59.

48. Landau, op. cit., p. 55.

49. Henry Kissinger, *The Necessity for Choice: Prospects of American Foreign Policy*, New York, Harper & Row, 1981. The revision of Kissinger's ideas on limited nuclear war was first published as 'Limited War: Conventional or Nuclear?' in 1960 in *Daedalus*, 89, no. 4. This was part of the collection published in early 1961 by Don Brennan (ed.), *Arms Control, Disarmament and National Security*, New York, George Braxiller, 1961.

50. *Necessity for Choice*, p.7.

51. For background on the origins of the missile gap and its eventual demise see Lawrence Freedman, *US Intelligence and the Soviet Strategic Threat*, London, Macmillan, 2nd ed., 1986.

52. *Necessity for Choice*, p. 15.

53. Ibid., pp. 12–14, 17.

54. Albert Wohlstetter, 'The Delicate Balance of Terror', *Foreign Affairs*, January 1959.

55. *The Necessity for Choice*, p. 18.

56. Ibid., p. 16.

57. Ibid., p. 59. On the origin of the concept of escalation and 'its influence on the strategic thought of this time see Lawrence Freedman, 'On the Tiger's Back: The Development of the Concept of Escalation' in Roman Kolkowicz (ed.), *The Logic of Nuclear Terror*, Boston, Allen & Unwin, 1987.

58. Ibid., pp. 59–60.

59. Ibid., p. 65.

60. Ibid., pp. 76–77.

61. Ibid., pp. 78–79.

62. Ibid., p. 81.

63. Ibid., pp. 81–6.

64. Ibid., p. 93.

65. *The Troubled partnership*, p. 93.

66. Ibid., p. 19.

67. Ibid., p. 109.

68. Ibid., pp. 181–4.

69. Henry Kissinger, 'American Strategic Doctrine and Diplomacy', in Michael Howard (ed.), *The Theory and Practice of War*, New York, Praeger, 1966, p. 291. Many of the paragraphs from this piece are found in the introduction and conclusion to the book on nuclear strategy Kissinger edited at this time. Henry Kissinger, *Problems of National Strategy*, New York, Praeger, 1965).

70. Henry Kissinger, *American Foreign Policy: Three Essays*, London, Weidenfeld & Nicholson, 1969, pp. 59–64. The relevant essay had first been published in *Agenda for the Nation*, Washington DC, The Brookings Institution, 1968.

71. In particular see Garthoff, op. cit., Gerard Smith, *Double Talk: The Story of SALT I*, Lanham, Maryland, University Press of America, 1980.

72. *Years of Upheaval*, pp. 999–1000.
73. Ibid., p. 1010.
74. Senate Foreign Relations Committee, *Strategic Arms Limitation Talks*, Washington DC, United States Government Printing Office, 1972, pp. 394–5.
75. Secretary of State Henry Kissinger, Press Conference of 3 July 1974. Richard Betts has noted that later he apparently repudiated this remark, claiming that it was due to 'fatigue and exasperation, not analysis'. US Senate Committee on Foreign Relations, *Hearings: The SALT II Treaty*, 96th Congress, 1st session, Part 3 (1979). Cited in Richard Betts, 'Elusive Equivalence' in Samuel P. Huntington (ed.), *The Strategic Imperative*, Cambridge, Mass., Ballinger, 1982. However, in his memoirs Kissinger did not repudiate the question but suggested that it was still relevant. *Years of Upheaval*, p. 1,029. As we have seen it was not out of step with his earlier views.
76. *Years of Upheaval*, p. 270.
77. For background see *Evolution of Nuclear Strategy*, chapter 25.
78. *Transcript of Secretary Henry Kissinger's Background Press Briefing*, 3 December 1974.
79. See Hersh, *The Price of Power*, pp. 147–56.
80. *American Foreign Policy: Three Essays*, p. 64.
81. *Years of Upheaval*, p. 999.
82. *The White House Years*, p. 216.
83. Richard M. Nixon, *United States Foreign Policy for the 1970s*, Washington DC, United States Government Printing Office, 18 February, 1970, pp. 54–5.
84. *The White House Years*, p. 217. Herken has McNamara's side of the story. McNamara is said to have told Kissinger that matters were not as bad as they seemed because it was possible to carry out selectively a portion of the plan, and there were five major options. He also warned that the SIOP provided an inappropriate response to a conventional invasion of Europe. According to Herken, Kissinger conceded to McNamara on leaving office that he had not made the SIOP any more appropriate. Herken, op. cit., p. 267.
85. *White House Years*, p. 217. Others were less sure. Deputy Secretary of Defence David Packard, when asked to clarify the meaning of 'sufficiency' replied: 'It means that it's a good word to use in a speech. Beyond that it doesn't mean a God-damned thing'. Quoted in Desmond Ball, *Deja Vu: The Return to Counterforce in the Nixon Administration*, California Seminar on Arms Control and Foreign Policy, 1974, p. 8.
86. Fred Kaplan, *The Wizards of Armageddon*, New York, Simon and Schuster, 1983, pp. 364–70.
87. Ibid., pp. 372–3.
88. See Lynn Etheridge Davis, *Limited Nuclear Options: Deterrence and the New American Doctrine*, London: International Institute for Strategic Studies, 1976; and Ball, op. cit.
89. *The White House Years*, pp. 218–20.
90. Both are reproduced in *For the Record*.
91. Ibid., p. 197.
92. Ibid., p. 239.

5 THOMAS SCHELLING

Phil Williams

The contribution made by Thomas Schelling to nuclear strategy was both immense and unique. Schelling brought to the subject a subtlety and sophistication which were rarely equalled let alone surpassed by other strategists. His work had a rare combination of rigour and imagination, and the contribution that he made to the understanding of deterrence, coercion and arms control was highly distinctive and of major importance. This is not to deny that some of Schelling's analyses were controversial, nor is it to argue that all his ideas were compelling or persuasive. The emphasis on the formalities of strategic logic and the sheer brilliance of many of Schelling's insights sometimes obscured fundamental political realities. Indeed, critics would argue that Schelling engaged in cerebral exercises in violence that were so elaborate that they overlooked practical constraints. Part of the reason for this was that Schelling was an intuitive rather than an empirical strategist, with a background in economics rather than history or political science. As a result he was perhaps overly dependent on models of rational decisionmaking and insufficiently attuned to the impact of the cultural or political context within which strategic decisions are often made. Yet, Schelling's legacy of insights and ideas into strategy is formidable. And even though it is possible to dissent from many of his arguments, it is impossible to deny the richness of his insights or the significance of his contribution. In view of this, the present chapter sets out to do three things. First, it outlines the assumptions which Schelling brought to the study of strategy — assumptions which were made explicit in *The Strategy of Conflict*. Second, it elucidates some of the key themes in Schelling's analysis of nuclear strategy and arms control — themes that were developed in *Arms and Influence* and in a co-authored book with Morton Halperin entitled *Strategy and Arms Control*. Finally it offers a critique and evaluation of Schelling's ideas and arguments.

The underlying assumptions

Schelling's contribution to strategic analysis reflected his background in economics. This was evident both in his highly formal approach to strategy and in his use of examples from economic life, whether competition between firms or disputes between management and labour. Schelling, in effect, attempted to develop a formal theory of conflict that was all-embracing. He believed that the same principles applied whether the conflict was a factory dispute or a confrontation between the superpowers. Indeed, Schelling's theorizing about conflict started from the assumption that conflict was both endemic and pervasive in social relationships. And rather than trying to abolish conflict, he was interested in identifying the kind of tactics that led to successful outcomes. As he described it, he was concerned with 'conscious, intelligent, sophisticated conflict behaviour' or with what he termed 'the strategy of conflict'.[1] Starting from the premise that any conflict would be characterized by the interdependence of both decisions and expectations about one another's behaviour, Schelling wanted to delineate what he described as correct conflict behaviour. His working assumption was that those involved in conflicts would behave rationally, and although he recognized that, in certain respects this was unrealistic, the caveat was outweighed by the conviction that the rationality assumption was conducive to theory.[2] Schelling did concede that whether or not the theory provided good insight into actual behaviour was a matter for subsequent judgement, but his main interest was very clearly in the development of theory.

In this connection, it is easy to see why game theory was so attractive to Schelling, encouraging him to develop what he termed a 'theory of interdependent decision'.[3] Game theory was 'concerned with games of strategy in which the best course of action for each participant depends on what he expects the other participants to do'.[4] For Schelling, therefore, it followed that the key was to influence the other player's assessment of what one's own behaviour was likely to be. Consequently, a strategic move was

one that influences the other person's choice in a manner favorable to one's self by affecting the other person's expectations of how one's self will behave. One constrains the partner's choice by constraining one's own behavior. The object is to set up for one's self and to communicate persuasively to the other player a mode of behavior (including conditional responses to the other's behavior) that leaves the other a simple maximization problem whose solution for him is the optimum for one's self, and to destroy the other's ability to do the same.[5]

At the same time Schelling recognized that the game was rarely one of pure competition. Indeed, the recognition that in most conflicts the adversaries shared common interests and a degree of mutual dependence was central to Schelling's thinking. In his view, most conflicts were variable-sum games in which adversaries engaged in both coercion and accommodation. While both adversaries had a common interest in reaching an outcome that was not mutually destructive, they differed over the precise form of the solution. As Schelling noted, the mix of conflict and cooperation could differ along a range from precarious partnership to incomplete antagonism. In most conflicts though coercive bargaining tactics were particularly important in influencing the adversary's expectations about one's own choices and likely behaviour. They were particularly important in 'distributional' bargaining where, although both sides were better off with a bargain than without one, a better bargain for one was a worse bargain for the other. Such a situation encouraged intense and often coercive bargaining, even though both sides recognized that they had a common interest in reaching some solution.

It was in this connection that Schelling developed some of his most distinctive ideas. Although he started from the assumption of rationality, he recognized that departures from rationality could take place in many different ways — and that these departures could sometimes prove a help rather than a hindrance in terms of the bargaining relationship. Acknowledging that in certain circumstances a careless attitude could pay off, Schelling was concerned with identifying and elucidating the 'strategic basis for certain paradoxical tactics'.[6]

While Schelling used game theory to elucidate many of his ideas, part of the attraction of this approach was its heuristic value. He was particularly effective in teasing out some of the points of contrast between zero sum conflicts and non-zero sum conflicts. In zero sum situations, for example, deception was an advantage as it was often necessary to keep the adversary guessing about one's actions. In variable sum or mixed motive games, however, it was advantageous to have a more transparent strategy that could be appreciated by the adversary. This fundamental assumption provided the basis for some of Schelling's analyses of communication in conflict, and his recognition of the fact that communication through action was necessary where the formal communication channels were incomplete or inadequate. Indeed, he argued that 'even with full verbal communication the pattern of action may speak louder than words'.[7]

If Schelling was one of the pioneers in the use of game theory for enhancing understanding of international conflict, he was far from slavish or uncritical in his approach and acknowledged its limitations as well as its insights. He recognized that the payoff functions should not dominate the analysis, and that the character of the game was changed by the amount of detail or context that was provided. He also underlined the importance of experience in determining such factors as the degree of trust between adversaries and acknowledged very explicitly that strategic principles relevant to successful choices could not be derived 'by purely analytic means from a priori considerations'.[8] Although not primarily an empirical analyst, Schelling nevertheless understood the importance of empirical evidence in explaining conflict behaviour. Indeed, Schelling's recognition of the limits of theory led him to pose some extremely interesting empirical questions. Among these were questions about coordinating the limits to a conflict when communication between the combatants was full, when it was non-existent or limited and when it was asymmetrical.[9] He also asked how dependent was a stable, efficient outcome on the extent to which the players were familiar with the setting of the conflict? In discussing this, Schelling pre-empted the argument that the details were irrelevant:

> there is no arguing that rational players have the intellectual capacity to rise above these details of the game and ignore them; the importance of these details is that they can be supremely helpful to both players and that rational players know that they may be dependent on using these details as props in the course of their mutual accommodation.[10]

If the context and details of the game were important, so too were the players and the patterns of play. Were similar temperaments and cultural backgrounds conducive to the discovery of mutually understandable and acceptable limits? How important were the opening moves in discovering stable patterns of behaviour or rules of the game? What kind of learning process could take place where there were no mutually accepted norms at the outset? Schelling not only saw these questions as important but accepted that they could only be answered with empirical evidence.

He also recognized that there were lots of uncertainties inherent in conflict situations and that these could be exploited by rational players. Indeed, one of Schelling's most illuminating discussions in *The Strategy of Conflict* was of what he termed 'strategy with a random ingredient'. When considering the 'randomization of threats and promises' Schelling highlighted the fact that a promise is costly when it succeeds, a threat when it fails.[11] When making a threat, there is always a risk that it might have to be carried out, and also a risk of inadvertent fulfilment even if the adversary is complying with one's demands. From a very formal mathematical analysis of randomization Schelling developed the notion of a 'fractional threat' — a threat that carries the risk but not the certainty of being carried out. This in turn provided the basis for his subsequent elaboration of 'the threat that leaves something to chance' — a concept that was one of Schelling's most distinctive and important ideas. If this idea, like many of his others, evolved out of formal game theory, Schelling developed it in a way which not only displayed great logic and rigour but also great imagination. Game theory may have provided the intellectual basis for some of Schelling's ideas, but it was his awareness of its limits and the skill and imagination with which he drew out the implications of the limits that provided such a distinctive and important contribution to strategic analysis.

The major ideas

Any attempt to encapsulate Schelling's major ideas in a few pages does a great disservice to the richness, subtlety and sophistication of his analysis. Nevertheless, it is possible to identify certain key ideas and themes that were not only central to Schelling's work but have provided an enduring intellectual legacy upon which later analysts have been able to build. Schelling's major theoretical work was *The Strategy of Conflict* and almost all the ideas that were subsequently developed, albeit in a less formalistic way, in *Arms and Influence* (a study replete with historical examples of Schellingesque behaviour) and in *Strategy and Arms Control* are discernible in this first book. Nevertheless, the other works are significant in that they helped to popularize these ideas in a form that was readily accessible even to those who were not versed in the subtleties of game theory. Furthermore, they exhibit the same concern with conceptual clarification, with identifying options and delineating logical possibilities in a variety of circumstances and with providing analytical clarity that characterized the first volume.

Schelling's ideas about conflict in non-zero sum situations were particularly suited to the nuclear age, where adversaries also had common interests in avoiding disaster. Indeed, in the first chapter of *Arms and Influence* he identified some of the changes that had taken place in war and diplomacy as a result of the advent of nuclear weapons. Schelling drew a distinction between brute force and coercion — a distinction between taking something and making someone give it to you — and focused on coercive diplomacy, where the behaviour of the adversary was influenced through the power to hurt and through threats to use that power. Schelling also argued that military power had been transformed with nuclear weapons — although not in the way generally believed. In his view, the difference between nuclear weapons and bayonets was 'not in the number of people they can eventually kill but in the speed with which it can be done, in the centralization of decision, in the divorce of the war from political processes' and in the fact that it could be done without first attaining military victory.[12] These developments gave states 'the power to hurt', which in turn, enhanced 'the importance of war and threats of war as techniques of influence, not of destruction; of coercion and deterrence, not of conquest and defence; of bargaining and intimidation'.[13] In other words, war had become a test of nerve and risk-taking rather than simply a contest of military strength, and military strategy had been transformed into the 'diplomacy of violence'.[14]

The difficulty, of course, is that the power to hurt was not exclusive. The Soviet Union, like the United States, possessed it in abundance. In such circumstances, the distinctive character of bargaining threats was that they might prove very costly in the event that they had to be implemented. Where one might prefer not to implement the threat, questions inevitably arose about credibility. Not surprisingly, therefore, Schelling developed a whole set of ideas related to the paradox that in a situation where both would suffer hurt, there were all sorts of bargaining advantages from being able to appear relatively impervious to dangers, risks or potential costs.

One way of increasing bargaining power was to lock or bind oneself into a situation or a course of action which placed the onus for avoiding a collision on the adversary. In *The Strategy of Conflict* Schelling identified 'an important class of tactics, of a kind that is particularly appropriate to the logic of indeterminate situations. The essence of these tactics is some voluntary but irreversible sacrifice of freedom of choice. They rest on the paradox that the power to constrain an adversary may depend on the power to bind oneself; that in bargaining, weakness is often strength, freedom may be freedom to capitulate, and to burn bridges behind one may suffice to undo an opponent'.[15] In other words, threats that would not be in one's interest to carry out can be made more effective by ensuring that in the event of a challenge there would be no alternative other than implementation. This theme was developed further in *Arms and Influence* where Schelling examined 'the art of commitment'. In this connection, Schelling argued that there is an important difference between the national homeland where credibility is more or less axiomatic and everything abroad where credibility has to be established and where it is necessary to incur and communicate a commitment if one's threats are to be credible. As he put it, 'The commitment process on which all American overseas deterrence depends — and on which all confidence within the alliance depends — is a process of surrendering and destroying options that we might have been expected to find too attractive in an emergency' and that ensure that the adversary has the 'last clear chance' to avert collision.[16] The process of commitment is one that Schelling discussed at some length. One form of commitment is of course military deployments, and here Schelling cites the example of West Berlin, where a small American contingent succeeded in deterring any Soviet encroachments. American troops could not defend Berlin, but could die for it, as Schelling put it, 'in a manner that guarantees that the action cannot stop there'.[17] He also accepts that although words are much cheaper than actions in international politics, statements are a form of commitment — especially where they involve reputation and therefore future credibility. Indeed, Schelling argues that commitments are interdependent, and that bargaining reputation is of major importance in determining the validity of commitments. As well as considering how states might undertake, accept or establish commitments, Schelling also considers ways in which they might be circumvented, discredited or dropped. He acknowledges, however, that the more success one has had in establishing commitments the more difficult it is to disengage from them:

> If commitments could be undone by declaration they would be worthless in the first place. The whole purpose of verbal ritualistic commitments, of political and diplomatic commitments, of efforts to attach honor and reputation to a commitment, is to make the commitment manifestly hard to get out of on short notice. Even the commitments not deliberately incurred, and the commitments that embarrass one in unforeseen circumstances, cannot be undone cheaply. The cost is the discrediting of other commitments that one would still like to be credited.[18]

Schelling relates the discussion of commitments to different kinds of threat and teases out some important distinctions between deterrent and compellent threats. Compellence is a more positive and dynamic form of threat in which one initiates an action that will cease only if the opponent complies with one's demands. 'To deter, one digs in . . . and waits — in the interest of inaction. To compel, one gets up enough momentum . . . to make the other *act* to avoid collision'.[19] Having established a clear distinction between the two types of threat, Schelling then shows how certain kinds of action — such as the United States' blockade of Cuba in the Missile Crisis — can combine elements of both. He also draws a distinction between compellent threats which exert steady pressure and those which increase risk. This leads him on very logically to a discussion of risk-manipulation.

Although Schelling develops the idea of manipulating risk most fully in *Arms and Influence*, he builds on his earlier work and in particular his discussion of threats that leave something to chance. The point about these threats, as he notes in *The Strategy of Conflict*, is that 'though one may or may not carry them out if the threatened party fails to comply, the final decision is not altogether under the threatener's control'.[20] Indeed, Schelling develops this theme brilliantly, arguing that the probability of inadvertent war rises with a crisis, and that both crises and limited war can be understood as generators of risk. The risk stems not from deliberate decision but from the dynamic processes involved. As Schelling notes:

> uncertainty exists . . . Violence, especially war, is a confused and uncertain activity, highly unpredictable, depending on decisions made by fallible human beings organized into imperfect governments, depending on fallible communications and warning systems and on the untested performance of people and equipment. It is furthermore a hotheaded activity in which commitments and reputations can develop a momentum of their own.[21]

Much the same is true of crises, and Schelling acknowledges that 'it is the essence of a crisis that the participants are not fully in control of events; they take steps and make decisions that raise or lower the danger, but in a realm of risk and uncertainty'.[22] The implication that Schelling draws from this though is that the risk and uncertainty can be used to intimidate the enemy. By creating 'shared risk' and increasing the probability that events might get 'out of control', it may be possible to compel the adversary to back down — especially if one has created the shared risk by an irreversible commitment.

Such techniques, are discussed by Schelling in terms of 'rocking the boat' or brinkmanship. His notion of the brink builds in uncertainty, and Schelling describes it not as a flat surface with a sharp precipice but as a curved slope on which there is some risk of slipping — a risk that increases as one moves closer to the edge. 'Brinkmanship is thus the deliberate creation of a recognizable risk of war, a risk that one does not completely control.'[23] This is, of course, a highly dangerous activity. Schelling recognizes that the last chance to avert disaster is not always clear but contends that this too is something that can be manipulated.

This analysis of risk enables Schelling to discuss American deterrence strategy in Europe in a way that is extremely illuminating. By moving beyond analyses which treated credibility in absolute terms, Schelling added a new dimension to assessments of extended deterrence. He recognized that credibility was a matter of degree, and that it did not require the United States to be willing to commit suicide on behalf of its allies. It was sufficient simply to structure the situation in a way that the Soviet Union would have to decide whether to initiate action that incurred a significant risk of escalation. As he noted, the danger of all-out war 'does not depend solely on whether the United States would coolly resolve to launch general war in response to a limited attack in Europe'.[24] The United States' military presence in Western Europe means that a Soviet attack would engage the United States in a local war — which could get out of control. This possibility of uncontrolled or uncontrollable violence is inherent in any clash between the forces of the two superpowers but is heightened as soon as nuclear weapons are introduced into the equation. Indeed, Schelling argues very strongly that nuclear weapons in Europe have to be understood as weapons of risk manipulation and nuclear bargaining rather than military weapons to be used for military purposes on the battlefield. He recognizes that their use would be akin to the chicken game — an analogy that he discusses at some length — but also contends that games of chicken are not always avoidable.   The concern with manipulating risk and exploiting uncertainty runs through Schelling's analyses. Yet he is also concerned with ways in which conflict might be limited or mitigated. To some extent this reflects his theoretical concern with the determination of outcomes in circumstances where communication is incomplete or impossible — a concern that leads into discussions of tacit bargaining and attempts to coordinate expectations around salient focal points. Schelling is especially intrigued by bargaining in a 'fluid and indeterminate situation that seemingly provides no logical reason for anybody to expect anything except what he expects to be expected to expect'.[25] In order for a decision to be reached 'these infinitely relative expectations must somehow converge on a single point, at which each expects the other not to expect to be expected to retreat'.[26] Schelling explains this convergence of expectations in terms of the 'intrinsic magnetism of particular outcomes, especially those that enjoy prominence, uniqueness, simplicity, precedent or some rationale that makes them qualitatively different from the continuum of possible alternatives'.[27]

This theoretical analysis has particular relevance to discussions of limited war, especially as such conflicts involve two distinct sets of bargaining processes — one concerned with the outcome, the other with the mode of conducting the war itself. Indeed, both in an appendix to *The Strategy of Conflict* and in *Arms and Influence* Schelling illustrates the relevance of these theoretical ideas to key policy issues. The idea of salient focal points, for example, is a key element in the discussion of limited war and the nuclear threshold. Taking his cue from the need to coordinate expectations, Schelling argues that this is much easier where there are qualitative distinctions or salient focal points which are relatively easy to recognize, to understand and to converge upon. The status quo ante, and natural boundaries such as rivers have the qualities that make it possible to regard them as thresholds. Thresholds are 'conventional stopping places or dividing lines. They have a legalistic quality, and they depend on precedents or analogy. They have some quality that makes them recognizable, and they are somewhat arbitrary. For the most part they are just "there"; we don't make them or invent them but only recognize them.'[28] They have a certain uniqueness as a stopping point or plausible limit and once this limit has been transgressed the stopping points become less obvious. Limits of this kind are likely to be all the more effective if they are 'qualitative and discrete rather than quantitative and continuous'; stable limits should have an 'evidently symbolic character'.[29] The nuclear threshold has this quality: even though the distinction between conventional and nuclear has been somewhat blurred in terms of the physics, in terms of the psychology it remains immensely powerful and important. Using nuclear weapons would be a 'symbolically discontinuous act' that would contravene precedent and the convention or tradition of non-use.[30]

In this connection, Schelling's analysis contains an illuminating although not fully developed analysis of rules and conventions. As Schelling acknowledges, the authority or effectiveness of the threshold is in the expectations themselves not in the thing to which the expectations have attached themselves.[31] He also contends that states might be prepared to accept limited defeat rather than breach the rules. 'The rules may be respected because once they are broken there is no assurance that any new ones can be found and jointly recognized in time to prevent the widening of the conflict.'[32] On the other hand, Schelling is attracted by the idea of limited reprisals as part of a coercive rather than strictly military approach to warfare and sees the attacks against North Vietnam as an example of this kind of approach. He also discusses how such an option might look when it involves the use of nuclear weapons at both the tactical and the strategic level. For Schelling, 'the purpose of introducing nuclear weapons in a tactical war that one was losing would not be solely, or even mainly, to redress a balance on the battlefield. It could be to make the war too painful or dangerous to continue.'[33] The use of nuclear weapons at the strategic level is something that he also sees in terms of risk manipulation, although he acknowledges that even the 'measured cadence of limited reprisal' cannot rescue war from impetuosity and give it a completely rational character.[34] From this it is only a small step to the argument that there are advantages in appearing to be 'on the verge of total abandon'. However rational the adversaries, they may compete to appear the more irrational, impetuous and stubborn.'[35]

Indeed, Schelling was sympathetic to the McNamara strategy of 1962 in which the secretary of defence suggested that war should be fought in the same way as wars in the past, that military forces should be the prime targets, that cities should be held as hostages and that deterrence should be extended into war itself. This is not to suggest he was uncritical. Schelling dissected the strategy rigorously, arguing that its various components were in some ways complementary and in others contradictory. He also considered how a limited strategic war might be brought to an end, recognizing that 'the last word might be more important than the first strike'.[36] Although it was essential to consider ways in which the war might be terminated, stable stopping points might be difficult to find — not only would they have to be physically recognizable, but also 'reasonably secure against double cross or resumption of the war'.[37] This made it all the more important that consideration of the ways that war might be terminated be a central part of peacetime planning.

If Schelling was concerned with how wars could be ended, he was also concerned with how they might begin and discussed the July crisis of 1914 as one in which technology had put a premium on haste, with disastrous results. From this he recognized the importance of being able to discriminate between measures that were essentially precautionary and those that were preparatory. This led to a discussion of stability which Schelling defined as 'the assurance against being caught by surprise, the safety in waiting, the absence of a premium on jumping the gun'.[38] Schelling also recognized that the stability problem had a dynamic dimension and was interested in restraining the 'dynamics of mutual alarm' in a crisis when both sides were placing forces on alert. This was a theme that he dealt with in *The Strategy of Conflict* in a very elegant and compelling essay entitled 'The Reciprocal Fear of Surprise Attack'.[39] In this Schelling argued that where surprise carried with it an advantage, it might be worth while to avert it by striking first. The implication of this was that a modest temptation might be compounded by interacting expectations since an 'objective source of basic anxiety generates a superstructure of subjective anxieties about each other's anxiety'.[40] In other words, the problem was not simply one of calculated advantage but also one of nervousness.

In practice, of course, much would depend upon both the warning and alert systems and the level and character of the strategic forces. In relation to the former, Schelling acknowledged that there was a fundamental design dilemma since warning systems can be imperfect in either direction, either being over-sensitive and responding to false alarms or being insufficiently responsive. As regards strategic forces, the problem was not simply related to one's own vulnerability, but also one's capability to put enemy forces at risk. 'The surprise attack problem when viewed as a problem of reciprocal suspicion and aggravated "self defence" suggests that there are not only secrets we prefer not to keep but military capabilities we might prefer not to have'.[41] One implication of this comment of course is that it was not a problem without solutions, and in this connection Schelling was enthusiastic about measures such as Eisenhower's Open Skies proposal that would offer a means of mutual reassurance. The other important implication was the recognition that it was not necessarily in the United States' interest for Soviet weapons to be vulnerable to a disarming first strike. In so far as the problem of pre-emption was one of nervousness then, it did not pay to make the Soviet Union nervous — even if this meant refraining from developing greater counter-force capability.

Some of these arms control themes were developed most fully in Schelling's co-authored book with Morton Halperin, entitled *Strategy and Arms Control*, in which the authors assess both the contribution and the limits of arms control. The basic approach of the book is that arms control is more closely related to military strategy than it is to disarmament. This is partly because the military relationship with potential enemies involves strong elements of mutual interest in avoiding a war that neither side wants, in minimizing the risk and the costs of the arms competition and in curtailing the scope and violence of war in the event that it occurs. Accordingly, arms control is defined as 'all forms of military cooperation between potential enemies in reducing the likelihood of war, its scope and violence if it occurs and the political and economic costs of being prepared for it'.[42] This broad definition of arms control is very close to that offered by Hedley Bull in *The Control of the Arms Race*, a book that Schelling and Halperin read in manuscript. Indeed, they arrive at many of the same conclusions as Bull, and together these two books established the basic philosophy of arms control.

One of the most remarkable aspects of the Schelling and Halperin analysis is that although it was written in a period of intense cold war, it recognizes that the problem was not simply one of Soviet aggressiveness and that it is the task of military forces to deter while avoiding provoking, desperate, preventive or irrational action. In short, the United States and the Soviet Union had a mutual interest in inducing and reciprocating restraint, in offsetting some of characteristics of modern weapons and military expectations and in ensuring that armaments and force postures did not exacerbate their underlying conflict. There was no hard distinction between arms control and force planning since arms control was a way of extending unilateral actions through joint understandings. Similarly, arms control could take different forms, ranging from a formal treaty with detailed specifications at one end of the scale through executive agreements, explicit but informal understandings, tacit under-standings to self-restraint that is consciously contingent on each other's behaviour at the other end.[43]

If the authors were critical of those who refused to consider collaboration with the Soviet Union, they were equally critical of those who espoused schemes of disarmament or who saw arms control as simply a way of saving money. Indeed, given that arms control was about promoting stability, and was concerned less with reducing capabilities than with reducing incentives that may lead to war, they recognized that rather than provide a way of saving money, it might actually cost more. Schelling and Halperin also acknowledged that reductions in numbers, under certain circumstances, could detract from rather than enhance stability: 'beyond a certain point further reduction may increase both the fears and the temptations that aggravate the likelihood of war'.[44] Much of course depends on force structure, and Schelling and

Halperin acknowledged that a diversified force structure could help to maintain stability.

If arms control was defined very broadly to include induced or reciprocated 'self control', whether negotiated or informal, Schelling and Halperin nevertheless acknowledged the need to treat arms control critically and to assess the impact of arms control on the military environment. They accepted that the results of arms control vary, that it can 'reduce tension or hostilities; it can reduce vigilance. It can strengthen alliances, collapse them, or make them unnecessary. It can create confidence and trust or create suspicion and irritation. It can lead to greater world organization and the rule of law or discredit them. And it evidently lends itself to the short run competition in propaganda'.[45] The consequences of particular arms control proposals were not self-evidently positive and had to be assessed in terms of their impact.

The most appropriate and effective arms control measures were those which promoted stability — something that Schelling recognized was partly a function of technology — and reduced both sides' expectations of attack. Closely connected to this was the possibility of accidental war, that is a war initiated in the belief that it has become unavoidable or had already started. For Schelling and Halperin, accidental war was pre-emptive war sparked by some unpredictable occurrence. Measures to reduce the urgency of quick action and the incidence of false alarm as well as steps to improve communications would minimize the prospects for surprise, making pre-emption less necessary and accidental war far less probable.

In relation to this, Schelling and Halperin recognized that one of the requirements in a crisis was working out a synchronized military relaxation, whereby de-escalation would not leave either side in a vulnerable and exposed position. Schelling himself was to develop this theme slightly in *Arms and Influence* where he argued that the requirements of inspection differed in crisis from non-crisis situations. In a crisis, it would be necessary to have observable or positive compliance: unlike longer-term inspection where the absence of evidence was generally regarded as a presumption that an agreement was being observed, there had to be some positive indicators that readiness was being relaxed and that neither adversary was exposing himself to danger.

The concern with stability also animated Schelling's and Halperin's approach to the arms race. Although not wildly enthusiastic about formal arms control, they argued that it would be beneficial if measures to slow down or stabilize the technological arms race, and to stop the spread of nuclear weapons to other states, could be approached cooperatively. Yet arms control had to be approached with three possibilities in mind — that an agreement would operate as planned, that one or both would cheat or that it would break down. Both cheating and breakdown could be more dangerous the lower the level of forces. The dangers of cheating, of course, could be minimized by an effective inspection system — deterrence through detection — although the difficulty with such a system (rather like the warning system) was on the one hand that it would miss violations and on the other that it would produce mistaken evidence that violation has occurred. It was important, therefore, to devise a system which would minimize false positives as well as false negatives. Even if cheating did not occur, however, they recognized that arms control might simply re-channel national armaments efforts in different directions.

The approach taken by Schelling and Halperin to formal systems of regulation and inspection ranged from the pragmatic to the sceptical. They were not convinced that detailed and precise regulation was necessary, especially in areas where less formal approaches were already operating effectively. They were also concerned about the unintended implications of arms control, and among other things considered whether arms control measures which helped to prevent the outbreak of a major war would make the world safe for local war. Although such a prognosis was superficially attractive, they concluded that concern about the arms control environment might pose an additional constraint upon the initiation of local war.

What was not foreseen, however, was that in an environment characterized by intense competition between the superpowers and involvement in local wars, if only by proxy, arms control would be vulnerable to political attack. In the event this was what happened with SALT II. Yet for Schelling the real problems with arms control as it evolved in the 1970s was not its political vulnerability but its underlying philosophy. Schelling and Halperin (along with Hedley Bull) had provided much of the philosophy which was to inform arms control efforts during the 1960s. During the 1970s, however, this philosophy appeared increasingly less relevant to the arms control experience. Schelling was subsequently to write a compelling paper entitled 'What went wrong with arms control?' in which he argued that during the 1970s the arms control process had become disorientated: 'What has been lost is the earlier emphasis on the character of weapons, and what has taken its place is emphasis on numbers, and specifically numbers within fixed categories, the categories having nothing to do with the weapon characteristics that most deserve attention'.[46] Although in many respects, this was simply a re-statement of Schelling's earlier arguments about stability, it also provided a powerful critique of the arms control process and a trenchant case for returning to the basic philosophy. The difficulty, of course, was that the process that Schelling and Halperin had regarded as essentially one of rational decision had been influenced by all sorts of political and bureaucratic factors. Nevertheless, Schelling's analysis was as pertinent to fundamental choices about strategy and arms control in the mid-1980s as the earlier work with Halperin had been. What can be said of Schelling's overall contribution to strategic thinking in the nuclear age?

Assessment and critique

Schelling's contribution to strategic analysis was immense. The skill and rigour as well as the novelty and originality with which he developed his arguments set new standards for strategic thinking. Furthermore, Schelling's treatment of almost any topic has a subtlety and nuance that are rarely matched. Perhaps one of Schelling's great strengths is that he can see all sides of a specific problem and is able not only to tease out implications that are not immediately obvious but also to identify various alternatives and the outcomes that are likely to result from each one.

Nevertheless, many of Schelling's ideas and arguments are open to criticism. Not surprisingly, some of the allegations that were directed at Herman Kahn were also directed at Schelling. The dispassionate tone with which he approached issues and options relating to nuclear war or to punitive strikes against North Vietnam led to charges that he was insensitive to ethical considerations and that he was an advocate of policies that bordered on genocide. Most of these charges were both intemperate and inappropriate. Yet there was a sense in which Schelling did allow his fascination with games of strategy and with the logic of winning to lead him into areas that could not be treated simply as 'games'. The defence against this is that although detachment was not an unmixed blessing, it was a prerequisite for the extremely rigorous way in which Schelling approached strategic issues.

If this rigour accounts for many of Schelling's insights, it was also a source of problems with at least some of his analysis. Schelling was a theoretical strategist rather than an empirical one. His background in economics was evident in the logic and skill with which his concepts were developed, yet he lacked the deep historical knowledge of a Bernard Brodie. As a result, the kinds of tactics that he developed and discussed had little appeal to policymakers who were much more aware of the risks. For Schelling, irrevocable commitments appeared to be an attractive and effective tactic; for policymakers engaged in a major confrontation, the major preoccupation was not with relinquishing but with maintaining freedom of action — both for themselves and for the adversary. Empirical studies of crises and their management by analysts such as Glenn Snyder and Oran Young subsequently revealed very clearly that the kind of irrevocable commitment that Schelling regarded as so effective was anathema to policymakers when the stakes of getting it wrong were very high.[47] Similarly, threats that left something to chance had little attraction for policymakers engaged in crisis management. Tactics that Schelling had elaborated with such care, if they were evident at all were used only very sparingly — and even then were hedged around with all kinds of restrictions and restraints.

This leads on to a closely related criticism: although Schelling was not oblivious to the risks and dangers inherent in many of the tactics he discussed, he was less concerned with risk reduction than with maximizing the coercive impact of actions. Part of the problem was that although Schelling was aware of the dynamics of conflict, and recognized the potential volatility of both war and crisis, his emphasis on the *strategy* of conflict led him either to minimize these dynamics or to treat them as something to be manipulated for bargaining purposes rather than to be contained and controlled. The attractions of manipulation almost invariably seemed to outweigh the dictates of prudence. This is evident in the following passage:

One does not always know what moves of his own would lead to disaster, one cannot always perceive the moves that the other side has already taken . . . one does not always understand clearly what situations the other side would not, at some moment, accept, in preference to war. When we add uncertainty . . . we are not so sure that disaster will be avoided. *More important, the risk of disaster becomes a manipulative element in the situation. It can be exploited to intimidate*[48] (emphasis added).

The same tendency is also evident when Schelling discusses the deliberate creation of risk. As he put it, 'If the outcome is partly determined by events and processes that are manifestly somewhat beyond our comprehension and control, we create *genuine* risk'.[49] The problem, of course, is that the party creating the risk is creating *genuine* risk for himself too — and it is not self-evident that he is any more prepared to accept or tolerate this risk than is the adversary. Similarly, although Schelling recognized the danger of simultaneous commitment in a confrontation, he still emphasized the advantages to be gained from making a commitment. The pitfall here, as with other tactics that he discussed, was that such moves were effective if only one side was using them, but if both sides were doing the same then there was a high probability that the confrontation would result in disaster. Indeed, it is arguable that if both Soviet and American decisionmakers had read Schelling on coercive bargaining and were prepared to act on Schellingesque precepts, the cold war would have been much more dangerous than it proved to be.

In practice, of course, the outcome of confrontations is not determined simply by bargaining skill, but also by such considerations as relative interests at stake. Indeed, one of the major shortcomings of Schelling's analysis of bargaining was that it focused so much on skill that it lost any real sense of context — and of the impact that context might have on the bargaining outcome. Although Schelling emphasized that details were important, his penchant for more abstract analysis meant that details that might have a major impact on the bargaining process were given scant attention in the analysis. Perhaps no omission was more important than that relating to the balance of interests in a superpower crisis — and the question of which superpower had more at stake. Relative propensity to take risks is a dimension that Schelling did not fully explore — and it is arguable that this is primarily a function of the balance of interests. The state with more at stake will generally be prepared to take higher risks than the one with less at stake.

Another closely related problem is that Schelling treated commitments as if they existed in both a policy and a political vacuum. As Alexander George and Richard Smoke pointed out in an empirical study of deterrence, commitments are less fundamental than interests.[50] This is not to deny that commitments embody, symbolize and accentuate interests. Nevertheless, commitments will generally vary in strength according to the strength of the underlying interests. This again was something that Schelling tended to overlook, especially in his discussion of the interdependence of commitments. It is much easier than Schelling acknowledged to differentiate between weak and strong commitments, and simply because a government relinquishes commitments based on marginal interests does not mean that the credibility of other commitments that are based on more durable and substantial interests will be challenged. Credibility does not depend on bargaining reputation alone but also on what one is protecting or defending. In this connection, cultural factors and considerations such as whether or not one is defending the homeland are of crucial importance yet figure only marginally if at all in Schelling's writings. Had they figured more fully, the analysis of punitive reprisals and coercive diplomacy — neither of which worked very effectively against North Vietnam — might have been rather different.

In all this the problem is not that Schelling's approach was either simple or simplistic. Perhaps more than any of his contemporaries Schelling was sensitive to the cross-pressures, the ironies, the paradoxes, the ambiguities and the tensions involved in nuclear diplomacy. Moreover, Schelling's analyses of different issues in strategy were interconnected in complex and interesting ways. This is evident, for example, in the way in which he and Halperin treated limited war as a form of arms control. The rather puzzling thing, however, is that although Schelling recognized that decision-makers face painful dilemmas and have to make difficult trade-offs between the need for coercive impact and the need for prudence — trade-offs that were explored most fully in the work of Glenn Snyder — he rarely explored the nature of these trade-offs, preferring instead to focus on maximizing coercive impact and the prospects for winning. This may be explained in part by the fact that the rigour with which Schelling analysed strategic problems was achieved by compartmentalizing these problems. Although he explores particular issues in a comprehensive and thorough way, and shows how tensions between different requirements have to be reconciled in the design of warning systems or monitoring and inspection systems, his concern with identifying the optimum design to meet competing or conflicting goals is rarely developed at a broader level. Schelling does not discuss the difficulties that can arise because different criteria pull strategy in different directions. There is, for example, little sense of how the requirements of crisis bargaining can be reconciled with the demands of escalation control. Similarly, there is little discussion about how the requirements of counter-force strategies, which may be a prerequisite for keeping war limited, might add to the 'reciprocal fear of surprise attack'. This is not so much a criticism as something to bemoan. Schelling, in some respects, was more sensitive to the dilemmas that plagued nuclear strategy than any of his contemporaries yet never addressed these dilemmas and problems as explicitly and as clearly as he might have done.

The problem was not that Schelling's ideas and arguments lack appropriate qualification — it is rather that he did not always follow through and accept fully the implications of the qualifications that he himself had made in passing. If one accepts, for example, that coercive bargaining is as dangerous as Schelling sometimes suggests, then the rational course might be not to play to win but rather to refrain from playing the game or to attempt to change its nature or its rules. Although Schelling flirts with this possibility, he does not develop it, preferring to focus once again on winning.

One implication of all this is that the major shortcomings of Schelling's analysis are less in the analysis itself — which is at times almost breathtaking in its brilliance — than in the underlying assumptions. His work is populated by an artificial strategic man concerned with maximizing his gains through coercion, compellence and the like. Yet strategic man is as much an unrealistic abstraction as is an economic man concerned only with maximizing profits. Although Schelling is clearly aware of this, he treats governments as rational monolithic actors and pays little attention to either bureaucratic and governmental bargaining processes or to broader public pressures that can constrain, alter or deflect policy. Closely related to this is the fact that although Schelling uses historical examples to great effect, especially in *Arms and Influence*, the richness of history and political science is not reflected in his work in a substantive as opposed to simply an illustrative way.

None of this is meant to deny the sheer intellectual virtuosity of Schelling's analyses nor is it to suggest that his work is of little relevance. On the contrary, where there is a stable structure and a stable set of expectations, then many of Schelling's arguments are extremely pertinent. The analysis of coercion and compellence is ultimately unconvincing, but many of the ideas he developed are much more persuasive in relation to deterrence. In emphasizing risk and uncertainty and acknowledging that violence was something which could develop a momentum and dynamism of its own, Schelling was accepting some of the most fundamental realities of the nuclear age. And while Schelling saw such possibilities as something to be exploited at least as much as feared, the notion of the volatility of military force, the inability to avoid 'threats that leave something to chance' and the dangers of inadvertent escalation enforced a fundamental prudence on policymakers. Indeed, this helps to explain why crises between the superpowers were so infrequent, why extended deterrence retained credibility even in an era of strategic parity and why policymakers were so reluctant to exploit the 'diplomacy of violence' that Schelling had identified. Perhaps the ultimate deficiency of Schelling's work is that the dangers he thought could be effectively exploited were precisely the dangers that policymakers were most anxious to avoid. A closely related irony is that although Schelling saw the virtues of counter-force strategy, his ideas about 'threats that leave something to chance' and the potential uncontrollability of military force provided the foundation on which subsequent critics of United States counter-force strategies, such as Robert Jervis, were to build so effectively.[51]

The other comment that might be made about Schelling is that although he recognized the cooperative elements of adversary relations, he often appeared more interested in the conflictual and the competitive aspects. There are some very incisive comments about cooperation between adversaries and about such factors as the development of trust which, in Schelling's view, is often achieved simply by the continuity of the relation between parties and the recognition by each that what he might gain by cheating in a given instance is outweighed by the value of the tradition of trust that makes possible a long sequence of future agreement.[52] In spite of this, it is Schelling's fascination with winning which provides the dominant strand in his thinking. There is invariably a suspicion when reading Schelling that he regarded cooperation as valuable not as a way of diminishing conflict but rather as a means of making the world safe for the conflict to continue. Concomitantly, it is possible to argue that if he had been as creative about conflict resolution as he was about winning, his contribution might have been even more significant.

In spite of the various problems or shortcomings with his work — or perhaps even because of them — Schelling's contribution to contemporary strategic thinking was both immense and unique. Schelling was rarely predictable and never bland, and his arguments were invariably highly provocative and intellectually exciting. His ideas about arms control, deterrence and stability were also of enduring relevance and very real value, and he left a rich vein of highly sophisticated argument and equally subtle analysis that subsequent generations of strategists could use, elaborate, criticize or qualify but could definitely not ignore.

Notes

1. Thomas C. Schelling, *The Strategy of Conflict*, London, Oxford University Press, 1960, p. 1.
2. Ibid., p. 2.
3. Ibid., p. 83.
4. Ibid., p. 9.
5. Ibid., p. 160.
6. Ibid., p. 17.
7. Ibid., p. 107.
8. Ibid., p. 163.
9. Ibid., p. 166.
10. Ibid., p. 167.
11. Ibid., p. 177.
12. *Arms and Influence*, New Haven Yale University Press, 1966, p. 20.
13. Ibid., p. 33.
14. Ibid., p. 34.
15. *The Strategy of Conflict*, p. 22.
16. *Arms and Influence*, p. 44.
17. Ibid., p. 47.
18. Ibid., p. 65-6.
19. Ibid., p. 72.
20. *The Strategy of Conflict*, p. 188.
21. *Arms and Influence*, p. 93.
22. Ibid., p. 97.
23. *The Strategy of Conflict*, p. 200.
24. *Arms and Influence*, p. 108.
25. *The Strategy of Conflict*, p. 70.
26. Ibid., p. 70.
27. Ibid., p. 70.
28. *Arms and Influence*, p. 135.
29. *The Strategy of Conflict*, p. 261.
30. Ibid., p. 258.
31. Ibid., p. 261.
32. Ibid., p. 77.
33. *Arms and Influence*, pp. 182-3.

34. Ibid., p. 183.
35. Ibid., p. 184.
36. Ibid., p. 204.
37. Ibid., p. 208.
38. Ibid., p. 235.
39. *The Strategy of Conflict*, p. 207.
40. Ibid., p. 211.
41. Ibid., p. 231.
42. Thomas C. Schelling and Morton H. Halperin, *Strategy and Arms Control*, New York, The Twentieth Century Fund, 1961, p. 2.
43. Ibid., p. 77.
44. Ibid., p. 57.
45. Ibid., p. 6.
46. See Thomas C. Schelling, 'What Went Wrong With Arms Control?' in O. Osterud (ed.), *Studies of War and Peace*, Oslo, Norwegian University Press, 1986, p. 102.
47. See Oran Young, *The Politics of Force: Bargaining during Superpower Crises*, Princeton, Princeton University Press, 1968, and Glenn Snyder and Paul Diesing, *Conflict Among Nations*, Princeton, Princeton University Press, 1977.
48. *Arms and Influence*, pp. 101–2.
49. *The Strategy of Conflict*, p. 201.
50. See Alexander George and Richard Smoke, *Deterrence in American Foreign Policy: Theory and Practice*, New York, Columbia University Press, 1974.
51. See R. Jervis, *The Illogic of American Nuclear Strategy*, Ithaca, Cornell University Press, 1984.
52. *The Strategy of Conflict*, pp. 134–5.

6 ANTHONY BUZZARD

John Baylis

To those who knew him Anthony Buzzard was both an admirable and an irritating man.[1] After a long and distinguished naval career, he was widely respected in the 1950s for his critique of the prevailing strategy of Massive Retaliation and his enunciation of an alternative doctrine of Graduated Deterrence. He was also admired as a devout Christian who wrestled continuously with the issues of morality in the nuclear age. Indeed the search for limitations in war and a more graduated concept of deterrence were inextricably linked to his deep concern about the ethical issues of nuclear war. His naval experience and after he retired his work for the World and British Councils of Churches meant that he was uniquely placed to provide the link between the strategists and the churchmen who put together the Brighton Conference in January 1957 which led to the foundation of the Institute for Strategic Studies.[2]

At the same time there is no doubt that he irritated not only those who rejected his strategic prescriptions but also many of his naval colleagues and even some of those within the so-called 'Commentators Circle' who supported many of his ideas on Graduated Deterrence.[3] He himself accepted that he had a 'bee in his bonnet'.[4] His growing frustration with what he saw as the dangerous weaknesses of British and Western defence policies in the mid- and late 1950s caused him to bombard politicians, civil servants, high-ranking serving officers, church leaders and the press with letters and articles advocating changes in policy based on his own superior strategic analysis.[5] The rather obsessive nature of Buzzard's proselytizing was not always well received, especially in the defence Establishment of which he was once a member.[6]

In his naval career Anthony Buzzard was mainly involved in gunnery, staff and naval/air appointments. Between 1941 and 1944 he served on the Strategic Joint Planning Staff which gave him access to many of the major strategic debates of World War II. His career prospered in the post-war period, and between 1951 and 1954 he held the post of director of naval intelligence (DNI) which brought him to the very centre of the discussions about British and Western nuclear strategy in this formative period of the early 1950s. As such, Buzzard was involved in the major debates about the British Global Strategy Paper of 1952, the Conservative government's Radical Review of defence between 1952 and 1954 as well as the American 'New Look' strategy of 1953 and the subsequent Massive Retaliation doctrine. To understand Buzzard's thinking it is important to understand the context of these debates about nuclear deterrence which characterized the post-war period.

Recognizing Britain's vulnerability in the nuclear age, the chiefs of staff began articulating a rudimentary doctrine of nuclear deterrence as early as 1946.[7] Initially this involved an emphasis on the threat to destroy Soviet towns and cities in retaliation for any aggression. It wasn't long, however, before a more discriminating approach to deterrence was adopted. While the United States was emphasizing an atomic offensive against Soviet industrial and population centres in the event of war, British military planners from 1947 onwards began to turn their attention to the need to threaten military targets (such as air bases, submarine and mine-laying bases) which particularly threatened Britain.[8] It was felt that the Strategic Air Offensive, designed to achieve a single war-winning blow against the Soviet Union, could be left to the United States while Britain concentrated on targets which were vital to limit damage to the United Kingdom itself.[9]

By the early 1950s, however, the American conception of deterrence demanded not only an emphasis on expanding and modernizing the Strategic Air Command with its nuclear missions but also building up vast conventional forces to meet those of the Soviet Union. Despite Britain's initial acceptance of this conventional build-up contained in the 1952 Lisbon Goals, economic circumstances demanded, and a different strategic logic suggested, a cheaper version of deterrence. For Sir John Slessor, the chief of the air staff, there was not 'the remotest chance' that NATO could build up the force requirements and the war reserves necessary for a conventional strategy.[10] For Slessor, the West should go 'nap on atomic air power', which in his view was 'the best chance of preventing war'.[11] Britain's new strategy (based on Slessor's thinking) was contained in the Global Strategy Paper which was produced by the chiefs of staff in late April and early May 1952. Although the paper emphasized the need for cold war forces and conventional capabilities in Europe, pride of place was given to nuclear deterrence. The report of the chiefs of staff on Global Strategy argued, however, that if deterrence failed and global war broke out, it would pass 'through an initial period of unparalleled intensity, which may last only a few weeks, followed by a prolonged phase during which all forms of activity are much reduced'.[12] As such the paper represented something of a compromise between the ideas of the RAF and those of the navy. For the RAF, priority had to be given to providing the capability in the form of the V-Bomber force to undertake effective 'blunting' missions against Soviet air and submarine bases.[13] The navy on the other hand, desperately searching for a role in the nuclear age, stressed the 'broken-backed warfare' concept and the vital role which would be played by the navy in the prolonged phase after the initial intense strikes had taken place.[14]

It was in the context of these strategic debates that Rear Admiral Buzzard's ideas evolved. As the Conservative government's Radical Review of defence between 1952 and 1954 forced significant cuts in the defence budget and modifications in the implementation of the Global Strategy Paper, so inter-service rivalry in Britain became more intense.[15] The Navy came under pressure as criticisms of the 'broken-backed warfare' concept mounted. Government ministers increasingly seemed to back the claims of the RAF with its stress on nuclear deterrence and the importance of the initial phase of any future war.[16] In July 1953 Rear Admiral Buzzard, as 'one of the ablest members of the Naval staff', was sent to see the minister of supply, Duncan Sandys, who was regarded as the main anti-naval member of the government. The purpose of the meeting was to give the minister 'a seminar on naval strategy'.[17] Sandys, however, remained unconvinced of the navy's case after a three-hour session and continued his campaign in favour of the strategic air offensive and against the carrier and cruiser forces. This was a campaign Sandys was to continue when he became minister of defence in 1957, and Buzzard, by this time a civilian, was to remain one of his staunchest critics.[18]

Buzzard's contribution to strategic analysis while he was director of naval intelligence was not confined to the inter-service debate about V-Bombers and carriers (although this debate did colour his wider thinking). In July 1953 he wrote a major paper in which he made a powerful critique of Western strategic doctrine as a whole.[19] In this paper, in which can be seen the genesis of his later ideas, he argued that the 'mass destruction policy', which would involve the immediate use of American

strategic airpower against Soviet industrial and population centres, would be unlikely
to achieve its desired results within six weeks as it was hoped. All of the estimates
from the joint intelligence board indicated, he argued, that it would take at least six
months, not six weeks, before attacks on Russian industries would deprive their
fighting forces of supplies. It was wrong, therefore, Buzzard argued, to rely on quick
results:

> . . . no one knows what the result of the initial air battle will be, much depends on
> such matters as who gets in the first blow, whether we have the necessary
> intelligence and what casualties to aircraft will be. What would be the accuracy of
> bombing and what would be the effect of deception, and what would be the effect of
> weapons of mass destruction, particularly on morale.[20]

According to Buzzard the 'mass destruction policy' made the avoidance of war much
more difficult because the incentive to strike first would become much greater. Just as
importantly, he believed, it also made the localization of any outbreak of hostilities
increasingly more difficult and it brought Russian retaliation to British ports and
cities with mass destruction weapons, at a time when the West would be at a much less
advanced stage of 'mobilization' than the Soviet Union.[21]

This assessment of the ineffectiveness and dangers of Western nuclear strategy led
Buzzard to formulate an alternative strategy of his own. This, he argued, would
involve using mass destruction weapons at the start of any war only against military
targets. Atomic bombs 'would be kept in the locker to deal with Russian industries and
centres of administration, if our own cities were attacked'.[22] Here we see an early
version of the 'city hostage strategy' which was to become popular with American
strategists later in the 1950s and 1960s. Buzzard's view was that this emphasis on
counter-force as opposed to counter-value targeting with atomic weapons:

> . . . would enable the maximum air effort to be made in the vital land campaign at
> the start, when it is of the utmost importance to buy time. It would also enable us to
> use chemical and atomic weapons, tactically, without fear of Russian retaliation
> with chemical weapons on our cities and ports. Only thus shall we obtain the
> freedom to work towards a strategy which will ultimately prove satisfactory both as
> a deterrent and for war winning purposes politically and militarily.[23]

In his paper Buzzard argued forcefully that this alternative strategy would help to
minimize the instabilities inherent in the existing strategy and would provide an
effective way to limit hostilities if they were to break out. Deterrence would be
enhanced, and an emphasis on the limitation of war would prevent total catastrophy if
deterrence did ever fail. Buzzard also believed that the concept of limited war had
another major advantage. By concentrating on counterforce targeting, the onus for
attacking civilian targets would be transferred to Russian shoulders. This, he believed,
would greatly improve allied morale given the public concern about the first use of
weapons of mass destruction against towns and cities. Once again Buzzard was
articulating an idea which was to become popular with later strategists and which was
to be emphasized in the McNamara doctrine in the early 1960s.

Buzzard's criticisms of Western strategic policies in 1953 were not, however, shared
by other members of the defence Establishment of the time where the efficacy of
deterrence through nuclear threats against Soviet cities was widely accepted and
enshrined from 1954 onwards in the American 'New Look' and the strategy of Massive

Retaliation. For the British chiefs of staff, like McGrigor, Dickson and the ex-chief of the air staff, Slessor, the key questions of the day concerned Britain's role in the counteroffensive, which forces should be involved and whether Britain required an independent targeting policy as Soviet technological developments weakened the credibility of the American nuclear guarantee.[24]

The fact that his views won few converts did not, however, deter Buzzard. He regarded the issues as being so important that he was not prepared to give up his campaign for an alternative strategy when he retired from the post of director of naval intelligence in 1954. He took up an appointment as group armaments adviser to Vickers and became an increasingly active member of various defence and disarmament commissions of the World and British Councils of Churches. By the mid-1950s he had helped to bring the debate about nuclear strategy out into the public domain with a series of letters to the press and a number of articles in various scholarly journals in Britain and the United States.[25] As a result of these letters and articles Buzzard became the leading exponent of his day of a Graduated Deterrence strategy.

Buzzard's starting point was his view that Massive Retaliation was incapable of dealing with the most likely threats to Western security. In his view 'deliberate and pre-meditated aggression on a world-wide scale or even a continental scale by the Communists' was largely out of the question.[26] The main menace to peace in his view arose from the problem of Communist subversion exploiting local nationalist difficulties. It was these kinds of conflicts which were most likely to escalate into direct military confrontation between East and West. What was required, according to Buzzard, was a defence policy which continued to deter deliberate aggression but which also provided the necessary local tactical strength to deter limited Soviet aggression and to deal with local nationalist quarrels. Buzzard's view was that the existing policy of Massive Retaliation was wholly inadequate to deal with these kinds of limited threats. A strategy which 'threatened to destroy civilization as a result of any aggression too powerful for our small conventional forces to handle' was likely to be regarded as a bluff by the Soviet Union.[27] Buzzard argued that such a strategy left room for misunderstanding and perhaps exploitation by the Soviet Union.

In a series of articles written in 1956 Buzzard developed some of the ideas presented in his 1953 paper when he was DNI.[28] Given the weaknesses of Massive Retaliation, he argued that what was required was an intermediate capability to deal with limited wars too great for Western conventional forces to handle. Graduated Deterrence would provide the option for intermediate action by establishing in peacetime a distinction between the tactical use of atomic weapons and chemical weapons on the one hand and the unlimited strategic use of the H-Bomb on the other. Buzzard suggested that in the event of a threat of aggression, too strong for the West's conventional forces but not warranting the use of the 'H' Bomb, Graduated Deterrence would allow the West to say to a potential aggressor: 'If you use aggression we will, if necessary, use atomic (and perhaps chemical i.e. gas) weapons against your armed forces, but we will not, on this issue use hydrogen or bacteriological weapons at all, unless you do, and we will not use atomic (or chemical) weapons against centres of population, unless you do'.[29] Buzzard accepted that given the realities of war certain exceptions to the definition of centres of population would have to be made, especially in terms of cities in the front line of the fighting and those with airfields in close proximity.[30] The main point, however, was that potential adversaries should be faced by realistic threats to deter aggression, and if deterrence broke down there should be every encouragement to show restraint.

One of the most powerful themes running through Buzzard's writings, apart from the need to improve the credibility of deterrence, is the importance he attached to morality in the developmment of strategic doctrine. Graduate Deterrence is portrayed as being morally superior to what he describes as the two extremes of Massive Retaliation and Unilateralism. Buzzard, as a military man and a devout Christian, was concerned to wrestle with the predicament in which Christians find themselves in the nuclear age. His solution to the moral dilemma is most clearly articulated in an article entitled 'The Christian Conscience and Modern War' written in 1964.[31] In this article, he accepts that massive retaliators and unilaterialists are both genuinely concerned with maintaining peace and preventing war. He suggests, however, that massive retaliators tend to feel that Christian ethics should be reserved for their personal lives and that government policy should pursue that which is expedient for the national interest. Unilateralists, on the other hand, tend to base their judgements on moral principles, with more sensitivity to their consciences and what seems morally right. Buzzard argues, however, that there is a third position, which he describes as a 'policy of moderation'. This is a position which in many respects underpins his concept of Graduate Deterrence. 'Moderators' take a moral stand somewhere between massive retaliators and unilateralists in which expediency and moral principle are not too far apart. Both are needed, he argues, 'because only expediency will enable the first steps to be taken in practice; and only moral principle, acting as guide lines, can ensure that these first steps are taken in the right direction'.[32]

In a section which has a great deal of contemporary interest Buzzard suggests that for the massive retaliator defence has become an end in itself and deterrence almost the sole means to that end. Unilateralists on the other hand are inclined to jump straight to nuclear disarmament on the assumption that this is an end in itself. In contrast Buzzard sums up the position of the 'moderator' (which is his own position) in the following way:

> All war is evil. We must therefore do all we can to abolish it, to prevent it, or at least to limit it. But there is another evil which has to be abolished, prevented or at least limited, and that is the evil of aggression, with the tyranny and injustice which follows it. We are in fact faced with a choice of evils — war or aggression.
>
> Our overall aim and criterion for choosing between these two evils can only be the good of humanity as a whole — concern for all our neighbours in the world. And this means striving to uphold justice, for, in a community, justice is the collective equivalent of the love which is the ethical aim of our relations with our neighbours as individuals. . .
>
> We have to balance, in the scales of justice, on the one hand, the evil of aggression and tyrrany, and on the other, the evil of fighting and war which results from resisting the aggressor or tyrant.[33]

On the basis of this moral position Buzzard emphasized the importance of the doctrine of the 'just war' in placing restraints on fighting. He accepted that the 'just war' doctrine had been abused in the past and in some respects was out of date in the middle of the twentieth century, but he insisted that it still contained four important basic principles which ought to condition our thinking about war in the nuclear age.

The first was the notion of restraint, in terms of both aims and means in war, 'so that it remains the lesser evil — the principle of proportion'.[34] Buzzard stressed the importance of limiting the aims and means in any conflict which might occur in order to make sure that the killing and suffering of war was never disproportionate to the issues at stake. Second, there was the 'principle of discrimination' — between military forces and civilians. For Buzzard, the direct and intentional attacks on civilians threatened in the Massive Retaliation doctrine, must be 'ruled out as absolutely wrong — except by way of reprisals'.[35] He believed strongly that such actions (like many of those against German and Japanese cities) could only be classed as murder. Buzzard does, however, draw a distinction between intentional attacks on civilians and indirect and unintentional killings of civilians which happen as a result of the secondary effect of a state's defence against an aggressor's military forces. The third principle is that of control. In Buzzard's view it was not possible to justify in moral terms methods which were likely to result in 'destruction becoming out of control of the human conscience'.[36] By this he meant actions which could lead to an uncontrolled spread or escalation of war, and the uncontrolled spread of suffering after a war, in terms of the genetic effects which might result. And finally, he stressed the importance of 'the principle of reprisal', or more accurately 'protective retribution'. Buzzard believed that although initiating indiscriminate methods of warfare could not be justified, 'resorting to such methods by way of reprisal for similar enemy action was permitted . . . as a means of stopping an enemy from indulging in such action'.[37]

On the basis of these principles Buzzard believed that morally the issue was clear. The West should not cause, or threaten to cause, more destruction than was necessary. This meant that the West's response to aggression should be strictly limited (in terms of weapons, targets, area and time) to the absolute minimum force which was necessary 'to deter and repel aggression, prevent any unnecessary extension of the conflict, and permit a return to negotiation at the earliest opportunity — without seeking total victory or unconditional surrender'.[38]

Buzzard's carefully thought out moral stance made him particularly critical of the defence policies pursued by the Conservative government of the day. Although he rejected the concept of Massive Retaliation on moral grounds, he believed that by the mid-1950s the United States at least was seeking to introduce limitations into their strategy in practice.[39] The British government by contrast, he believed, were moving in the other direction towards an even more full-blown massive destruction policy than the one contained in the 1952 Global Strategy Paper. Buzzard believed that the government was obsessed by the idea of total war and largely ignored the issues raised by more limited conflicts.[40] After the Sandys' White Paper of 1957, Buzzard even went as far as formally resigning from his local Conservative Party in protest over the dangers and immorality of existing defence policy. In his letter of resignation he complained bitterly that the government's handling of defence policy, including their actions in the Suez crisis, were no longer acceptable to him.

> They are, in my view, ignoring absolutely fundamental moral principles, as well as basic political and military factors and there comes a point at which one's conscience just cannot continue to subscribe to the policy presented . . . there are certain things that one must not tolerate.[41]

He believed passionately that existing policies were so flawed that they could well result either in a disastrous war or in the dissolution of the Western alliance.[42] As a result, Buzzard's constant refrain throughout the period of the late 1950s and early 1960s was that there was a desperate need for a change of heart, a new spirit in the approach to the whole business of war, 'particularly in the government machinery where strategy and policy are made'.[43]

Despite his repeated criticisms of the Sandys' doctrine, as the earlier argument suggested Buzzard was no supporter of the Campaign for Nuclear Disarmament (CND) which emerged in the late 1950s in Britain. Buzzard was prepared to give up Britain's independent nuclear deterrent under certain circumstances but not on moral grounds. He argued that nuclear weapons were not intrinsically evil in themselves. What mattered was how states used or intended to use them. Indeed he saw some positive moral value in possessing nuclear weapons: 'For the fear which they have struck into all men's hearts is making us more reluctant to war to achieve our ambitions. Nuclear weapons have reduced the prospects of prolonged, world-wide, conventional conflict like World War II, which, do not let us forget, killed tens of millions.[45]

Buzzard argued that to disarm unilaterally while a potential adversary continued to possess nuclear weapons might well be morally irresponsible. Conventional war might be more likely in such circumstances, and the West's enemies might be tempted to use nuclear weapons as 'we had used them at Hiroshima and Nagasaki when we had a monopoly of those weapons'.[46] Buzzard believed that nuclear deterrence did not necessarily defy any basic moral principles. A nuclear strategy which helped to keep the peace (provided it was governed by the limitations he laid down) was acceptable in moral terms.

Apart from this powerful moral case for Graduated Deterrence, Buzzard also argued that there were strong political arguments in its favour. Because Graduated Deterrence would provide an effective intermediate deterrent against the most likely threat of local aggression the Western deterrent posture as a whole would be strengthened, he believed, and there would be more latitude for diplomacy. Buzzard believed that the option for intermediate action would enhance the West's ability to negotiate with the Soviet Union from a position of local tactical strength. Such an ability, he believed, was becoming increasingly important in the late 1950s as strategic stalemate between the two superpowers approached.[47]

Just as importantly, Buzzard believed that because Graduated Deterrence was less drastic than Massive Retaliation it would help to reduce tension and build up trust between East and West. In this early version of confidence-building measures as an important aspect of security, Buzzard argued that Graduated Deterrence would be less frightening and intimidating to the Soviet Union than the threats of immediate annihilation contained in the Massive Retaliation doctrine.[48] Buzzard believed that it was necessary to take into account these genuine Soviet fears. While not under-estimating the Soviet threat to Western interests, like his friend George Kennan, he favoured a process of dialogue with the Soviet Union which he hoped would contribute in the longer term to disengagement.[49] The announcement of a new strategy, Buzzard argued, would demonstrate to the Eastern bloc that the West genuinely wished to limit all possible use of nuclear weapons. It would constitute an assurance of the West's sincerity. Whether or not the Soviet Union responded would then be an important test of their sincerity in negotiations, especially disarmament negotiations.

Buzzard believed that by relying more on tactical strength to match Soviet tactical forces, Graduated Deterrence would convert Western security requirements into terms more comparable to those of the Soviet Union itself. This convergence in terms of strategic concepts would be more likely, he suggested, to lead to balanced, stage-by-stage reductions in armaments.[50] This idea that greater symmetry in strategic concepts between East and West would help to break down the barriers of mutual misunderstanding and encourage the process of disarmament was to reappear again in the late 1970s and early 1980s.[51] Indeed many of Buzzard's disarmament proposals have something of a contemporary ring about them. He argued, for example, in favour of a test-ban agreement. He urged the opening of negotiations 'for the demilitarization of space before it is too late'. And he urged cuts in numbers of strategic nuclear weapons and the level of conventional forces in Europe. Buzzard even went as far as to argue that 'the surest road to ultimate disarmament probably lies through Graduated Deterrence'.[52] Whether he actually believed in the practical possibility of complete nuclear disarmament, however, is not altogether clear.

Buzzard believed that Graduated Deterrence would not only contribute to greater security through encouraging disarmament, it would also have specific military advantages for the West. By barring hydrogen bombs and the mass destruction of cities, he argued, both East and West would benefit enormously on an absolute basis. NATO, however, would gain more. Both would benefit because (unlike under the existing strategy) there would be restraints on the use of weapons of mass destruction against most cities, industries, communication centres and ports. The West, however, would gain most, Buzzard suggested, because of its greater dependence on ports 'which form such bottlenecks and such ideal targets for nuclear and chemical weapons'.[53] This advantage would be particularly important in the crucial early stages of a war because the mobilization and deployment of the Allied forces were always likely to be much less advanced at the start than those of the Warsaw Pact. Another gain, he argued, would result from the fact that cities could still be attacked with high explosives, and in terms of technique and precision attack the Allies were superior. Faced with local aggression the West would be able to utilize its superiority in atomic weapons, as well as exploiting the great defensive properties of these weapons. Such a policy, he believed, would help particularly to redress the tactical balance of power and improve the West's ability to hold territory.

Taking into account this range of moral, political and military considerations, Buzzard believed that Graduated Deterrence was 'infinitely superior to Massive Realiation'.[54] He was, however, aware that criticisms could be made of Graduated Deterrence and many of his early writings in particular are taken up with trying to deal with the major objections which came from diverse quarters.

One of the major critics of Buzzard's Graduated Deterrence thesis, as one might expect, was Sir John Slessor. In books, articles and public debates with Buzzard in the mid-fifties Slessor went out of his way to argue that the attempt to impose limitations on the use of hydrogen weapons was neither desirable nor possible.[55] For Slessor, Graduated Deterrence was a dangerous policy for a number of reasons: first, because it would undermine deterrence and make war more likely. Any attempt to graduate deterrence, Slessor believed, could well cause 'a would-be aggressor to believe that the game might conceivably be worth the candle'.[56] If the Soviet Union believed that it would be immune from attacks by hydrogen weapons it might well decide to utilize its conventional superiority to over-run Western Europe. To Slessor the threat of horrendous destruction was more likely to deter.[57]

Slessor was not alone in this criticism of Graduated Deterrence. On the instructions of the Chiefs of Staff (COS) Committee the Joint Planning Staff (JPS) undertook a detailed study of Buzzard's ideas in late 1955 to 'determine whether the adoption of such a policy would strengthen our aim of preventing war'. As a result of their study, which included discussions with Buzzard himself, the JPS produced a report which was considered by the COS committee on the 13 December. The report was highly critical of Graduated Deterrence. In their view there were

. . . practical objections to declaring distinctions between tactical and strategic targets as proposed by Graduate Deterrence. A determined Communist drive would only be stopped by nuclear attack, not only on targets close to the front line of the land armies, but also on air fields, communication centres, bases and perhaps cities, many of them remote from the front line. The distinction between tactical and strategic targets thus becomes impracticable.[58]

The view of the JPS was that Graduated Deterrence would weaken deterrence not strengthen it. In their view there was no case for giving up the policy of Massive Retaliation. This judgement was conveyed to Buzzard by the First Sea Lord Mountbatten, on 2 January 1956. In his letter Mountbatten confirmed that the chiefs of staff saw practical objections to drawing distinctions between tactical and strategic targets for nuclear weapons. They felt it would be against Britain's interests to reduce its deterrent value by drawing any definite dividing line between small and large nuclear weapons. This was also the view which had been expressed by the cabinet in April 1955.[59]

Slessor's public criticisms of Buzzard's ideas were very much those of the defence Establishment. Apart from weakening deterrence Slessor also argued that Graduated Deterrence was dangerous in other respects. He rejected, for example, Buzzard's claim that atomic weapons were capable of holding 175 or so Soviet divisions if deterrence ever broke down. According to Slessor, atomic weapons had not redressed the tactical balance of power, as Buzzard was arguing, and it was dangerous to believe that they had.[60]

Another worry which Slessor expressed (and which was contained in the JPS report) was that Buzzard had ignored important political considerations in his search for an intermediate capability. To say that atomic weapons would only be used in the area of the front line, or against cities in the battle zone, would not, he suggested, be acceptable to the Germans, especially if Soviet cities were to be largely immune from attack by nuclear weapons.[61] The strength of Slessor's argument on this point would seem to be confirmed by the reluctance of all West German governments to move away from the Massive Retaliation if the 1960s in favour of a more graduated flexible strategy. The need to give nuclear weapons a high profile to deter all wars (conventional and nuclear) was an important aspect of the West German approach to Western strategy.

In an attempt to deal with some of these criticisms, Buzzard vigorously refuted the charge that Graduated Deterrence would undermine deterrence and make war more likely. In his view it was the credibility of Massive Retaliation which was suspect based as it was on the unbelievable threat to commit suicide. Graduated Deterrence, he argued, was more likely to be credible against aggression because the Soviet leaders would know that 'our deterrent — not necessarily being suicidal — would be less likely to bluff, and that we would be more united in our determination to retaliate'.[62] He also pointed out that the risk of hydrogen bombs being used and the destruction of Soviet cities remained, even with Graduated Deterrence. The Soviet Union would still have to reckon with the risk that war might escalate and its cities might be devastated.

There is certainly something to be said for Buzzard's argument on this point, especially his critique of the inadequacies of the all-or-nothing approach to Massive Retaliation in the emerging age of strategic parity. Where Buzzard's argument is more contentious, however, is on Slessor's point that trying to draw distinctions betwen the tactical and strategic uses of nuclear weapons is impractical. Slessor argued that even if distinctions could be drawn, it would be unlikely that they would be adhered to for very long. Echoing a broadcast made by ex-Prime Minister Clement Attlee, on 10 June 1954, Slessor argued that in real wars when the existence of nations was at stake any weapon would be used in the last resort.[63] He didn't believe that the Soviets would be likely to refrain from bombing with nuclear weapons the ports and main rail centres through which the West would be bringing its reinforcements and supplies. In a major war when the very survival of the state was at stake, Graduated Deterrence would not, he believed, prove practical. The rules would soon break down. 'In the last resort no nation is going to accept defeat with the hydrogen bomb still in its armoury.'[64]

The chiefs of staff were also of the same opinion. In early 1954 they spent some time considering the possibility of limiting a nuclear war and came to the conclusion that while both sides would do everything they could to prevent the escalation of local wars to all-out global wars, it was unrealistic to expect that warfare could be limited if tactical nuclear weapons were used. In their view: 'if such weapons could be used they would go some way towards redressing the balance in numerical superiority which the Soviet land forces will always enjoy. However, we doubt if their use is practical, because of the risk that it would lead to unlimited war once the moral and practical restrictions on the use of any nuclear weapons had been removed'.[65]

Buzzard accepted that the task of making useful distinctions between hydrogen and atomic weapons and of defining centres of population and their geographic limits was a difficult one. He argued, however, that provided there was sufficient study of the problems of drawing distinctions, they were not insuperable.[66] Once distinctions had been worked out in peacetime the task of securing limitations in war would become more manageable. For Buzzard the crucial point was that both sides would have every incentive possible to make sure that tactical atomic war did not escalate to all-out nuclear holocaust. Both sides would recognize that they must not allow the conflict to get out of hand. If they did, the consequences would be utterly devastating. Buzzard spelled out his position on this question very clearly in a reply to a letter from Alun Gwynne Jones on 5 April 1962. The future Lord Chalfont had questioned his attempt to draw clear distinctions between tactical and strategic uses of nuclear weapons. In his reply Buzzard said:

I agree with you that the distinction between the various types and uses of atomic weapons is difficult and unlikely to last for any length of time. I agree too, that the distinction between conventional and tactical atomic weapons is more important and indeed quite crucial.
Nevertheless so long as there remains a real danger of tactical atomic warfare and particularly so long as we remain — as we must — in a position where we might have to threaten the first use of tactical atomic weapons, I do not see how one can escape the responsibility of making all possible preparations for distinctions in the types and uses of tactical weapons.[67]

Buzzard has a point, states involved in an atomic war would clearly have every incentive to keep the conflict limited and states do have a responsibility to think about how best this can be done. The question, however, remains whether it is reasonable to expect that nuclear wars will remain limited and whether it is reasonable to plan on that basis. Although belligerents undoubtedly would have a major incentive to maintain limitations, a very strong case can be made that in the fraught, unpredictable and highly charged atmosphere of nuclear war this would prove to be extremely difficult, if not impossible. If the chances are very great that escalation will occur, is it wise to adopt such a policy? Even some of Buzzards close friends in the 'Commentators Circle' who shared many of his ideas questioned this aspect of Graduated Deterrence. Liddell Hart, who corresponded regularly with Buzzard, was one who felt that this was a weak link in his thinking. He felt that Buzzard was 'much too optimistic when he argued that there was no reason why tactical weapons should spread to H-Bombing in a war of limited aims'.[68] Liddell Hart also quoted the chief strategic planner in the Pentagon who claimed:

. . . to have a very gloomy feeling about how a war would develop after the first fission bomb had been dropped — tactically or otherwise. There would, of course, be reprisals in the same fashion and, I greatly fear, the result would be a gradual drift towards greater and greater frightfulness and then final disaster.' [69]

P. M. S. Blackett was another who told Buzzard that if atomic weapons were used, he did not believe 'there would be any reasonable prospect of the fighting not spreading to total global war'.[70] Michael Howard also felt that Buzzard was too rational, in his belief that 'it was possible to calibrate exactly degrees of force in a manner which would be understood and respected by both belligerents engaged in all the confusion of war'.[71] Michael Howard's explanation was that Buzzard was a sailor and therefore had no understanding of the Clausewitzian concept of 'friction'!

It would be wrong, however, to believe that Buzzard was unaware of the possibility that limited atomic warfare might escalate to total war. He accepted that it was conceivable that wars could get out of control. Buzzard dealt with this problem by suggesting that if there was a threat of wars becoming utterly total and indescriminate the West could always, and should always, accept a cease-fire,, 'if necessary on the enemy's terms'.[72] In such circumstances Buzzard clearly accepted that it was better to be 'red than dead'. Again the moral strand in Buzzard's thinking is clear. In a letter to George Kennan on the 2 May 1958 he argued that:

> . . . we have no moral right to commit our children to suicide rather than Communist occupation, if it should come to that choice. More emphatically still, we have surely no right whatever to commit to death, disease and deformity, the millions of people and children in the neutral countries of the world who will have no say or concern with our quarrel with the Communists.[73]

Despite these arguments, however, Buzzard continued to argue that both sides would be desperately anxious to avoid total war. He genuinely believed that there was a good chance that 'the dangerous emotional factors could be kept under control by pre-conditioning'.[74]

It is easy to be critical of Buzzard on this point. It is less easy to provide a viable alternative. By the mid-1950s there was a growing number of Western strategists who rejected Massive Retaliation. A consensus was beginning to emerge that it was necessary to find an intermediate level of response to aggression if deterrence was to retain any credibility. The argument, however, was over what form this intermediate level of response should take. There were those at the time, like P. M. S. Blackett, who believed that the West should confine itself to conventional forces only, putting much more effort into stronger and more mobile forces.[75] Such arguments reappeared in the 1980s with the debates about the need for reform of NATO strategy.[76] Buzzard himself provided a penetrating critique of non-nuclear deterrence on both economic and strategic grounds. Sufficiently large conventional forces to match those of the Soviet Union, he argued, would be very costly in terms of both manpower and matériel.[77] It was unlikely that Western governments would be prepared to make the necessary sacrifices to improve conventional forces to the level required. In this respect he was right. On strategic grounds Buzzard argued that it was necessary to pose unacceptable risks to the Soviet Union. This, he believed, could only be done with nuclear weapons. The threat of nuclear reprisals was necessary against a nuclear adversary:

> . . . in order to make the Communist leaders realise that if they should try to spread
> or

escalate a limited conflict serious risk to vital Russian targets would be involved. We don't have to tell them just how much risk and just how far we would go, but we have to make it clear that it would be far enough to make any attempt to test us on this matter a thoroughly unworthwhile exercise for them.[78]

This is not to say that Buzzard was opposed to the improvement of the West's conventional forces. He told Blackett in February 1950 that the West must be prepared to deal with every local limited issue with conventional forces only 'up to the hilt'.[79] It was necessary to improve conventional forces as far as possible. But, he argued, it was also important to let a potential aggressor know that 'if pressed too far, we would, if absolutely necessary, initiate tactical atomic warfare for really serious local limited issues'.[80] Buzzard's position was that the West should try and defend with hard-hitting mobile streamlined conventional forces but should keep the tactical atomic threat overhanging the situation in order to prevent the Soviet Union from daring to make use of its massive conventional power.

Buzzard's writings in the 1950s suggest that he was not in favour of what strategists now call a 'no-first-use' declaration. He was, however, to revise his ideas to a certain extent on this matter in his later writings. As he became more and more preoccupied with the moral issues of peace and war in the nuclear age, he became increasingly worried about the government's emphasis on the early-use of nuclear weapons.[81] By 1963 he was arguing that it was important for the West 'to escape as far, and as fast as possible' from its reliance on the first use of tactical nuclear weapons and to make the necessary sacrifices to achieve this.[82] Increasingly, movement in the direction of no-first-use was becoming an important objective. His dilemma remained, however. He still believed that nothing should be done to undermine deterrence by easing Soviet calculations. As such he stopped short of recommending a formal 'no-first-use' declaration, arguing that the government should not 'announce in advance just how far they would go'.[83]

This illustrates another aspect of Buzzard's position. It demonstrates his continuing concern to make sure that his proposals for reform remained within the realms of practical politics. To those who advocated a conventional deterrent strategy and unilateralism he pointed out that there was little chance of Western governments adopting such policies. He told Blackett in February 1958 that it was inconceivable that the American and British governments would move: 'straight from "Massive Retaliation" to conventional forces only in one step. So it seems to me that we should do our damnedest to persuade them to take the first step in the right direction that is in fact practical'.[84]

It was no good, he argued, putting forward policies which their proponents regarded as right but which were unlikely to be adopted in practice. 'For my part', he said, 'I am determined to put forward something which does stand a reasonable chance of being accepted.'[85]

This emphasis on pragmatism and the need to take account of political reality is an important aspect of Buzzard's contribution to the strategic debate. He was not alone in this. His concern to treat concrete situations within a context and his reluctance to 'theorize in the abstract' helped to produce what Armstrong has described as a distinctive British approach to nuclear strategy.[86] John Garnett has commented elsewhere that:

. . . whereas there is a fundamental, almost timeless quality, about some American strategic theory, its British counterpart is very firmly related to specific problems facing the British government. The theoretical formulations of deterrence analysis by G. Snyder or A. Wohlstetter have no counterpart in the British literature. Nor is there any British equivalent to the theorizing of T. C. Schelling on threats and bargaining, or H. Kahn on 'escalation' theorizing which is at such a fundamental level of enquiry that it can be applied in any historical time scale. One is tempted to make the distinction between 'pure' and 'applied' strategic thought, and to comment on a British tendency to avoid the former.[87]

Buzzard, with his specific criticisms of Massive Retaliation and his constant lobbying of the British government to adopt his carefully worked out alternative strategy of Graduated Deterrence is a good example of this more concrete British approach to strategic thought.

Despite its concrete form, Graduated Deterrence was never accepted by the British or any other Western government in its 'pure' form. It was, however, one of the most influential alternative strategies of the 1950s and a strong case can be made that Buzzard's ideas have had a profound influence on strategic thought right down to the present day. Not only was Buzzard at the forefront of the campaign against Massive Retaliation, his writings helped to pioneer thinking about limited war in the nuclear age. Although the theory of limited war is usually associated with other more famous American strategists (some of whom are dealt with elsewhere in this volume), Buzzard's contribution was just as important, and he deserves greater recognition than he has received. 'The Buzzard Papers' at Churchill College, Cambridge, reveal the extent of his influence on various American writers, including Henry Kissinger, Albert Wohlstetter, Arnold Wolfers, Paul Nitze and Thomas Schelling.[88] Buzzard was in regular correspondence with Henry Kissinger, for example, throughout 1955 and 1956 when the latter did much of his pioneering work. Kissinger and Buzzard on a number of occasions exchanged articles and also commented in detail on each other's ideas.[89] Kissinger expressed himself in one letter to be in almost complete agreement with Buzzard on the ideas expressed in his article in *World Politics* in 1956.[90] He also asked Buzzard for help with British attitudes towards the nuclear question for some of his own research.[91] In another letter in 1955 Paul Nitze argued that his own recent article in *Foreign Affairs* had been stimulated by discussions with Buzzard.[92] Tom Schelling was another who expressed the debt he owed to Buzzard in the development of his own ideas on the theory of limited war.[93] Buzzard was a frequent visitor to the United States to talk to various defence groups, and such was the interest in his ideas that in the summer of 1958 he received an invitation from A. W. Marshall to visit the prestigious RAND Corporation in Santa Monica, California to discuss Graduated Deterrence with a number of influential American strategists who were working there.[94]

To assess the influence of any single individual on the strategic debates of the 1950s and early 1960s is inevitably rather difficult. A strong case can be made, however, that Buzzard's campaign to introduce a greater degree of rationality and credibility into nuclear strategy did play an important part in the evolution of Western strategic thought away from Massive Retaliation and towards the McNamara doctrine of the early 1960s. Michael Howard has written, with some justification, that Buzzard's ideas of Graduated Deterrence were in many respects the true precursors of the whole concept of Flexible Response.[95] It could be added that the ideas of limited nuclear war contained in the Schlesinger doctrine of 1974, President Carter's PD59 in 1979 and the counterveiling strategic concepts of the Reagan administration in the 1980s also owe a great debt to the Buzzard thesis.[96]

In the limited number of assessments of Buzzard's contribution to strategic thought which have been written there has been a tendency to be rather critical of his ideas.[97] Some of these criticisms are certainly justified. In particular his ideas remained rather rigid and inflexible on the question of the possibility of drawing distinctions between the tactical and strategic uses of nuclear weapons. In many ways he was overly optimistic about the chances of preventing a limited war from escalating into an all-out nuclear holocaust. Nevertheless, even though criticism can be made of some of his ideas, Buzzard presented a well-thought out and coherent alternative strategy at a very early stage of the debate about Massive Retaliation. It was an alternative which although not accepted in its entirety would appear to have had a major influence on other strategic thinkers in Britain and the United States. It would also seem to have played an important part in helping to create a climate of debate in which major changes occurred in Western strategic policies along generally similar lines to those proposed by Buzzard.

Just as important as his ideas about Graduated Deterrence was the stress he placed on the importance of morality in nuclear strategy. Buzzard accepted that it was necessary to think about the unthinkable, but he never lost sight of the need for moral principles to guide statesmen and soldiers in the development of their strategic plans. His campaign for 'a new spirit in the approach to the whole business of war' came at a time in the 1950s when few strategists gave much attention to questions of morality.[98] His attempt to reconcile expedience and moral principle, while not acceptable to all, made an important contribution to the moral debate in the late 1950s and early 1960s. His concern to ensure that unilateralists should not go unchallenged in their claims to the moral high ground was just as relevant in the debates of the 1980s as it was in his own day.

Anthony Buzzard was without doubt one of the major spokesmen of a distinctively British approach to strategic doctrine in the 1950s. Indeed a strong case can be made that the debate which he more then anyone else generated with his ideas about Graduated Deterrence was the last major British contribution to the theory of nuclear deterrence. As a number of writers have pointed out, from the late fifties onwards the British debate about nuclear strategy was to be increasingly influenced by American-generated ideas and concepts.[99] Buzzard, together with Blackett, Slessor and Liddell Hart contributed to the formulation of many of those ideas and concepts, but increasingly American strategists, like those dealt with elsewhere in this volume, were to assume and retain the centre of the strategic stage. In most studies of the development of Western nuclear strategy in the formative period of the 1950s and early 1960s the names of Bernard Brodie, Albert Wohlstetter, Henry Kissinger, Herman Kahn and Thomas Schelling are rightly emphasized. It is the contention of this chapter that Anthony Buzzard deserves a place in this list of masters of strategic nuclear thought.

Notes

1. Letter to the author from Michael Howard, 15 May 1986.
2. For an insight into Buzzard's role at the Brighton Conference see the correspondence, especially with the Reverend Alan Booth contained in the Buzzard Papers, held in the Churchill College Archives, Cambridge (hereafter referred to as *BZRD*).
3. The 'Commentators Circle' consisted of a small discussion group of leading defence correspondents in the 1950s. The members included Basil Liddell Hart, Sir John Slessor, Richard Crossman, George Wigg and John Strachey as well as Sir Anthony Buzzard. They are credited with 'no little influence in developing informed opinion and colouring the tone

of the mass media' in the mid- and late 1950s. See L. W. Martin, 'The Market for Strategic Ideas in Britain: The "Sandys Era" ', *American Political Science Review,* **LVI**, no. 1, 1962.

4. Letter from Buzzard to Lord Cunningham, 12 March 1953, *BZRD*, Box 25.

5. *The Buzzard Papers* contain hundreds of letters to leading political, military and church leaders of the day expressing Buzzard's criticisms of existing strategic policies and explaining the nature of his own strategic ideas.

6. See E. Groves. *From Vanguard to Trident: British Naval Policy since World War II*, London: Bodley Head, 1987.

7. See M. Gowing, *Independence and Deterrence*, Vol. I, London, Macmillan, 1974, p. 169.

8. See J. F. Schnabel, *The History of the Joint Chiefs of Staff*, Vol. I, 1945–47, Wilmington, Michael Glazier Inc., 1979 and K. W. Condit, *The History of the Joint Chiefs of Staff*, Vol. II, 1947–49 Wilmington: Michael Glazier Inc., 1979. See also N. J. Wheeler, 'British Nuclear Weapons and Anglo-American Relations, 1945–54', *International Affairs*, **62**, no. 1, Winter 1985/6; Gregg Herken, *The Winning Weapon*, New York, Knopf, 1980; and D. A. Rosenberg, 'The Origins of Overkill: Nuclear Weapons and American Strategy, 1945–60', *International Security, 7*, no. 4, Spring 1983.

9. *Defe* 4/64, COS(53), 24th Meeting, 17 July 1953.

10. *Defe* 4/55, COS(52), 5 July 1952.

11. Ibid.

12. See the discussions about the Global Strategy Paper in E. Groves, op. cit.

13. Ibid.

14. Ibid.

15. Ibid.

16. Ibid.

17. Ibid.

18. For Buzzard's criticisms of Sandys see *BZRD*, Box 24, especially the letter from Buzzard to Lord Beveridge, 27 May 1958.

19. *ADM* 205/93, paper by director of naval intelligence, 6 July 1953.

20. Ibid.

21. Ibid.

22. Ibid.

23. Ibid.

24. See *Defe* 4/64, COS(53) 24th meeting, 17 July 1953. See also N. J. Wheeler, op. cit.

25. See in particular 'Massive Retaliation and Graduated Deterrence', *World Politics*, no. 2, January 1956 and 'The Crux of Defence Policy', *International Relations*, Vol. 5, No. 1, 1956.

26. 'Massive Retaliation and Graduated Deterrence', op. cit.

27. See Buzzard, Slessor and Lowenthal, 'The H-Bomb: Massive Retaliation or Graduated Deterrence?' *International Affairs*, **32**, no. 2, 1956.

28. See in particular the articles in *World Politics, International Relations*, and *International Affairs*, op. cit.

29. 'The H-Bomb: Massive Retaliation or Graduated Deterrence?', op. cit.

30. For a discussion of the distinctions between tactical and strategic uses of nuclear weapons and the exceptions see 'The Crux of Defence Policy', op. cit.

31. 'The Christian Conscience and Modern War', *Worldview*, March 1964. A copy is contained in *BZRD*, Box 35.

32. Ibid.

33. Ibid.

34. Ibid.

35. Ibid.

36. Ibid.

37. Ibid.

38. Ibid. See also 'The Christian Dilemma on Nuclear Weapons', and 'The Moral Aspects of Modern War', *BZRD*, Box 49/3.

39. See 'The Crux of Defence Policy', op. cit. for a discussion of the significance of a speech made by John Foster Dulles on 8 December 1955.

40. Letter from Buzzard to Alastair Buchan, 15 February 1957, *BZRD*, Box 25.

41. Letter from Buzzard to H. M. Hodges, 23 June 1958, *BZRD*, Box 24. Buzzard remained in sympathy with the government's approach to domestic economic policy.
42. Ibid.
43. Ibid.
44. In 1964 Buzzard was arguing that 'the valid arguments for an independent British deterrent are overridden by the need to centralize the control of nuclear weapons, in order to prevent their proliferation to more and more countries (who could claim similar arguments to ours for independence)'. He also accepted the argument that there was a need to save all possible money for better defensive conventional forces, 'so helping to escape from our present reliance upon the first use of tactical atomic weapons'. There were, however, conditions. These were that France should also give up her nuclear weapons and no other Western country started making nuclear weapons. Buzzard does not discuss what Britain should do if France refused to give up her weapons. See Buzzard's letter to *The Times*, 9 February 1969, *BZRD*, 8/1.
45. 'The Christian Conscience and Modern War', op. cit.
46. Ibid.
47. 'Massive Retaliation and Graduated Deterrence', op. cit.
48. Ibid.
49. Letter from Buzzard to George Kennan, 2 May 1958, *BZRD*, Box 24.
50. 'Massive Retaliation and Graduated Deterrence', op. cit.
51. See F. W. Ermarth, 'Contrasts in American and Soviet Strategic Thought' in D. Leebaert, *Soviet Military Thinking* London, Allen and Unwin, 1981.
52. 'The Christian Conscience and Modern War', op. cit.
53. 'Massive Retaliation and Graduated Deterrence', op. cit.
54. Ibid. Buzzard also believed that 'although there would be no relief from our present defence expenditures, Graduated Deterrence would give us better security for our money'.
55. See in particular *The Great Deterrent*, London, Cassell, 1957; *Strategy for the West*, London, Cassell, 1954 and 'The H-Bomb: Massive Relatiation or Graduated Deterrence', op. cit.
56. 'The H-Bomb: Massive Retaliation or Graduated Deterrence', op. cit.
57. Ibid.
58. *Defe* 4/81, COS (55), 104th Meeting, Minute 2, 13 December 1955. The JPS argued that Buzzard's ideas were constantly envolving and it was not possible 'to follow the flight of the Buzzard'. The report came to four conclusions: first, 'that the threat of massive retaliation is the only effective deterrent to Global War both now and in the future'; second, that 'there would be little, if any advantage in making a declaration of intent affecting Limited War'; third, that 'it is impossible to draw a clear division between tactical and strategic targets for nuclear weapons'; and fourth, that 'it is not possible to draw any definite dividing line between small and large nuclear weapons'.
59. Letter from Mountbatten to Buzzard, 2 January 1956, *BZRD*, Box 26. Mountbatten's arguments are almost indentical to the cabinet statement of 7 April 1955. C(55) 95 and CM (55) 1st, item 4.
60. 'The H-Bomb: Massive Retaliation or Graduated Deterrence', op. cit.
61. Ibid. This view was also expressed by the Joint Planning Staff in the report prepared for the chiefs of staff in December 1955; op. cit.
62. 'Massive Retaliation and Graduated Deterrence', op. cit.
63. 'The H-Bomb: Massive Retaliation or Graduated Deterrence', op. cit.
64. Ibid.
65. *Defe* 4/70, JP 54, note 11, 6 May 1954: COS Committee: UK strategy, note by directors of plans.
66. 'Massive Retaliation and Graduated Deterrence', op. cit.
67. Letter from Alan Gwynne Jones to Buzzard, 4 April 1962 and letter from Buzzard to Alan Gwynne Jones, 5 April 1962, *BZRD* Box 1.
68. Letter from Liddell Hart to Buzzard, 10 February 1956, *BZRD* Box 24.
69. Letter from Liddell Hart to Buzzard, 6 January 1956, *BZRD* Box 24.
70. Letter from Buzzard to P. M. S. Blackett, 17 January 1958, *BZRD*, Box 24.
71. Letter from Michael Howard to the author, 15 May 1986.

72. Letter from Buzzard to P. M. S. Blackett, 24 February 1958, *BZRD*, Box 24.
73. Letter from Buzzard to George Kennan, 2 May 1958, *BZRD*, Box 24.
74. Letter from Buzzard to P. M. S. Blackett, 24 February 1958, *BZRD*, Box 24.
75. Letter from Buzzard to P. M. S. Blackett, 17 January 1958, *BZRD*, Box 24.
76. See for example *Defence without the Bomb: the Report of the Alternative Defence Commission*, London, Taylor and Francis, 1983.
77. 'The H-Bomb: Massive Retaliation or Graduated Deterrence', op cit.
78. Letter from Buzzard to Canon R. H. Preston, 27 May 1958, *BZRD*, Box 24.
79. Letter from Buzzard to P. M. S. Blackett, 24 February 1958, *BZRD*, Box 24.
80. Ibid.
81. See Buzzard's Coventry Cathedral Address, 16 June 1963, *BZRD*, Box 35.
82. Ibid. See also a letter from Buzzard to J. Godber, 19 February 1962, *BZRD*, Box 1.
83. 'The Christian Conscience and Modern War', op. cit.
84. Letter from Buzzard to P. M. S. Blackett, 24 February 1958, *BZRD*, Box 24.
85. Letter from Buzzard to P. M. S. Blackett, 17 January 1958, *BZRD*, Box 24.
86. De Witt Armstrong, *The Changing Strategy of British Bases*, unpublished Ph.D. thesis, Princeton University, 1960, p. 32.
87. J. C. Garnett, 'British Strategic Thought' in J. Baylis (ed.), *British Defence Policy in a Changing World*, London, Croom Helm, 1977, pp. 162–3.
88. In particular see *BZRD* Boxes 2, 24, 25, 26 and 49/3.
89. In a letter to Kissinger on 16 June 1955 Buzzard commented on the former's article in *Foreign Affairs*, 'Military Policy and Defense of the "grey" Areas', and said that 'we have arrived at similar conclusions. Kissinger told Buzzard in a letter on 18 July 1955, 'We seem to agree substantially . . . your analysis is somewhat more systematic than my own', *BZRD*, Box 25.
90. Letter from Kissinger to Buzzard, 16 February 1956, *BZRD*, Box 25.
91. Letter from Kissinger to Buzzard, 27 April 1956.
92. The discussions had taken place at a conference in Garmisch. See letter from Nitze to Buzzard, 4 November 1955, *BZRD*, Box 25.
93. Letter from T. C. Schelling to Buzzard, 8 April 1958, *BZRD*, Box 24.
94. See the correspondence between Buzzard and Paul Nitze, Albert Wohlstetter and A. W. Marshall in July and August 1958, *BZRD*, Box 2. Buzzard's ideas were also discussed by Kissinger's Harvard Defence Group, *BZRD*, Box 2. As Colin S. Gray has written, 'In the mid-1950s Rand truly was the center of US excellence in strategic studies', *Strategic Studies: A Critical Assessment* London Aldwych Press, 1982, p. 16.
95. Letter from Michael Howard to the author, 15 May 1986.
96. Buzzard would probably not have supported the massive build-up of American military forces in the 1980s or concurred with the American lack of interest at the time in the arms control process. Buzzard rejected the search for military superiority and favoured a process of dialogue leding to arms control agreements. For Buzzard, security could not be achieved through military power alone. He believed that defence policy and arms control had to be effectively integrated. See letter from Buzzard to J. Godber, 19 February 1962, *BZRD*, Box 1.
97. Apart from Slessor's criticisms, there is an interesting critique of Buzzard's ideas in A. J. R. Groom, *British Thinking about Nuclear Weapons*, London, Frances Pinter, 1974.
98. This point was made by Denis Healey in a letter to the author on the 23 June 1986.
99. This is a point which is developed by Clark and Wheeler in *The British Origins of Nuclear Strategy 1945–1955*, Oxford, Clarendon Press, 1989.

7 P. M. S. BLACKETT*

Michael Howard

Professor P. M. S. Blackett possessed two characteristics which, in combination, set him apart from all other strategic thinkers of his time. In the first place he was, as he himself put it, 'the only atomic scientist to have been brought up as a professional fighting man'. He was educated at the Royal Naval College at Dartmouth, served in the Royal Navy throughout World War I and participated in the last great battle between European navies at Jutland in 1914. Throughout his life he retained the naval officer's disciplined habits, laconic speech and concern for operational efficiency. Secondly he was a political radical: in no sense a revolutionary but a man driven by a passion for social justice and disgusted by the squalor and waste, as he saw it, of free-enterprise capitalism. He was too clear-sighted to share the uncritical reverence for the Soviet Union which characterized so many intellectuals of his generation in the twenties and thirties; but neither did he accept the equally uncritical admiration, more general in the late forties and fifties, for the ideals and the policies of the United States. His primary quality was an abrasive independence of mind; but it was one which co-existed with a respect for the 'conventional wisdom' of military leaders who bore such frightening responsibilities and who had learned their job the hard way.

Blackett's thinking thus developed out of polemic directed against two opposite targets: initially the professional fighting men who did not think hard enough about the implications of their experience; then increasingly, professional thinkers whose elegant formulations did not in his view take sufficient account of military experience and the nature of the real world.

His distinctive contribution to strategic ideas came less from his brilliance as a scientist than from his personal experience of war, and the healthy scepticism which that experience had given him of all theories based upon either unstated or unverifiable hypotheses.[1] The five adolescent years which he spent in the Royal Navy between 1914 and 1919 equipped him not only with a stern sense of what was practically possible and necessary in warfare but with first-hand knowledge of what war was like; with an understanding of that Clausewitzian element of 'friction' without which all theories of war are meaningless. In his writings Blackett referred repeatedly to the Battle of Jutland, when the vessel on which he was serving, the *Barham*, steamed past a great oily patch littered with flotsam and the bobbing heads of survivors where the battle-cruiser *Queen Mary* had been destroyed by a single German salvo a few moments before. 'There's something wrong with our bloody ships today, Chatfield,' Admiral Beatty had calmly remarked about the disaster. In fact there was something wrong with the Royal Navy as a whole: the way it designed its ships, the way in which it thought about war, the way in which it waged war. It worked too much on hunches and unverified assumptions. It did not take enough trouble to find out about its enemy. It did not sufficiently base its tactics on hard reasoning from

* This chapter is based on the Blackett Memorial Lecture to the Operational Research Society in 1984, reprinted in the *Journal of Operational Research Society*, **36**, no 2., pp. 89–95.

observable phenomena. When Blackett returned to the services as a scientific adviser in World War II, it was with the object, as he put it, of 'encouraging numerical thinking and helping to avoid running the war on gusts of emotion'.

Blackett spent most of the inter-war years at Cambridge, where his pioneer work on nuclear physics in the Cavendish Laboratory was to gain him a Nobel Prize. During World War II his combination of naval and scientific experience enabled him to pioneer, if not indeed to invent, 'operational research' at the Admiralty, where he made particularly notable contributions in the field of convoy warfare. But although his work with the navy constituted his major contribution to allied victory, it was his thinking about air warfare which was to have more lasting significance for students of strategic thought.

Blackett's debut in this field came as early as 1935. In that year he joined the Committee on Air Defence set up under Sir Henry Tizard. The work of that body on the potentialities of radar was to revolutionize air warfare by revising hitherto unquestioned assumptions about the ineluctable superiority of the offensive in the air. Radar, and the general development in defensive technology, might not prevent the bombers from getting through, but it could make it impossible for them to do so except at prohibitively high cost. The balance between the offensive and defensive in the air could therefore be restored, as indeed it was in 'the Battle of Britain' in 1940. There was one dissenting voice on that Committee — that of Sir Frederick Lindemann, later Lord Cherwell. Cherwell was defeated but returned to the charge a few days later when, as scientific adviser to the prime minister, he constituted himself the major advocate of the strategic bombing offensive as the primary means of winning the war.

The controversy over the effectiveness of strategic bombing between Cherwell and the air staff on the one side and Tizard and Blackett on the other has been amply recorded. To a large extent in shaped Blackett's attitude towards the possibilities and limitations of air warfare in the early years of the nuclear age. Like Tizard, Blackett was deeply sceptical of the claims Cherwell put forward for the destructive capabilities of strategic bombing, believing (rightly, as he subsequently showed) that these overestimated the true capability of RAF bomber command by a factor of six. Hostility to strategic bombing was in any case deeply engrained in Blackett's old service, the Royal Navy, which desperately needed aircraft for the Battle of the Atlantic, and Blackett would have been less than human if he had not allowed their needs to weigh with him very considerably. But it was on a basis of tough numerical analysis that he showed that bomber command could not possibly perform all that it promised; and he was one of the first people to give publicity to the results of the post-war United States' Strategic Bombing Survey which so devastatingly measured those expectations against actual achievement.

This experience made Blackett sceptical about the belief, current in the immediate aftermath of the dropping of atomic bombs on Hiroshima and Nagasaki, that nuclear weapons would transform the nature of war; that the inflated claims of the early prophets of air power, that bombing would end the war in a matter of weeks, if not days, would at last come true. In his work *Military and Political Consequences of Atomic Energy*, published in 1948, Blackett pointed out that some 3 million tons of ordinary bombs had been dropped on the enemy by allied aircraft during World War II. So 'since one atomic bomb of the 1945 type produces about the same material destruction as 2000 tons of ordinary bombs', he argued, 'it is [thus] certain that a very large number of atomic bombs would be needed to defeat a great nation by bombing alone . . . , [and] a long-drawn out and bitter struggle over much of Europe and Asia, involving million-strong land armies, vast military casualties and widespread civil war would be inevitable'.[3] The allied bomber offensive had achieved results only once it had achieved total command of the air; but the development of jet-powered fighters and improved AA weapons would make this increasingly difficult to obtain. So very large numbers of aircraft (and in consequence of bombs) would be needed to overcome the resulting attrition. In any case, Blackett pointed out, 'a huge number of atomic bombs would have been necessary to inflict on Russia as much damage as she actually suffered by the German invasion'. In consequence, he concluded, 'a war between America and Russia would be of world wide extent and would be a war of all arms, and probably of very long duration'.[4]

These sombre predictions were, as we now know, shared by both American and Soviet military planners. Blackett made the shrewd but unpopular diagnosis that these calculations explained the Soviet determination to maintain its grip on Eastern Europe as a defensive glacis, in the same way as they led the American military to urge the retention of as much as possible of Western Europe to provide bases for their nuclear striking forces. Equally unpopular was his view that the 'Baruch Plan' for the international control of nuclear weapons had been quite understandably rejected by the Soviet Union, since it would have placed that country in a permanent position of nuclear inferiority to the United States and its Western allies. But most unpopular of all was the advice which he gave the British government, in November 1945, not to go ahead with the manufacture of its own nuclear weapons. To do so, he said, would be a dissipation of scarce resources; it would not produce stockpiles on a sufficient scale to be effective; and it would invite Soviet pre-emption against Western Europe. It would be better, he suggested, that Britain should set an example of what was eventually to be termed 'non-proliferation' and use both her military and scientific resources more productively.[5]

It was typical of Blackett that his analysis, while leading him to agree with the professional military assessment of the nature of a new war, led him also into questioning the political judgements in which their strategic recommendations were based. He was by no means alone in the immediate post-war years in seeing a deep divergence of interest between Britain and the United States as well as between the United States and the Soviet Union. Those were the years when the two nations were deeply at odds over such issues as the treatment of occupied Germany, Jewish immigration into Palestine and, not least, the terms on which the United States was to underwrite British financial solvency. But whereas this sense of divergence led the government to press ahead with its plans for an independent British bomb, it made Blackett, like many of his colleagues in the Labour Party, favour, at least for a time, the creation of a 'third force', if not actual neutralism. He was, in consequence, thereafter suspect as an adviser in Whitehall — or at least in the ministry of defence.

All these assessments, political and military, were to be overtaken by events. Blackett's incipient neutralism, like that of many socialists in Western Europe, was shattered by the events of 1948 shortly after the publication of *Military and Political Consequences*: the coup in Czechoslovakia, the breach between Yugoslavia and the Soviet Union, the Berlin blockade. Thereafter Blackett never seriously doubted the need for the Western alliance, though he remained persistently critical both of its strategies and of its policies.

No less important than the changes in the political scene were those which were simultaneously taking place in the technological. Blackett did not foresee — at that stage no one could — how rapidly both American and Soviet scientists would develop what was then referred to as 'the superbomb'. But, unlike most of his contemporaries, he did guess in 1948 that 'a period of five years from now is the latest possible date at which none could reasonably expect that the USSR would not possess at least some atomic bombs'. As for further developments, Blackett saw the attractiveness of smaller and lighter nuclear bombs which could be carried in smaller and faster aircraft 'or as the warhead of a V2 weapon of reasonable size', but the technical problems seemed to him in 1948 likely to be so immense 'that no type of pilotless aircraft or rocket is likely to be useful for attack at a range of 1000 miles on such a small target as a single factory or an atomic bomb plant for at least very many years'.[6] He wisely did not set a figure on this negative prognosis. It took, in fact about a quarter of a century for missiles of this capability to be produced.

In the early 1950s there came the development of thermonuclear weapons, the order of magnitude of whose destructiveness rendered out of date all the calculations on which Blackett and the professional military had hitherto based their strategic analysis. Paradoxically, their advent appeared providential to defence planners in the West who had been wrestling with the insoluble problem of how to sustain a capacity to fight a global war on a peacetime economy. First the United Kingdom, in 1953, then the United States, in 1954, announced their intention of developing force-structures intended not to fight a war but to deter one by their capacity to inflict inescapable and unacceptable damage on any 'aggressor'. Since they did so at a moment when the Soviet Union was rapidly acquiring the capacity to retaliate in kind, it did not take an analyst of Blackett's stature to perceive the problems inherent in such a policy. It was indeed out of the critique of this concept of 'massive retaliation' that the whole corpus of nuclear theory was to develop on both sides of the Atlantic. In the United States, scholars like Herman Kahn, Henry Kissinger, Thomas Schelling and Albert Wohlstetter developed concepts of great depth and sublety which still constitute the basic texts for the subject. In Britain, a small group attacked the problem: Alastair Buchan, Denis Healey, Rear-Admiral Sir Anthony Buzzard and the veteran military analyst Captain B. H. Liddell Hart. But it was Blackett's experience and incisiveness that largely dominated their thinking, and it is his work that best bears re-reading.

Again, Blackett's strategic analysis was based on and reinforced by historical experience. He was scornful of the argument set out in the British Defence White Paper of 1954 that superior Western technology would enable the West to counter the Soviet advantage in manpower. He knew that it was exactly this kind of assumption which had led to the disasters at Jutland and elsewhere in World War I. Technological superiority, he wrote, was 'something to strive and to hope for, but not too often to rely on for planning purposes'.[7] A few years later he was to take issue with the young Henry Kissinger on the same grounds. In his book *Nuclear Weapons and Foreign Policy* Kissinger had contrasted 'the flexibility and self-reliance of an American officer-corps "drawn from a society in which individual initiative has traditionally been encouraged" with the rigidity of Soviet military organisation'. This Blackett described as 'plain poppycock'. 'To one who remembers similar beliefs about British personal and technical superiority current before World War I and remembers the outcome', he wrote, 'I can only comment, "this is where I came in" '.[8]

The main problem posed by a doctrine of 'massive retaliation', as Blackett was not alone (although he was among the first) in perceiving, was that a strategy based on initiating a nuclear strike lacked credibility as a deterrent unless one was ready and willing to absorb the adversary's subsequent nuclear counter-blow. Neither the United States nor the British governments were prepared to complement their offensive deterrent posture with the protective domestic measures necessary to make it credible. Blackett was particularly scornful of the British government's allocation of £50 million to civil defence. The Defence White Paper of 1956, when announcing this, explained that 'within the proportion of our resources that can be made available for home defence, the Government's aim will be to take the precautions without which, should the worst happen, ordered society could not survive'. 'The concealed assumption', Blackett pointed out, 'is that the funds made available . . . are in fact adequate to enable ordered society to survive an all-out atomic war . . . This is one example among others where a flagrant lack of quantitative thinking has been glossed over by a suave phrase.' [9]

Blackett thus took issue with the attempt of the government of the day to persuade the population that Britain could fight a nuclear war and, in any meaningful sense, survive. But it was in this very impossibility of survival, reciprocally, that he saw salvation. Like Winston Churchill himself, Blackett believed that safety might be 'the sturdy child of terror'. The concept of 'Mutually Assured Destruction' as a basis for security was not to be formulated by Robert McNamara until nearly a decade later, but it underlay the arguments which Blackett put forward in the Lee Knowles Lectures which he delivered at Cambridge in 1956. 'A strategic atomic stalemate is already in existence', he then stated. We should therefore 'act as if atomic and hydrogen bombs have abolished total war and concentrate our efforts on working out how few are needed to keep it abolished'. [10] Although some years were to pass before this doctrine was categorized as 'minimal deterrence', it did not in principle diverge very far from the action policy of the British government of the day or the declaratory policy of the American government under President Eisenhower. In practice, 'how few' was to be determined as much by productive capability as by perceived targeting need. In the case of the United States enough (to paraphrase Eisenhower) proved to be plenty.

Like many others, Blackett took some time to make up his mind about the feasibility of using nuclear weapons in a tactical or battlefield role. In 1948, like his friend Robert Oppenheimer in the United States who was working on the famous 'Project Vista', he was interested in exploring their usefulness against such military targets as those which had been provided by the Normandy landings, against ports and airfields and against large naval units at sea. Six years later, official thinking caught up with him when NATO forces began to introduce tactical nuclear weapons to strengthen the defence of Western Europe. Blackett observed at the time that 'NATO planners must be greatly inhibited as to whether wider Strategic considerations will actually allow their use'. [11] But in his Lee Knowles lectures he gave an on the whole benevolent survey of the various proposals for 'Graduated Deterrence' which were currently advocating the limited use of nuclear weapons in preference to the immediate unleashing of all-out nuclear war. Two years later, however, he came out firmly against them. In a lecture delivered at Chatham House in April 1958, he stated flatly that once the Soviet Union had attained nuclear equality, any attempt to persuade or compel her to conform to Western ideas of limited war were bound to fail. Indeed, he suggested, the Soviets 'may now be in a position to try to force the West to comply with their own set of rules for limited war, which in certain circumstances might well exclude the use of tactical weapons'. In any case, he thought it 'on the whole unlikely that Britain and America would in fact initiate the use of tactical nuclear weapons if a limited war broke out in Europe. I think that at the last minute they would leave the land forces to fight without nuclear weapons.' [12]

The following year indeed, in an article published in the New Statesman in December 1959, Blackett was quite explicitly advocating what would now be termed a 'No First Use' policy. In practice, he considered,

the West would accept limited defeat rather than take the three risks inherent in initiating tactical nuclear war: the risk of accelerating defeat in the field; the risk of obliterating the people whom one is attempting to defend or protect; and the risk of starting the process of escalation towards total war.[13]

In consequence he considered that 'NATO would be well-advised to announce that in no circumstances would it initiate the use of tactical nuclear weapons, though it would use them if the Soviet forces did'. In general, indeed, he suggested that ever since the World War II, the West had 'committed a vast military blunder in neglecting adequate preparation for land warfare in the mistaken view that atomic weapons would do instead'.

This was a view which Blackett had been developing throughout the 1950s. Nuclear weapons, he believed, were politically and militarily sterile. Their only utility was reciprocally to deter their use. He cited as evidence Henry Kissinger's complaint in 1957 that 'we have never succeeded in translating our military [nuclear] superiority to political advantage'.[14] To attain or defend political objectives one needed conventional forces; and the gravamen of Blackett's charge against Western defence policy as a whole in the 1950s was

that by concentrating so much material effort on the deterrence, by threat of atomic bombardment of the USSR from a full-scale attack on Europe, it weakens our ability to play an effective role in many parts of the world where minor wars may and do continually occur. So by reducing relatively the land forces, tactical and transport aircraft etc. required to fight minor wars, we may find it more difficult to prevent such minor wars spreading into bigger wars. In this way, the policy of the Great Deterrent may make a major war more rather than less likely.[15]

This was a view which naturally commanded much sympathy within the British armed forces themselves. Their capacity to deal with what they called 'brush-fire wars' was ruthlessly cut back by defence ministers of both parties, who, from Duncan Sandys onwards, were more concerned with balancing their shrinking budgets than with maintaining a capacity for global intervention by conventional forces whose costs soared increasingly year by year. In the United States, where identical opinions were being voiced by experts as disparate as the young Professor Henry Kissinger and the veteran General Maxwell Taylor, it found even more influential support. It convinced, among others, the incoming President J. F. Kennedy, who took advantage of a Congress panicked into generosity in the aftermath of the first Sputnik flight to restore the conventional capabilities which his predecessor had so drastically reduced.

As a result, the United States had the resources to fight their war in Vietnam which makes one wonder whether Blackett and those who thought like him were right after all. That experience suggested indeed that while conflicts in the Third World could certainly not be resolved by Western nuclear power, they could not necessarily be resolved by Western conventional forces either. Against the Vietnam disaster are to be set the successful British interventions in Kuwait in 1961, East Africa in 1964, Borneo in 1965 and, come to that the Falkland Islands in 1982. But the success of those operations was the result of a precise limitation of objective and skilful management of forces which a more lavish provision of resources might have done little to improve and much to adulterate. Like other critics then and since, Blackett urged the improvement of the conventional defences of Western Europe, but the continuing inability of these, judged by any ordinary military standards, to match their Soviet opponents without that recourse to tactical nuclear weapons which Blackett condemned suggests that the nuclear balance was in fact remarkably stable.

Indeed towards the end of the 1950s Blackett found himself having to defend his belief in the stability of the nuclear balance against attack from another quarter. Partly as a result of the foundation of the Institute for Strategic Studies in 1958 and its annual conferences which assembled strategic thinkers from both sides of the Atlantic; partly in consequence of the early Pugwash conference which provided an international forum for scientists as well as strategists, Blackett and other British thinkers became familiar at the end of the decade with the highly sophisticated strategic analysis in progress at the RAND Corporation and on the Charles River at Harvard and MIT. It might have been thought that the meticulous approach adopted by such analysts as Thomas Schelling would have appealed to Blackett's own scientific bent, but it did not. It affronted all the pragmatic instincts he had developed during his long association with the armed services. It was based, to his way of thinking, on a complete lack of understanding of the realities of war. The theory of deterrence, he complained in 1959, had brought into existence

> an excessively complicated set of theoretical and numerical arguments essentially dealing with such problems as the extent to which a military threat which one dares not implement can deter an enemy from an action which you do not want to take, or force him to do something that you want him to do. The ramifications of such theories and calculations have reached scholastic subtlety and are expressed in a formidable jargon . . . theorising which, however necessary it is, in my view is hardly likely to provide the military and civil heads of governments with the basis of practical decisions in a crisis.[16]

Two years later, in 1961 Blackett returned to the charge. The 'models' on which American strategic analysts had based their calculations were subtle and elaborate but bore little relation to the real world. The problem was to know whether 'the model which has been constructed is sufficiently like the real events which it purports to represent to allow conclusions which have much relevance to executive action'. The conclusions of operational analysis always had to be checked against 'the conclusions reached in a more intuitive manner by attempting to envisage the situation as a whole'. In World War II he calculated that in only about one-tenth of cases could operational research add anything to the decisions reached by military staffs 'through the exercise of their traditional judgement and wisdom'. If operational research staffs cannot improve on military conclusions based on rough calculation, he said, they should keep quiet: 'never should they fall into the trap of decking out what is essentially only a hunch with pseudo-scientific backing'.[17]

All this was preliminary to a ferocious critique of the highly influential article which the American analyst Albert Wohlstetter had published in the periodical *Foreign Affairs* in January 1959 under the title *The Delicate Balance of Terror*. This article summarized the conclusions of a study which Wohlstetter had carried out at the RAND Corporation for the United States Air Force on the basing modes of Strategic Air Command, and he had come to some highly disturbing conclusions. The bases from which the United States Air Force intended to launch their nuclear strikes against the Soviet Union, Wohlstetter had shown, were highly vulnerable to a pre-emptive attack. Further, little or no provision had been made for the organization of effective command and control of strike forces in the aftermath of such an attack. The requirements for a credible deterrent force were thus far more complex and extensive than had generally been believed. It had to be large enough for a substantial proportion to survive a surprise attack and strike back against an adversary whose defences were prepared, whose population was largely sheltered through effective measures of civil defence and whose regime was sufficiently ruthless to accept enormous damage in pursuit of their totalitarian aims of world conquest. This meant a very large force indeed: deterrence, argued Wohlstetter, could not be obtained on the cheap.

Again, it might have been expected that Blackett would have had some sympathy with Wohlstetter's position, if not with his arguments. Like Blackett himself in his earlier years, Wohlstetter was trying, by cool analysis, to counteract some of the irrational assumptions that underlay much of his government's strategic planning. Curiously enough his arguments paralleled many of those that Blackett had used during World War II. Like the Royal Air Force before the war, the American Strategic Air Command had a deeply instinctive commitment to the principal of the offensive that made them overlook the resources available to the defence, the extent to which those resources might counteract the effectiveness of the attack and the need in any force planning to keep the two in perspective. Paradoxically Blackett now found himself occupying the position which he had begun his career as a strategic analyst by attacking: the belief that the bomber would always get through.

The passion with which Blackett attacked Wohlstetter — a passion which was to be heartily reciprocated — was due in part to the circumstances in which Wohlstetter's article was published. It appeared at the height of the panic in the United States about the so-called 'missile gap' — the belief that the Soviet Union had a commanding lead over the United States in the production and deployment of intercontinental ballistic missiles. This belief was exploited in the presidential campaign of 1960 by a Democratic Party which, within a few months of coming into office, had to admit that no such gap existed. None the less, huge appropriations were voted to expand the strategic nuclear forces of the United States by land, sea and air in order to meet the enormous requirements which, according to the Wohlstetter thesis, were needed if the United States was to maintain a credible posture of deterrence.

Of all Patrick Blackett's writings on nuclear strategy, that which best repays re-reading is the article, 'A Critique of Some Contemporary Defence Thinking', which appeared in *Encounter* magazine in April 1961 and is reprinted in his collection, *Studies of War*. With a distinctive mixture of numerical analysis and tough common sense, he demolished the assumption on which the theory of the missile gap was based, and with controlled passion he attacked what he saw as the political presuppositions which underlay Wohlstetter's analysis. In the first place, he pointed out, it was utterly unrealistic to assume that any government, however ruthless, would consider launching a surprise attack in the certain knowledge that it could not escape retaliation on a scale which *at best* was likely to involve some 20 million casualties, with all the economic destruction that would go with them. In the second place, a force on the scale visualized was bound to be seen by the Soviets as posing the threat of a pre-emptive strike against their own forces; for one could not expect the Soviets to attribute to the West any more benign intentions than the West attributed to them. Inevitably they would respond. To accept the idea that stability could only be obtained by 'a great increase of expenditure on research and development of long range missiles and a large increase in their invulnerability', wrote Blackett, 'is likely to lead to wrong allocations of priorities as well as a worsening of the international atmosphere'. It would destroy all hope of effective arms control agreements and open the way to 'an endless and increasing arms race'.[18]

But Blackett's passion was fuelled also by his own political preconceptions. His political radicalism made him instinctively hostile to the assumption which so many American analysts took for granted: that the Soviet Union was a revisionist power implacably bent on world conquest, restrained only by the military strength of the United States and likely quite ruthlessly to take advantage of any weakness regardless of cost. That was a view which, like many Europeans, he regarded as highly unrealistic. He never became sympathetic to the Soviet Union or hostile to the United States: he had too many friends and associates in the American scientific community to wish to see transatlantic bonds weakened, and he held aloof from the manifestations of neutralism which began to reappear on the British left after 1958 with the establishment of the Campaign for Nuclear Disarmament. But he grew increasingly unsympathetic to the whole trend of Western strategic thinking as it developed in the 1960s and gradually ceased to contribute to it. In 1964 he became an adviser to the new Labour government with special responsibility for the development of technological education, a field of public policy where he felt that he could make a more immediate impact; and he devoted himself to this and to his scientific research until his death in 1974.

Blackett's attention to strategic problems was at best intermittent. One of the most brilliant physicists of his generation, if not indeed of the century, his main energies were devoted to his research, to the teaching and administration involved in running large university departments in Manchester and London and to the general activities in the scientific community which earned him the presidency of the Royal Society in 1965 and the award of the Order of Merit in 1967. This detachment from 'the strategic community' which was developing among largely American, largely full-time analysts in 'think-tanks' meant that his contributions were increasingly those of an educated layman rather than a strategic specialist in his own right, reiterations of 'conventional wisdom' rather than refinements of or new insights into theory. But he feared not only that theory was becoming increasingly remote from the real world, but that if it was allowed to run unchecked it would bring into being a new and dreadful world in which expenditure on weapons would become ever greater, and the dangers of war through inadvertence ever more probable.

The debate between Blackett and Wohlstetter was thus to be of fundamental importance to the development of strategic studies, and it is not settled yet. 'Minimal deterrence' as expounded by Blackett was based on a calculation not of military but of political probabilities. It assumed that the prospect of nuclear war *in itself*, without any assessment of what level of destruction might or might not be 'tolerable', would be enough to deter the Soviet Union or any other revisionist power from initiating war as a deliberate instrument of policy. In consequence little if any thought need be devoted to the actual conduct of such a war, to the selection of targets or to the protection of populations — to anything in fact except the preservation of a stable second-strike capability, capable of destroying the adversary's most vulnerable centres.

In terms of political realities such a doctrine is highly persuasive. The kind of meticulous strategic analysis carried on by Wohlstetter and his colleagues does not occur among political and military decisionmakers, whatever their ideologies. Their calculations are very much more crude, and at times of crisis they are likely to be very crude indeed. The bare possibility of the annihilation even of a single city, of a holocaust of a million or so civilians, of the unpredictably terrible economic and ecological consequences of a dozen thermonuclear explosions on one's own territory is likely to freeze the blood of the most fanatical aggressor, let alone statesmen so cautious, careful and prudent as those characteristic of the Soviet system. Beyond that initial catastrophe, few political leaders are likely to look, and all are likely to treat its avoidance as their overwhelming priority.

But though such a doctrine may be politically realistic, it is militarily inadequate. It does not even address itself to the issue of greatest importance to the peoples of Western Europe: how, in a world of stable nuclear deterrence, is their continent to be defended against Soviet conventional or even localized nuclear attack? Politically speaking such an attack may appear highly improbable; but its deterrence in military terms depends ultimately on the threatened use of American nuclear weapons against the territory of the Soviet Union — a course of action which, if the concept of mutually assured destruction is correct, would be suicidal and in consequence incredible. Strategic analysts are bound therefore to consider the implications of initiating a nuclear strike; the targets against which it would be directed, the responses it would be likely to evoke. They are bound also to consider the eventuality of an attempt to pre-empt such a strike, an attempt inspired not by Soviet aggressiveness but by Soviet fears. Political leaders may prefer not to peer beyond the curtain of the first dreadful nuclear exchange, but strategists have a professional obligation to think about the unthinkable.

Nevertheless the consequences of such thinking were much as Blackett had foretold; an endless and increasing arms race, and the complication, to the point of impractability, of all prospects of arms control. The technological developments of the 1970s, in particular the improvement in the accuracy, miniaturization and control of all missile systems would in any case have made the maintenance of effective minimal deterrence, as Blackett conceived it, a far more difficult matter than he could ever have imagined. Still, the requirements specified by Wohlstetter and his colleagues for the stabilization of the 'delicate balance of terror' involved the creation of a force structure which was not only enormously expensive but itself destabilizing in that it inevitably led to the creation of a first-strike capability to which the Soviet Union was predictably bound to respond in kind.

Blackett's contribution to strategic thought lay not in any specific theory or theories, nor even in any startlingly original insights into the new problems of the nuclear age. It lay in the quality of mind that he brought to bear on them; the scientist's capacity for hard reasoning based on observable data combined with a solid common sense and understanding both of war and of politics which was rare among his more fluent and sophisticated American contemporaries and which has, alas, grown still rarer. The only figure of comparable quality was the late Bernard Brodie — a man, curiously enough, who also came to strategic studies from a background in naval affairs. Like all the rest of us, Blackett explored blind alleys and put forward ideas which, on reflection, he wisely abandoned. But his final warning is one of continuing relevance.

I have not the slightest doubt [Blackett wrote in 1961] that the main danger today is not from the rational act of responsible statesmen, but is due to essentially irrational acts of irresponsible, frightened, humiliated, revengeful, or just mad people — or perhaps, more likely still, from the confused actions of well-meaning people overwhelmed by complex circumstances beyong their mental or moral ceiling.[19]

Little has changed over twenty-five years.

Notes

1. P. M. S. Blackett (1962) *Studies of War, Nuclear and Conventional*, Edinburgh, Oliver & Boyd, p. 75.

2. Ibid., p. 74.
3. P. M. S. Blackett *Military and Political Consequences of Atomic Energy*, London, Turnstile Press, 1948, pp. 4–5.
4. Ibid., pp. 53, 55.
5. M. Gowing *Independence and Deterrence: Britain and Atomic Energy 1945–52*, Vol. I, London, Macmillan, 1974, pp. 194–206.
6. P. M. S. Blackett *Military and Political Consequences of Atomic Energy*, p. 49.
7. P. M. S. Blackett *Studies of War, Nuclear and Conventional*, p. 43.
8. Ibid., p. 62.
9. P. M. S. Blackett *Atomic Weapons and East-West Relations*, Cambridge University Press, 1956, pp. 24–5.
10. Ibid., pp. 5, 100.
11. P. M. S. Blackett *Studies of War, Nuclear and Conventional*, p. 43.
12. Ibid., pp. 64–5.
13. Ibid., p. 84.
14. Ibid., p. 57.
15. Ibid., p. 45.
16. Ibid., p. 92.
17. Ibid., pp. 128–30.
18. Ibid., p. 141.
19. Ibid., p. 141.

8 ANDRÉ BEAUFRE

François de Rose

What strikes one in the work of General André Beaufre is the range and variety of the parameters he brought into play in his reasoning, demonstrations and conclusions. I shall mention here only those aspects of Beaufre's career which most decisively helped to shape his ideas.

As a student at the military academy of Saint-Cyr, he was amazed at the absence of political culture in the teaching he received. Consequently, after having served as a lieutenant in the Rif War in Morocco, he entered France's senior military academy, the Ecole de Guerre, and at the same time enrolled at the Paris Ecole des Sciences Politiques. Thus one trait of his character was already apparent: the refusal to take anything for granted that he had not sifted through his own study and judgement. After the hard-won victory of 1918, the French army was reckoned, or at least it reckoned itself, to be the best in the world. Beaufre saw its weaknesses and questioned the ideas that were presented to him as axiomatic.

In the last weeks before World War II, he was a member of the Franco–British military mission which went to Moscow seeking Soviet cooperation in anticipation of Hitler's aggression. Stalin made his cooperation conditional on the right of passage through Polish territory — and this Warsaw refused. Beaufre realized then that it is impossible to square a political circle at the military level. It was Ribbentrop who signed with Molotov the agreement to partition Poland.

In 1940, the French army collapsed. But, as Beaufre observed, it had lost in one month more than twice as many dead as in the worst periods of World War I. So it was not the fighting soldier who was responsible for the defeat but the military command which had neither understood nor foreseen what was to happen. The defeat was due to years of intellectual sloth and political incoherence.

After the war, Beaufre served in Indochina, where he gained insight into the conditions of combat between large Western units and guerrillas, an experience which was later reinforced in Algeria. But between his service in these two wars, he commanded the land forces in the Franco–British Suez operation. Here too, he was able to observe the extent to which a lack of clarity in the political definition of the objective to be attained and a lack of diplomatic preparation and of understanding of the new international dimension of certain conflicts can transform victory on the ground into political defeat.

He took early retirement in 1961 after having served in the integrated general staff of NATO which he was thus able to observe in operation and after having represented France on the Permanent Military Group in Washington.

The lessons of these experiences were combined with the resources of an acute intelligence, equally gifted for imagination and reflexion — both analytic and synthetic — and for forward-looking thinking grounded in extensive knowledge of the past, a lucid understanding of the present and intuition as regards the future.

The result was a systematic study of strategic problems which he set out in several books and numerous articles, in particular in the journal of the Institut Français des

Etudes Strategiques which he set up in Paris shortly after Alastair Buchan founded the London-based Institute for Strategic Studies.

His first book, *Introduction à la Stratégie*, was published in 1962, thirteen years before his death. Liddell Hart described this first work as the most comprehensive, carefully formulated, up-to-date treatise on strategy published in this generation, superseding on many points all earlier works.

The period was crucial. The leaders of the major powers were declaring their wish for *détente*, and de Gaulle launched his famous slogan: '*Détente, entente, coopération*'.

Did Beaufre believe in *détente*? Certainly not in the sense in which public opinion understands it for he was convinced that the rivalry between countries with different political and economic systems will not melt away. But he saw *détente* as a total strategy, generally conducted in the indirect mode, and orientated towards the future.

For our present purpose, four books are essential in order to understand General Beaufre's thinking and to assess the impact of his ideas on modern military thought. They are: *Introduction à la Stratégie*, which has already been mentioned, *Dissuasion et stratégie* (1964), *Stratégie de l'action* (1966), and *Stratégie pour demain* (1972).

I shall here endeavour to present a synthesis of their arguments, considering successively Beaufre's ideas on operational strategy at the conventional and nuclear levels, deterrence and the strategy of direct and indirect action.

Operational strategy

Operational strategy is 'the art of the dialectic of wills using force to resolve their conflicts'.[1] The strategist's objective is to impose his will — not to win battles.

Beaufre postulates that 'strategy is not a doctrine but a method of thinking'.[2] His whole *oeuvre* stems from the conviction that 'in all human affairs, it is the idea that must dominate and direct'. France was defeated in 1940 because, after 1918, it was not 'strategy' that was taught but '*a* strategy' which was thought infallible and was already false. Any strategy can be best in one situation and very bad in another.

War has become total war, conducted in every field — political, economic, diplomatic and military. The same is true of cold war. Strategy therefore has to be total strategy. It cannot be left to soldiers alone. It is no longer simply the art of using forces to attain a result determined by politics. It is 'the art of making force contribute to achieving the goals of politics', and force here includes not only military might but all the factors involved in the confrontation between the protagonists. Winning is no longer defined by victory in battle. It is the adversary's acceptance of the conditions one seeks to impose on him. It is a psychological event.

The means are very varied: they range from the threat, if the sheer disparity of forces allows it, through diplomatic or economic pressures, successive actions (Hitler's strategy from 1936 to 1939) or long-lasting conflicts (decolonization, generalized guerrilla campaigns) to outright military victory.

Strategic reasoning must combine the psychological and material elements of the situation by an abstract, rational operation of the mind involving analysis and synthesis. This is the method which Beaufre himself applied to conventional military strategy, nuclear strategy and indirect strategy.

Conventional military strategy

Setting out the elements of conventional military strategy, Beaufre recalls that the capacity to produce a decision by force of arms is a function of the operational possibilities resulting from armament, the methods of war, replenishment of supplies etc. One of the essential elements of military strategy has always been to understand, more rapidly than one's adversary, the changes in warfare and in the relationship, in offensive and defensive terms, of the elements on which victorious battles depend: line of battle, firepower, the possibilities of overwhelming the opposing forces, of bluff or surprise, the psychological elements, discipline, confidence, morale — in short, all the components which go together to force a decision.

On land, the aim is to disrupt the enemy forces. At sea and in the air, the aim is the physical destruction of the enemy since there is no ground to be won.

In military warfare, battle is only one stage, a completion. The forces have to get within combat range. The whole set of dispositions and manoeuvres constitutes the operations. For a long time, operations and battle were linked. Then, they evolved in relation to the possibilities of movement and the elements of power conditioning the opportunities for envelopment, break-through and exploitation of the terrain which give hostilities their character as a war of movement or of position and attrition and which condition the volume of the forces and duration of the conflicts.

These factors evolve over time, both intriniscally and in relation to one another, and these variations may be accelerated and can intervene in the course of a conflict as was the case in the course of World War II. They condition offensive and defensive capacities, strategic mobility (outside the conflict zone) and tactical mobility (in combat).

These considerations show the fundamental difficulty of the military art: its variability. Every attempt to look into the future must both be based on experience of the past and invent the adaptation of this experience to the new means of war. Every innovation implies a major risk. But all routine is condemned in advance to failure.

In this game, 'at once conjectural and terrible, the key is provided by the transformation and adaptation of operational strategy'.[3]

Nuclear strategy

Applying these considerations to nuclear weapons, Beaufre emphasizes their power, which is no longer linked to the mass and range of the vectors. It amounts to an almost total mobility.

Against this unprecedented danger there are, theoretically, only four types of counter-measure: preventive destruction (direct offensive means); interception; protection (direct defensive means); and the threat of retaliation (indirect defensive means).

The first of these, the idea of preventive destruction, lasted only a few years. The second and third do not offer sufficiently complete safeguards. The fourth, the threat of retaliation, is valid as a basis for deterrence.

But the irrationality of nuclear conflict creates a margin of freedom of action, that is scope for minor actions in which the stake is too small for the threat of retaliation to be credible. It is therefore necessary to suppress this margin of freedom of action, which means presenting a system of forces capable of countering the operations which the adversary might try to conduct within the margin. It is a question of avoiding the all-or-nothing dilemma while maintaining the threat of rising to the highest levels of violence. This is the role of tactical nuclear weapons.

Except for the case in which one side has acquired the capacity to disarm the other

completely, conflict is likely to begin with relatively limited actions. This is what led
to the doctrine of flexible response which aims to provide an effective riposte while
containing the conflict within certain limits. It is an 'inevitable' strategy but one
which none the less raises objections from the countries likely to become the theatre
of hostilities and also because to accept the hypothesis of limited conflict is perhaps in
itself an invitation to engage in it.[4]

It follows from these parameters that:

(i) Nuclear strategy is necessarily conceived in terms of total war. An implicit
strategy, conducted more or less intuitively by a kind of 'dead reckoning', gives
way to a strategy which has to be scientifically total and which becomes an
intellectual discipline that is indispensable at the level of political leadership and
indeed for the national elites in general.

(ii) But at the same time one must not become locked in a dogmatism closely tied to
the circumstances of the day. In less than two decades we have moved from
American nuclear monopoly to strategic parity between the superpowers,
through the stages of sputnik, the 'missile gap' and the emergence of tactical
nuclear weapons. One therefore has to rise to a total strategy encompassing not
only the nuclear phenomenon but also those that follow it: militarization of
space, chemical weapons and the minor forms of indirect strategy.

(iii) Finally, it follows from the changed character of defence problems that
'preparation is more important than execution' [5] since possession of superior
means is more decisive than the way they might be used. It is the opposite of
Napoleon's dictum that: 'War is a simple art that is entirely a matter of
execution.' The idea of security takes on the abstract character of keeping one
step ahead in preparation. 'Manoeuvre of forces becomes a manoeuvre of
potentials in which the qualitative factor is far more important than the
quantitative factor, which means that the assessment of a situation is increasingly subjective.' [6] The time scale extends, and looking into the future becomes
an absolutely vital discipline. The time lags are much greater still in the political
field. The Soviet Union did not begin to draw dividends from the Congress of
Baku (1920) until Mao's victory in 1949!

(iv) The evolution of nuclear strategy shows the growing importance of strategies
complementary to that obtained by the threat of atomic retaliation. Nuclear
balance does not remove the need for conventional forces.

(v) If war were to break out, it would be as a result of miscalculation, since 'Hara-
kiri is no policy'. It would therefore have a good chance of remaining limited.
There is a growing move away from the type of full-scale conflict seen in the
nineteenth century and in the two world wars. The same is true of crisis
management, as the Cuba affair showed. But these minor actions take on new
and greater importance because of the results of indirect strategy which may
become apparent only in the long term but which can none the less change the
global balance.

Nuclear weapons make peace more stable. Short of 'a trick of fate or biological
predestination', the likelihood is of increasingly controlled use of force in support of
increasingly sophisticated politico-strategic manoeuvring. But the struggles now
shifted into a minor key will have become permanent. 'Major war and true peace will
then have died together.' [7]

Indirect strategy

'The object of indirect strategy is not to take on the enemy in a direct trial of strength but to gain the upper hand in this balance of forces before the decisive test of the crisis by manoeuvering and not by fighting'.[8] Ideally, it would make fighting superfluous. It is the mode of action imposed when the nuclear risk excludes direct confrontation. It is also the necessary instrument of a strategist who is not strong enough to defeat his enemy on the terrain chosen by the latter. It achieves its objective by means other than military victory. Its success depends on the protagonists' freedom of action. With nuclear weapons, that freedom of action is considerably reduced in ·areas where the two sides confront each other, as they do in Central Europe. But in other areas it has allowed major changes such as those which have taken place in Korea, Indochina, Hungary, Suez, Cuba — not to mention all those which have occurred since Beaufre wrote.

Indirect strategy combines external manoeuvres with internal manoeuvres. External manoeuvres are conducted on a global scale. They aim to paralyse the adversary by pinning him down, like Gulliver, with countless commitments. Thus psychology here plays a major role in combining political, economic, diplomatic and military means. By playing on moral factors, it seeks to give the adversary a guilty conscience, appealing to sections of internal opinion and turning against him his own moral, humanitarian or legal values. At the same time, if the adversary is engaged in external conflict, political and military advisers, weapons and possibly 'volunteers' are sent in; in extreme cases, threats of direct action or retaliation are brandished, as in the Suez affair.

The importance of this psychological aspect in indirect strategy is that it can neutralize the reality of the facts. Thus, the Soviet Union, which imposed its will by force on its satellites, took over the platform of peace. The world's last colonial power exploited anti-colonialism and demanded the elimination of the nuclear weapons that it produces in great quantities.

Internal manoeuvres conducted in the region where one seeks to obtain a result will combine, in varying proportions, material forces, moral forces and the time factor. They seek either to win a rapid decision or, by 'salami tactics', to gain a succession of objectives. In the case of a guerrilla campaign, which has to be able to rely on external supplies and the proximity of a sanctuary, military inferiority has to be offset by a growing superiority in psychological strength as the conflict continues. It will call for moral support from the outside world while expanding terrorist acts against the populations so as to enlarge the scope of its threat.

In short, the more that nuclear strategy succeeds, through its precarious balances in strengthening overall deterrence, the greater use will be made of indirect strategy. 'Peace will be less and less peaceful.'[9]

The key for both sides is freedom of action. Every vulnerability offers an opening to the adversary. The real game of indirect strategy has to take place at the level of preliminaries. In this game, brainpower replaces force.

To define strategy, Beaufre proposes the formula:

$$S = KF\psi T$$

where S is strategy, K is the factor specific to each particular case, F is the material forces, ψ the moral or psychological forces and T is time.[10] In direct strategy, F is the key factor. In indirect strategy, ψ predominates.

We therefore have to learn indirect strategy since strategy is unintelligible if it is limited to the military sphere. It is a perpetual process of invention, the evolving character of which was little appreciated until recent years, so much so that some theories even assumed that strategy operated on constants, with only tactics needing to evolve. There can be no modern strategy without powerful research facilities.

Deterrence

Bilateral deterrence

Studying deterrence in relation to direct and indirect strategy, Beaufre observes that nuclear weapons mean that it is no longer possible to engage in a conflict with the idea that the prize to be won justifies the price that will be paid for it. The objective is no longer sought through military victory but through indirect strategy.

Since deterrence consists in preventing the adversary from taking the decision to use his weapons, it will be based on study of the combination of the material realities and the political, social and moral psychological factors. But there are two forms of deterrence: the defensive form, consisting of preventing the adversary from launching an operation against oneself and the offensive form designed to prevent the adversary from opposing an action one wishes to undertake.

The key to nuclear deterrence is the capacity for riposte, whereas the ability to minimize the riposte is the key to nuclear initiative. The first strike should therefore be primarily a counter-force attack and the second strike should be aimed primarily at the enemy's resources. Stability depends on the dialectic of second strikes.[11]

Since this stability is sufficiently attained as soon as the risk is out of proportion to the prize, we have cold war in the sensitive zones and limited war in the peripheral zones. But, at the same time, deterrence allows acts directed against another country which previously would have led to war. It follows that since peace is more stable in the form of non-war, cold war allows many actions that would previously have been unthinkable.

In the confrontation between a superpower and a medium-sized power, Beaufre assigned no absolute value to the 'equalizing power of the atom', unlike France's other great strategic theorist, General Gallois. Beaufre considered that if one of the protagonists could destroy 15 percent of the potential of the other, as against 90 percent in the opposite direction, there would be deterrence only if the latter could not accept that 15 percent loss. But the former would have only defensive deterrence and would not be able to intervene on behalf of a third party. In short, indirect defensive deterrence is difficult to obtain. Here Beaufre seems to have had a premonition of the debate in the 1980s on the capacity of the two European nuclear powers to extend the scope of their deterrence and offer a nuclear 'guarantee' to their non-nuclear allies; and he was sceptical as regards such a capacity.

Even in the case of the United States, a nuclear guarantee could not mean a return to the threat of massive retaliation, reciprocal suicide being irrational. Therefore, to maintain the credibility of the risk, while McNamara was secretary of defence, the United States announced the concept of the limited counter-force initiative, intended as a warning and designed to bring about a compromise and protect friendly populations while respecting those on the other side.[12]

Beaufre regarded this concept as unconvincing and even dangerous if it were to render limited nuclear war acceptable. He even feared a rehabilitation of violence at other levels if the nuclear balance became too stable. In this respect, subsequent developments in the rivalry between the superpowers and the two alliance systems which face each other in Europe have not justified his anxiety; the risk of escalation has ensured the maintenance of deterrence at the lower levels of their direct confrontation.

However, Beaufre highlights the seeming paradox whereby the Soviet Union has an indirect offensive strategy for which it only needs to have a defensive nuclear force, that is a counter-city retaliatory force, whereas the United States, having an indirect defensive strategy, requires an offensive, that is counter-force, nuclear capability.[13] It has to be recognized that the Soviet Union now has the means for a disarming first strike, particularly in Europe, giving it the complete range of strategy, both offensive and defensive.

However, taking his analysis further, Beaufre considers that as nuclear weapons become more numerous, counter-force capability is bound to become less and less effective. Nuclear stabilization would thus steadily increase, and deterrence at other levels should take on ever greater importance, perhaps eventually becoming predominant. His foresight was remarkable, in view of the calls by senior NATO officials in the 1980s for enhanced conventional means, particularly through use of the new technologies.

While deterrence at the nuclear level is based on the risk of immediate mutual destruction, at the conventional level the problem is less simple. The risk is then that of losing the war because one side wins a necessarily unilateral victory. It is the hope of success that creates instability. Here, however, we are no longer in the field of certainties or virtual certainties but in that of assessments and of confrontation with the opposing strategy.

If in nuclear strategy one deters by the threat of unacceptable retaliation, in conventional strategy one can deter only by making the enemy fear defeat. It follows that the 'conventional arms race creates insecurity because it encourages the hope of victory, whereas the build-up of nuclear weapons gives the certainty of mutual destruction'.[14]

This having been said, deterrence does not prevent cold war. But it aims to prevent certain reactions to acts of cold war by depriving the adversary of his freedom of action while maintaining that of the initiator of the action.

This type of struggle is won essentially on a world scale. It follows that once deterrence is capable of preventing the use of conventional or nuclear weapons, 'the level of cold war is that of total strategy and the modern operational level par excellence'.[15]

But nuclear weapons can deter from minor actions only if they are closely linked with conventional weapons. It is interesting to note in this respect that, when Beaufre was writing, the risk most often discussed was that of premature or excessive use of tactical weapons through automatic application of pre-established plans. It is the opposite that is generally feared in Europe today, either through an American refusal to use tactical weapons, on the principle of 'no first use', or through excessive delay in taking the decision.

Multilateral deterrence

Multilateral deterrence is the problem raised by the existence of third-country nuclear forces.

In the dialogue between a 'weak' and a 'strong' nuclear power, the 'weak' power cannot deter its 'strong' adversary unless it can inflict unacceptable damage and unless the stake is of vital importance for itself. But the 'weak–strong' dialogue has to be assessed in relation to the balance between the two superpowers because they will have an interest in calming the situation whenever, for them, the stake is marginal whereas it is essential for the 'weak' state. There will none the less remain a *de facto* solidarity between the weak state and its powerful ally.

In this, Beaufre took a contrary view to the leaders of the United States. At that time, Washington was strongly critical of France's effort to acquire nuclear weapons. 'An unfriendly act,' President Kennedy even went so far as to call it, and McNamara described third-country nuclear forces as 'ineffective, unnecessary and dangerous'.[16]

Beaufre replied that they were not ineffective if they strengthened solidarity between allies; and that they would be useless only if the great ally's commitment to use its own nuclear forces was irrevocable. But when its interests are marginal, there has to be doubt. On the contrary, Beaufre considers, third-country forces strengthen the solidarity of alliances through the *de facto* solidarity which they create. This was written ten years before the Ottawa Declaration of 1974 which acknowledged that the French and British nuclear forces have a specific deterrent role in contributing to the overall strengthening of Alliance deterrence. As for 'danger', it could only result from an act of folly on the part of the weak: it is not clear why a country should seek its own destruction.

What does create a problem is the absence of consultation and coordination among the nuclear allies. Such coordination should not imply either abdication of the responsibility of decisionmaking or any right of veto. Each party must understand that it is part of a whole while remaining independent. 'The only way for an independent force not to be dangerous is to be allied but not integrated.'[17]

In short, Beaufre considers that third-country forces increase organic solidarity among allies, tend to reduce the area of the cold war by covering certain zones that would be marginal for other powers and complicate the task of a possible aggressor.

In fact, the theoretical reasoning which leads him to conclude the necessity for such coordination has not been confirmed by events, at least as far as the French forces are concerned, since no consultation has taken place with the United States or NATO regarding plans for their use.

Beaufre also thought that interdependence and solidarity within an alliance would increase the reciprocal influence of the various allies. He was no doubt influenced by the example of Great Britain, which has sought to keep up a special relationship with Washington. This has not been either the experience or the ambition of France.

However, Beaufre recognized that we are still in the early stages of reflection on the new era that the world has entered with the coming of nuclear weapons and of a situation in which peace can only be the 'permanent interplay of deterrence'.[18] But, to prevent catastrophe, the threat has to remain credible, so a risk has to remain and be carefully preserved. This contradiction is 'the essential mystery of the new age which seems to secrete both the power of man and the safeguards which must prevent him for misusing it'.

In passing, Beaufre is led to wonder whether the absolute primacy of nuclear weapons is not liable to damage the military vocation and the recruitment of officers, if their skills become anachronistic. His answer is, however, that while conflict in Europe is unlikely, the Third World poses formidable problems, the more so as it assimilates our techniques. The work of defence will remain the indispensable complement to economic prosperity and cultural progress.

Moreover, while it is true that, in the zones covered by deterrence, situations as politically absurd as Berlin or Quemoy become stable, with 'military stability almost completely covering political instability', outside these zones there is great freedom of action especially for non-nuclear powers: 'Joining the nuclear club means giving up irresponsible innocence'.[19]

Beaufre emphasized that, at the time when he was writing, the geographical limits of the deterrent action of nuclear weapons were not well defined, the corollary being that the degree of freedom of action thereby restored to conventional weapons was equally undefined. An answer was subsequently given, with the Soviet Union's interventions in Africa through its Cuban surrogates and its direct invasion of Afghanistan, not to mention its interventions in its satellite allies.

Faced with such initiatives, the Western countries need to conceive a world strategy at the service of a policy which likewise has to be defined. From this standpoint, strategy is a foreshadowing of action. It does not aim to forecast the future but to construct it.

So it is for politicians to define the goals which strategy must seek to achieve in a 'shrinking and over-populated world': avoiding conflict between the United States and the Soviet Union, seeking the most stable world system possible (which Beaufre did not expect to be achieved through the United Nations or by disarmament), looking towards a multi-polar world in which a coherent Europe, with an identity of its own, will again be a world power, linked to the United States in defence but having recovered its political independence; China is another of these poles.

At the level of indirect strategy, Beaufre considers that the Western countries must re-establish a minimum of cohesion enabling them to take initiatives. Recognizing that not all the allies are equally interested, he urges consultation among those who feel most concerned.

Instead of asking 'What is going to happen?' politicians should start to ask 'What must we do?'.[20] The world cannot continue to drift blindly on now that it has the capacity to destroy itself, on the premise that the essential role of modern strategy is manoeuvre in time, just as manoeuvre in space was the role of classical strategy.

Rising to philosophical reflection, he suggests that

> Nature reproduces at the collective level, with atomic weapons, the equivalent of what it has achieved at the individual level with pain — the safeguard of life and the suffering of the living.[21] The nuclear danger can then be seen as a natural mechanism preventing human societies from using their destructive power beyond a certain degree of violence, a step towards a more peaceful or a less cruelly thoughtless world.

The strategy of action

Insisting that he had no wish to enter the arena of politics, Beaufre none the less put forward clear ideas regarding the requirements which preparation for modern confrontations must satisfy, although, because of the staggering technological changes in the areas of equipment and information, the problems encountered are more intractable than ever before.

Quite apart from the nuclear factor, Beufre argued that the world was entering a new form of contest for which the lessons of the two world wars are outdated. Forces will necessarily be small in volume since mobility counts for more than firepower; the relationship which counts most from now on is that between 'agilities'. Hence the primacy of the air offensive which, if it is capable of securing victory, becomes the essential element in the outcome, land battle being no more than the exploitation of this victory.

This is the strategy of the *fait accompli*, to which Western Europe is unfortunately very vulnerable because of the narrowness of its territory and the geographical, psychological and political factors which make it unsuitable for defence and therefore for deterrence when under threat by guerrilla action. To render the outcome of such an enemy air offensive inconclusive is therefore a matter of 'life and death'.

But even if this result were achieved, it does not follow that the consequence would be prolonged conflict. This is for the reason already mentioned, the narrowness of the territory, but also because of the reactions of public opinion and the fear of nuclear escalation. Thus in all circumstances conventional warfare would have to achieve its objectives in a matter of days.

Given the conventional superiority of the Warsaw Pact, NATO would have to resort to use of tactical nucler weapons. Beaufre did not contest the need for recourse to these weapons, but doubted whether they could ensure the defeat of the enemy. It is therefore necessary to consider how they help to prevent conflict, that is contribute to deterrence. To do this, it is necessary to establish the probability of their use, which in his view 'flexible response' does not do. Without urging renunciation of tactical nuclear weapons but taking account of the unpredictability of the reactions of troops subjected to nuclear attack and of populations terrified by the fear of annihilation, Beaufre considers it necessary to raise the nuclear threshold considerably in the event of conventional attack by the enemy. But one also needs to consider the use of 'clean' nuclear weapons. Thus, even if he does not use the term, Beaufre seems to envisage the enhanced radiation weapon.

In short, since massive retaliation is not credible, deterrence in Europe has to be based on the one hand on improved conventional forces and on the other hand on the credibility of generalized, timely use of tactical nuclear weapons.

Having said this, and assuming that deterrence is consolidated in this way, there remains the need to be able to act at the level of total strategy where deterrence and action are both opposite and complementary: opposite because action is the positive act of doing something and deterrence, which prevents someone else from doing something, is a negative act; complementary because the two are closely linked and yet asymmetrical. For, while deterrence can be achieved without action, action always involves a degree of deterrence towards the adversary or third parties. But above all, the strategy of deterrence, if it succeeds, is purely conjectural whereas the strategy of action cannot avoid the material verification of the means that it uses.

While deterrence can still be maintained with only an 'infinitesimal amount' of credibility, the strategy of action necessarily entails technical and psychological testing. The margin of possible error has to be much narrower because whereas deterrence can be based on a doubt, action has to produce a real certainty in the opposing camp that it would be catastrophic to pursue the struggle.

However, while changes in the system of international relations demand the extension of strategy and will increasingly do so, this in no way implies an extension of the military sphere at the expense of the political. On the contrary, 'the notion of total strategy tends to diminish strictly military strategy, subordinating it very closely to an overall strategic idea, itself directly governed by a political vision and implemented by politicians'.[22]

That is, in any case, what faces us on the other side. In Marxist–Leninist thought, there is no distinction between the sphere of politics and that of total strategy. The Soviets have completely merged the two. It is therefore indispensable for us to understand the system of thought with which we are confronted. The adoption of total strategy does not necessarily mean that the procedures used in conflicts are automatically extended to political disputes. Indeed, it is the application of the methods of strategy to the political sphere which makes it possible to avoid using military force, recourse to the military often being merely the result of the absence of an appropriate political concept.

'Winning the war' is not a political goal, as Liddell Hart has shown; it is the kind of peace that follows the war that is the real political goal[23] if one is tempted or obliged to resort to war. But action does not always or necessarily mean resorting to hostilities. Action, 'in its simplest definition, always rests on the dialectic between the possible gains and losses, the balance struck between the hope of success and the fear of the risks incurred'.[24]

The parameters involved in this equation are numerous. It is they which make possible the political diagnosis needed for the strategy of action, a diagnosis which has to be much more complete than for the strategy of deterrence. They will determine the forms of the action, from the most violent to the most insidious.

On the basis of this analysis, the key element of action is will-power, the will of the would-be-actor and the will of the intended target of the action. Often, too, 'inevitabilities' intervene. A train is not stopped in ten yards, and likewise action is set in an infinitely complex environment the components of which have an inertia of their own that can make one a prisoner. It is therefore almost always by intervening very early that one can modify the course of events or influence their unfolding. Hence the need for foresight, as opposed to the traditional and mistaken 'wait and see'.

Does this amount to saying, as Marxists do, that there is a 'direction of history' inexorably dragging the world towards so-called 'progressive' formulae? When he was writing, twenty years ago, Beaufre was impressed by the impact of the ideological dynamic of the Soviet Union and China. It was the period when the Third World was strongly influenced, economically and politically, by the Marxist model. The dynamic of events seemed to favour the development and spread of that ideology, and the West seemed to have no comparably compelling idea to set against it. And it is a paradoxical fact that the advocates of a materialist view of history are the most skilful in using the resources of ideology and psychology. The Soviet Union's successes in Angola, Mozambique, Ethiopia, South Yemen, Vietnam and Laos; Moscow's influence over Syria, Iraq and Libya in the 1970s and early 1980s seemed to confirm Beaufre's prediction, although the economic failure of the Soviet system and the collapse of communism in the late 1980s has significantly tarnished the prestige of Marxism–Leninism in the 1990s.

At the time when Beaufre was writing, however, the Western countries seemed unable to respond on the ideological level by attacking the weak points of the opposing system and to providing an answer to the needs of those whom they wished to convince. They appeared to Beaufre to lack 'a body of liberal thinking responding to the immediate needs (on matters of economics, social organization or political constitution) of Third World countries'.[25]

Beaufre also felt the West incapable of responding to overt aggression. He therefore advocated the creation of mobile intervention forces which predated the later rapid intervention forces of the United States and France, capable of acting wherever necessary but exerting a constant deterrent effect and therefore having a stabilizing value simply by virtue of their existence.

At all events, while politics can be progressive or conservative, strategy cannot be either but can only be guided by the concern to use the most effective means available in the prevailing situation — the 'conjuncture' — with a view to achieving the political goal assigned to it.

The importance which Beaufre attaches to the conjuncture leads him to analyse the 'mechanics' of action, in other words the inventory of the possibilities and constraints that will intervene, before action is unleashed, at the level of political decisionmaking.

Comparing the situation in the two world wars, he observes that in 1914–18 the impossibility of achieving a breakthrough or envelopment created a 'desperately stable' situation, in which the outcome was finally decided only by attrition of forces combined with economic measures (blockade) and psychological measures (propaganda on the domestic front). In World War II, the outcome for France in 1940 was essentially decided by mobility and the possibilities of a breakthrough which created an essentially unstable strategic situation.

After Hiroshima, the situation was one in which stability at the nuclear level, owing to the existence of invulnerable retaliatory forces, was counterposed to instability at the conventional level owing to the opportunities for actions using very mobile forces and for achieving a breakthrough.

The political environment involves several actors or players: the state which seeks to act; the states whose interests coincide to a greater or lesser extent with the action envisaged; the main adversaries which constitute the obstacle to be overcome in order to achieve the end in view and the rest of the world, which has no interests directly affected by the action envisaged but which may exert a favourable or unfavourable influence.

The assessment of this situation will determine the scope for decision and action available in relation to the adversary and to third countries. This leads to the political diagnosis of the chances of achieving the goal that is in view. This was the analysis Hitler made before the invasion of Czechoslovakia which led him to neutralize France and Britain by psychological and material action to shatter Czechoslovak resistance both materially and psychologically. Conversely, France and Britain failed to make such an analysis before they launched the Suez expedition without having secured political cover regarding the reactions of the United States, the Soviet Union and the United Nations.[26]

It was the latter experience, as well as those in Indochina and Algeria, which led Beaufre to rationalize his concept of total strategy, whether applied in the direct mode, that is essentially military action based on the use or threat of use of military force — or in the indirect mode in which the outcome in view has to be attained essentially by non-military means — or in which these means play only an ancillary role.

However, even in direct-mode strategy, the use of military force represents only part of the action and must be supported in the political, diplomatic and economic fields, with the operational phase being kept as short as possible in order to achieve a *fait accompli*.

This being so, direct-mode operations are very unlikely between the two alliance systems of the East and West, unless the nuclear balance were to become so perfect that nuclear deterrence lost all credibility.

Hence the primordial importance of the way the cold war has been conducted. At the same time it has to be remembered that in indirect as in direct strategy, the defensive attitude of withstanding the enemy's initiative cannot lead to any satisfactory political solution. Any defence that is not conducted with a view to a counter-attack is worthless.

Only offensive action counts. . .[27] This crucial idea has hitherto been largely ignored in the West, partly as a result of passivity but mainly because the phenomena of indirect strategy were little known there. Strategists have never known how to analyse these problems and have often wrongly concluded that the only alternatives were to give in or to engage in military adventures.

It is not certain that if Beaufre had to judge the two decades which have passed since he wrote those lines, he would be inclined to think that we have made great progress in understanding the forms of contemporary struggles.

His reflections finally led him to ask whether the total strategy whose function is to implement a political vision is itself strategy or politics. The answer is that it achieves the extension of the rigorous methods of strategy to international politics of which Lenin perhaps gave the first example and from which Marxism–Leninism has drawn its philosophy of action. It therefore behoves Western leaders to make themselves fully aware of the mechanisms of action instead of the 'intuitive approximations' with which they have hitherto been satisfied.

Beaufre was then led to compare strategy and economic management, the two basic and essential techniques of state governance. They cannot be considered separately because they are closely interdependent: the economy provides the means of strategy, and strategy directly impinges on the economy through the cost of armaments, their technological spin-off and the economic disruption resulting from conflicts.

However, though Beaufre gives this central place to analysis of the elements of a situation, nothing could be further from his approach than *esprit de système* or the idea that history unfolds with mathematical rules of logic. It is passions that lead men and the springs of action used by idealists, patriots, ambitious or greedy leaders have been religion, nationalism, democracy and freedom, material progress and social justice.

He himself was not immune to passions, even if cold reasoning and clarity of expression relate him to the best writers in French literature. The influence of Descartes is never far from his mental process and the way he expresses it. But the wound suffered by the 1940 disaster had never completely healed which explains the almost desperate application he devotes to his search for understanding the future.

It may not be generally realized outside France but, from a certain point of view her defeat then was something unique in her history. In centuries of wars against Spain, Austria, England, Germany, her fate, whether victorious or vanquished, had always settled the final result, not only for herself but for Europe as well. In 1940 for the first time, her collapse did not mark the end of the fighting. War went on and, whatever the courageous feats of her resistance fighters, she was eventually to be rescued by the victory of Britain, the Soviet Union and the United States and then saved. Similarly the Western half of the continent was prevented from becoming a part of Stalin's empire by the presence of American forces on the line that divides West from East.

Furthermore, French colonial days were over, having ended with defeat in Indochina and withdrawal from Algeria. There was therefore a danger that the French might lose interest in defence matters or no longer feel responsible for their own security, leaving it to the United States, both at the conceptual and material levels.

It can be reasonably argued that the building of the *force de frappe* and the withdrawal from NATO's integrated military structure (replaced by cooperation agreements between NATO and French forces' commanders) were very instrumental in restoring, in the minds of the French people, the feeling of their responsibility for their own security which has made them less vulnerable to pacifist movements than other European nations.

Beaufre's writings also contributed to that end, convinced, as he was, that the national humiliation suffered in the early phase of World War II was primarily owing to a failure to grasp the changes that had taken place in the relation of forces and the new factors of power. It was a defeat of the mind; of the military leaders and the political class and even more generally of the elite of the nation.

But that did not lead him, unlike most other French military writers, to consider that France's security presents a special case in Europe, allowing for, or rather requiring unique solutions. Such a point of view was exemplified, for instance, in the

1972 official White Paper or referred to in many political pronouncements claiming France's 'independent' posture on deterrence and defence. Beaufre never separates the problem of France from the wider context of the Atlantic Alliance although keeping complete freedom in his judgements *vis-à-vis* NATO's strategy.

He also differs from British and American strategists in that his approach is much less focused on the immediate and most tangible aspects of the Soviet threat — not that he minimises or underestimates Moscow's military programme and achievements. But opposition and conflict of power being the essence of international society, the problem is to master the rules of the new era which apply to both East and West, but which seem to have been better understood by the Kremlin. He does not therefore, concentrate on strategies meant to check Soviet nuclear and conventional doctrines and armaments but rather to fathom the depth of the 'new ocean of problems' we have embarked upon.

In this perspective he makes a distinction between global and total strategy. The first, most generally referred to by other writers, has a predominantly military meaning extended worldwide to match Soviet expansion. The second, which of course includes the first, adds the other parameters (especially political, economic, psychological, cultural) of which the Soviets have made such good use in their offensive against the West and in developing countries.

No doubt, this is not all that novel, but what is new is that modern weapons have achieved a destructive power of such magnitude that the use of force between nations which possess these weapons can no longer be considered as the natural continuation of other policies. Military power will not disappear from the picture, but other factors will play a greater role in shaping the fate of the world as essential parts of total strategy, whether of deterrence or action, whether the action be direct or indirect.

Furthermore, it is not merely 'the giant shadow of nuclear deterrence' which imposes the strategy of action in the indirect mode. Such strategy corresponds to a profound shift in modern attitudes towards violence, no doubt as a result of the absurd great wars we have experienced in this century. As man becomes increasingly powerful, he tends to reject the paroxysmic use of force. If this tendency continues, while power is deployed to the benefit of deterrence, action will increasingly have to be confined to the use of indirect-mode strategy because this strategy alone makes it possible to achieve significant results through a more or less measured use of force, even to the point of being limited to abstract manoeuvres solely at the level of political decisions. Total strategy in the indirect mode is likely to be the strategy of the future. The danger would be for the Western nations to see in this new situation only its 'non-war' aspect, freeing them from the nightmare of an apocalypse and taking that state of affairs for granted, thus leaving the road wide open for the Soviet strategy of 'victory without war'.

Nothing is fixed once and for all in human rivalries, and this is more true than ever in view of the fantastic, unpredictable developments of the scientific and technological factors which play an increasing part in determining and modifying the hierarchy of the powers. None the less, the message Beaufre has left us is one of confidence in the future, a confidence based on the twofold belief in the durability of deterrence and the primacy of the mind — of which his whole *oeuvre*, committed to thinking the unthinkable and rationalizing the irrational, gives an example that has lost none of its persuasive power and freshness.

Notes

1. *Introduction à la stratégie*, Paris, Economica, 1962, p. 16.
2. Ibid., p. 11.
3. Ibid., p. 62.
4. Ibid., pp. 78–9.
5. Ibid., p. 89.
6. Ibid.
7. Ibid., p. 93.
8. Ibid., pp. 93–4.
9. Ibid., p. 115.
10. Ibid., p. 117.
11. *Dissuasion et stratégie*, Paris, Armand Colin, 1964, pp. 36–7.
12. Ibid., p. 39.
13. Ibid., pp. 47–8.
14. Ibid., p. 56.
15. Ibid., p. 63.
16. Ibid., p. 95.
17. Ibid., p. 102.
18. Ibid., p. 113.
19. Ibid.
20. Ibid., p. 204.
21. Ibid., p. 116. In a philosophical essay entitled 'The Nature of Things', Beaufre explains that it is pain and fear of pain that makes man avoid dangers. Without the warning of pain, they would rush to their deaths.
22. *Stratégie de l'action*, Paris, Armand Colin, 1966.
23. Ibid., p. 18.
24. Ibid., p. 27.
25. Ibid., p. 111.
26. In a book published under the title *L'expedition de Suez*, Beaufre, who was the commander-in-chief of the French forces, discusses the lessons of well-conducted but politically ill-conceived and supported campaign.
27. *Stratégie de l'action*. p. 122.

9 V. D. SOKOLOVSKII

*S. Neil MacFarlane**

In the 1960s and 1970s many assumed that strategies based on mutual assured destruction were a logical outcome of adjustment to the advent of nuclear weapons. The pain that a nuclear power could inflict on its adversaries even in defeat, and the consequent irrationality of a conscious choice to do battle, created a radical disjuncture between war and politics for those possessing this technology. Nuclear weapons — and, given the possibility of escalation, conventional ones as well — became means of deterring an enemy rather than being instruments to be used in the pursuit of a state's objectives at the enemy's expense. Perhaps as a result, the Western powers have had great difficulty in developing coherent plans for how to fight a major war and, more importantly, in relating strategic options and plans to forces in being.[1]

Since the character of nuclear technology itself was perceived to determine this evolution, it transcended the particular characteristics of different nations' historical and cultural backgrounds. Just as we had come to see these truths, so the Soviet Union would ultimately join us in the embrace of deterrence based on mutual assured destruction.

Yet the developing Soviet discussion of nuclear war and strategy seems at variance with these expectations. Soviet military writers have been far more preoccupied than we with how to fight such a war should it occur and with the relation of military strategy to the attainment of concrete political objectives, even in the nuclear context. These perspectives are deeply rooted in the historical development of Soviet military thought and Soviet Marxism–Leninism.[2] Both have contributed to a view of nuclear weapons and the relationship between war and politics in the nuclear age which is distinctly Soviet. Although there are currently signs of change in Soviet perspectives on nuclear weapons (see below), Soviet thinking about nuclear weapons remains in many respects quite different from Western thinking.

Marshal V. D. Sokolovskii played a prominent role in the definition of Soviet perspectives on nuclear weapons and nuclear war. Sokolovskii's military career spans the entire history of the Soviet armed forces, from the revolution through to the approach to parity with the United States in the late 1960s. Sokolovskii trained as a teacher and joined the Red Army in 1918. During the Civil War, he fought on the eastern, southern, and Caucasian Fronts and rose to regimental command. Subsequently, he served in the campaigns against the Basmachi in Soviet Central Asia. During the 1930s he rose to command of a rifle division, and then — avoiding the extensive purge of the officer corps in the late 1930s — to chief of staff of the Moscow Military District. In April 1941, he joined the General Staff.

During the war, he was active in command positions on the western, Ukrainian and Byelorussian fronts. He was named a Hero of the Soviet Union for outstanding performance during the Berlin operation which brought the European war to a close.

* The author wishes to acknowledge the support of the University of Virginia and the Berkeley/Stanford Program in Soviet International Behavior in the preparation of this chapter.

After the war, he replaced Marshal Zhukov as commander of Soviet forces in Germany and chief of the Soviet military administration there. In the 1950s, as chief of the General Staff and first deputy minister of defence (1952–59), he oversaw the substantial modernization and restructuring of Soviet forces. In 1956, he was elected to membership of the Central Committee of the Communist Party of the Soviet Union and was re-elected at the 21st, 22nd and 23rd congresses. In 1960, he retired from active service and turned his attention to questions of military strategy, heading the authors' collegium which produced *Military Strategy* in 1962.

Military Strategy, prepared under the editorial supervision of Marshal V. D. Sokolovskii, and published in three editions (1962, 1963, and 1968) is a seminal work in the post-war development of Soviet strategy. Its relevance as an indication of *contemporary* Soviet thinking on the questions of the nature of war and appropriate strategy in such a war may be questioned in a number of respects.[3] Yet it is the first systematic attempt by prominent Soviet military theorists to develop a coherent body of strategic principles on how to fight a war in the nuclear age.[4] Though it did not have the status of official doctrine (see below), its conclusions on central issues of nuclear strategy seem to reflect rather closely those in statements and works having this status during the 1960s. The theory developed in the book, moreover, matched closely soon-to-be-developed Soviet capabilities. Finally, although its direct significance in Soviet strategy and force planning may have been ephemeral, it arguably had a significant impact on the Western perception of the Soviet threat. For all these reasons, the volume deserves close attention in the study of the evolution of strategic thought in the nuclear age.

This examination of Sokolovskii's work begins with a discussion of the historical and political context in which it was written. It goes on to consider the substance of the work, notably the image of future war contained therein and the proposed Soviet strategic response to this image. It concludes with an examination of developments in Soviet strategic thinking and practice since the last edition of *Military Strategy* in an attempt to assess the work's significance and continuing relevance to the analysis of strategy in the nuclear age.

Before moving on to the body of the analysis, three methodological issues should be addressed. First, with regard to the content of the book, in addition to their assessment of the 'revolution in military affairs' associated with the advent of nuclear weapons, Sokolovskii and his colleagues discuss a number of other aspects of strategy such as the possibility and nature of limited war, the organization of the armed forces and the relationship between military and civilian authorities. Given the constraints of space and the focus of this collection, the analysis centres on the nuclear aspect of Sokolovskii's work.

Second, it is somewhat inappropriate to include Marshal Sokolovskii in a volume of this type since *Military Strategy*, of which he was the 'responsible editor', is the product of a collegium of authors,[5] many of whom contended with one another in the Soviet debate on nuclear weapons which preceded the publication of the collective work. Sokolovskii's own position in these debates is not entirely clear, though the dominant thrust of his major work — *Military Strategy* — suggests that he sympathized with the resistance of more traditional officers to more conclusions concerning the implications of nuclear weapons for conventional forces (see below). Some have attributed his retirement at the end of the 1950s to disagreement with a political leadership ostensibly devoted to deep cuts in conventional forces. However, it has also been reported that he had heart problems during this period. Some of his co-authors, meanwhile, appear to have supported Khrushchev's advocacy of radical change in the structure of the Soviet armed forces (see below). In subsequent work,

Sokolovskii, in conjunction with his frequent co-author Lt.-General Cherednichenko, displayed a certain degree of unhappiness with the state of Soviet strategic thought, of which his own book was a dominant element.[6] In many respects, *Military Strategy* reflects not so much a resolution of debates concerning nuclear weapons as an embodiment of them, with many key issues left unresolved.

Third, the Soviet military establishment has a far more formal definition of 'strategy', its relation to 'doctrine' and the relationship of both to politics than do many Western authors. Cruder discussions of the Soviet threat[7] frequently miss this point. None the less, it is of some importance in the assessment of that threat. It is also relevant to the assessment of the significance of this work. The *Soviet Military Encyclopedia* defines military doctrine as the body of views that a state holds on the 'purposes and character of a possible war, on the preparation of the country and the armed forces for it and also on the methods of waging it'.[8] Doctrine has two dimensions:

(1) *the political* — dealing primarily with the political purposes and political character of war and the relationship between military needs and the political, economic, and social organization of the state and population;
(2) *the military-technical* — dealing with the methods of waging war, the organization of the armed forces, procurement, readiness and so on.

In theory, the former is dominant. Responsibility for the definition of doctrine lies with the party leadership in accord with the principle of military subordination to party control.

However, in the development of the military–technical aspect of doctrine, the party relies on the development of 'military science' by the General Staff and the military academies. Military science is in turn comprised of strategy, operational art and tactics.[9] It is worth defining where Sokolovskii's book fits into this schema. As the title implies, it is not a statement of doctrine, though doctrine sets the scene for much of the analysis. It is a book about strategy, a concept the authors define as: 'a system of theoretical knowledge dealing with the laws of war as an armed conflict in the name of definite class interests'.[10]

Drawing upon Lenin's remarks on Clausewitz, the authors go on to note that since war 'is a tool of politics', the relation of military strategy to politics is one of complete dependence of the former on the latter. It is policy that sets the strategic aims. Strategy suggests how to realize them.

The importance of this kind of distinction becomes clearer when one considers, for example, the discussion in Sokolovskii of how to fight and *win* a nuclear war through massive simultaneous counterforce and countervalue strikes, which may be pre-emptive in character. This is not a very comfortable scenario from the point of view of those of us who would be on the receiving end. But it is not necessarily an indication that the Soviet leadership thought or thinks that it might be desirable to fight such a war.[11] Sokolovskii's contribution to Soviet *military science* (or, for that matter, subsequent discussions of war fighting by Soviet military intellectuals) is not a sufficient basis for confident conclusions about this aspect of Soviet military doctrine. Instead, it represents an attempt by a group of prominent serving officers to provide a strategy for fighting such a war successfully as one element of the definition of doctrine by others. One might well interpret Soviet strategy as elaborated in Sokolovskii's book as serving the policy aim of avoiding catastrophic war, that is to say, as a basic prop of a doctrine not of the prosecution of war but of its prevention.

For that matter, this distinction might seem wrongheaded to Soviet strategic thinkers, since it is through the development of strategies which suggest to the enemy that one might be able to prosecute war successfully that one prevents it.

The historical and political context

There are three important contextual factors which influenced the writers of *Military Strategy*:

1. the 'revolution in military affairs' associated with the development of nuclear weapons and their procurement by the Soviet armed forces;
2. the budget battle over the appropriate size of the armed forces and their nature in the nuclear age;
3. developments in American strategy and doctrine, and in relations between the two superpowers.

With regard to the first, the Soviet Union tested an atomic device in 1949, and the atomic weapons began to reach units of the armed forces in 1953. One might have expected some evolution of Soviet military strategy in this period to take account of these new capabilities. However, there was little evidence of such a process in the public Soviet literature. This was due largely to the doctrinal stance of Stalin himself and his close control of Soviet military affairs.[12]

For whatever reason (success in the previous war by conventional means, a sense of inferiority to the United States in atomic weaponry), Stalin chose to denigrate the significance of the atomic revolution. He also belittled the strategic significance of putative surprise strikes with atomic weapons, emphasizing instead the continuing significance of permanently operating factors (the stability of the rear, morale in the armed forces, the quantity and quality of divisions, the armament of the army and the organizing ability of command personnel) in war. He explicitly denied the proposition that the war had become non-inevitable in the conditions prevailing in the early 1950s.[13]

With Stalin's death, Soviet military thought was 'destalinized', first rather tentatively, and after 1956 with greater confidence. Stalin's own role in stifling the development of military science was amply criticized. Soviet military writers began to assess in far greater detail and with some originality the nature and objectives of war in the nuclear age and the roles of nuclear and conventional weapons and of surprise in such war.[14] In the meantime, the doctrine of the inevitability of war was revised by Khrushchev himself at the 20th party Congress. By implication, he ascribed this change to the Soviet attainment of a strategic nuclear capability (however primitive it might have been at the time): 'But war is not fatalistically inevitable. Today there are mighty social and political forces possessing formidable means to prevent the imperialists from unleashing war, and if they actually try to start it, to give a smashing rebuff to the aggressors and frustrate their adventurist plans.'[15]

From such statements, it is reasonably clear that Soviet doctrine — whatever the character of Soviet strategy — was deterrent in character. As he consolidated power in the late 1950s, Khrushchev increasingly attempted to translate this deterrent doctrine into policy concerning the size and makeup of the armed forces. In this effort, he was apparently motivated by a desire to reduce the level of human and material resources devoted to the military in order to facilitate more growth. The Politburo created a new branch of the armed forces in 1959, the Strategic Rocket Forces. They gave it operational control of Soviet missiles with a range greater than 1,000 kilometers. Doctrinal pronouncements of the period made it clear that this service was to play the crucial role in restraining (*sderzhivanie*) Western aggressiveness. If war occurred none the less, this service was to be the primary instrument in the attainment of Soviet objectives. The role of traditional services such as the ground forces and navy, by contrast, was somewhat ambiguous and clearly secondary. This had the felicitous implication that levels of investment in these services could be reduced.

Khrushchev took this issue up at a plenum of the Central Committee of the Communist Party of the Soviet Union (CPSU) in December 1959 and unveiled a new military policy in remarks to the Supreme Soviet in January 1960.[16] He noted that in his view, missiles would be the dominant element in any future war, that conventional arms were consequently becoming obsolete, and that first strike strategies based on surprise were unfeasible because of residual capabilities likely to survive such an attack. He then announced shifts in force structure to the detriment of the traditional conventional forces as well as the party's intention to reduce military manpower by approximately one-third.

This innovation and its precursors met with considerable resistance from some military officers, for a number of reasons. One source was the bureaucratic interest of the military elite. Fewer soldiers meant fewer command positions and a diminution of the presence of the military in Soviet politics and society. Another presumably was martial culture. As a matter of course, the military elite preoccupied itself with how to fight war rather than with essentially political notions of deterrence.

The retirements of a number of leading military officers in the spring of 1960 suggested that, initially, Khrushchev had the upper hand in this dispute. As noted earlier, Sokolovskii's retirement during this period may suggest that he was among those resisting the trend of Khrushchev's military policy.

Although Khrushchev's line met with considerable initial success, external events conspired to weaken his hand. As long as the policy of peaceful coexistence appeared to be bearing fruit in a relaxation of tension with the United States, it was difficult for military officers to point to imminent external threats in defending their position. But in May of 1960, the downing of an American U-2 brought with it the cancellation of the Paris summit and a considerable worsening of the Soviet–American diplomatic relationship. This provided the military with ammunition in their attempts to dilute Khrushchev's effort to reallocate resources within the military away from conventional arms of the Soviet services and towards the missile forces and, more generally, away from the military and towards the civilian sector.

With the election of President Kennedy later in the year, things took an even worse turn from Khrushchev's perspective. The new administration chose radically to increase American defence spending, speeding up the Polaris programme and seeking to develop a more balanced military posture through the buildup of conventional forces. This presumably was a rational response to the erosion of the credibility of the doctrine of massive retaliation which resulted from the Soviet development of a degree of intercontinental delivery capability. It is ironic, however, that it should have occurred just as Khrushchev was attempting to implement a new military doctrine which resembled rather closely that of the Eisenhower administration in its stress on nuclear capabilities and assured destruction, coupled with cutbacks in conventional forces. These developments in American defence policy were accompanied by considerable tension in 1961 around Berlin.

Changes in American procurement brought with them the articulation of a new doctrine — that of flexible response, with its stress on the development of capabilities and plans to wage war at a variety of levels below that of a general nuclear exchange. These changes strengthened the arguments of those already seeking to maintain balance in Soviet forces structure. Defence Minister Malinovskii, for example, argued in a much cited speech at the 21st party Congress in October 1961 that final victory in a future war would require the 'combined action of all arms and services'.[17] He also took a far less sanguine view than did Khrushchev a year earlier of the question of surprise attack, noting that it was a realistic possibility, implying that under certain circumstances pre-emption might be necessary and arguing therefore for high levels of readiness. As Dinerstein, Goure and Wolfe pointed out, this position had fundamentally different implications with regard to peace-time force levels than did that of Khrushchev[18], and constituted a rejection of the force reductions advocated by the general secretary a year earlier. The fact that Malinovskii articulated these statements at a party congress and was not effectively rebutted suggests that the balance of opinion in the Soviet Union had shifted towards those resisting such a radical restructuring in the Soviet Armed Forces.

The analysis thus far ignores a further dimension to the consideration of the impact of nuclear weapons and new means of delivery on Soviet strategy. It is incorrect to view the military as a monolithic entity, uniformly opposed to the kinds of strategic innovation Khrushchev was advocating. Indeed, to judge from the military literature of the early 1960s, the advent of the ICBM in particular had fostered considerable disagreement between traditional and more innovative sectors of opinion in the military establishment. A number of more radical military thinkers (for example. General N. A. Talenskii) maintained for instance that nuclear technology had rendered previous concepts of war obsolete and that the successful development of strategy necessitated the discarding of traditional doctrine and its focus on the experience of past wars. Attention, according to these writers, should focus instead on the working out of new strategic principles based on the utilization of nuclear weapons. A notable aspect of the discussion was the revision of perspectives on the possibility and significance of surprise in war. Writers such as Marshal P. Rotmistrov held that the advent of nuclear weapons had rendered it possible to draw significant advantage from surprise attack. He therefore envisaged a role for massive pre-emption in order to prevent it.[19] More traditional military thinkers, by contrast, favoured an approach to strategy based heavily on Soviet historical experience. They criticized the group just mentioned for underestimating the significance of experience accumulated in past wars.[20]

Sokolovskii's volume of 1962 was an attempt to develop a more or less coherent general statement on Soviet strategy in the context of these technological, and internal and external political conditions influencing the development of Soviet strategic thought. Given the complexity of the factors impinging on the analysis, it is not surprising that many critical issues were papered over or left unresolved. The book, rather than constituting a definitive conclusion to the debates of previous years, is instead a compromise document embodying the lowest common denominator on which these authors could agree and which was politically acceptable at that point in time. Indeed, the compromise in the volume was in some respects incomplete. In chapter 7 on defence preparation, for example, the authors argue that nuclear missile forces can reduce expenditure for military preparation in peacetime since their presence permits 'a significant cutback in production of other types of armament without lowering the firepower of the armed forces'.[21] This is consistent with Khrushchev's preferences of 1959–60. But it is very difficult to square with comment elsewhere in the book (see below) stressing the necessity of high levels of peacetime readiness and the need for substantial non-nuclear forces.

The general position on strategy and force posture taken in the volume in many respects reflects what Raymond Garthoff once referred to as the 'enlightened conservatism' of officers such as Malinovskii and Sokolovskii himself[22] — a willingness on the one hand to accept that the advent of nuclear weapons and modern means of delivery had fundamentally altered the character of war, but that traditional land forces in particular would have a significant role to play none the less, and, therefore, that they could not be gutted as nuclear capabilities grew.

Sokolovskii's *Military Strategy*[23]

This discussion focuses on a number of aspects of the treatment of war and nuclear weapons in the Sokolovskii volume:

(1) What, in the authors' view, was the impact of nuclear technology on future war? Could such a war be won in the nuclear age? Was it to be limited or general, short or protracted, counterforce or countervalue?

(2) What was the role of surprise in war and, by extension, what were the authors' attitudes on the question of pre-emption?

(3) What forces were necessary to fight this future war? Was military superiority a requirement of Soviet strategy in the nuclear age? Was defence possible or desirable in a strategic nuclear war?

With regard to the first of these issues, it is clear that the authors of this work took the view that nuclear weapons and modern means of delivery had brought a revolution in military affairs which profoundly affected the nature and conduct of war, rendering obsolete many of the traditional modes of Soviet strategic thinking. They rejected the previous stress in Soviet strategy on the successive defeat of enemy forces in the field followed by the occupation of the enemy's rear. In a related vein, they raised doubts about the continuing relevance of associated concepts derived from the World War II experience, such as economy of force, concentration of forces along the decisive axis, final victory being the cumulation of partial victories and so on.

The war envisaged in this work was one in which the basic political stake was the destruction of one or the other social system. Given these stakes, war between the socialist and imperialist camps was unlimited, global and inevitably nuclear in character. The weight of comment concerning local and limited war options — while not conclusive — suggests considerable skepticism on prospects for avoiding escalation from small-scale conflicts involving the two camps to general war.[24] Despite their recognition of the high levels of probable damage to both sides in such a war, they maintained emphatically that this *did not* break the link between war and policy:

the political aims of participants in a future world war will be achieved not only by a defeat of armed forces, but also by the complete disorganization of the enemy's economy and by lowering the morale of his population. Therefore, the essence of war as a continuation of politics by means of armed violence . . . appear[s] today more clearly than in the past, and modern means of coercion assume ever increasing importance.[25]

In other words, the policy aim of world war in the nuclear age remained unchanged. What had changed, in the author's view, were the means available to pursue this end and the strategic objectives of military action. The authors noted that in World War II, the strategic goals of the war were attained not through attacks on the deep rear of the adversary, but by defeating his forces in land theatres and by seizing his vitally important economic regions and political-administrative centres. The advent of nuclear weapons and their deployment in large numbers, by contrast, raised the question of whether the Soviet armed forces should aim at 'the defeat of the enemy's armed forces (as in the past) or the annihilation, destruction, and devastation of objectives in the enemy's rear for the purpose of disorganizing it':

> Soviet strategic theory gives the following answer: Both these goals should be achieved simultaneously. The annihilation of the enemy's armed forces, the destruction of objectives in the rear and disorganization of the rear will be a single continuous process of the war. Two main factors serve as the basis for this answer: the need to defeat the aggressor decisively in the shortest possible time, for which purpose it will be necessary to deprive him of the military, political, and economic means of waging war; secondly the real possibility of achieving these goals simultaneously with existing weapons.[26]

The primary targets in the enemy's rear were his strategic nuclear capabilities. Indeed, targets in the rear were of first priority, the centre of gravity of war having shifted from the zone of contact between the adversaries to 'deep within the enemy's home front'.[27] In other words, nuclear war was to be global in character with simultaneous counterforce and countervalue strikes, both in the theatre of military operations and in the enemy's homeland.

It followed that many of the traditional methods of combat developed in World War II were in need of radical revision. The authors cautioned that the attempt to use these methods unchanged was 'extremely dangerous'.[28] The previously paramount role of ground forces was downgraded, their place being taken by the newly formed Strategic Rocket Forces.[29] Even in principal land theatres, the defeat of the enemy was to be the result mainly of nuclear missile strikes.[30] The concepts of 'strategic defence' and 'defensive strategy' were decisively rejected, given that the adversary was preparing an offensive war which could be countered only by 'decisive active operations by our armed forces'.[31]

However, this did not constitute a rejection of attempts to defend the homeland (through both anti-aircraft and anti-missile systems) against nuclear attack. The authors characterized such efforts as an extremely important military operation since it was necessary to the preservation of effective political and military command and control and to the limitation of damage to Soviet forces deployed in the rear (for example the Stratetic Rocket Forces) and to the economy.[32] But the authors were emphatic in stressing the primacy of strategic offensive action.

The great explosive power and efficient means of delivery of nuclear weapons brought up the question of surprise in contemporary warfare, as noted above. The question is addressed most clearly in the discussion of the periodicity of nuclear war. Although retreating from previous suggestions in the literature that surprise was one of the 'decisive conditions of the attainment of success not only in battles and operations, but also in war as a whole',[35] the authors clearly did not subscribe to Khrushchev's rather summary dismissal of the problem in January of 1960.[34] Instead, they took the middle road, noting the decisive importance of the initial period of war and the remaining danger of surprise attack, and drawing from this a conclusion similar to that of Marshal Malinovskii in his speech at the 21st Party Congress and congenial to a military establishment concerned about the effects of Khrushchev's proposed manpower reductions to the effect that high levels of peacetime readiness were a necessity.[35]

But there was some ambiguity on just how decisive the initial period was. The favoured formulation was that the initial period would determine the course of the war but not its outcome. The latter was of course predetermined: 'This war will inevitably end with the victory of the progressive Communist socio-economic system over the reactionary capitalist socio-economic system which is historically doomed to destruction.'

This was the result not only in a general sense of the laws of history, but more specifically of the 'balance between the political, economic, and military strengths of the two systems, which has changed in favour of the socialist camp'. The authors cautioned, however, that 'victory will not come by itself. It must be thoroughly prepared.' [36] Apparently, what the authors were suggesting in the distinction between the course and the outcome of the war was that while the outcome was inevitable, the ease with which it was achieved and the costs incurred in achieving it were strongly affected by events in the initial period of massive nuclear strikes.

This leads to the question of pre-emption. The discussion of surprise suggests that if the imperialists achieved it, this could seriously complicate the Soviet route to victory. The authors suggested, moreover, that hostilities might be shortened considerably through the effective and massive use of nuclear missiles in the initial stages of war. This suggests a belief that the state which goes first may have significant advantages. Such a conclusion is supported by the emphasis in their discussion in the first two editions of the book of targeting on the destruction of enemy missiles on the ground prior to launch.[37] Thus, although the authors did not go so far as to advocate pre-emptive or preventive first strikes,[38] the weight of their argument seems to lead in this direction.

This is in turn related rather closely to the question of the duration of war. Here, the authors appear to waffle. The analysis clearly implies that a world war can be won quickly. The rejection of the notion of economy of force and the stress on the massive and unreserved quality of the initial exchange support this conclusion. However, the authors hedge their bets, noting that: 'in order to protect the interests of our country it is necessary to develop and improve both methods and weapons to attain victory over the shortest possible time and with minimum loss. At the same time, it is necessary to make serious preparations for a long war.' [39]

This is presumably related to the argument between traditionalists and modernists in the military establishment and between the military and civilian leaderships with regard to the appropriate size of forces-in-being on the one hand and resource allocation between nuclear and conventional systems on the other. If it were accepted that war would necessarily be a short, nuclear paroxysm then presumably there would be little necessity to prepare the 'human and material resources' [40] for prolonged hostilities.

This brings us finally to the question of the relationship between conventional and nuclear forces in modern war. The weight of the argument thus far suggests that the importance of ground forces and of the European theatre of operation — which in World War II had been the central focus of Soviet strategy — had been considerably downgraded. In and of itself, this favoured the position of those who believed that such forces and other conventional services such as the air force and surface navy were no longer necessary and could be sacrificed to the budgetary axe. But the authors, again presumably reflecting some sort of compromise between the military and political leaderships on the one hand, and modernists and traditionalists within the military on the other, were careful not to draw this conclusion. On the contrary, they emphasized that although the role of such forces was no longer dominant, it remained essential:

> Soviet military strategy concludes that, in spite of the extensive introduction of nuclear weapons and the latest types of military equipment, a future world war will require massive armed forces. . . . We cannot fail to point out the complete bankruptcy of modern bourgeois theories, which advocate — for class reasons and out of fear of arming the masses — the idea of waging war with small professional armies that are technically well equipped.[41]

Elsewhere, the authors repeat Malinovskii's 1961 formulation concerning the necessity of a 'multi-million' mass army.

One might well ask just what this multi-million ground force was for (other than the subjugation of Eastern Europe — an end not mentioned in the Sokolovskii work). The function of ground forces in land theatres was to seize whatever theatre nuclear capabilities of the adversary they could lay their hands on in order to minimize the effectiveness of enemy use of such weapons in the theatre. Beyond this, they were to finish the job of the nuclear forces by taking important political, economic and military objectives in the theatre and establishing 'proper' order in occupied zones.[42]

In short, to the extent one can infer conclusions about doctrine from discussions of strategy, it appears that the traditonal services had won the argument with Khrushchev on manpower levels and the continuing importance of conventional arms of the service. This conclusion is confirmed by Soviet procurement and force size in the period subsequent to the publication of the first edition. The dual emphasis on large numbers of highly capable nuclear weapons and on the maintenance of a massive highly mobile conventional capability at a high level of readiness set the stage for the prolonged Soviet buildup of nuclear and conventional forces in the 1960s and 1970s.

The issue of the appropriate size of the services leads to the final question of whether nuclear and conventional superiority were deemed necessary to the attainment of victory. In the view of the authors, *overall* qualitative and quantitative superiority (*preimushchestvo*) was a necessity in the achievement of Soviet political and strategic objectives in modern war.[43] Since rocket nuclear weapons played the leading role in solving the fundamental problems of future war: 'creating and constantly maintaining quantitative and qualitative superiority (*prevoskhodstvo*) over the enemy in this type of armed conflict and in the method of using it are two of the most important problems for the armed forces today'.[44]

The work itself changed to some extent as it passed from its first to its third edition, in response to technological developments and to Western and Soviet criticisms of it. Several of these changes have been mentioned in some detail in preceding notes. It suffices to note the most important here. In the first place, the authors' views on pre-emption and surprise seem to have evolved. The 1968 edition evinced far less concern about the prospect of successful surprise attack (see note 35). This appears to be related to the development of more sophisticated and capable warning systems. It followed that pre-emption was a less significant option, and references to it disappeared in the last edition. As argued in note 36, this omission may also have reflected Soviet awareness of the damaging effects that the embrace of pre-emption (even in qualified form) had on Soviet–American relations. Even if it was an option to be considered, it made little sense to air it publicly. Some have argued that the evolution of the work suggests also a growing interest in local war and conventional options. While it is clear that such an evolution is reflected in the broader Soviet military literature, it is not so obvious in Sokolovskii, where statements concerning the necessity of preparing for local limited options were present from the first through the third editions (see note 24).[45]

In summary, Sokolovskii and his colleagues did not hold a future world war to be inevitable. But they apparently felt it necessary to develop a strategy defining how to fight one should it occur in the nuclear age. Their vision of such a war was global, and all-out in character. It would involve combined arms operations using all services and both conventional and nuclear weapons. The strategy they proposed — and which, given the repeated publication of the book, apparently enjoyed official backing — involved simultaneous nuclear strikes against both military and civilian targets in both theatres of operations and in the enemy rear. Attacks against military targets, and in particular the enemy's strategic nuclear capabilities, had first priority. Their strategic objective was total victory. The work maintains that this objective is possible despite the likelihood of bearing significant costs in its pursuit. They advocated efforts to achieve military superiority through the development of massive nuclear and conventional capabilities as a necessary condition of achieving this aim. They argued also for the development of effective strategic (in our sense of the word) defence as a means of ensuring the survivability of their political and social system and military capabilities in a wartime environment. In short, it was a strategy for fighting and winning a nuclear war.

In order to distinguish this body of work from American discussions of the topic, it is worth mentioning a number of concepts which were absent from or criticized in Sokolovskii's work. The authors rejected the proposition that the nuclear era was different from previous eras in military history in that the incomparable explosive power of nuclear weapons meant that they could not be instruments of a rational politics of force. The implication that such weapons were therefore useful only as a deterrent met the same fate. These Soviet writers did not accept the proposition that the security of the state could or should be based on a mutual hostage relationship resting on invulnerable second-strike capabilities.

They did not seriously consider the possibility of a conventional phase in a major war between East and West. Such a war would inevitably and immediately become nuclear. For similar reasons, there was no consideration of firebreaks, tacit or explicit communication in war, limited nuclear war and intra-war deterrence. The authors recommended the massive and indiscriminate use of strategic nuclear weapons at the outset of the conflict.

Finally, there was no treatment of the concept of arms control as a means of channelling the development and procurement of nuclear weapons in stabilizing directions. In short, there are clear and substantial differences between this body of strategic theory and contemporaneous and subsequent American consideration of the impact of nuclear weapons on military strategy. In this Soviet view, despite their explosive power, nuclear charges are essentially weapons to be used like any other in the attempt to defeat the enemy.

None the less, it would be incorrect to infer from this discussion of the nature of future war, of the necessity of preparing to fight it and of the 'winnability' of such a conflict that the Soviet Union wanted or intended to fight such a war. The book suggests little about Soviet intentions at the time or later. The then (and currently) prevailing doctrine concerning the non-inevitability of war suggests that the prospect of world war was not viewed with any great enthusiasm by the Soviet leadership or by the authors of this work. The polemic between the Soviet and Chinese parties in 1963 indicates an official Soviet view that the dangers of the nuclear age necessitated efforts to stabilize and improve relations with the United States and the avoidance of actions carrying a serious prospect of provoking war. Finally, whatever the authors may have said about the possibility of victory, they knew that the strategic balance was unfavorable to them, that any initiation of such a war would consequently be unwise, that the effort to achieve superiority was by no means assured of success and that any such success was liable to be a matter for the distant future. It seems safer to conclude that this elaboration of Soviet strategy served two functions:

1. reducing the likelihood of war through the attempt to demonstrate to putative adversaries some evidence of a Soviet capacity to wage it. It was apparently the Soviet view that the formulation of strategies and the acquisition of capabilities to wage war successfully were a means of preventing war.
2. providing the Soviet state with strategic options should war occur.

The impact of Sokolovskii

Sokolovskii's *Military Strategy* has had important effects on both Soviet and Western strategy and policy with regard to nuclear weapons. On the Soviet side, it has been cited as recommended reading for officers while its principal editor has been eulogized as a key figure in the revolution in military affairs occasioned by the introduction of nuclear weapons.[46] *Military Strategy* reflected and perpetuated a number of continuities in military writings which have relevance today, among them the emphasis on the offensive, combined arms operations and unified military doctrine, a concept of deterrence based on credible war-fighting capabilities, the development of strategies which were practical should deterrence fail, and the necessity for a multimillion armed force with balanced conventional and nuclear capabilities.

However, it does not appear to be the case that: 'the basic content of Soviet doctrine has remained relatively stable since the early 1960s when the initial post-Stalin debates finally produced the broad policy consensus reflected in Marshal Sokolovskii's *Voennaya Strategia*'.[47]

Sokolovskii's work may have approximated Soviet strategy in the 1960s. The development of Soviet force posture in the mid- and late 1960s suggested a desire to match Soviet capabilities to the analyses contained in the book.

Yet Sokolovskii's work apparently did not fully resolve many of the issues animating the debate which had preceded its publication. As has been noted above, the book was in many respects a compromise document. It sought to underline the significance of the nuclear revolution in strategy, but its authors avoided the radical Khrushchevian conclusions that the development of such weapons made war unwinnable while rendering more traditional military capabilities obsolete. As such, Soviet writers have subsequently attacked it from two sides.

The first concerns the revival of more traditional missions for Soviet forces. There is evidence of interest in the development of substrategic conventional and nuclear war options which rely on intra-war deterrence at the strategic level. Sokolovskii's work was criticized very soon after it appeared for having gone too far in its focus on strategic nuclear capabilities. In a review of the book in *Krasnaya Zvezda* in late 1962, General of the Army P. Kurochkin contested the authors' view on the strategic significance of the 'revolution in military affairs', criticizing them for excessive concentration on strategic missiles to the detriment of other forces.[48] This line of criticism reflected dissatisfaction with the all-or-nothing approach outlined in *Military Strategy* and brought a search in the late 1960s and 1970s for new capabilities which would allow the diversification of military options. In turn, these new capabilities brought efforts at a revision of the strategy outlined in Sokolovskii's work.[49]

Several episodes in this evolution deserve mention. The attainment of parity or essential equivalence in strategic nuclear weapons removed the spectre of American escalation dominance and arguably made the contemplation of lower-level violence easier. The introduction of large numbers of MIRVs from the mid-1970s onward allowed a considerable expansion in target coverage and multiple coverage of significant targets. The deployment of Delta SSBNs in protected home waters gave the Soviet Union a viable second-strike capability. This made intra-war deterrence possible. The deployment of SS20s in large numbers in Europe made possible an autonomous theatre nuclear option. Improvements in conventional capabilities from the mid-1960s on allowed more serious consideration of purely conventional scenarios. Soviet forces began to exercise purely or protracted conventional options in the late 1960s.

These developments in force posture reopened discussion of a number of issues in Sokolovskii's work. The SSBN deployment brought a reformulation of the concept of all-out nuclear war in some writings. By the mid-1970s, some Soviet writers were arguing that a world war would inevitably be nuclear and global but not necessarily all-out in character. Targeting of both counterforce and countervalue options was deemed possible but not inevitable. It was considered feasible to hold back counter-value attacks in order to deter the adversary during war. As a result, protraction of war was taken more seriously, and the critical significance of the initial period of war drawn into question. This in turn implied a resurrection of the principle of economy of force in the initial stages. With increasing emphasis on the SSBN and the concomitant expansion of the surface navy, the role of the navy in overall strategy was considerably enhanced.

Changes in force posture in Europe led to further revision in some circles. In the late 1970s, a number of Soviet military writers began to contemplate the possibility of confining conflict to a single theatre. Escalation to global war was no longer deemed inevitable. The expansion and improvement of conventional capabilities in the theatre brought with it some consideration as early as the late 1960s of the possibility of a conventional phase in a major war. In 1967, for example, the *Dnepr* exercise began with a purely conventional phase, in contrast to the conception of the initial period of war outlined in the Sokolovskii work. In 1969, Defence Minister Grechko made this official by noting that units should be prepared to fight with or without nuclear forces. As the years passed, military writers began to discuss the possibility that war in the theatre could remain conventional throughout.[50] In the 1980s, the discussion extended still further, some writers entertaining the possibility that general protracted conventional war in widely separated theatres could be stable and not escalate to the level of nuclear exchanges.

Many of these trends were summarized in a work by General M. A. Gareev in 1985[51], in which he specifically criticized Sokolovskii's work for exaggerating the significance of the development of nuclear weapons and for its unifocal attitude towards modern war; questioned the massive and indiscriminate use of nuclear weapons in war; stressed the growing possibilities for fighting a long conventional war and the consequent significance of economy in the use of force; emphasized the primacy of theatre rather than global war and of partial victories as building blocks for victory in war; and advocated counterforce rather than countervalue targeting in theatre operations. In other words, with the passage of time and the development of more flexible capabilities, the discussion of *strategy* (as opposed to doctrine) shifted back towards a greater emphasis on theatre rather than global war, on conventional as opposed to nuclear capabilities and towards counterforce rather than mixed targeting.

This reflects presumably not only the growing technological sophistication of both nuclear and conventional weapons but also lingering resistance on the part of officers involved in conventional forces to their downgrading in strategic planning. It is important to note that writers participating in this development — despite their desire to diversify options — generally continue to stress the war-fighting role of nuclear weapons, at both theatre and strategic levels, even though they tend to accept that the role of strategic forces is deterrent in character. Nor have they abandoned the proposition that the use of strategic nuclear forces can be decisive in character.[52] In certain instances, indeed, important Soviet military writers embrace the possibility of victory being attained through surprise first strikes in a war of short duration. In the most recent edition of *Military Art*, for example, the authors asserted that: 'The presence of nuclear weapons and powerful groups of military forces at highest levels of readiness when used in surprise, now as never before, permit a situation in which surprise can have a decisive influence on the course *and even the outcome* (italics added) of war.[53]

The second line of criticism of Sokolovskii is more radical in character, postulating that the advent of strategic nuclear capabilities on both sides has rendered traditional conceptions of global (nuclear) war as a continuation of politics obsolete.[54] In 1964, N.M. Nikolsky argued that the presence of massive nuclear capabilities on both sides meant that nuclear war had 'negated itself'. Victory was no longer possible, and general war could no longer be considered an instrument of policy.[55] Although Nikolsky was forced to retreat from this position in 1965, his position regained its respectability in the aftermath of Leonid Brezhnev's Tula speech of January 1977.[56] In this and more clearly in subsequent statements, Brezhnev and others expressed the view that to expect victory in nuclear war was insane and that the effort to attain a superiority which carried some prospect of such victory was pointless. The effort to achieve victory through a surprise first strike would bring 'unavoidable retaliation'.[57] More recent comment on nuclear weapons and nuclear war — which are characterized as the most significant threat to human civilization — suggests that the current leadership shares such perspectives, at least in public.

Associated with this perspective on nuclear weapons is a growing stress on the mutuality of security (the notion that one side cannot be secure while the other is not),[58] on strategic stability[59] and in concepts of 'reasonable sufficiency' in strategic nuclear and conventional capabilities.[60] Sufficiency in the current lexicon of the Soviet political leadership apparently means that: 'At each crucial level of the military balance . . . the two sides should have armed forces only adequate for defending against possible aggression, not forces permitting either side to carry out offensive operations against the other.[61]

The Soviet acceptance of an INF treaty eliminating this category of nuclear weapons altogether, and of deep cuts in strategic systems, indicates that the leadership may take the view that there is little point in building beyond a level of guaranteed mutual destruction and that doing so may induce American behaviour which, from the Soviet perspective, is counterproductive. This recalls Khrushchev's views of the late 1950s and early 1960s on military capabilities.[62]

Growing interest in 'reasonable sufficiency' of conventional forces deployed in Europe parallels this trend in nuclear thought. In a 1987 article, for example, a civilian researcher and a retired general (and co-author of the Sokolovskii volume) reinterpreted the significance of the battle of Kursk to stress the success in this instance of defensive rather than offensive strategy and tactics. They went on to note that recent developments in conventional weaponry had created a situation in Europe where the balance between offense and defence in armoured warfare favoured the latter. This made it possible in their view to think seriously about concepts of 'non-provocative defence' such as those articulated by the Western peace movement.[63] The fact that such views were published not merely in media for foreign consumption, but in professional journals in Russian and, for that matter, in *Kommunist*[64] — the CPSU Central Committee's main theoretical organ — suggested that they were meant to be taken seriously in internal Soviet debate on these subjects. They seemed to reflect a desire to reallocate material, and research and development resources towards the modernization of the civilian sector of the economy which is again similar to that of the Khrushchev period.

This line of argument is clearly difficult to square with the first line of criticism, emanating primarily from military thinkers. The tension between them suggested a persistent disagreement between elements of the military command on the one hand and elements of the civilian leadership on the other concerning the utility and role of nuclear weapons, the Politburo returning to a conception of mutual assured destruction similar to that articulated by Khrushchev, and many military officers resisting this trend for bureaucratic, institutional and presumably cognitive reasons. It is considerations such as these, along with disagreements on the necessity of building and maintaining a force capable of fighting and winning at any level of war in conditions of rapidly evolving conventional technologies and at a time of severe investment constraints in the Soviet Union which may have been at the root of Ogarkov's departure from his post as chief of the General Staff of the Soviet armed forces,[65] and what has been an abnormally high rate of turnover at the highest levels of the Soviet military since Gorbachev took office. Gorbachev appears to be using incidents like the Chernobyl disaster (which resulted in the sacking of the chief of the civil defence programme) and the Mathias Rust affair (in which Defence Minister Sokolov and the chief of the Soviet air defence system Marshal Koldunov were fired) to staff the upper echelons of the armed forces with individuals whom he judged to be more receptive to evolving civilian views on war and defence. This trend has been significantly extended as a result of the failed coup d'etat in August 1991.

Dinerstein, Goure and Wolfe noted in their introduction to the first edition of Sokolovskii that: 'Perhaps the cardinal point to be mentioned here is that the strategic outlook that emerges from the pages of this work reflects a broad shift from past preoccupations with theatre land warfare to a central focus on the problems of global strategic war.'[66]

The evolution of Soviet capabilities and discussions of the military-technical aspect of doctrine (strategy, operational art and tactics) since then suggests several modifications to this conclusion. First, the more traditional Soviet focus on conventional theatre land war has retained considerable vitality. Soviet military theorists have spent considerable effort since the appearance of the book in developing strategy, operational art, and material capabilities to conduct a war at this level. Moreover, much of the subsequent development of Soviet thought on nuclear weapons has focused on how to integrate them on a limited basis in a local war in the theatre while avoiding escalation to a general nuclear exchange. This indicates that in a number of important respects, Sokolovskii's elaboration of military strategy may be less relevant than it once was. None the less, Soviet military writings on general nuclear war in the late 1980s suggested a continuing fidelity to war fighting and to the possibility of victory which is reminiscent of the Sokolovskii approach and which suggested its continuing influence on Soviet military thought.

In the meantime, development of the political aspect of doctrine since the appearance of the Sokolovskii volumes suggests growing scepticism about the usability of nuclear weapons, about the possibility of victory in nuclear war, concern over the danger of escalation and doubts about the wisdom of a strategy based on the offensive. Strategists associated with civilian institutions meanwhile show increasing interest in modification of military–technical aspects of doctrine to render them more responsive to these concerns (for example Kokoshin's and Larionov's discussion of defensive tactics and strategy cited above). These modifications reflect not only doubts about the feasibility of realizing Soviet political objectives through major war between the two social systems and concern about the provocative and apparently counterproductive character of attempts to develop the means to do so, but also a concern to reduce the military burden on the Soviet economy, or more modestly, to prevent any significant increase in that burden during a period of rapidly evolving military technology and changing East-West relations.

The overall impression one gets from this tension between strategy and political doctrine today and between the institutions responsible for their elaboration is that there is today no settled Soviet doctrine concerning nuclear weapons or on the character of war in the modern era. The period is in this sense superficially similar to that of the late 1950s when the Soviets were adjusting to the advent of operational nuclear capabilities. There would appear to be room in the current context for a new attempt at synthesis to supersede that of Sokolovskii and his colleagues. But the political situation and in particular civil–military relations at the moment do not appear sufficiently settled to permit such a synthesis to be achieved.

None the less, the fact that some aspects of Gorbachev's own views on nuclear weapons follow logically upon a trend in thinking among his predecessors dating back to the achievement of parity and Brezhnev's Tula speech suggests that the leadership's apparent aversion to nuclear war may be reasonably broadly based. Assuming that the Soviet characterization of the relationship between political and military–technical aspects of doctrine and between doctrine and strategy continues to hold, we may assume that the Soviets are moving away from conceptions of deterrence based on war-fighting capabilities and towards a more 'minimalist' conception of deterrence. Such a conclusion is supported by the successful conclusion of INF and CFE negotiations.

If, as seems likely, this is the direction in which the Soviets are moving, then in this sense, too, Sokolovskii's influence may be perishable. But confident conclusions on the evolution of Soviet strategy must await the outcome of the profound changes taking place in the aftermath of the failed coup. There remain many uncertainties including the future of the Soviet Union itself. When that is resolved, the Soviet Union, or what remains of it, is likely to retain substantial numbers of nuclear weapons. There will then be a need for a new Sokolovskii to emerge to take stock of the new military thinking which has characterized the late 1980s and early 1990s.

Notes

1. On this point, see L. Freedman, 'The first two generations of nuclear strategists' in P. Paret (ed.), *Makers of Modern Strategy*, Princeton, Princeton University Press, 1986, pp. 735–78.
2. For reasons discussed below, this does not necessarily mean that Soviet writers have rejected deterrence. It suggests instead that, historically, they have had a rather different view of its requirements.

3. See, for example, J. McConnell, 'The irrelevance today of Sokolovsky's book *Military Strategy*', CNA Research Memorandum CRM 85-35, Alexandria, Virginia, Center for Naval Analyses, 1985.
4. As the authors point out, for that matter, theirs was the first volume in the *open* literature to address the problem of military strategy in its entirety since A. Svechin's *Strategia*, published in 1926 (V. D. Sokolovskii, *Voennaya Strategia*, Moscow: Voennoe Izdatel'stvo, 1963, p. 9).
5. Marshal of the Soviet Union V. D. Sokolovskii, Col. A. E. Belyaev, Col.-General A. I. Gastilovich, Col. V. D. Denisenko, Major General I. G. Zavyalov, Major General V. V. Kolechitskii, Col. V. V. Larionov, Col. G. M. Nykrov, Col. I. V. Parot'kin, Major General A. A. Prokhorov, Col. A. S. Popov, Col. K. I. Sal'nikov, Col. A. N. Shimanskii, Major General M. I. Cherednichenko, Col. A. I. Shchegolev.
6. V. Sokolovskii and M. Cherednichenko, 'O sovremennoi veonnoi strategii', *Kommunist Vooruzhennykh Sil* (1966), no 7, pp. 59-66.
7. Richard Pipes, 'Why the Soviet Union thinks it could fight and win a nuclear war', *Commentary* (July 1977), pp. 21-34.
8. *Sovetskaya Voennaya Entsyklopedia*, II, Moscow, Voennoe Izdatel'stvo, 1976, p. 184.
9. For a useful discussion of the relationship between these various concepts, see D. Holloway, *The Soviet Union and the Arms Race*, (New Haven, Yale University Press, 1983), pp. 29-31.
10. V. D. Sokolovskii (ed.), *Military Strategy* (first edition), (New York: Praeger, 1963), p. 13.
11. Behavioural evidence and published materials since 1956, and more strongly since the mid-1970s, suggest that this is not the case.
12. Compare Major General S. Kozlov, 'The development of Soviet military science after World War II', *Voennaya Mysl*, 1964, no. 2, p. 35. As cited in Holloway (op. cit., note 9), p. 28. On his control of military affairs, see Khrushchev, as cited in V. Aspaturian, 'The stalinist legacy in Soviet national security decisionmaking', in J. Valenta and W. Potter (eds), *Soviet Decisionmaking for National Security*, London, George Allen and Unwin, 1984, pp. 28-9, 59.
13. See J. V. Stalin, *Sochinenia* IV, pp. 148-51. Holloway notes (op. cit., note 9, p. 31) that the fact that Stalin felt it necessary to underline this point suggests that there may have been some questioning of it at the time.
14. For a discussion of these debates, see R. Garthoff, *Soviet Strategy in the Nuclear Age*, New York, Praeger, 1962, pp. 61-96.
15. *Pravda*, 15 February 1956.
16. The remarks are reproduced in *Pravda*, 15 January 1960.
17. *Pravda*, 25 October 1961.
18. H. Dinerstein, L. Goure, and T. Wolfe, 'Introduction' in V. Sokolovskii (ed.), *Soviet Military Strategy*, Englewood Cliffs, Prentice Hall, 1963, pp. 18-19.
19. As cited in Holloway, op. cit., note 9, p. 37.
20. Dinerstein, *et. al.*, op. cit., note 18, pp. 20-4.
21. As cited in R. Garthoff, 'Introduction', in V. D. Sokolovskii, *Military Strategy: Doctrine and Concepts*, New York, Praeger, 1963, pp. xii-xiii.
22. Ibid., pp. x-xi.
23. In examining Sokolovskii's work, I have used the Praeger version of the 1962 edition (V. D. Sokolovskii (ed.), *Military Strategy*, New York, Praeger, 1963) and the Russian language versions of the 1963 and 1968 editions (V. D. Sokolovskii (ed.), *Voennaya Strategia*, Moscow, Voennoe Izdatel'stvo, 1963 and 1968). The three editions are designated in subsequent notes by the year of the Russian edition: 1962, 1963, and 1968.
24. In the 1962 edition, for example, the authors note that:

    > In either case [direct attack on the socialist camp or the unleashing of local war against a nonsocialist country where basic interests of the socialist countries are at stake], the start of war by an aggressor will obviously lead to a new world war in which the socialist countries will be on one side and the imperialist and capitalist countries on the other. [1962, pp. 181; 1963, p. 232; 1968, 226].

    There was some evidence of discomfort among the authors regarding this point. Elsewhere in the work, they noted that 'the armed forces of the socialist camp must be prepared for small-scale wars that could be unleashed by the imperialists', and called for study 'of the means of conducting such wars in order to prevent them from developing into a world war and in order to achieve a quick victory over the enemy' (1962, pp. 182–3; 1963, p. 234; 1968, p. 228). When subsequent to the publication of the first edition, Western scholars noted the unequivocal character of Soviet views on escalation, members of the author's collegium responded by misquoting their own work to the effect that escalation was possible rather than inevitable. See T. Wolfe, *Soviet Strategy at the Crossroads*, Cambridge, Mass., Harvard University Press, 1964, pp. 123–4. It may be that the first assertion reflects a concern to deter the West from involvement in local conflicts through the threat of escalation, while the second reflects a more practical concern not to foreclose any military options which might be useful. Alternatively, the tension between the two may be another manifestation of dispute between traditional and more innovative thinking in the military or between the military and civilian leaderships (in the Khrushchev period) over resource allocation. Whatever the case, the work is incoherent on this point.

25. 1962, pp. 168–9; 1963, pp. 216–17; 1968, pp. 210–1. See also 1962, p. 172; 1963, p. 220; 1968, p. 214.
26. 1962, p. 195; 1963, pp. 249–50; 1968, p. 244. See also 1962, p. 285; 1963, p. 378; 1968, p. 348.
27. 1962, pp. 204, 278; 1963, pp. 366, 260; 1968, p. 340.
28. 1962, p. 277; 1963, p. 364; 1968, p. 332.
29. 1962, pp. 278, 280; 1963, pp. 366, 369; 1968, p. 339.
30. 1962, p. 198; 1963 p. 250; 1968, p. 245.
31. 1962, p. 282; 1963, p. 371; 1968, pp. 341–2.
32. 1962, pp. 283, 295–8; 1963, pp. 372–3; 1968, pp. 343.
33. Marshal Rotmistrov, as cited in note 19.
34. Khrushchev, as cited in note 16, noted that: 'The state which suffers the attack, if, of course, we are speaking of a sufficiently large state, will always have the possibility to deliver the proper rebuff to the aggressor.'
35. 1962, p. 198; 1963, pp. 252–3; 1968, pp. 247. The references to surprise in the 1962 and 1963 editions were deleted from the 1968 references to 'attacks' and 'strikes' by the adversary. This change presumably reflected increasing confidence in warning systems. As the 1968 edition noted:

   possibilities of averting a surprise attack are constantly growing. Present means of reconnaissance, detection, and surveillance can opportunely disclose a significant portion of the measures of direct preparation of a nuclear attack by the enemy and in the very first minutes locate the mass launch of missiles and the takeoff of aircraft belonging to the aggressor and, at the right time, warn the political leadership of the country about the impending danger. Thus, possibilities exist not to allow a surprise attack by an aggressor, to deliver nuclear strikes on him at the right time [1968, p. 337].

   One is left wondering just what the phrase 'the right time' means. (See the discussion of pre-emption below). The comment on the significance of the initial period and the necessity of readiness remained unchanged in the 1968 edition.
36. 1962, p. 203; 1963, p. 258; 1968, p. 253.
37. 1962, p. 278; 1963, 366. The formulation is omitted in the 1968 edition. This omission may have reflected an awareness that arguments of this type served as ammunition for those in the United States advocating the deployment of an ABM system. It may also have reflected the hardening of American silos and the growing salience of submarines in the American triad, both of which rendered the first strike option somewhat less credible than it might have been earlier. However, depending on how one interprets their discussion of surprise in the 1968 edition (see note 34), there remains evidence that the authors continued to think about the possibility of pre-emptive first strikes.
38. As Malinovskii had appeared to do in 1961 in his remark that the Soviet Union had to be ready to 'break up the aggressive designs [of the enemy] by dealing him a crushing blow *in time.* (R. Malinovskii, *Izvestia*, 25 October, 1961).

39. 1962, 204; 1963, 261; 1968, 255–6.
40. 1963, 261.
41. 1962, p. 201; 1963, p. 256; 1968, p. 251.
42. 1962, pp. 281, 288–9; 1963, 369, 383–4; 1968, 340, 351–3.
43. 1962, p. 235; 1963, p. 314; 1968, p. 309.
44. 1962, p. 226; 1963, p. 303; 1968, p. 298.
45. Holloway (op. cit., note 9, p. 41–2 and 190), for example, notes more Soviet interest in local wars, citing the third edition of Sokolovskii to the effect that Soviet forces had to be prepared not only for world war, but also for local wars. As was seen in note 24, however, this statement appears also in the first and second editions. It cannot, therefore, be used as evidence of a Soviet change of mind. For a systematic comparison of the three editions, see H. Scott, ed., *Soviet Military Strategy*, London, Macdonald and Jane's, 1975.
46. As cited in ibid., pp. xxiv, xix.
47. B. Lambeth, 'Soviet military policy' in R. Kolkowicz and E. Mickiewicz (eds.), *The Soviet Calculus of Nuclear War*, Lexington, Mass., Lexington Books, 1986, p. 32.
48. General P. Kurochkin, *Krasnava Zvezda*, 22 October 1962. This review is reprinted in translation in an appendix to the Dinerstein, Goure, and Wolf version of the 1962 edition (op. cit., note 18).
49. This process is admirably summarized in McConnell, op. cit. (note 3), pp. 4–12. The discussion which follows draws to a considerable extent on McConnell's work.
50. This was by no means the only view aired, however. In other works, it appeared quite clear that early and quite possibly first use of theatre nuclear forces was envisaged.
51. *M. V. Frunze — Voennyi Teoretik: Vzglyady M. V. Frunze i Sovetskaya Voennaya Teoria*, Moscow, Voennoe Izdatel'stvo, 1985.
52. See, for example, Ogarkov's characterization of defensive nuclear strikes in *Vsegda v Gotovnsti k Zashchite Otechestya*, Moscow, Voenizdat, 1982, pp. 32–4.
53. Lt.-General P. A. Zhilin, (ed.), *Istoria Voennogo Iskusstya*, Moscow, Voenizdat, 1986, p. 407.
54. To some extent this development was prefigured in Clausewitz's own reservations about total war. See P. Paret, 'Clausewitz' in P. Paret (ed.), *The Makers of Modern Strategy*, Princeton, Princeton University Press, 1986, p. 199.
55. See N. M. Nikol'sky, *Osnovnoi Vopros Sovremennosti: Problema Unichtozhenia Voin*, Moscow, 1964.
56. *Pravda*, 19 January 1977.
57. L. Brezhnev, *Pravda*, 21 October 1981.
58. M. S. Gorbachev, 'Political report of the CPSU Central Committee', *Pravda*, 26 February 1986, as translated in *Foreign Broadcast Information Service*, Soviet Union. III. 26 February, 1986, p. 29.
59. See A. G. Arbatov *et. al.*, 'Yadernoe oruzhie i strategicheskaya stabil'nost', *SShA: Politika, Ekonomika, Ideologia*, 1987, no. 10, pp. 17–24.
60. Gorbachev, op. cit. (note 58), p. 34.
61. Robert Legvold, 'Gorbachev's new approach to conventional arms control', *The Harriman Institute Forum*, **I**, no. 1 January 1988, p. 4.
62. The most obvious difference between the thinking of the late 1950s and that of the current period lies in the prevailing conception of the triad. Khrushchev's focus lay on the role of the land-based Strategic Rocket Forces. Soviet military writers currently stress Strategic Nuclear Forces, including the submarine force and, to a lesser extent, manned bomber capabilities. The current doctrinal stress on a balanced triad reflects technological developments since Khrushchev's time (notably the development of a large submarine force) and the apparent shift in Soviet leadership thinking away from nuclear war fighting and towards deterrence based on a diverse array of survivable second-strike forces. The parallel between this development and traditional American conceptions of deterrence is striking, though the evidence suggests that many in the Soviet military conceive of these forces as providing a deterrent shield allowing the exercise of conventional warfighting options. For a brief discussion highlighting the transition in Soviet strategic thought to the concept of Strategic Nuclear Forces, see the summary of a talk on 'Soviet Civil-Military Relations' by Dr Rose Gottemoeller on 3 June 1987 in *Meeting Report*, The Kennan Institute

for Advanced Russian Studies, Washington, DC, The Wilson Center, 1987.

63. A. Kokoshin and V. Larionov, 'Kurskaya Bitva v svete sovremennoi oboronitel'noi doktriny', *Mirovaya Ekonomika i Mezhdunarodnye Otnoshenia*, 1987, no. 8, in particular pp. 32–3, and 40.

64. V. Zhurkin, S. Karaganov, and A. Kortunov, in 'Vyzovy bezopasnosti — starye i novye', *Kommunist* 1988, no 1, p. 46 argue, for example, that the avoidance of war in Europe now demands a considerable reduction in the level of military confrontation there. In this context, they argue that the INF treaty not only signifies the elimination of two classes of nuclear weapons, but is also a concrete step in the direction of giving the military doctrines of the two sides a strictly defensive (*strogo oboronitel'nogo*) character. Such an evolution in their view still requires a significant rethinking of many concepts of strategy and operational art 'beginning with a reevaluation of the quantitative need for certain types of weapon (for example, the tank).' Gorbachev himself has also noted that there 'should be a change in armed forces with a view to imparting an exclusively defensive character'. As cited in Legvold, op. cit., note 61, p. 4. Just how this would be done is of course problematic.

65. For a useful discussion of the dispute between Ogarkoy and the political leadership, see T. Hasegava, 'Soviets on nuclear-war-fighting', *Problems of Communism* (July-August 1986), pp. 68–79. The fact that Ogarkov continued to argue that victory was possible in global nuclear war after his dismissal and was permitted to publish in the military press suggests that his dismissal did not resolve the issue. In April 1985, for example, while accepting the dangers associated with nuclear war, he noted that such a war would continue 'until complete victory against the enemy' was achieved. N. Ogarkoy, *Istoria Uchit Bditel'nost* (Moscow, 1985), p. 77, as cited in ibid., p. 78. In this sense, Ogarkov prefigures the surprising endorsement, of the possibility of victory contained in Zhilin's 1986 work (op. cit., note 53, p. 407).

66. Dinerstein, *et al.*, op. cit. (note 18), pp. 3–4.

INDEX